Hiking the San Francisco Bay Area

Linda A. Hamilton

FALCONGUIDES ®

GUILFORD, CONNECTICUT
HELENA, MONTANA
AN IMPRINT OF THE GLOBE PEQUOT PRESS

FALCONGUIDES®

All interior photos by the author
Maps by Ben Pease © Morris Book Publishing, LLC

ISSN: 1542-0663
ISBN 978-0-7627-1206-9

Manufactured in the United States of America
First Edition/Fourth Printing

To buy books in quantity for corporate use
or incentives, call **(800) 962–0973**
or e-mail **premiums@GlobePequot.com.**

Table of

Contents

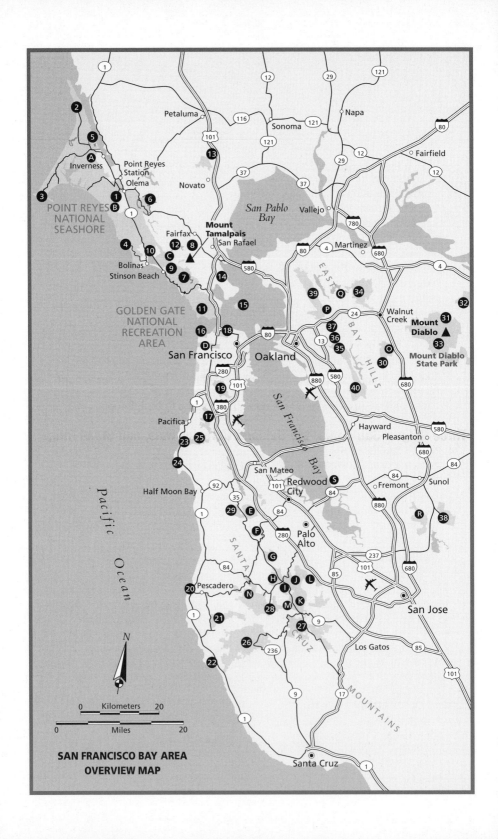

SAN FRANCISCO BAY AREA
OVERVIEW MAP

The Northern Santa Cruz Mountains

Mount Diablo and Las Trampas Foothills

Three Ridges: San Pablo, the Oakland/Berkeley Hills, and Sunol Ridge

Preface

On the day I became a hiker, I was one mad six-year-old. Cross-legged in a circle, I listened frustrated to the other first graders rattle off their religions. It was about the time when children learn they have a religion. I didn't know what mine was. With hands on hips, I confronted my mother. To my surprise, our family had a religion, and she told me what it was. I couldn't wait to share this revelation at school.

The next day, when the topic came up again, I was ready. Pulling back my shoulders, I declared proudly, "I'm a pedestrian."

My mispronunciation became closer to the truth. Since I was six, walking has been my self-declared doctrine. I love the outdoors. So it is no wonder I wound up writing this book.

It seems an appropriate basis for a religion, if you think about it. Hiking feeds the spirit. Doctors write about its capacity to heal mind, body, and soul. Coexisting with the wilderness requires rules of behavior that translate well into positive ways of living. And I can't think of a prettier cathedral than a forest of 2,000-year-old redwood trees.

Born and raised in the East Bay, I watched the San Ramon Valley grow from scattered ranches and countryside to thriving cities and suburbs—and traffic jams. People sometimes don't believe me when I tell them that we didn't know what a traffic backup was when I was first driving in 1981.

Recently, my husband and I discussed the possibility of moving away, discouraged by the high real estate costs and crowds. Then I started investigating the idea of writing a book about hiking, an activity many people associate with wilderness areas like the Sierras and not a major metropolis like the Bay Area. I soon discovered the beautiful and varied open space in this region. *Hiking the San Francisco Bay Area* has reawakened for me a love and appreciation for this wild, diverse, historical, and beautiful place.

Taking a closer look at the hills and trails I adore, I found the history and spirit of the San Francisco Bay Area embodied in the open space. Still alive in our parklands are the stories of peaceful native life, of exploration, of survival and destruction, of staking claim and prospering in a new land, of the tough physical existence of western living and the genteel traditions of the San Francisco elite.

Having grown up here, I had my haunts, my regular trails, and hardly deviated from them. Then I left for college and came back with the eye of a traveler. It was time to explore, and I started to learn just how much was out there. The South Bay became a kind of miracle to me while researching for this book. And I admit it here: Admiring the majestic shape of Mount Tamalpais my whole life, I didn't climb it until I was well into adulthood. The day I did, I fell in love with the mountain and, coincidentally, with the man who took me there. We had our first kiss on the deck of West Point Inn, a stunning view of the bay below us. Before this book was finished, that man became my husband.

I am grateful for the experience of creating *Hiking the San Francisco Bay Area* and hope that in sharing it with others, I can guide people to the places of magic and beauty one can only see by foot in the Bay Area. You too may join me in saying, "I'm proud to be a pedestrian." Happy hiking!

Map Legend

Roads

≡80≡ Freeway/ Interstate Highway

≡(101)≡ U.S. Highway

—(1)— State Highway

——— Other Road

=== =: Unpaved Road

Trails

- - - - - - Selected Route

- - - - - Trail or Fire Road

——— Paved Trail or Bike Path

· · · · · · · Optional Trail Route

|||||||| Steps

⟶ Direction of Travel

Water Features

Body of Water

River or Creek

Intermittent Stream

Marsh or Wetland

Waterfalls

Spring

Land Management

Parks and Preserves

Watersheds

Trailhead

Picnic

Visitor Center/ Information

Parking

Rest Room

Telephone

Water

Lodging

Campground

Ranger Station

Gate

Bridge

Tunnel

Mountain/ Peak

Pass/ Gap

Stables

Building/ Point of Interest

Locator Number

Major Airport

Interpretive Panel

N

True North
(Magnetic North is
approximately 15.5° East)

Acknowledgments

have many thanks to give for the completion of this book. First, thanks to my parents, Bob and Nancy Parker, for instilling my love of hiking and supporting me in my dream to become a professional writer. Oh, and for my fancy new hiking boots. Next time I'll wear them in first so I don't find myself hiking in wool socks with shoes in my hands. I love you both very much.

My big brother, David, Shari, and Jessalyn provided constant support and answered my obscure questions when I didn't know whom else to call. I feel blessed. Thanks to my best buddy, Michelle, and Trevor, the fabulous retriever, for their company, cheerleading, sushi, laughter, and love. My new family, the Hamiltons, make me so proud of the name I now bear. Bob, Dona, Ann, Holly, Tom, Kathy—thank you for thinking of me so often during the writing of this guide. I love you all.

Thanks to all the friends and family that joined me on the hills and put up with my talking into a tape recorder and suddenly changing directions to explore a new path. Denise, I led you into the woods after dark and you still did the makeup for my wedding; thank you for your friendship. Thanks also to all those people who suggested their favorite hikes. Many showed up in the book.

The feedback I received from my writing groups was invaluable. Thanks, folks. Thanks to my 7:00 A.M. friends for their courage and kindness. Thanks to Scott Adams at The Globe Pequot Press for the opportunity to write this book and for your patience at the end when I needed the pressure of a deadline.

I am grateful to all the wonderful innkeepers that provided a roof over my head and a hot shower after hiking in the rain. There are so many beautiful and friendly places to stay around the Bay Area. Thank you to the hiking guides and everyone at Skylonda Lodge. What a great experience! Paul, thanks for showing me the ropes at Purisima. To all the rangers, naturalists, docents, and historians in Bay Area parks, I sing your praises. You answered my endless questions on the phone, recommended books, suggested routes, told me park legends, and shared your enthusiasm for the outdoors. Thanks to Walter Bennett Cameras in Oakland for picture-perfect developing.

Doug, my wonderful husband, I thank you above all for your patience with an impossible project, for backrubs and I love you calls. I'm grateful that you represented us at social functions and took up the slack of dealing with "life" close to deadline. Thanks for hiking with me on our honeymoon, and most of all for being you, a great teacher, my partner, and the love of my life.

Introduction

Welcome to the wild variety of hiking in the San Francisco Bay area. No other metropolis in the world offers so much open space so close to a major city. Whether you like it wet, dry, high, low, perfectly level, or mountain goat steep, there's something nearby for you. Hiking is a wonderful way to discover the beauty of the Bay Area. Beyond the daily commute, beyond the sleepy suburbs, beyond the familiar tourist attractions, there are places where no roads go, where you can look out at nothing but hillsides or ocean or take in the sights of the city from a lofty perch. Reach out and touch the trunk of a giant redwood or stick your hand into cool creek water, and you can almost feel the rich history of this place. The trails in this book lead you to roaring waterfalls, silent glades, and wind-whipped mountaintops. They'll show you quiet meadows covered with wildflowers, swarming with butterflies, and deep, verdant forests where ferns grow lush and colossal trees stand like pillars holding up the sky. And they'll take you to places to breathe anew.

The purpose of this guide is to offer readers an opportunity to explore the San Francisco Bay Area's many facets. It was hard to create a perimeter for the hikes. The beauty of Northern California continues in all directions. Nonetheless, the epicenter, if you will, is the San Francisco Bay Bridge, and all the hikes, with only a couple exceptions, are within an hour and a half's weekend drive from there. Within this range, the book features the most diverse, exhilarating, and beautiful hikes around the bay, hikes that do justice to the history, natural diversity, and character of this region. There are hikes here for every level of experience, some with options for families and longer hikes. Though all the features are day hikes, many chapters provide ideas for exciting overnight excursions. All are complemented by travel information listing some of the best bed-and-breakfasts, restaurants, and posthike activities available in this magnificent coastal region.

Northern California Weather

Possibly no other region in this country displays as many varieties of weather simultaneously as does the San Francisco Bay Area. The weather is every bit as varied as the landscapes. It can be sunny on the Las Trampas Ridge, raining on Mount Tamalpais, snowing on Mount Diablo, foggy on Sweeney Ridge, and windy on Montara Mountain all at once. On any one hike you can experience severe changes in temperature and humidity as trails take you abruptly from one ecosystem to the next. Atmospheric forces and geologic formations come together to form the area's unique combination of forest, river, ocean, bay, and hills, one of the most prominent phenomena being the jet stream causing the famous summer fog that pours over the Golden Gate Bridge.

That thick summertime fog, along with mild winters, helps to buffer large temperature swings and accounts for the milder climate in the coastal regions that sustains the temperate rainforest of coast redwoods. For a hiker, the chilly fog, which can occur in winter too, often lies thick on the mountains in the morning and comes in fast in the afternoon. The average temperature in San Francisco ranges between 50° F and 60° F. East of the bridge averages are five to ten degrees higher as you head inland.

Flora and Fauna

With as many microclimates and diverse weather patterns as the Bay Area has, it's no wonder the vegetation and wildlife vary as much as they do. Of the over 5,000 native plants in California, more than a third of them are endemic to the state, a high percentage of those occurring in the Bay Area.

The coast is famous for its redwood trees—the tallest living things on earth. Under the thick canopies of these giants, sword ferns carpet the forest floor, occasionally making room for clover-like redwood sorrel. Shady hills may feature a mixture of madrone, California bay, tan oak, big-leaf maple, and pungent California laurel. The coastal bluffs alternate between brushy chaparral, coastal scrub, and forested headlands, depending very much on the local microclimates. In Point Reyes National Seashore, over 700 plants have been identified. South-facing sunny slopes often host oak savanna with wildflower-filled, grassy meadows. Sagebrush, manzanita, and knobcone pines are characteristic of dry sandstone ridges, where plants must be able to tolerate the meager precipitation and intense summer heat.

Wildlife in the region is easily as impressive as the flora. Invertebrates, many endemic, are very abundant in the muddy, bottom sediments of the San Francisco Bay Estuary, an area rich in plant and wildlife. The marbled murrelet and spotted owl, for example, are limited to old-growth forests. Wetlands, scattered along the coast, around the San Francisco Bay Area provide important feeding and breeding grounds for migratory birds traveling the Pacific Flyway. Sandhill cranes, snow geese, and American coots all stop on their way. Osprey nest in the tops of tall trees near the rivers they fish. Grassy hillsides all over the Bay Area support raptors like red-shouldered hawks and golden eagles and the small mammals and birds upon which they feed.

Tule elk, once numbering in the tens of thousands, were hunted to near extinction before being protected. On the road to recovery, they now survive on Tomales Point in Point Reyes. Mountain lions, seldom seen, roam throughout the area, wherever deer are abundant. Bobcats, coyotes, ravens, raccoons, and skunks are also common. Exotic wild pigs, once released by hunters, are multiplying, causing a big problem in the area. They plow through land like rototillers, digging up roots for their supper.

Seals and sea lions are a common sight along the coast and in coastal estuaries. Harbor seals are the most visible, but California and northern sea lions are also abundant. The largest of the lot, northern elephant seals, hang out and breed on the beaches of Año Nuevo. Whale watchers can observe the yearly migrations of the gray whale from a high spot along the coast, like Point Reyes and Bodega Head.

While threatened by logging, agricultural runoff, dams, and overdevelopment, a few of the Bay Area's rivers still host seasonal trout and salmon runs. Coho salmon and steelhead trout make their way from the ocean up rivers and streams to spawn in the headwaters where they were born.

Among the area's endangered species are the San Francisco garter snake, the California clapper rail, the California least tern, the San Joaquin kit fox, the salt marsh harvest mouse, and the red-legged frog.

Wilderness Restrictions/Regulations

The San Francisco Bay Area has a combination of county, state, and national parks, preserves and reserves, and open space. These lands have important biological, cultural, economic, and recreational value. Permits, access quotas, and fees are part of the effort to balance human use without compromising the health and wild character of the wilderness.

Regulations vary, so it's important to check out rules about dogs, parking, fees, and trail use before departing. They are almost always posted at trailheads. Call ahead about backpacking rules and restrictions. Please heed this advice, follow regulations, and get required permits. It may seem like a pain, but with millions of people living in or visiting the Bay Area, wilderness is becoming an increasingly precious commodity. Help keep the wilderness wild.

How to Use This Guide

T ake a close enough look and you'll find that this little guide contains just about everything you'll ever need to choose, plan for, enjoy, and survive a hike in the San Francisco area. Stuffed with over 300 pages of useful San Francisco–specific information, *Hiking the San Francisco Bay Area* features forty mapped and cued hikes, nineteen honorable mentions, and everything from advice on getting into shape to tips on getting the most out of hiking with your children or your dog.

Here's an outline of *Hiking the San Francisco Bay Area*'s major components.

What You'll Find in This Guide

Each region begins with a **Section Intro,** where you're given a sweeping look at the lay of the land. Each hike begins with an **Overview.** These short summaries give you a taste of the hiking adventures to follow. You'll learn about the trail terrain and what surprises each route has to offer. Following the Overview you'll find the quick, nitty-gritty details of the hike: where the trailhead is located, hike length, approximate hiking time, difficulty rating, type of trail surface, land status, the nearest town, canine compatibility, and what other trail users you may encounter. The **Getting There** section gives you dependable driving directions from a nearby city right to where you'll want to park, and directions by public transportation where available. The **Hike Description** is the meat of the chapter. Detailed and honest, it's a carefully researched impression of the trail. In the **Miles/Directions** section mileage cues identify all turns and trail name changes, as well as points of interest. The **Hike Information** box is a hodgepodge of information. In it you'll find trail hotlines (for updates on trail conditions), trail schedules and use fees, local outdoor retailers (for emergency trail supplies), and a list of maps available to the area. It also gives some recommendations for where to stay, what to eat, and what else to see while you're hiking in the area. Each regional section ends with a **Honorable Mentions** section detailing some of the hikes that didn't make the cut, for whatever reason—in many cases it's not because they aren't great hikes, but because they're overcrowded or environmentally sensitive to heavy traffic. Be sure to read through these. A jewel might be lurking among them.

Don't feel restricted to just the routes and trails that are mapped here. Be adventurous and use this guide as a platform to dive into San Francisco's backcountry and discover new routes for yourself. One of the simplest ways to begin this is to just turn the map upside down and hike the course in reverse. The change in perspective is often fantastic, and the hike should feel quite different. With this in mind, it'll be like getting two distinctly different hikes on each map.

For your own purposes, you may wish to copy the directions for the course onto a small sheet to help you while hiking, or photocopy the map and cue sheet to take with you. Otherwise, just slip the whole book in your backpack and take it all with you. Enjoy your time in the outdoors and remember to pack out what you pack in.

How to Use These Maps

Overview Map. This map (see page iv) shows the location of each hike in the area by hike number (or in case of Honorable Mentions, by letter).

Profile Map. This helpful profile gives you a cross-sectional look at the hike's ups and downs. Elevation is labeled on the left and right, mileage is indicated on the top. Road and trail names, towns, and points of interest are shown along the route.

Route Map. This is your primary guide to each hike. It shows all of the accessible roads and trails, points of interest, water, towns, landmarks, and geographical features. It also distinguishes trails from roads, and paved roads from unpaved roads. The selected route is highlighted, and directional arrows point the way. See The Art of Hiking in the back of this book for more information about maps and navigation.

Hike Information (included in each hike section)

Trail Contacts: This is the direct number for the local land managers in charge of all the trails within the selected hike. Use this hotline to call ahead for trail access information, or after your visit if you see problems with trail erosion, damage, or misuse.

Schedule: This tells you at what times trails open and close.

Fees/Permits: What money, if any, you may need to carry with you for park entrance fees or tolls.

Maps: This is a list of other maps to supplement the maps in this book.

Other important or useful information will also be listed here such as local attractions, outdoor retailers, contacts for hike tours, and selected nearby accommodations and restaurants.

Getting around San Francisco

Area Codes

The Bay Area is split into six area codes: **415** (San Francisco and North Bay), **510** (Oakland), **925** (East Bay), **408** (San Jose and Silicon Valley), **831** (Santa Cruz), and **650** (San Mateo County). The North Coast (Sonoma and Napa) is **707**.

Roads

In California, call **CalTrans** at (800) 427–ROAD or visit them at www.dot. ca.gov/hg/roadinfo for road conditions, closures, and construction status. Also look up www.ceres.ca.gov/flood/fmap/ncal.html for updated flood and weather-related road information.

By Air

The airports in the area are **San Francisco International Airport** (SFO), **Oakland International Airport** (OAK), and **San Jose International Airport** (SJO). SFO often has delays due to fog. Construction at the airport has not ceased since its conception in 1927, so leave time to navigate around the airport by foot and car. The other two smaller airports are easier choices if accessible from your destination.

To book reservations online, check out your favorite airline's Web site, or search one of the following travel sites for the best price: www.cheaptickets.com, www.expedia.com, www.previewtravel.com, www.priceline.com, www.orbitz.com, www.travel.yahoo.com, www.travelocity.com, or www.trip.com. Many of these sites can connect you with a shuttle or rental service to get you from the airport to your destination.

From the Airport

SFO Transportation Hotline provides information on transportation alternatives to SFO. Bus service to SFO is available from the Colma BART Station via the BART-SFO (800-736-2008). You can find a list of operators at www.flysfo.com/ transport/services/gt_tsv_search.asp.

For other bus service to SFO, call SamTrans at (800) 660–4287. For details on the free Caltrain-SFO shuttle, call (800) 532–8405; www.caltrain.com/samtrans/. AirBART provides frequent shuttle service to Oakland International Airport from the Coliseum BART station, (510) 562–7700; www.transitinfo.org/Airports/ AirBART.html.

By Bus

Greyhound services most major towns and cities in California. Schedules and fares are available online at www.greyhound.com or by phone at (800) 231–2222. A few areas that are off the Greyhound routes are connected to the network by local buses.

To connect to a live operator for the **Bay Area transit system** information or for recorded current traffic and incident information, call TravInfo at (510) 817–1717; www.transitinfo.org.

MUNI provides service within San Francisco with diesel buses, trolley buses, Muni Metro streetcars, historic streetcars, and the world-famous cable cars. Muni's eighty-one routes include sixteen express lines. Bicycle racks are available on some buses. Service operates twenty-four hours, daily. (415) 673–6864 or (415) 923–2000; www.transitinfo.org.

AC Transit covers Alameda and Contra Costa Counties. (510) 817–1717; www.actransit.org.

Golden Gate Transit provides regional bus service in San Francisco, Marin, and Sonoma Counties. Service is also available between Marin and Contra Costa County. (415) 455–2000; www.transitinfo.org.

SamTrans covers the South Bay and Peninsula. (800) 660–4BUS; www.transitinfo.org/SamTrans/. Santa Clara Valley Transportation Authority. www.vta.org.

By BART or Train

BART (Bay Area Rapid Transit) serves San Francisco, Alameda, Contra Costa, and Northern San Mateo Counties through five interconnected rail lines and thirty-nine stations. There is bus service to all thirty-nine stations. (510) 465–2278 www.bart.gov.

Regional services include **Caltrain**, a commuter rail that runs down the San Mateo Peninsula from San Francisco to San Jose and Gilroy. (800) 660–4287 or (650) 508–6448; www.caltrain.org. **Altamont Commuter Express** (www.acerail.com) operates rush hour service from Stockton to San Jose.

Since the early 1990s, California has aggressively worked to expand Amtrak rail service by providing new trains and connecting them to off-line cities with coordinated bus connections. **Amtrak's Capitol Corridor** trains provide frequent service between San Jose, Oakland, and Sacramento; **Amtrak Thruway Buses** connect these trains to many other destinations, including San Francisco, Napa Valley, Santa Cruz, and Lake Tahoe. There's a free shuttle for passengers between its Emeryville Station (the main station for the San Francisco Bay Area) and various San Francisco locations. Amtrak information and reservations are available online at www.amtrak.com or by phone at (800) 872–7245.

The **Coast Starlight** train starts in Los Angeles and serves Oakland, Sacramento, Redding, and Dunsmuir on its way to Seattle. The **California Zephyr** is a long-distance train that starts in Chicago and ends in Oakland, stopping in Sacramento and Truckee. **San Joaquin trains** run from Oakland to the Central Valley, with bus connections to Yosemite National Park and Los Angeles.

By Ferry

Alameda/Oakland Ferry provides service to San Francisco (daily) and Angel Island (seasonal). (510) 522-3300; www.transitinfo.org/AlaOakFerry/.

Harbor Bay Maritime provides weekday commuter ferry service between Harbor Bay Isle and San Francisco and seasonal service to 3Com Park. (510) 769-5500; www.harborbayferry.com/.

Golden Gate Ferry provides round-trip service to the San Francisco Ferry Building from Larkspur and Sausalito. (415) 455-2000; www.transitinfo.org/GGT.

Other services include **Angel Island–Tiburon Ferry Service** (415-435-2132; www.angelislandferry.com/); **Blue and Gold Fleet Pier 39–41** ferries to Sausalito, Oakland, Angel Island, Vallejo (415-773-1188; www.blueandgoldfleet.com/); **Red and White Fleet** ferries to Sausalito, Tiburon, and Angel Island (415-546-2628; www.redandwhite.com/).

By Bicycle, Car Pool, or Shuttle

Berkeley TRiP Commute Store offers public transit and bicycling information and sells transit tickets and passes. (510) 644-7665; public-safety.berkeley.edu/trip/.

RIDES for Bay Area Commuters provides car pool, vanpool, bicycle, and other transit information and assistance. (800) 755-7665; www.rides.org/.

Emery Go-Round provides free shuttle service between Emeryville and Mac-Arthur BART in Oakland. www.transitinfo.org/EmeryGoRound/.

Muni has installed bicycle racks on about ten routes. (415) 673-6864.

Call the **Commuter Hotline** for more information on the San Francisco Bicycle Program. (415) 585-2453.

With Disabilities

Dial-a-ride programs provide door-to-door transportation for people with impaired mobility. House of operation, fares, and wheelchair accessibility vary. MV Transportation (415) 468-4300; Paratransit Services (415) 543-9650; East Bay Paratransit provides service. (510) 287-5000 or (800) 555-8085. Yellow Paratransit Program (415) 282-2300; www.transitinfo.org/Access/.

Visitor Information

You can get information for the whole Bay Area at the **San Francisco Visitor Information Center** at Market and Powell Streets, on the lower level of Hallidie Plaza, near the Powell Street BART station. Call (415) 391-2000 for information, (415) 391-2001 for recorded events information. You can also call (415) 561-4323; www.sfvisitor.org/ or www.sfgate.com/traveler/guide/.

Alameda County www.co.alameda.ca.us/.

Half Moon Bay Coastside Chamber of Commerce and Visitors' Bureau, 520 Kelly Avenue, Half Moon Bay. (650) 726-8380; www.halfmoonbaychamber.org.

Marin County Convention and Visitors Bureau. www.visitmarin.org/.

City of Oakland Convention and Visitors Bureau. www.oaklandcvb.com/.

Santa Clara County Convention and Visitors Bureau, 1850 Warburton Avenue, Santa Clara. (800) 272–6822; www.santaclara.org/.

Santa Cruz County Conference and Visitors Council, 1211 Ocean Street, Santa Cruz. (831) 425–1234 or (800) 833–3494; www.santacruzca.org/.

San Mateo County Convention and Visitors Bureau. www.smccvb.com/.

Tri-Valley Convention and Visitors Bureau. (925) 846–8910; www.trivalley cvb.com/visitorinfo.html.

For California visitor information or a travel brochure, call the California Division of Tourism at (800) GOCALIF, or visit their Web site at www.gocalif.ca.gov. The state's official site is www.ca.gov.

Important Phone Numbers

Police and Fire: **911**

Information: **411**

Information (any area code): **(xxx) 555–1212**

Local pay phone calls are 35 cents or 50 cents, depending on the carrier.

Point Reyes

Point Reyes National Seashore features unique elements of biological and histori-cal interest in a spectacularly scenic panorama of thunderous ocean breakers, open grasslands, bushy hillsides, and forested ridges. The biological diversity stems from a favorable location in the middle of California and the natural occurrence of many distinct habitats. Nearly 20 percent of the state's flowering plant species are repre-sented on the peninsula, and over 45 percent of the bird species in North America have been sighted.

But Point Reyes is much more than this.

Even the drive into Point Reyes on Sir Francis Drake Boulevard feels like a journey into a romantic past or some faraway, mystical place. On your drive, you pass Spirit Rock Meditation Center, considered by its devotees as a center of energy. People who have fallen in love with Point Reyes might say the same thing about this National Seashore. And Point Reyes has lots of lovers. But even with over two million visitors every year, you don't feel crowded here or rushed. People travel to Point Reyes for serenity, contemplation, and the sheer beauty of the place.

It's a dramatic strait where the North American Plate meets the Pacific Plate, epicenter of the 1906 San Francisco earthquake, a narrow peninsula that is in con-stant movement as it shifts northward a few inches each year. Here, ridges of damp redwood forests meet warm ocean beaches, with sandpipers scurrying along dain-tily over foamy sand, doubling their number in the reflection of the water. Rocks protect pools that at low tide reveal millions of creatures: starfish, anemones, and clams that cling to the watery stones and hide in crevices in this co-op home.

Point Reyes is home to one of the most spectacular wildflower displays on the West Coast, of thousands of acres charred by fire and in determined and inspired rebirth, young pine forests in thick clumps stretching branches up toward the sky. The northern point protects a herd of tule elk, grazing freely here as they once did all along the Northern California coast when the Miwok Indians lived here. Arti-sans gather here in the historic towns of Point Reyes Station, Inverness, and Olema, towns that seem to have more bed-and-breakfasts than garages. Every-where you look are living watercolors, photo-realistic at sunny noon, at misty dawn impressionistic, in rain-drenched fading light abstract. The lighthouse boasts the foggiest and windiest place on the Pacific, its light struggling to pierce the thick white mist, while across Tomales Bay, sunshine bathes a grassy path as equestrians sway upon their saddled horses.

This is Point Reyes.

1

Mount Wittenberg and Bear Valley Loop

Overview: *The hike starts in lush forest of Douglas fir and oak trees. You then follow the ridgeline, with views of Drake's Bay and the Pacific Ocean. The trail descends to the treeless, stark beauty of coastal bluffs. Have lunch on a tiny, idyllic beach. Then walk through wind-manicured scrub, with views of blue-rippled ocean. Head inland through a fairy-tale woodland of chalk white alders and follow a meandering stream. End up back at the Bear Valley Visitor Center.*

County: Marin
Start: 0.2 mile up Bear Valley Trail from the end of Bear Valley Parking Lot
Length: 12.3-mile loop
Approximate Hiking Time: 6 hours
Difficulty Rating: Strenuous
Trail Surface: A steep dirt path through forest and meadow, climbing 1,300 feet, takes you to a flat ridge top. Descend gradually on single-track dirt trail to coastal bluffs. Dirt trail through

sea scrub follows a strip of the Pacific, then heads inland on a flat, wide, double-track dirt-and-gravel trail, following the creek back to the trailhead.

Land Status: National seashore
Nearest Town: Olema
Other Trail Users: Hikers only; equestrians okay on weekdays; mountain bikers on most of Bear Valley Trail
Canine Compatibility: No dogs allowed

Getting There

By Car: From San Francisco, take U.S. Route 101 north. Exit at Sir Francis Drake Boulevard (for the cities of Fairfax and San Anselmo), and continue west on Sir Francis Drake to Olema. From the Richmond/San Rafael Bridge, take the Sir Francis Drake exit and stay on Sir Francis Drake until it ends at Olema and Highway 1. To get to the visitor center, turn right in Olema onto Highway 1, then make an almost immediate left onto Bear Valley Road. Continue on Bear Valley Road for less than a half mile—you'll see the visitor center entrance on the left. Turn in and park by the center.

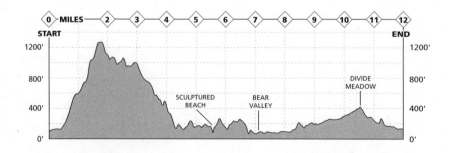

Mount Wittenberg and Bear Valley Loop

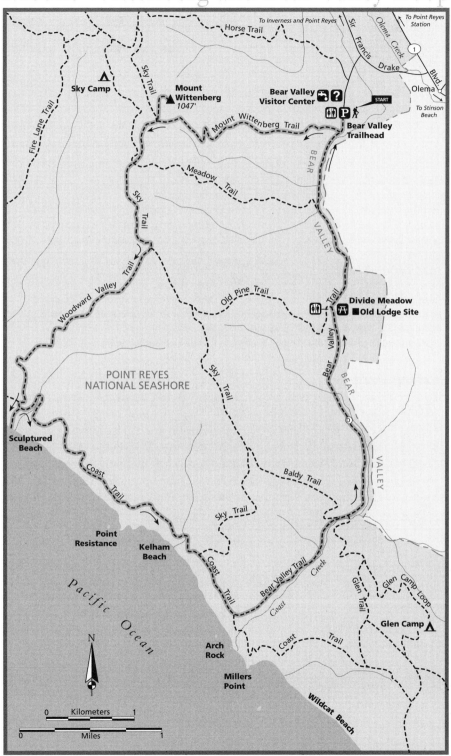

Horse Trail

To Inverness and Point Reyes

To Point Reyes Station

Olema Creek

Sir Francis Drake

Blvd.

To Stinson Beach

Olema

Sky Trail

Sky Camp

Fire Lane Trail

Mount Wittenberg
1047'

Bear Valley
Visitor Center

START

Bear Valley
Trailhead

Mount Wittenberg Trail

Meadow Trail

Sky Trail

Woodward Valley Trail

Old Pine Trail

Bear Valley Trail

Divide Meadow
Old Lodge Site

BEAR VALLEY

POINT REYES
NATIONAL SEASHORE

Sky Trail

Sky Trail

Baldy Trail

Sculptured
Beach

Coast Trail

Point
Resistance

Kelham
Beach

Coast Trail

Bear Valley Trail

Coast Creek

Glen Trail

Glen Camp Loop

Glen Camp

Pacific Ocean

N

Arch
Rock

Millers
Point

Coast Trail

Wildcat Beach

0   Kilometers   1

0   Miles   1

By Public Transportation: From San Rafael, take the Route 65 Inverness–P.R.N.S.–San Rafael. For times and more information, contact Golden Gate Transit (415–455–2000; www.goldengatetransit.org).

Hike Description

The Bear Valley Visitor Center makes a comfortable starting point for this long, but very enjoyable, hike. Wander through the bookstore, grab a map, talk to a ranger, and take advantage of the full facilities.

A brief meadow jaunt brings you to the Mount Wittenberg Trail, the only uphill portion of the hike and a good 1,300-foot climb, pleasantly graded but steady. At 1,407 feet, Mount Wittenberg is the highest point on Point Reyes Peninsula. It was named for a father and son who leased land here for a large—and hilly—dairy ranch in the 1860s.

Douglas firs along the Woodward Valley Trail

Thick, lush Douglas fir and oak forest—with the occasional endangered Bishop pine—canopies the dirt trail textured with angular roots and surrounded by healthy maidenhair, chain, and appropriately named five-fingered ferns. It's a fairly popular weekend trail, but less so than the flat, wide, and easy Bear Valley Trail. On a weekday after a good rain, you may share the trail only with browsing deer, skittering squirrels, and birds hopping through trees and foraging the ground for food. Bird life here is unparalleled in North America. Over 400 species of birds are attracted to the peninsula's mild climate, diversity of habitat, varied topography, and location on the western edge of a continent.

Sky Trail takes you along the ridge where, through the trees, you get your first glimpse of ocean to the northwest with Drake's Bay and the Estero de Limantour hugging the Limantour Spit. A stand of tall, charred Bishop pine trunks stand eerily on hills to the west, a testament to the devastating 1995 Mount Vision fire. But here and on Woodward Valley Trail you can see young Douglas firs and Bishop pines reinvigorating the forest. Bishops, like Monterey and knobcone pines, are known as fire pines. It takes fire to "hatch" the seeds from their cones and start new growth. To tell the difference between the Bishop pine and Douglas fir, take a look at the cones and the needles. Bishop pines have two long needles per cluster and large cones. Douglas firs have short needles that poke out from the branch like a bottlebrush and small, waxy-looking cones.

The Woodward Valley Trail takes you through hillside valleys, bathed with afternoon sunlight and through about a 6-foot-wide corridor with woodland on either side, mostly new-growth Douglas firs. Views open up to the expanses of the Pacific Ocean. As you descend toward the Coast Trail, the surrounding trees disappear and the salty, misty smell of the sea strengthens.

The Coast Trail offers the stark beauty of the bluffs, the contemplative view of the Pacific, and the mesmerizing sound of the waves lapping rhythmically on the shore. Yellow and blue-purple coast bush lupine add color in the spring, along with golden-yellow lizard-tail, coast fiddleneck, and gumplant. Pink bursts of sea thrift color the early summer.

A short detour to Sculptured Beach offers a great lunch and napping spot if the wind is calm. Winter rains feed two creeks, which stream across the sand into the ocean, creating a wet barrier that isolates the little coarse-sand beach. It takes its name from the jutting water-carved rocks exposed at low tide.

The Coast Trail section of the hike ends at Arch Rock. This arch is typical of Northern California's coastline, known as a submerged coastline, meaning that in the past 10,000 years or so the ocean level has risen to inundate former valleys. These flooded valleys have consequently been battered and carved away over the past 10,000 years, leaving sea stack, sea caves, and arches like this one well worth visiting.

Bear Valley heads inland again, following the Coast Creek, which cascades toward the ocean. Pretty mountain springs tumble down rocks on the opposite banks, feeding the creek. Alder trees with chalk-white bark lean over the water.

Soon after the Coast Creek turns away from the path out of earshot, you come upon Divide Meadow, with picnic tables, log seats, and rest rooms available beside the inviting expanse of mowed grass. In late August the far end of the meadow displays bright pink "naked ladies," old-world amaryllis lilies probably planted by owners of the hunting lodge that stood here long ago. Bear Valley Road brought early 1900s travelers by horse-drawn carriage from Olema to the popular hunting lodge. Presidents William H. Taft and Theodore Roosevelt belonged to the club, which disbanded when this became a preserve in 1976.

On all these trails, in wooded Woodward Valley and on Mount Wittenberg, in the scrub of the Coast Trail and especially in Bear Valley's sloping meadows, you will undoubtedly see native black-tailed deer and the exotic axis and fallow deer. Shy and graceful, axis deer were brought here in the late 1940s from India for hunting. They have a reddish brown coat with small white spots, a white bib chest, and a dark stripe running the length of their backs. Bucks shed their antlers every winter. A hunter named Ottinger bought a herd of the fallow deer from the San Francisco Zoo and brought them here in the 1950s for more game. Native to the Mediterranean region, individuals may be charcoal, light brown, chocolate brown, spotted, or the most stunning, pure white. White fallow deer grazing on a green meadow look a bit like mythical unicorns from a distance. Males drop their antlers in April. Despite their dense population around Wittenberg, the foreign deer do not compete directly with the native black-tail, which browse, pawing and digging for food, while axis and fallow graze goatlike on the grassland.

Bear Valley after Divide Meadow is probably the single most traveled trail in Point Reyes, but returning near dusk, most tourists have already gone to town for cocktails and oysters. The Bear Valley Creek, running inland away from the coast, accompanies you the rest of the way along with borders of oak, bay, and Douglas fir, and high banks that allow you a close-up look at the vegetation and insect life here. White milkmaids, yellow buttercups, and pink checkerbloom brighten the grasslands in spring, but it's a favorite winter walk too.

Miles/Directions

0.0 START from the parking lot at Bear Valley Visitor Center. Walk to the end of the lot, west toward the driveway to the old Morgan Ranch. The double-track Bear Valley Trailhead heads west across the meadow.

0.2 Turn right onto Mount Wittenberg Trail.

2.0 To continue on the Mount Wittenberg Trail, turn left. It becomes Sky Trail toward Woodward Valley Trail (1.1 mile).

2.4 Trailhead for Sky Trail and Meadow Trail. Continue straight on Sky Trail 0.7 mile to Woodward Valley Trail.

3.1 Woodward Valley Trailhead. Turn right, heading 1.8 miles to Coast Trail. **Option:** For a shorter hike, continue straight on Sky Trail. Turn left onto Old Pine Trail, right onto Bear Valley Trail, and back to visitor center, 6.7 miles.

4.9 Turn left onto Coast Trail.

5.4 Detour to Sculptured Beach. Turn left onto single-track trail that leads to beach.

5.6 Sculptured Beach. Return on the same path to Coast Trail.

5.8 Turn right on Coast Trail. After the second wooden bridge, watch for Arch Rock. Pass the trailhead for Sky Trail.

8.3 Trailhead for Bear Valley Trail. Turn left, heading inland along Coast Creek.

10.7 Divide Meadow. Continue on Bear Valley Trail.

12.1 Bear Valley Trailhead. Continue to visitor center and parking lot.

12.3 Bear Valley Visitor Center, parking lot and starting point.

Hike Information

🖊 Trail Contacts:
Point Reyes National Seashore/ National Park Service, www.nps.gov/pore/recreation/recreation.htm or www.nps.gov/pore
Bear Valley Visitor Center, Point Reyes Station, CA (415) 464–5100

🕐 Schedule:
Open year-round sunrise to sunset

💲 Fees/Permits:
No fees

❓ Local Information:
West Marin Chamber of Commerce, P.O. Box 1045, Point Reyes Station, CA 94956 (415) 663–1200; www.pointreyes.org
Point Reyes National Seashore Association, Point Reyes Station, CA (415) 663–1200; www.ptreyes.org or www.pointreyes.net
Coastal Traveler, www.coastaltraveler.com/w01_cover.html

📍 Local Events/Attractions:
Kule Loklo (0.5-mile walk from Bear Valley Visitor Center) (415) 464–5100
Marin French Cheese Factory, 7500 Redhill Road, Petaluma, CA (707) 762–6001

🛏 Accommodations:
Camping at Point Reyes (415) 663–8054; www.nps.gov/pore/recreation/camping/camp2.htm

Hostelling International—Point Reyes (off Limantour Road, P.O. Box 247, Point Reyes Station, CA 94956 (415) 663–8811; www.norcalhostels.org
Neon Rose Cottage, Point Reyes Station, CA (415) 663–9143; www.neonrose.com
Casa Mexicana, 11800 State Route 1, Point Reyes Station, CA (415) 663–8463

🍴 Restaurants:
Olema Inn and Restaurant, U.S. Route 1 & Sir Francis Drake Boulevard, Olema, CA (415) 663–9559
Olema Farm House, 10005 State Route 1, Olema, CA (415) 663–1264
Station House Cafe, 11180 State Route 1, Point Reyes Station, CA (415) 663–1515

🛒 Local Outdoor Retailers:
REI—Corte Madera, 213 Corte Madera Town Center, Corte Madera, CA (415) 927–1938; www.rei.com

🚶 Hike Tours:
Bear Valley Visitor Center, Point Reyes Station, CA (415) 464–5100
Marin Agricultural Land Trust, www.malt.org/event.htm

🅝 Maps:
www.nps.gov/pore/pphtml/maps.html
USGS maps: Inverness, CA; Drake's Bay, CA

2   Point Reyes National Seashore: Tomales Point

Overview: *There's something about the stark beauty of the coastal bluffs, often appearing and disappearing in sheets of wispy fog. The Victorian-built whitewashed buildings of Pierce Ranch stand isolated and haunting on the green hills. Springtime wildflowers add bursts of color along the trail. Hiking Tomales Point is invigorating and mysterious, so that your blood starts pumping before even setting out. Though hikers, as a rule, are generally unsatisfied with a return-trip single trail, the crashing of the Pacific against the shore and the majestic rocky sculptures and sea cliffs offer a contemplative view that's worth revisiting.*

County: Marin
Start: Right of the Historic Pierce Point Ranch at the end of Pierce Point Road
Length: 9.2-mile round trip
Approximate Hiking Time: 4.5 hours
Difficulty Rating: Moderate
Trail Surface: Double-track dirt trail rises and

falls moderately through grassland and scrub. A single-track dirt trail (1.6 miles) leads to the point
Land Status: National seashore
Nearest Town: Inverness
Other Trail Users: Hikers only
Canine Compatibility: No dogs allowed

Getting There

By Car: From San Francisco, take U.S. Route 101 north. Exit at Sir Francis Drake Highway (for the cities of Fairfax and San Anselmo), and continue west on Sir Francis Drake to Olema. From the Richmond/San Rafael Bridge, take the Sir Francis Drake exit and stay on Sir Francis Drake until it ends at Olema and Highway 1. To get to the visitor center, turn right in Olema onto Highway 1, then make an almost immediate left onto Bear Valley Road. Pass the visitor center. At the end of Bear Valley Road, turn left on Sir Francis Drake Boulevard. Pass the town of Inverness. The road curves westward. Turn right on Pierce Point Road, where you see the sign for Kehoe and McClures Beaches and Tomales Point. Take it to the Pierce Point Ranch, and park in the lot in front of the buildings.

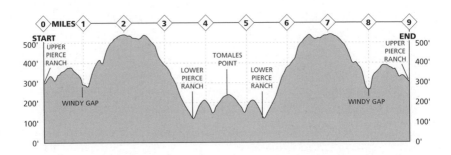

Tomales Point

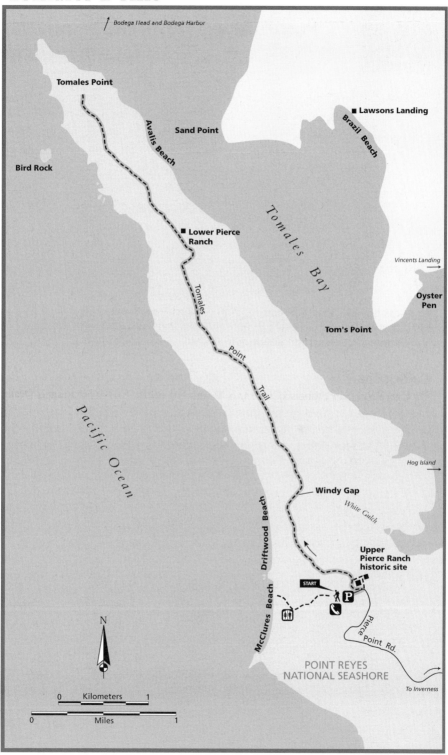

Bodega Head and Bodega Harbor

Tomales Point

Avalis Beach

Sand Point

Lawsons Landing

Brazil Beach

Bird Rock

Tomales Bay

Lower Pierce Ranch

Vincents Landing

Oyster Pen

Tomales

Point

Tom's Point

Trail

Pacific Ocean

Hog Island

Windy Gap

White Gulch

Driftwood Beach

Upper Pierce Ranch historic site

START

McClures Beach

N

Pierce Point Rd.

POINT REYES NATIONAL SEASHORE

To Inverness

Kilometers
0   1

Miles
0   1

By Public Transportation: From San Rafael, take the Route 65 Inverness–P.R.N.S.–San Rafael bus. You will have to bike or hitch a ride out to the trailhead. The park service runs a shuttle on weekends in summer. For times and more information, contact Golden Gate Transit (415–455–2000; www.goldengatetransit.org).

Hike Description

The point's rich pasture caught the eye of a farmer named Solomon Pierce, who began a dairy here in 1858. Pierce and his son Abram produced fine butter, which was shipped to San Francisco from a wharf they built on Tomales Bay. For seven decades, the point remained in the Pierce family. In post–gold rush San Francisco, if a proprietor displayed the sign POINT REYES BUTTER, shoppers knew they were getting the best.

The walk begins at Upper Pierce Ranch at the Pierce family house, barn, and outbuildings, now maintained by the National Park Service. You can wander through the grounds and read about its history on interpretive signs. The path, the old ranch road, wanders over the green hills, which are seasonally sprinkled with yellow-orange poppies and tidy tips, orange fiddleneck, and purple iris.

Tomales Point is the northernmost boundary of Marin County and Point Reyes National Seashore and makes you feel as if you've reached the end of the world in some ways. The point is literally splitting away from the Bolinas Ridge, separated by Tomales Bay, which follows the San Andreas Fault line, where the Pacific and the North American plates move past each other in opposite directions.

Views from this trail are superb, starting with the beach and surf to the west. You can see the occasional fishing vessel bobbing on the ocean. In February and March, you can spot molting elephant seals on the isolated patches of sand below the cliffs. As you crest the ridge and meander a saddle, you can see the eastern side, Tomales Bay, little Hog Island in the bay, and the village of Dillon Beach, oyster central. The old ranch road descends to the site of Lower Pierce Ranch, marked by a pond and a eucalyptus grove, the only trees on this part of the bluff. This is where the "official" trail ends. But a well-worn social trail takes you out to a high vista point that looks down on Bird Rock, occupied by cormorants and white pelicans. From there, a faint path takes you to the very top of Tomales Point for stirring views of Bodega Head and Tomales Bay, a worthwhile destination point for hikers. If you are trekking with children or are short on time, you can turn around at any point on the trail and still get a good sense of the area. The main highlight of this trail: the tule elk.

Sailing past the Point Reyes Peninsula in the year 1800, explorers saw large herds of tule elk roaming through open grasslands. As a matter of fact, for thousands of years, as many as 500,000 tule elk thrived in California, from the lush open country of the Central Valley to the grassy hills on the coast. This particular species (*Cervus elaphus nannodes*) occurs nowhere else. The Miwok Indians lived peacefully with the herds. But following the gold rush of 1849, the new settlers hunted the elk nearly to extinction and took over their habitat for agriculture and livestock

A pacific-side view from the trail—wow!

grazing. By 1870, fewer than ten tule elk survived.

In 1874, ranch workers draining a marsh to create new agriculture fields near San Luis Obispo discovered this last remaining herd. None had been seen for the last four years. The landowner, Henry Miller, felt compelled to protect the elk, and by 1905, their population had grown to 140. When the elk began eating Miller's crops and trampling his fences, he captured some and moved them to other locations in California. This was the first time the animals were moved for conservation.

The state awarded the elk complete protection in 1971. In the spring of 1978, two bulls and eight cows were brought in from the San Luis Island Wildlife Refuge near Los Banos and set into a three-acre enclosure on the point while they adjusted. They obviously liked their new coastal views; six of the cows bore calves that summer. By fall, seventeen elk were released to enjoy 2,600 acres of open grassland and coastal scrub on Tomales Point. By 1998, over 500 elk lived on the bluffs and more than 3,000 in different parts of California. The Point Reyes herd is one the largest

Hike Information

🅘 Trail Contacts:
Point Reyes National Seashore/ National Park Service, www.nps.gov/pore/recreation/ recreation.htm or www.nps.gov/pore
Bear Valley Visitor Center, Point Reyes Station, CA (415) 464–5100

🅞 Schedule:
Open year-round sunrise to sunset

🅢 Fees/Permits:
None

🅠 Local Information:
West Marin Chamber of Commerce, P.O. Box 1045, Point Reyes Station, CA 94956
(415) 663–9232; www.pointreyes.org
Point Reyes National Seashore Association, Point Reyes Station, CA 94956
(415) 663–1200; www.ptreyes.org or www.pointreyes.net
Coastal Traveler, www.coastaltraveler.com/w01_cover.html

🅠 Local Events/Attractions:
Bike rentals: David L. Barnetts Cycle Analysis, Rentals and Repairs (415) 663–9164
Blue Waters Kayaking, 12938 Sir Francis Drake Boulevard, Inverness, CA (415) 669–2600
Horseback riding: Five Brooks Stables, 8001 State Route 1, Olema, CA (415) 663–1570

🅛 Accommodations:
Camping at Point Reyes
(415) 663–8054; www.nps.gov/pore/ recreation/camping/camp2.htm
Hostelling International—Point Reyes (off Limantour Road), P.O. Box 247, Point Reyes Station, CA 94956 (415) 663–8811; www.norcalhostels.org
Rosemary Cottage, 75 Balboa Avenue, Inverness, CA (415) 663–9338
Terry's Homestay Atop Inverness Ridge, Point Reyes Station, CA (800) 969–1289
West Marin Lodging Network, 11434 Shoreline Highway, Old Creamery Building, Suite 17, Point Reyes, CA (415) 663–9543
Inverness information: www.pointreyes.org/inverness.html

🅘 Restaurants:
Manka's Restaurant, Callendar Way and Argyle, Inverness, CA (415) 669–1034

🅠 Local Outdoor Retailers:
REI—Corte Madera, 213 Corte Madera Town Center, Corte Madera, CA (415) 927–1938; www.rei.com

🅗 Hike Tours:
Bear Valley Visitor Center, Point Reyes Station, CA (415) 663–1092 or (415) 464–5100
Marin Agricultural Land Trust, www.malt.org/event.htm

🅝 Maps:
www.nps.gov/pore/pphtml/maps.html
USGS maps: Tomales, CA; Drake's Bay, CA

---

of the twenty-two in the state. Watch for one bull and his harem and a gang of bachelor bucks grazing by the trails, common socialization for the elks.

Coyotes and mountain lions will target elk calves, but an elk's flailing, hard hooves can easily kill a coyote and damage a lion. Neither type of attack has ever been documented in the park, so the elks live pretty much predator free. However, some are stricken with an illness contracted by cattle that weakens their immune system, making the dry season particularly hard to survive. You may see a ranger out on the bluff researching this phenomenon by taking samples from a carcass.

The point is also home to an amazing number of hawks and falcons that rest on the scrub looking for moles and rabbits. Big black ravens sit in pairs on the blanched rock outcroppings that give the grassy ridge top a sort of Stonehenge feel.

There are no facilities at the ranch, but a short drive will take you to rest rooms and the trailhead to McClures Beach. A short, steep, downhill 0.6-mile walk brings you to this small cove with its intense surf. The rocks at either end of the beach add to the drama and danger. It is tempting to venture around the southern corner to explore the adjacent beach, but it can only be safely accessed during the outgoing low tide.

Miles/Directions

0.0 START from the parking lot at Upper Pierce Point Ranch.

1.0 Windy Gap (Driftwood Beach below)

2.0 Highest point (535 feet). To the east is Tom's Point, jutting out into Tomales Bay; to the north, Brazil Beach.

3.0 Lower Pierce Ranch. Sign leads to Tomales Bay. To the east is Sand Point, with the town of Dillon Beach just north. Between the two is the University of Pacific Marine Station of Biological Science.

4.0 Trail to western edge of point overlooking Bird Rock. Several faint trails heading northwest lead to Tomales Bluff, the tip of the point.

4.6 Tomales Point (255 feet above sea level) and view of Bodega Bay. Turn around and head back the way you came.

9.2 Upper Pierce Ranch and parking lot.

3 Point Reyes National Seashore: Lighthouse and Chimney Rock Trails

Overview: *These are two short, exhilarating hikes. The lighthouse walk features marine wildlife and plant life that can survive harsh weather conditions. The lighthouse (open from 10:00 A.M. to 4:30 P.M., Thursday to Monday, weather permitting) is the best place in Marin to watch gray whales migrating from Alaska to Baja California. On a clear day, you can see out to the Farallon Islands. Chimney Rock boasts one of the best wildflower displays on the coast and is the site of shipwrecks dating to 1585. Along the Chimney Rock Trail, towering 500-foot cliffs provide spectacular coastline scenery. A short drive is required to get to the Chimney Rock trailhead from the lighthouse.*

County: Marin
Start: These two short hikes start at the end of Sir Francis Drake Highway in Point Reyes National Seashore.
Length: 1.2 and 1.8 miles
Approximate Hiking Time: 2 hours for both
Difficulty Rating: Easy

Trail Surface: Paved road, lighthouse stairs, and viewing platform; single-track dirt pathway under cypress trees, overlooking cliffs. Wind and fog are likely.
Land Status: National seashore
Nearest Town: Point Reyes Station
Other Trail Users: Hikers only
Canine Compatibility: No dogs allowed

Getting There

By Car: From San Francisco take U.S. Route 101 north. Exit at Sir Francis Drake Boulevard (for the cities of Fairfax and San Anselmo), and continue west on Sir Francis Drake to Olema. From the Richmond/San Rafael Bridge, take the Sir Francis Drake exit and stay on Sir Francis Drake until it ends at Olema and Highway 1. Turn right onto Highway 1 and proceed about 100 yards. Take the first left turn at Bear Valley Road. In about a mile, at the stop sign, Bear Valley Road becomes Sir Francis Drake Boulevard once again. Continue straight on Sir Francis

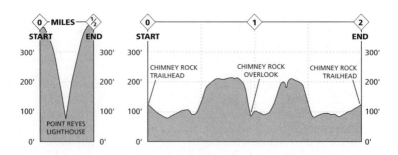

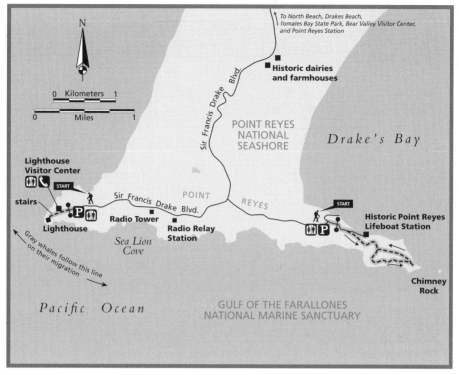

Drake Boulevard about 20 miles until it ends at the lighthouse parking lot. The driving time from the Bear Valley Visitor Center is about forty-five minutes.

By Public Transportation: From San Rafael, take the Route 65 Inverness–P.R.N.S.–San Rafael. For times and more information contact Golden Gate Transit (415) 455–2000, www.goldengatetransit.org.

Hike Description

For hard-core hikers who need a calf-burner grade to feel authentic, this could be a redefining experience. The lighthouse and Chimney Rock are proof that short hikes can be equally rewarding.

The forty-five-minute drive to the lighthouse from the Bear Valley Visitor Center hardly seems that long. The western end of Sir Francis Drake Boulevard takes you past Inverness and serene Tomales Bay, through rolling valleys, and beside ocean dunes. Historic dairy farms along the way post their dates of origin. Try to identify the oldest of these picturesque old cow haunts. The creameries here still supply people around San Francisco with milk and cheese. You pass several other trailheads and turnoffs to Point Reyes beaches, some with great tide pools. At one point, the road follows the crest of a ridge, dropping off on either side. You can admire both the white cliffs in Drake's Bay that Sir Francis thought looked like Dover and the vast Pacific Ocean that puts human life on a different scale.

Check at the Bear Valley Visitor Center (open Thursday to Monday from 10:00 A.M. to 5:00 P.M.) to see if you can drive all the way to the lighthouse parking lot. On weekends, when good weather brings more tourists out, you may have to park at Drake's Beach and take a shuttle to the lighthouse.

The lighthouse parking lot is small, so an early arrival is recommended. Park and walk up the paved lighthouse service road. If clear, most of the 11 miles of Point Reyes beach are visible from here. You can watch the tide ebb and flow, smell the fresh sea air, and hear the waves splash on the sand.

In 1981, this 948-nautical mile area became the Gulf of the Farallones National Marine Sanctuary. The preserve stretches from the beach all the way to the Farallon Islands and includes marshes, mudflats, a tidal zone, and deep ocean waters. It is home to numerous seabirds, diving birds, stellar and California sea lions, elephant seals, porpoises, dolphins, whales, harbor seals, flounder, halibut, Pacific herring, and invertebrate species. Tide pooling, clamming, fishing, boating, and wildlife observation activities are encouraged.

Before you reach the lighthouse itself, you can learn about the human history, wildlife, and plant life of the area in the Lighthouse Visitor Center. If you're visiting during gray whale migration, you may especially enjoy the facts about these large baleen mammals.

Point Reyes Lighthouse

Those strange cement domes across from the visitor center were built in 1870 for catching and storing rain for drinking water and steam for energy up here when lightkeepers kept their lonely watch. During drought, keepers had to buy water from ranchers on the peninsula.

From the viewing platform past the visitor center you can watch a whale 30 to 50 feet in length breaching, hurling itself out of the water and landing smack on its back. This is one of the best places in Northern California to see whales (short of being on a boat). It's on high ground above the water with breakers just offshore. When whale spotting, look for spouting (that's when a whale exhales air through its blowhole and the air rises 10 to 15 feet, condensing into a white vapor). Bring binoculars.

This is the foggiest area on the West Coast and one of the windiest. Rangers say this with some pride, so you may hear it often while visiting Point Reyes. More important than the beacon from the lighthouse here is the fog signal. The housing for the system is open to the public. Over the years, the fog signals have gone from bells to whistles to electric foghorns. The current automated system produces a sound every 30 seconds (a D sharp).

Even with the foghorn, boats still wreck here. Typically, a year doesn't go by without a wreck of a personal vessel, fishing craft, or other boat. It has always been very dangerous for ships, dating back to the first reported wreck, the *San Augustin* in 1595. During the gold rush of the 1840s, mariners lost $1 million in ships and cargo and called for the lighthouse to be built. A committee of mariners paid $6,000 for the land, and the lighthouse was completed in 1869. But even afterwards, the treacherous coastline took its toll: The ship *Samoa*, and the oil freighter *Richfield*, and the sailing ship *Haddingtonshire* all went down. Not until electric and radar navigation were perfected did these tragedies happen less frequently.

The sea adventures of Henry Dana, Jules Verne, and Robert Louis Stevenson come to mind as you descend the stairs. Ahead of you is an isolated whitewashed lighthouse, small on its narrow precipice. (The lighthouse isn't always open; inquire at the visitor center.) Though completely functional, the lighthouse is now used only for interpretation and is lit every other Saturday. On those Saturdays, you can call at 10:00 A.M. to reserve space for a group of up to eight. The first twenty-five people get to go out to the lighthouse at night.

The lens is made up of 1,032 dazzling prisms that refract or reflect light out to sea, creating 1,000 watts. On a clear night it can be seen 24 nautical miles out. A weight-and-pulley system starts the gears running and creates a flash pattern every five seconds.

When you're ready to head back up, you will have a different view of the 310 steps you came down, equivalent to a thirty-story building. Here's your calf-burner if you want it. If taking it more leisurely, several benches on the way offer rest points.

Back on the lighthouse service road, interpretive signs on the right tell you about the few plants that manage to thrive in the harsh conditions here. Pale green lichens and salal with its thick and glossy leaves are native as is the bright orange algae on the boulders by the road. The wife of a lightkeeper once planted a small garden nearby, but with no success. Wind blew away new sprouts.

Hike Information

📞 Trail Contacts:
Point Reyes National Seashore/ National Park Service, www.nps.gov/pore/recreation/recreation.htm or www.nps.gov/pore/ **Bear Valley Visitor Center,** Point Reyes Station, CA (415) 464–5100

🕐 Schedule:
Open year-round sunrise to sunset. Lighthouse stairs and exhibits (weather permitting), 10:00 A.M. to 4:30 P.M., Thursday through Monday.

💲 Fees/Permits:
None for parking or hiking; shuttle bus $3.50 per person on weekends from New Year's to Easter when the weather is good.

❓ Local Information:
West Marin Chamber of Commerce, P.O. Box 1045, Point Reyes Station, CA 94956 (415) 663–9232; www.pointreyes.org/ **Point Reyes National Seashore Association,** Point Reyes Station CA 94956 (415) 663–1200; www.ptreyes.org/ or www.pointreyes.net/ **Coastal Traveler,** www.coastaltraveler. com/w01_cover.html

💡 Local Events/Attractions:
Clem Miller Educational Center (415) 663–1200; www.ptreyes.org/clem/center. html **Morgan Horse Ranch** (next to the Bear Valley Center), Point Reyes Station, CA (415) 663–1763

🛏 Accommodations:
Backpacking Camps at Point Reyes (415) 663 8054; www.nps.gov/pore/ recreation/camping/camp2.htm **Hostelling International—Point Reyes** (off Limantour Road), P.O. Box 247, Point Reyes Station, CA 94956 (415) 663–8811; www.norcalhostels.org **Inns of Marin** (415) 663–2000; www.innsofmarin.com **Point Reyes Lodging** (415) 663–1872; www.ptreyes.com

🍴 Restaurants:
Gray Whale Pizza & Pasta, 12781 Sir Francis Drake Boulevard, Inverness, CA (415) 669–1244 **Perry's Delicatessen,** 12301 Sir Francis Drake Boulevard, Inverness Park, CA (415) 663–1491

🚵 Local Outdoor Retailers:
REI–Corte Madera, 213 Corte Madera Town Center, Corte Madera, CA (415) 927–1938; www.rei.com

🚶 Hike Tours:
Bear Valley Visitor Center, Point Reyes Station CA (415) 464–5100 **Marin Agricultural Land Trust,** www.malt.org/event.htm

Ⓝ Maps:
www.nps.gov/pore/pphtml/maps.html **USGS Maps:** Tomales, CA; Drakes Bay, CA; Inverness, CA

Before driving to the Chimney Rock trailhead, two pit toilets are available in the lighthouse parking lot.

Chimney Rock

The drive is fifteen minutes and well marked to the Chimney Rock Trailhead. Facing the trailhead, to your left is Drake's Bay, named for sixteenth century explorer Sir Francis Drake.

Available for touring is the Lifeboat House on the beach of Drake's Bay. The U.S. Life Saving Service built the first fully equipped station in Point Reyes in

1889. The station moved to its current site on Drake's Beach in 1912. Check it out either before or after the Chimney Rock hike.

A lot of trade and commerce used to take place here. Ships would motor or sail over the landbar during high tide into Limantour and Drake's Bay to a little inlet called Scooter Bay. The dairy workers would meet the ships on scooters, carrying butter, cheese, and dairy products that the vessels would take back to San Francisco.

On the bluffs, especially in spring, you will see a beautiful West Coast wild-flower display. Yarrow, baby blue eyes, cobweb thistle, flowering flax, beautiful purple Douglas iris, yellow footsteps of spring, violet and yellow bush lupine, orange California poppy, red Indian paintbrush, large star linanthus, and seaside daisy grow in thick clumps on the hillsides sloping to the sea.

An easy walk on the single-track trail to the end of the bluff brings you to Chimney Rock, a rock outcrop resembling a chimney stack that marks the meeting point of Drake's Bay, the headlands, and the sea. This is another spot to watch whales. Also, you can observe the elephant seals molting or mating on isolated beaches below.

Hiking on the Overlook Trail offers views of headland reserves, the Farallon Islands 20 miles off the point, and, of course, shipwrecks of the last two centuries. Along the Pacific side of the bluff, waves crash against the cliffs below you. You are at different times 50 to only 5 feet from the edge.

The hike may be short, but it is very satisfying and leaves you with energy to go tidepooling, walking on a beach, or loitering around Point Reyes Station.

Miles/Directions

0.0 START at the lighthouse parking lot. Walk uphill past the gate on the paved road to the lighthouse.

0.1 Point Reyes Beach is below (not accessible from paved trail).

0.5 Visitor Center. Head down the stairs to the lighthouse.

0.6 Lighthouse. Head back up stairs.

0.7 Back to visitor center. Head back down service road to parking lot.

0.8 Interpretive sign about local plant life.

1.2 Back to car. Drive to Chimney Rock Trail. To reach the trailhead, drive out the way you came about 1.5 miles and turn left, following the signs to Chimney Rock.

0.0 Chimney Rock trailhead.

0.3 Junction with Underhill Road. Continue straight. U.S. Coast Guard Lifeboat Station below.

0.9 End of the bluff, overlooking Chimney Rock. Head back on Overlook Trail.

1.4 Overlook area. Turn right onto trail toward Drake's Bay.

1.5 Junction with Chimney Rock Trail. Turn left and follow it back to car, or continue down to tour Lifeboat Station, then take road back to the trail head.

1.8 Back to parking lot.

4 Point Reyes National Seashore: Palomarin Trailhead to Alamere Falls

Overview: *The trail from Palomarin on the southwestern edge of Point Reyes National Seashore takes you through coastal bluffs with Pacific views. Then it takes you through the shade of a Douglas fir forest, past streams and quiet lily-covered ponds. There are two lakes on the featured hike, four if you plan to hike at low tide. The highlight of this hike is 50-foot Alamere Falls. During low tide, you can take the beach all the way back. Otherwise, you travel back the way you came. Bring plenty of water, binoculars for marine and coastal wildlife, and a long-sleeved shirt, pants, and Technu if you take the narrow poison oak–laden path to the falls from the Coast Trail, which is definitely worth it if the tide is high. Weather is changeable.*

County: Marin
Start: Palomarin Trailhead for the Coast Trail at the end of Mesa Road
Length: 8.8 miles round trip
Approximate Hiking Time: 5 hours
Difficulty Rating: Moderate with a strenuous 0.1 climb down to the beach at the falls and back up
Trail Surface: Double-track dirt trail goes along open coastal bluffs past ponds, creeks, and lakes and through woodland. A narrow, single-track trail leads to Alamere Falls. A rutted, steep shale and sandstone bluff heads to Wildcat Beach at the falls.
Land Status: National seashore
Nearest Town: Bolinas
Other Trail Users: Equestrians
Canine Compatibility: No dogs allowed

Getting There

By Car: From San Francisco, take U.S. Route 101 north to the Highway 1 north/Stinson Beach exit. From the Richmond/San Rafael Bridge, take the Sir Francis Drake Boulevard exit to Route 101 south (toward San Francisco), and take the Highway 1 north/Stinson Beach exit. Follow signs to Highway 1, Panoramic Highway, and Mount Tamalpais. Drive up the windy foothills of Mount Tam. There are two splits. Stay left at both of them on Highway 1 to Stinson Beach. The highway takes you over the ridge and starts heading north along the coast through

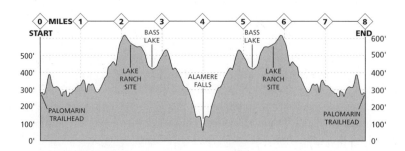

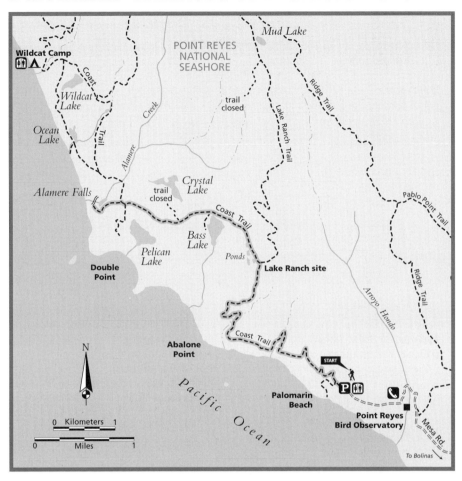

Wildcat Camp

POINT REYES
NATIONAL
SEASHORE

Mud Lake

Wildcat
Lake

Coast

Creek

trail
closed

Ridge Trail

Ocean
Lake

Trail

Alamere

Lake Ranch Trail

Alamere Falls

trail
closed

Crystal
Lake

Coast Trail

Pablo Point Trail

Bass
Lake

Pelican
Lake

Ponds

Lake Ranch site

Double
Point

Ridge Trail

Arroyo Hondo

N

Coast Trail

Abalone
Point

START

Pacific

P

Palomarin
Beach

Point Reyes
Bird Observatory

Mesa Rd.

0   Kilometers   1

0   Miles   1

Ocean

To Bolinas

the town of Stinson Beach, then past the Bolinas Lagoon on your left. At the end of the lagoon, turn left on Olema-Bolinas Road. If you miss it, turn left on Horseshoe Hill to get back to Olema-Bolinas Road. Turn right on Mesa Road at the stop sign and take it for 4 miles. It becomes a gravel road and passes the Point Reyes Bird Observatory. At the end of Mesa Road is the gravel parking lot for the Palomarin Trailhead.

By Public Transportation: Follow transit directions for Stinson Beach, except continue on GG bus #63 to its terminus at the Audubon Canyon Ranch entrance. From there, you need a bicycle or a ride to the trailhead. Only one morning bus travels to the preserve, and only one travels back in the afternoon. Make sure you are at the Marin City transfer stop (Donahue and Terners) for the 9:28 A.M. bus, and leave the preserve on the 3:05 P.M. bus. For more information, contact Golden Gate Transit (415–455–2000; www.goldengatetransit.org).

Hike Description

The obscure trailhead, past the Point Reyes Bird Observatory at the end of a pot-holed dirt road, bodes of good things from this hike—and they hold true. At first, you walk by 3-foot grassland between tall, soldier-like rows of eucalyptus. The Australian natives were probably planted as windbreakers for a ranch built on this spot, though there is a colorful but unlikely legend that people planted patches of eucalyptus around the Bay Area to create a habitat for imported koalas.

Past the turnoff for charcoal-shaded Palomarin Beach, you walk stark coastal bluffs through fields of yellow lupine, peach-orange monkeyflowers, broom, coffeeberry, coyote brush, and California sagebrush. Rabbits streak across the trail early morning and late afternoon. Binoculars help you see the sea lions and various seabirds bobbing above a kelp bed in the surf below, while the white water crumbles and dissolves against rock and sand. In March, those binoculars may even help you spot gray whales as they migrate north along the coast. If it's clear, the Farallon Islands seem only a long leap away. A marine preserve stretches from the Point Reyes National Wilderness across the sea to the Farallones. Farther south, you may see fishing vessels or freighters making their way into the San Francisco Bay.

The Coast Trail heads inland, passing over numerous finger creeks. You enter a forest of mature Douglas firs shadowing out most plants except moisture-loving ferns and grasses. Where sunlight gets through, you can see wild strawberries and manroot. Branches of Alamere Creek are on either side of the path. You'll come upon a series of still ponds to the left, with green lily pads growing on their surface. Then comes Bass Lake.

One of the most romantic spots in the Bay Area, Bass Lake is also a popular swimming hole in summer and a good place to fish. It may be overrun on summer weekends, but in winter and on some weekdays, it is quiet and invites long gazing. Ducks skim the water, making streaks of silver on the black mirror surface.

Pelican Lake offers a wonderful illusion. The freshwater lake is backed by two hillsides called Double Point that slope down in a V and kiss just at the lake's surface, revealing the Pacific backdrop. It looks like the lake is suspended just above the sea.

Alamere Falls is an amazing sight, especially after it rains. It is one of two coastal falls in California. (Its sister, McWay Falls, is a more accessible attraction at Big Sur.) Here in Point Reyes, wide Alamere Creek tumbles over a bluff, creating two smaller waterfalls on the hillside, then drops straight off the edge of a cliff 40 feet onto exposed rock and Wildcat Beach. At its heaviest flow, the falls are 25 feet across. During drier times, it may split into two narrower falls. As the tide rises, the salty surf comes up to meet the fresh water flowing in. A favorite lunch spot is on the cliff beside the falls. Getting there is an adventure. From Wildcat Camp, past serene Ocean Lake and the narrow end of Wildcat Lake, you can hike the beach the entire way within an hour of low tide. But that takes careful planning. From the Coast Trail, a narrow, marked, but unmanaged single-track dirt trail with lots of scrub threatening to overgrow the path takes you to the top of the falls. Wear a

Hikers discussing Alamere Tidefall on the beach

long-sleeved shirt and long pants for this jaunt. To get to the bottom of the falls and see the largest drop to the beach properly, you have to cross over the cascading stream. Even in rainy winter, the crossing is not too wide, but it requires a jump and looks intimidating because of the roiling waters. The trail also involves a climb down water-rutted canyons and slivering rock banks to view the upper and lower part of the 50-foot falls. But it is well worth it if you miss low tide.

Stop by the Point Reyes Bird Observatory on the way out. If you stay the night in Bolinas, the lagoon supports an amazing variety of water birds. The Audubon Canyon Ranch has more information and guided bird watching. Also, the town of

Hike Information

Trail Contacts:
Point Reyes National
Seashore/National Park Service,
www.nps.gov/pore/recreation/
recreation.htm or www.nps.gov/pore
Bear Valley Visitor Center, Point Reyes Station, CA (415) 464–5100

Schedule:
Open year-round sunrise to sunset

Fees/Permits:
None

Local Information:
West Marin Chamber of Commerce,
P.O. Box 1045, Point Reyes Station, CA
94956, (415) 663–9232;
www.pointreyes.org
Point Reyes National Seashore Association, Point Reyes Station, CA 94956
(415) 663–1200; www.ptreyes.org or
www.pointreyes.net
Coastal Traveler,
www.coastaltraveler.com/w01_cover.html

Local Events/Attractions:
Audubon Canyon Ranch, 4900 Highway
1, P.O. Box 577, Stinson Beach, CA 94970
(415) 868–9244; www.egret.org
Bolinas Museum, 48 Wharf Road,
Bolinas, CA 94924 (415) 868–0330;
www.bolinasmuseum.org
Point Reyes Bird Observatory, Mesa
Road, Stinson Beach, CA 94970 (415)
868–0655; www.prbo.org

Accommodations:
Camping at Point Reyes (415)
663–8054; www.nps.gov/pore/recreation/
camping/camp2.htm
Hostelling International—Point Reyes
(off Limantour Road), P.O. Box 247, Point
Reyes Station, CA 94956 (415) 663–8811;
ww.norcalhostels.org
Smiley's Schooner Saloon and Hotel,
41 Wharf Road, Bolinas, CA (415)
868–1311
Thomas White House Inn, 118 Kale
Road, Bolinas, CA (415) 868–0279;
www.thomaswhitehouseinn.com

Restaurants:
Blue Heron Inn, 11 Wharf Road, Bolinas, CA
(415) 868–1102
Coast Cafe, 46 Wharf Road, Bolinas, CA
(415) 868–9984

Local Outdoor Retailers:
REI—Corte Madera, 213 Corte Madera
Town Center, Corte Madera, CA (415)
927–1938; www.rei.com

Hike Tours:
Bear Valley Visitor Center, Point Reyes
Station, CA (415) 464–5100
Marin Agricultural Land Trust,
www.malt.org/event.htm

Maps:
www.nps.gov/pore/pphtml/maps.html
USGS maps: Bolinas, CA; Double Point,
CA; Inverness, CA

Bolinas is charming and unique. Its culture combines the influences of old hippies, the invigorating physical life of living on the coast, small town gossip, young surfers, and out-of-town tourists trying to get away from the city.

Miles/Directions

0.0 START from the parking lot for the Palomarin Trailhead. The trailhead is on the east side of the parking lot next to the rest rooms. Climb the stairs and turn left onto Coast Trail.

0.1 Pass trailhead for Palomarin Beach (0.6 mile to beach). Continue on Coast Trail.

2.2 At the junction with Lake Ranch Trail, stay to your left on Coast Trail.

2.8 Bass Lake. Admire it from the trail, or take the narrow trail on the north side of the lake.

3.1 Pass the trailhead for Crystal Lake Trail. (*Note*: Be careful; trail is overgrown.) If it is accessible when you pass, you can reach the lake in less than 0.5 mile. Stay on Coast Trail.

3.6 Pelican Lake and Double Point. Continue on Coast Trail.

3.9 Trailhead for Alamere Falls Trail. Turn left onto trail to cliffs above beach. (*Note*: Watch for poison oak.) **Option:** Time it so you reach this point just before low tide and continue on Coast Trail. Take the left (west) loop of Ocean Loop Trail past Ocean Lake and Wildcat Lake, then back to trail down to beach. Follow beach back to Alamere Falls, and go up trail just before falls. Return to Coast Trail on Alamere Falls Trail.

4.3 Top of Alamere Falls. Cross stream below second falls for trail down to beach. (*Note*: Be careful; loose rock.)

4.4 View of falls from Wildcat Beach. Return by same trail.

4.5 Return to Coast Trail via Alamere Falls Trail.

4.9 Turn right on Coast Trail, and retrace your steps past the lake to Palomarin.

5.2 Pass Pelican Lake.

6.0 Pass Bass Lake.

6.6 Stay on Coast Trail past the junction with Lake Ranch Trail. (If it's really clear to the west, you can see the Farallon Islands.)

8.8 Palomarin Trailhead and parking lot.

5

Tomales Bay State Park: Heart's Desire Beach to Shell Beach

Overview: *The hike encompasses three of the park's four beaches. An extra mile gets you to Indian Beach as well. Between beaches, each more isolated than the last, the trail takes you through a thick, damp woodland of oaks, bays, alders, willows, and Bishop pines. On the beaches, you can sort through shells and stones and watch California sea lions poke their torpedo-shaped noses above the water. Clam digging and fishing (with license) are other options.*

County: Marin
Start: Johnstone Trailhead at Heart's Desire Beach past the main entrance of Tomales Bay State Park
Length: 8.0-mile round trip
Approximate Hiking Time: 4.5 hours
Difficulty Rating: Moderate
Trail Surface: Single-track dirt trail through oak, bay, madrone, and Bishop pine woodland from beach to beach
Land Status: State park
Nearest Town: Inverness
Other Trail Users: Mountain bikers and equestrians
Canine Compatibility: No dogs allowed except in picnic areas on leash

Getting There

By Car: From San Francisco, take U.S. Route 101 north to Sir Francis Drake Boulevard exit, then west on Sir Francis Drake. From the Richmond/San Rafael Bridge, take the second exit, Sir Francis Drake Boulevard, and follow it west. Take Sir Francis Drake Boulevard 15 miles until it ends at Highway 1 in Olema. Turn right on Highway 1 and take the first left on Bear Valley Road (toward the Bear Valley Visitor Center). Continue past the visitor center. At the stop sign, Bear Valley once again meets up with Sir Francis Drake Boulevard. Turn left and follow the boulevard until it splits again. Stay right on Pierce Point Boulevard (signs to Tomales Bay State Park). Turn right at the main entrance to Tomales Bay State Park (sign to Heart's Desire Beach). Go past the kiosk and turn left into Heart's Desire parking lot (there is additional parking down the road to the right).

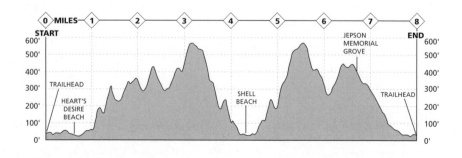

Tomales Bay State Park

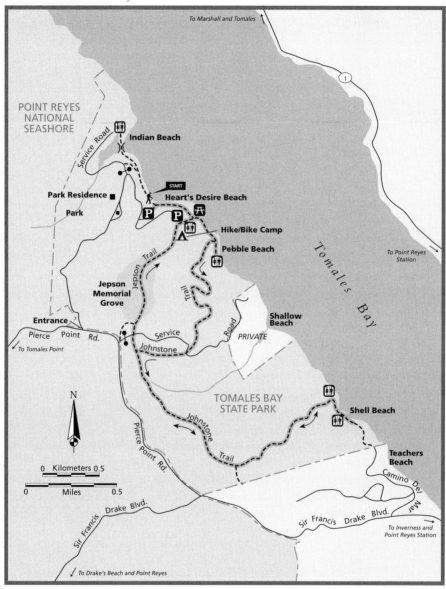

To Marshall and Tomales

POINT REYES
NATIONAL
SEASHORE

Service Road

Indian Beach

Park Residence

Park

START

Heart's Desire Beach

P   P

Hike/Bike Camp

Pebble Beach

Jepson Trail

Jepson
Memorial
Grove

Trail

Tomales Bay

To Point Reyes
Station

Entrance

Pierce   Point   Rd.

To Tomales Point

Service Road

Johnstone

Shallow
Beach

PRIVATE

N

TOMALES BAY
STATE PARK

Johnstone

Shell Beach

Pierce Point Rd.

Trail

Teachers
Beach

0   Kilometers 0.5

0   Miles   0.5

Camino Del Mar

Sir Francis Drake Blvd.

Sir Francis Drake Blvd.

To Inverness and
Point Reyes Station

To Drake's Beach and Point Reyes

By Public Transportation: From San Rafael, take the Route 65 Inverness–P.R.N.S.–San Rafael bus. You will have to bike or hitch a ride out to the trailhead. The park service runs a shuttle on weekends in summer. For times and more information contact the Bear Valley Visitor Center (415–464–5100) and Golden Gate Transit (415–455–2000; www.goldengatetransit.org).

Hike Description

The Coast Miwok people inhabited this region for 3,500 years, making a living of fishing, digging for clams and oysters, collecting edible and medicinal plants, and hunting game for food and clothing. Tomales Bay State Park was a homeland for many tribes.

The word *Miwok* means "people" in the Sierra Miwok language. The Coast Miwok who lived by Tomales Bay used the term *mítcha* or *mítchako*. The Támal-ko, the Indians of the Tomales, had more than one hundred village sites on the Point Reyes Peninsula. Eleven of them were at Shell Beach and Indian Beach. The self-guided nature trail on the way to Indian Beach tells some of the Miwok story, focusing on Native American uses of local plants.

As you wander the beaches, you can picture the natives making their homes here. Imagine them going about their daily routines in the sheltered coves, beaches, tidal marshes, and Bishop pine forests on the western shores of Tomales Bay. The Támal-ko ate Washington clams and used basket or heart cockles and bay mussels for tools and jewelry as well as food. They made other tools out of chert stone and formed sinker stones, probably for fishing nets, from obsidian. Archeologists have also found leaf-shaped obsidian spearheads, fired clay balls, and some clam disk beads, which may have been used as a kind of money.

Juan Rodriguez Cabrillo, a Portuguese navigator sailing under the flag of Spain, was the first European to see Point Reyes in 1542, though his crew did not come ashore anywhere in Northern California. English explorer Sir Francis Drake was the first foreigner to weigh anchor in Drake's Bay when his ship, the *Pelican*, needed repairs in 1579. He was exploring this land in the name of her majesty Queen Elizabeth I. (On the trip home he renamed the ship the *Golden Hind*. The queen knighted him upon its decks after the two-year voyage.) To the Miwoks, Drake may have looked like a ghost. They believed that to the west, from which the Europeans came across the Pacific Ocean, was *úute-yómi*, the "dead home." A line through the surf led to the far-off place in the west where the dead could be with Old Man Coyote, the creator ('Oye-'Oyyis).

The Spanish arrived next in 1595 but didn't settle in until the late 1700s, when they released cattle onto the grasslands and sought to convert the Miwoks to Christianity in nearby missions. Most of the Indians died from disease brought by the new settlers. Remaining descendants try to keep old stories and traditions alive, but they are very few. Russian and German scientists explored the area in the early 1800s, identifying many previously unknown plants.

Throughout the Point Reyes Peninsula, in the little towns of Point Reyes Station, Olema, Inverness, and Marshall, you can see the influences of all these different cultures. From landmark names (for example, Olema comes from Miwok, Point Reyes the Spanish, Drake's Bay from you-know-who) to ranching and dairy traditions and building styles, you can find adopted customs unique to this rich and isolated coastal community.

Heart's Desire Beach

Real estate developers in the 1940s began to purchase large areas of beachfront land, but local residents and conservation groups said, "No way!" As a result of their grassroots efforts, Tomales Bay was formally dedicated and opened to the public in 1952.

The area offers hiking, fishing, boating (nonmotorized boats may be launched at Heart's Desire Beach), swimming, ten camping sites with cold showers, and four beaches, all with rest rooms and each with its own character. Indian Beach, with its interpretive signs along the half-mile path, makes for a great family hike. Heart's Desire Beach, the trailhead and most accessible beach, is a great swimming and picnic beach, but tends to get crowded on summer weekends. The romance that its name implies is definitely attainable on less busy weekdays and quieter cool winter afternoons.

Pebble Beach, a mile past Vista Point picnic area, is a secluded swimming cove aptly named for its colorful stones decorating the sand. Shell Beach, the final destination of the hike, consists of two small beaches separated by rock outcrops covered with black-shelled mussels and white barnacles. Being 4 miles from the main entrance, it is the quietest of the beaches and offers the most. The scattering of shells in the sand are fun to look at, as are the clear mounds of jellyfish that plant themselves on the beach in low tide. And there are other sea creatures to find in the crevices of rocks and buried in sand. California sea lions frequent the bay waters as do a variety of waterfowl. Brandt's cormorants can be spotted drying themselves on the rocks. Puffins, great blue herons, and sandhill cranes add a more exotic feel to the bay view.

The thick woodland, wet ravines, and pastoral meadows that you glimpse are home to foxes, raccoons, badgers, weasels, chipmunks, rabbits, bobcats, wood rats, moles, coyotes and black-tailed deer. Spotted owls fly by at dusk. Coveys of quail waddle over the afternoon trail. Goldfinches and towhees hop from branch to branch. The hammer of a woodpecker echoes through the trees as a meadowlark whistles a few bars of its favorite melody. Lots of lizards skitter over stumps in summer, as monarch butterflies stretch their wings around blossoming wildflowers.

The two adjoining trails that make up this hike are named for lovers and protectors of plants. Botanist professor Willis Linn Jepson (1867–1946) founded the School of Forestry and funded the Jepson Herbarium at the University of California, Berkeley. The author of the esteemed *Manual of the Flowering Plants of California* is honored by the Jepson Trail. Way ahead of his time, he wrote an article in 1893 describing how native California plants were being crowded out by alien plants. One of the finest remaining virgin groves of Bishop pine in California is in the park's Jepson Memorial Grove. The Jepson Trail takes you right through it.

Conservationist Bruce Johnstone, a Marin County planner, and his wife, Elsie, worked long and hard to preserve Tomales Bay and place part of it in a state park. Johnstone Trail leads from Pebble Beach to Shell Beach. A plaque trailside pays them tribute. The beautiful path is shared with mountain bikers.

Miles/Directions

0.0 START from the parking lot for Heart's Desire Beach. Walk to the left end of the beach to Johnstone Trailhead.

0.1 Picnic area for Heart's Desire Beach.

0.2 Vista Point group picnic area. Follow Johnstone Trail to Pebble Beach.

0.4 Bear left to Pebble Beach. Return to single-track Johnstone Trail to Shell Beach.

0.5 Turn left, continuing on Johnstone Trail to Shell Beach. Bridge crosses creek. Trail heads uphill at a moderate grade. Lawson's Landing to the east.

1.5 Trailhead and junction with paved fire road. Cross paved road, staying on single-track dirt trail, now the Johnstone/Jepson Trail.

1.7 Trailhead for Jepson Trail (to take on the way back). Go straight, continuing on Johnstone Trail (to Shell Beach, 2.5 miles). Look for wild strawberries, lilies, mushrooms, and rare western leatherwood scrub. The flat trail starts to rise moderately. Viewing benches along the way.

4.2 Shell Beach—final destination. The wooden steps and path lead to Shell Beach. (Beyond that there is a 0.2-mile trail to Camino del Mar Drive.)

6.7 Back to Jepson Trail. Turn left. In less than 0.1 mile, pass over paved access road, and continue on Jepson Trail to Jepson Memorial Grove.

7.7 Jepson Trail ends at parking lot for Vista Point. Walk across parking lot to Vista Point picnic area.

7.8 In Vista Point picnic area, turn left onto single-track Johnstone Trail.

8.0 Back at Heart's Desire Beach and parking lot. **Option:** Take self-guided 0.9-mile nature trail loop on other side of the beach to Indian Beach.

Hike Information

① Trail Contact:
Tomales Bay State Park, Star Route, Inverness, CA 94937 (415) 669–1140; cal-parks.ca.gov

◐ Schedule:
Open year-round from 8:00 A.M. to sunset

⑤ Fees/Permits:
$2.00 per car when kiosk attended

❷ Local Information:
West Marin Chamber of Commerce, P.O. Box 1045, Point Reyes Station, CA 94956 (415) 663–9232; www.pointreyes.org
Point Reyes National Seashore Association, Point Reyes Station, CA 94956 (415) 663–1200; www.ptreyes.org or www.pointreyes.net
Coastal Traveler, www.coastaltraveler.com/w01_cover.html

♀ Local Events/Attractions:
Bike Rentals: David L. Barnetts Cycle Analysis, Rentals and Repairs (415) 663–9164
Blue Waters Kayaking, 12938 Sir Francis Drake Boulevard, Inverness, CA (415) 669–2600
Horseback Riding: Five Brooks Stables, 8001 State Route 1, Olema, CA (415) 663–1570

⊖ Accommodations:
Camping at Tomales State Park (415) 669–1140

Hostelling International—Point Reyes (off Limantour Road), P.O. Box 247, Point Reyes Station, CA 94956 (415) 663–8811; www.norcalhostels.org
Holly Tree Inn and Cottages, P.O. Box 642, Point Reyes Station, CA 94956 (415) 663–1554 or (800) 286–HOLL; www.hollytree.com
Inverness information: www.pointreyes.org/inverness.html
West Marin Lodging Network, 11434 Shoreline Highway, Old Creamery Building, Suite 17 Point Reyes, CA (415) 663–9543

⑪ Restaurants:
Hog Island Oyster Farm, Marshall, CA (415) 663–9218
Tony's Seafood, 1883 Highway 1, Marshall, CA (415) 663–1107

⊕ Local Outdoor Retailers:
REI—Corte Madera, 213 Corte Madera Town Center, Corte Madera, CA (415) 927–1938; www.rei.com

⑪ Hike Tours:
Tomales Bay State Park, Star Route, Inverness, CA (415) 669–1140
Marin Agricultural Land Trust, www.malt.org/event.htm

Ⓝ Maps:
Tomales Bay State Park, Star Route, Inverness, CA 94937 (415) 669–1140; cal-parks.ca.gov
USGS maps: Inverness, CA; Drakes Bay, CA; Point Reyes NE, CA: Tomales, CA

6

Samuel P. Taylor State Park: To the Top of Barnabe Peak

Overview: *Starting off by Devil's Gulch Creek, Bill's Trail gently ascends to the top of Barnabe Peak and past a 30-foot waterfall. At the lookout, the 360-degree view takes in Tomales Bay to the Pacific Ocean, the towns of San Geronimo and Lagunitas, and isolated Kent Lake and Peters Dam in the Marin watershed. The fire roads on the way down allow you to enjoy those vistas a while longer.*

County: Marin
Start: Devil's Gulch Horse Camp on Sir Francis Drake Boulevard
Length: 7.1-mile loop
Approximate Hiking Time: 3.5 hours
Difficulty Rating: Moderate
Trail Surface: Paved fire road for 0.1 mile takes you to single-track dirt trail up the mountain at about a 5 percent grade through forest.

Reach the top of the mountain and return on dirt fire roads through grasslands.
Land Status: State park
Nearest Town: Olema
Other Trail Users: Mountain bikers and equestrians on fire roads; hikers only on Bill's Trail
Canine Compatibility: Dogs on leash on fire roads only

Getting There

By Car: From San Francisco, take U.S. Route 101 north. Exit at Sir Francis Drake Highway (for the cities of Fairfax and San Anselmo). From the Richmond/San Rafael Bridge, take the Sir Francis Drake exit and continue west. Take Sir Francis Drake past the town of Lagunitas into a wooded area (about 15 miles from Highway 101). The trailhead is past the main entrance to Samuel P. Taylor Park, but you might want to take the left into the main entrance (signs for picnicking and camping warn you that it's coming up) to pick up trail maps and information. If so, just park in the fifteen-minute area by the kiosk to avoid paying fees. Continue another mile (past the Madrone Camp) to Devil's Gulch Horse Camp, and park in the gravel lot on the left side of the road. Cross the street to the trailhead.

By Public Transportation: From San Rafael, take the Route 65 Inverness–P.R.N.S.–San Rafael bus. For times and more information, contact Golden Gate Transit (415–455–2000; www.goldengatetransit.org).

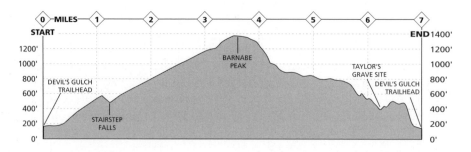

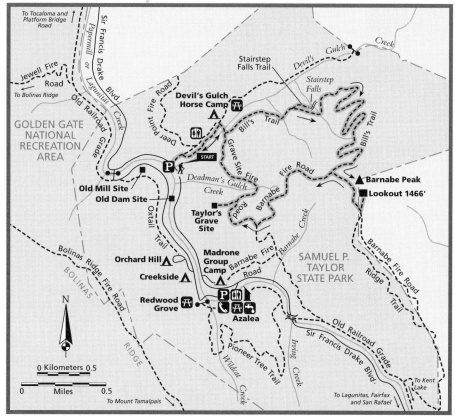

Hike Description

There are many firsts in this park's history. Samuel Penfield Taylor (1827–1896) was ahead of his time in advocating responsible land use and recreation. On this site, he started the first paper mill on the West Coast and the first overnight camp for city dwellers. He established one of the first major towns on the Point Reyes Peninsula (Taylorville, long gone), built the first fish ladder in the West, and developed the first "modern" grocery bag as we know it today. He prospered, recycled . . . *and* rescued a mule. Now, that's California spirit.

In 1874, Taylor built a rustic hotel in what is now the Redwood Grove picnic area to house friends and business associates. They brought their friends and then, with the opening of a narrow-gauge railroad to serve the isolated Tomales Bay region, the general public started showing up. Taylor enlarged the hotel and added tent cabins and a dance pavilion big enough for a thirty-piece brass band. He and his wife called it Camp Taylor. It was the first campground for city children and their parents in the state of California. By 1888, over 3,000 people came to Camp Taylor each year.

Taylor's son James took over management of Camp Taylor in 1888 and added more facilities and a third floor to the hotel, renaming it Hotel Azalea for the blooms covering the banks of Lagunitas, then called Papermill Creek. It burned down in the early 1900s and was not reconstructed. But the state park service purchased the land in 1946. Samuel P. Taylor was one of the first parks in the United States to offer camping as part of its recreation program.

It's hard to believe all this bustle took place here as you walk through the quiet forests and picturesque picnic areas. There is a self-guided nature and history trail (2 miles plus) in the main part of the park that would be a great option for a short hike or if you have the energy after the featured hike or are staying the night. Enjoy a dip in the swimming hole—a favorite for over half a century—in warm weather.

Samuel P. Taylor is divided in two by Sir Francis Drake Boulevard. The featured hike is opposite the campground, passing the area where Taylor and his family lived and where his gravesite is today, enclosed by a white picket fence. The easy climb through serene forests takes you to the top of Barnabe Peak (1,466 feet), which is indeed named for a mule.

View from bridge across Devil's Gulch Creek

He was a retired army mule who had crossed the plains with General John C. Fremont's troops. Taylor found the old, white burro at the San Francisco Presidio, named him Barnabe, and brought him back to Camp Taylor, where he became a favorite pet of the children and guests. A smart old ass, Barnabe often escaped his corral and trekked up to the top of the mountain to graze on the plentiful grasslands. And so the peak, which he claimed, took his name.

Recently when livestock from a neighboring farm hopped the fence to graze the pristine grasses of the park, the rangers did not grant them the same privileges, although the sight of a white llama on the slopes looked like Barnabe's ghost.

Today the inhabitants of Barnabe Peak—except for the rangers who man the Fire Lookout Station—are all wild. Red-tailed and red-shouldered hawks, kestrels, vultures, and ravens circle the skies. You may spot a fox, bobcat, or badger. Skunks, gophers, squirrels, mice, and snakes also make this home. Black-tailed deer are the most commonly seen big animals.

Miles/Directions

0.0 START from the dirt and gravel parking area on the side of the road across from the Devil's Gulch Horse Camp. Cross the street onto the paved fire road past the gate to start the hike. Devil's Gulch Creek is on the right.

0.1 Turn right onto the unnamed, single-track dirt trail. To your left up the hill is the horse camp.

0.2 Turn right to cross the bridge over Devil's Gulch Creek, then left onto Bill's Trail to Barnabe Peak (4 miles to peak). The trail takes you over several numbered bridges that cross over cascading creeks and springs that flow down the mountain and into Devil's Gulch Creek.

1.2 Trailhead to Stairstep Falls. Turn left to the falls.

1.4 Stairstep Falls. Head back the way you came to Bill's Trail.

1.6 Turn left, continuing up Bill's Trail to Barnabe Peak. A moderate grade, the path makes a series of hairpin turns. Watch for views of Tomales Bay to the west.

4.6 Junction with Barnabe Fire Road. Turn right up the hill to reach fire lookout tower.

4.8 Fire lookout tower. Head back the way you came on Barnabe Fire Road.

5.0 Pass the trailhead to Bill's Trail, staying on the double-track dirt Barnabe Fire Road. Forest is on your right.

6.0 Trailhead. Turn right on Gravesite Fire Road.

6.1 Trail to Taylor's gravesite (0.1-mile round trip). Return to the Gravesite Fire Road.

6.2 Continue left on Gravesite Fire Road toward forest and Devil's Gulch. (*FYI*: Fire road may be muddy and washed out in places after winter storms.) You are passing through Deadman's Gulch (watch for narrow seasonal streams).

6.4 Trailhead. A watershed access road to the right is closed to visitors. Take the double-track Deadman's Gulch Trail to the left. Trail meets up with Gravesite Fire Road heading down to Devil's Gulch and the bridge.

6.9 Back at the bridge. Turn left after the bridge onto the single-track trail you came in on.

7.0 Trail meets paved fire road. Take this back out to Sir Francis Drake Boulevard.

7.1 Cross Sir Francis Drake Boulevard back to parking lot.

Hike Information

🟢 Trail Contact:
Samuel P. Taylor State Park, P.O. Box 251, Lagunitas, CA 94938 (415) 488–9897; cal-parks.ca.gov/DISTRICTS/marin/sptsp233.htm

🕐 Schedule:
Open year-round sunrise to sunset

🟢 Fees/Permits:
No fees (entrance to main picnic areas and campgrounds is $2 per car)

❓ Local Information:
West Marin Chamber of Commerce, P.O. Box 1045, Point Reyes Station, CA 94956 (415) 663–9232; www.pointreyes.org
Point Reyes National Seashore Association, Point Reyes Station, CA 94956 (415) 663–1200; www.ptreyes.org or www.pointreyes.net
Coastal Traveler, www.coastaltraveler.com/w01_cover.html

🟡 Local Events/Attractions:
Morgan Horse Ranch (next to Bear Valley Visitor Center), Point Reyes Station, CA (415) 663–1763
Point Reyes Lighthouse (415) 669–1534

🛏 Accommodations:
Camping (800) 444–7275; www.ReserveAmerica.com/usa/ca/samu

Coastal Getaways, P.O. Box 681 Point Reyes, CA 94956 (888) 663–9445; www.coastalgetaways.com
Rosemary Cottage, P.O. Box 273, 75 Balboa Avenue, Inverness, CA 94937 (415) 663–9338; www.rosemarybb.com
Vacation Rentals: A1vacations.com or 10kvacationrentals.com
Point Reyes Lodging (415) 663–1872; ptreyes.com

🍽 Restaurants:
Olema Inn and Restaurant, U.S. Route 1 and Sir Francis Drake Boulevard, Olema, CA (415) 663–9559
Taqueria la Quinta, Third and Highway 1, Point Reyes Station, CA (415) 663–8868

🏕 Local Outdoor Retailers:
REI—Corte Madera, 213 Corte Madera Town Center, Corte Madera, CA (415) 927–1938; www.rei.com

👥 Hike Tours:
Samuel P. Taylor State Park, P.O. Box 251, Lagunitas, CA 94938 (415) 488–9897; cal-parks.ca.gov/DISTRICTS/marin/sptsp233.htm

🟢 Maps:
USGS maps: San Geronimo, CA

Honorable Mentions:
Point Reyes

A. Point Reyes National Seashore: Inverness Ridge

A hike through Inverness Ridge takes you to the beginnings of a forest. Still in recovery from the 1995 Mount Vision fire, the area feels new. Everywhere, plants compete for precious sun and soil. Young Bishop pines grow in fast, healthy crowds on the hillsides around the charred remains of their ancestors who died in the flames. You can look out at hillsides and valleys all the way to the sea, now vibrant green, and imagine it the way it looked after the firestorm finally died, everything ashen gray and smoldering. The surroundings on Drake's View and Bucklin Trails illustrate a story of devastation and renewal all around you.

The 7-mile loop starts off Limantour Road. Take Muddy Hollow Road to the Bayview Trail. Turn left onto Drake's View Trail to the Inverness Ridge. Turn left for 0.5 mile along the ridge and left down Bucklin Trail, which affords great views of Drake's Bay and the ocean. Back on Muddy Hollow Road, turn left again and follow it 1.4 miles back to the trailhead.

To get there from Highway 101 west, take the Sir Francis Drake Boulevard exit west. Where it ends in Olema, turn right onto Highway 1. Take the first immediate left on Bear Valley Road (you can pick up a map at the visitor center on the way). Take Bear Valley Road to Limantour Road. Turn left onto Limantour Road. Turn right onto Muddy Hollow Road, which ends shortly at the trailhead. For more information, check out the Point Reyes National Seashore/National Park Service Web site at www.nps.gov/pore/recreation/recreation.htm or www.nps.gov/pore, or call the Bear Valley Visitor Center, Point Reyes Station at (415) 464–5100.

B. Point Reyes on Rainy Days

It rains a lot here. And when it does, it's usually windy too.

The last place you want to be on a stormy, wet day is the lighthouse. It sounds romantic, and it certainly would give you a taste of the life of the lonely, isolated, and weather-beaten lighthouse keepers of Point Reyes. But it's also one of the foggiest, windiest places in the world. Besides, on really socked in days, rangers will close this area to tourists.

In light rain or mist, most of the hiking trails are stunning. Light rain is great Point Reyes weather, darkening the hue of the forest, adding sparkle to leaves and crystal-hung spider webs. But the heavy stuff, gloomy sheets of rain and ice-chill winds may require hiking on asphalt. Luckily, Point Reyes offers fascinating paved hikes.

Park at the Bear Valley Visitor Center, take in the slide show, then head across the parking lot to the Earthquake Trail. A 0.6-mile loop starts almost on the epicenter of the great San Francisco earthquake of 1906. Interpretive signs along the way show you how the right slip fault line actually works and illustrates how Point Reyes is traveling north on the Pacific Plate, while the North American Plate moves west at the speedy rate of several feet per century. You can also walk 0.5 mile to Kule Loklo, a modern rendering of a Miwok village.

Oh, and there are the surroundings: a meandering creek, pretty wooden farm fences, scrub oaks and shrub, meadows, and grassy hills. Remember, it's bad luck to step on a banana slug. They'll be looking for pavement on rainy days too.

Mount Tamalpais and Its Foothills

The people of Marin County love their mountain. Mount Tamalpais is an important part of the Bay Area's western skyline. Its foothills rise from the towns of Fairfax, Mill Valley, and San Anselmo to the east and end at the Pacific Ocean and the resort town of Stinson Beach to the west. Traveling up the mountain and down to the sea, a hiker can find a little bit of everything.

Fifty miles of trails within the park connect to a larger, 200-mile-long trail system. On the slopes are deep canyons with redwoods and Douglas firs, cascading creeks, grassland meadows, and ridges of manzanita and sandstone. An outdoor amphitheater hidden in trees hosts musicals to the public every summer. A hiker can enjoy miles of trails in the friendly Mount Tam watershed, exploring pristine lakes. Also within the mountain's folds is Muir Woods, the nature lover's cathedral, with redwoods 500 years old covering 560 acres, filling the area with a rich aroma of citrusy needles and moist earth.

Also here are the Marin Headlands, with one of the best places in Northern California to watch raptors. Trails lead you through not only pretty countryside but also the rich history of the vaqueros (cowboys), Portuguese dairy farmers, military movements, and early seafarers. From Point Bonita Lighthouse, the cityscape and Golden Gate Bridge prompt lots of picture taking.

Mount Burdell, a distant cousin above Novato, gives the hiker a smaller mountain to climb, with meadows and a view into quarrying days. Nearby Olompali State Park is the site of a major Miwok Indian village that dates from A.D. 1100 to 1300.

Miwok Indians once inhabited the valleys and foothills of the mountain. New settlers were drawn to Mount Tam too, making their way up to the East Peak on the "world's crookedest railroad," to dance and drink or just admire the views. The rails gone, the route of the train is now a trail for hikers and mountain bikers, who are also drawn up the canyons and hillsides as the "Sleeping Maiden" emerges out of the fog and everyone in the valleys below seems to sigh.

7 | Muir Woods: Bootjack Trail to Dipsea Trail Loop

Overview: *On the first mile of your hike in Muir Woods, you'll have to contend with lots of camera-swinging tourists. Overwhelmed by the ancient trees and touched by the sheer tranquility of the place, many walk as if in a cathedral, whispering and respectful. People point and stare up into the high redwood branches and truly marvel at this popular National Monument. Venturing past the milling masses on paved paths, you are rewarded with solitude. There for your discovery are ridge trails lined with young pine trees dripping with grandfather's beard, bay and alder woodlands with flitting bushtits and hammering woodpeckers, sunny meadows, bridged streams with feathery ferns, hills full of huckleberries, and panoramic views of the Pacific. No picnicking is allowed in Muir Woods proper, but there are plenty of places along the trails beyond to stop for lunch.*

County: Marin
Start: Muir Woods National Monument main entrance
Length: 6.3 miles
Approximate Hiking Time: 3.5 hours
Difficulty Rating: Moderately strenuous

Trail Surface: 1 mile of paved pathway, then well-maintained, mostly single-track dirt trail
Land Status: National monument
Nearest Town: Mill Valley
Other Trail Users: Equestrians
Canine Compatibility: No pets allowed

Getting There

By Car: Go to Highway 101 between the Golden Gate Bridge and Interstate 580 turnoff (12 miles north of the Golden Gate). Exit Highway 1/Stinson Beach (there will be a sign for Muir Woods at this exit). Drive about 0.5 mile. At the stoplight, turn left. Drive about 2.7 miles. At the top of the hill, turn right toward Muir Woods/Mount Tamalpais. Drive about 0.8 mile. At the four-way intersection, turn left toward Muir Woods (oncoming traffic has the right of way). Continue down the hill about 1.6 miles. The Muir Woods parking lot will be at the bottom of the hill, on a sharp turn, on your right. Roads to the park are steep and winding; vehicles over 35 feet long are prohibited.

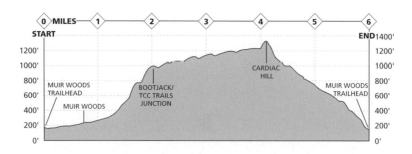

Muir Woods

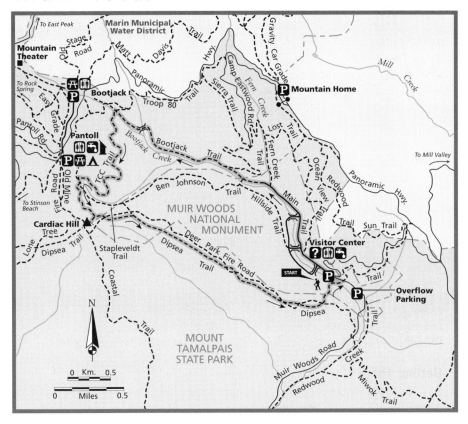

By Public Transportation: Golden Gate Transit bus #63, which runs weekends and holidays only, makes stops at the Mountain Home Inn, Pantoll, Bootjack, and Stinson on the Panoramic Highway. From there it is a steep 1.8-mile hike to Muir Woods. Call Golden Gate Transit for a schedule (415–923–2000).

Hike Description

"This is the best tree lover's monument that could possibly be found in all the forests of the world."—John Muir

Early in the 1850s on Mount Tamalpais came the crashing sound of felled virgin redwoods and giant Douglas fir trees. Lumber was in high demand for the booming new metropolises around San Francisco and Sacramento following the 1849 California gold rush. But because of inaccessibility caused by the steep slopes around it, the majestic old-growth forest in Redwood Canyon—now Muir Woods—survived. It is the only stand left in the Bay Area. Today's visitors mumble thanks as they wander down the path of giants.

Main Trail in Muir Woods—touristy for a good reason!

In the twentieth century, water shortages in the ever-growing Bay Area resulted in plans to dam Redwood Creek and create a reservoir. The huge trees were to be logged, then the canyon flooded. Hearing this disturbing news, wealthy Mount Tam landowner and avid outdoorsman William Kent asked his wife, Elizabeth, "If we lost all the money we have and saved the trees, it would be worthwhile, wouldn't it?" In 1905, they bought 611 acres and in 1908 donated 295 acres, the heart of the canyon, to the American people. They insisted that the grove be named for their friend John Muir, champion of the nation's environmental movement. Agreeing, President Theodore Roosevelt proclaimed it a National Monument.

Now, the monument attracts 1.8 million admirers every year. On summer weekends, the visitor center is packed, the roads are slow and the parking lot is an obstacle course. (Try a weekday, or arrive before 10:00 A.M. for a day hike or after 4:00 P.M. for a sunset stroll.) But even with the crowds, these giants, some more than 1,000 years old and over 200 feet tall, inspire and amaze even those averse to crowds. Traveling beyond the paved pathways, you may feel as if you know some great secret.

Summer is the season of fog, azaleas, and aralias. Elk clover shrubs stretch their stalks and sprout tiny white flowers. With an abundance of nuts and flowering plants, gray squirrels scamper everywhere. Wilson's warblers and chestnut-backed chickadees preen and chirp.

Fall tends to be the warmest time of year, attracting ladybugs on the horsetail ferns and crayfish in Redwood Creek. Beautiful monarch butterflies pass through on their migration to the central coast of California and Mexico, where they winter. Purple thistles appear in golden grasslands. Turning maple leaves and red-leafed poison oak bring fall colors to the trail. When rains start to fall, more than one hundred kinds of mushrooms appear on the soaked forest floor, some popping up overnight and lasting only a few hours, others growing slowly and remaining for weeks.

During winter, steelhead salmon (migratory rainbow trout) and flashing silver or coho salmon migrate up Redwood Creek to spawn. After spending most of their adult lives at sea, they always return to their birthplace to lay their eggs. They guard their nests for a week or so, then die. Juvenile salmon live in the stream for over a year, feeding on insects, unhatched salmon eggs, and each other before the ocean calls them. Once in the Pacific, they undergo a radical physiological and behavioral change, converting from solitary freshwater fish to schooling saltwater ones. According to park naturalists, Muir Woods salmon are unique, representing one of the last truly wild, genetically distinct populations of salmon in California. Best viewing occurs a few days after a heavy storm.

Coming out of the canyon up Cardiac Hill, the open ocean view is startling. If clear, it is expansive. Rolling fog provides an equally dramatic sight. This is

Muir Woods Seeds of Knowledge

The widest tree in Muir Woods is 13.5 feet in diameter.

Muir Woods was the seventh National Monument, the first created from land donated by a private individual.

Muir Woods is the only old-growth coastal redwood forest in the North Bay Area and one of the last on the planet.

Nearly two million acres of forest once covered a narrow strip along the coasts of California and Oregon. Today, 97 percent of it has been destroyed or altered.

An 800-year old redwood tree toppled in Cathedral Grove on July 8, 1996. Fifty awestruck visitors watched as the 200-foot monarch fell with a roar that could be heard a half mile away in the parking lot. It caused no damage or injuries and was left where it fell to provide nutrients for the soil, nesting for birds, and bedding for plants.

Hike Information

📞 Trail Contacts:

Muir Woods National Monument, Mill Valley, CA 94941
Ranger's office (415) 388–2595; Nature Hotline (415) 388–2596;
www.nps.gov/muwo
Muir Woods Visitor Center (415) 388–7368 or (415) 388–7059;
www.visitmuirwoods.com

🕐 Schedule:

Open year-round 8:00 A.M. to sunset unless otherwise posted

💲 Fees/Permits:

Adults, $2.00; children 16 and under, free. National Park Annual Pass, $50; Muir Woods Annual Pass, $15. No charge for parking

❓ Local Information:

Mill Valley Chamber of Commerce, 85 Throckmorton Avenue, P.O. Box 5123, Mill Valley, CA 94941 (415) 388–9700;
www.millvalley.org

📍 Local Events/Attractions:

Marin Theatre Company, 397 Miller Avenue, Mill Valley, CA (415) 388–5200
Mill Valley Fall Arts Festival (September), P.O. Box 300, Mill Valley, CA 94941 (415) 381–8779
Mill Valley Film Festival (October), Film Institute of Northern California, 38 Miller Avenue #6, Mill Valley, CA 94941 (415) 383–5256
Mountain Play Association, P.O. Box 2025, 177 East Blithedale Avenue, Mill Valley, CA (415) 383–1100
Sweetwater Saloon and Music Club, 153 Throckmorton Avenue, Mill Valley, CA (415) 388–2820; www.sweetwatersaloon.com

🛏 Accommodations:

Camping: Mount Tamalpais State Park (415) 338 2070
Bed and Breakfast Exchange of Marin, 45 Entrata, San Anselmo, CA (415) 485–1971
Mill Valley Inn, 165 Throckmorton Avenue, Mill Valley, CA (415) 389–6608
Mountain Home Inn, 810 Panoramic Highway, Mill Valley, CA (415) 381–9000;
www.mtnhomeinn.com

🍴 Restaurants:

Buckeye Roadhouse, 15 Shoreline Highway, Mill Valley, CA (415) 331–2600;
www.buckeyeroadhouse.com
Dipsea Cafe, 200 Shoreline Highway, Mill Valley, CA (415) 381–0298
Frantoio Ristorante, 152 Shoreline Highway, Mill Valley, CA (415) 289–5777
Mill Valley Cantina, 651 East Blithedale Avenue, Mill Valley, CA (415) 381–1070
Stefano's Pizzeria, 8 East Blithedale Avenue, Mill Valley, CA (415) 383–9666

🏔 Local Outdoor Retailers:

Any Mountain, 71 Tamal Vista Boulevard, Corte Madera, CA (415) 927–0170
REI—Corte Madera, 213 Corte Madera Town Center, Corte Madera, CA (415) 927–1938

👥 Hike Tours:

Muir Woods National Monument, Mill Valley, CA 94941
Ranger's office (415) 388–2595; Nature Hotline (415) 388–2596

🅝 Maps:

Muir Woods National Monument (415) 388–2596; www.nps.gov/muwo
USGS maps: San Rafael, CA; Bolinas, CA

a great area to enjoy a picnic before the descent back into woodland.

If you don't want to bring a picnic, you can lunch at the Muir Woods Cafe (415–388–7059) after the hike and buy a redwood seedling in the park's shop to start your own forest of giants. Facilities are available only at the start of the hike.

Miles/Directions

0.0 START at Muir Woods parking lot. Follow the main trail along Red wood Creek. Bohemian Grove has some of the tallest trees in the park. Pass three bridges.

0.9 Take Bootjack Trail along Redwood Creek. Path narrows and turns to dirt. Trail begins to climb. Steps help with ascent.

2.3 Van Wyck Meadow. Look for the large rock centerpiece and misspelled "population sign." Take the trail to the left of the meadow, (posted TO STAPLEVELDT TRAIL), a TCC (Tamalpais Conservation Club) path. Bridge crosses creek.

2.8 Manzanita stand. To the left is view of Mount Tam.

3.7 Go left to stay on TCC Trail. Shortly after, you come to a trail marked TO STAPLEVELDT TRAIL, BEN JOHNSON AND DIPSEA. Take it to the right. Cross a bridge, and come to another junction; take trail to Pantoll, Dipsea, and Ben Johnson. Stay right to Dipsea.

4.1 Junction with Dipsea Trail. Turn right to climb uphill (about 200 feet) to Cardiac Hill. **Option:** Coastal Trail heads down to Stinson Beach. Or, backtrack down Cardiac Hill and follow Dipsea Trail to Muir Woods. This will take you to Deer Park Fire Road for 0.3 mile.

4.5 Junction with Dipsea Trail. Stay right on Dipsea Trail, which crosses over Deer Park Fire Road several times.

4.7 Cross over grassy hillside called Hogsback. (*FYI:* Layered dress recommended, especially in summer.)

5.9 Dipsea Trail crosses Deer Park Fire Road, then bears left.

6.2 Dipsea Trail Bridge. Cross the creek. Turn left.

6.3 Back in parking lot of Muir Woods.

In Addition: The Magic of Redwoods

Peering upward at a redwood

What is it about redwoods? Walking through a grove of the giant, straight, red-barked trees can be a magical experience. But other than their obvious height, which is humbling in itself, what is it about these trees that capture the imagination and create a sense of awe?

The coastal redwoods *(Sequoia sempervirens)* are the tallest living things on earth (some over 360 feet tall) and grow only here in the Northwest, from Monterey County along the coast to Curry County in southwestern Oregon. But this was not always the case. In the age when dinosaurs roamed the earth, redwood forests covered the Northern Hemisphere. Imagine a brontosaurus lumbering through them and their large scale makes sense. One of the amazing things about coastal redwoods is that, while the earth has shifted and reformed all around them, these trees have barely changed at all since the Jurassic period 170 million years ago. They are a link to an ancient past, well before humans set foot on soil.

Glacial advances created a cooler, drier climate than the redwoods could stand, everywhere but here, where the fog keeps them cool and moist in summer, and mild, wet winters keep the freeze away. The needles of the tree collect the moisture and drop it onto their roots like rain. Redwoods have two ways of reproducing. One way is by seed from their small cones. But just as often, a new trunk begins as a sprout from the base of an old tree. These redwood sprouts create a burl ring, a dense mass of living shoots. The burl settles into the soil and grows wider with the new trunk, awaiting some sort of biological signal before shooting upwards to the sun. If we measured the age of a redwood by its roots, it could be 8,000 years old. Unidentified under the needle-carpeted floor in Muir Woods may be the oldest living woody plant on earth.

The rings of new trees are called family or fairy circles. Some people claim a spiritual connection standing in the middle of one. What we know for certain, is that the trees in the circle are not separate individuals. All the trees make up one single living entity, and you are standing in the middle of it.

Repeated wind and fire do sometimes bring the trees crashing down, but not time. Unlike higher animals and other plants, redwoods do not seem to suffer physiological aging. They change as they get older, their growth slows down, but there is no inevitable deterioration like we experience as humans. They may be as close to immortal as anything on earth.

The height, the majesty, the contrasting red and green, how the canopy shelters a soft floor of shade-loving and moisture-loving plants, the ancient stillness, our tendency to personify the trees—all these characteristics help to create the magic we often feel in the redwoods. People who feel it strongly will go to any means to keep that magic alive.

8

Phoenix Reservoir: Tucker and Bill Williams Trails

Overview: *Beside a sparkling lake, admire a Victorian log cabin and watch fishermen trying to land big-mouth bass. Below the branches of madrones, redwoods, bays, maples, and oaks, meander along a pleasant trail with wildflowers most of the year, wild iris in spring. Under the shade of the redwoods in Bill Williams Ravine, discover a dam built in 1886, and feel in this deepest part of the canyon very much "away" from it all.*

County: Marin
Start: In the parking lot of Natalie Greene Park in Ross
Length: 3.5 miles
Approximate Hiking Time: 2 hours
Difficulty Rating: Moderate
Trail Surface: A gravel road along the lake to single-track dirt trail through dry chaparral and

mostly damp, shaded canyons, crossing the stream several times, and back to double-track dirt and the road again
Land Status: Municipal water district
Nearest Town: Ross
Other Trail Users: Mountain bikers and equestrians around the lake
Canine Compatibility: Dogs on leash

Getting There

By Car: From Highway 101 north of the Golden Gate Bridge, take Sir Francis Drake Boulevard west. From the Richmond/San Rafael Bridge, take the second exit after the bridge on Sir Francis Drake Boulevard and continue into the town of Ross. In Ross, take Lagunitas Road left to Natalie Greene Park past the tennis courts. The parking lot holds about twenty cars, and it fills up fast. Back out near the tennis club there is additional street parking. If you end up parking here, take the trail on the left side of the street up to the hill. It will drop down to the main parking lot.

By Public Transportation: Golden Gate Transit General Information (415) 455–2000.

Hike Description

In 1905, dairy ranchers damned the Phoenix Dam that eventually created the reservoir. Built across the old Shaver stagecoach road, the dam was going to cut

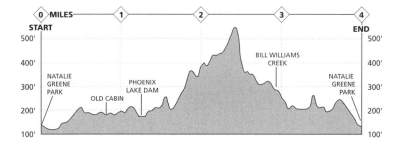

Phoenix Reservoir

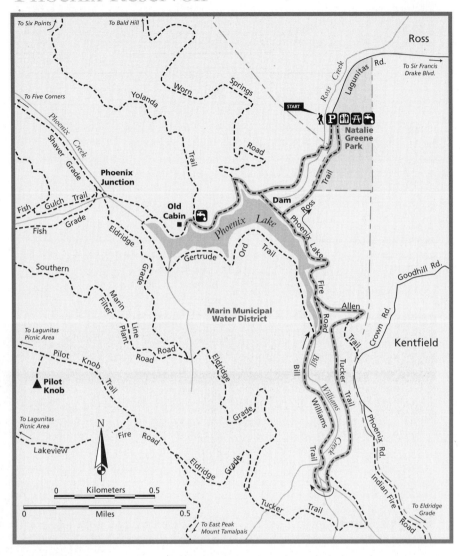

To Six Points
To Bald Hill
Ross
To Five Corners
To Sir Francis Drake Blvd.
Ross Creek
Lagunitas Rd.
Yolanda
Worn
Springs
START
Natalie Greene Park
Phoenix Creek
Shaver Grade
Phoenix Junction
Trail
Road
Ross Trail
Fish
Gulch Trail
Grade
Fish
Eldridge
Old Cabin
Dam
Ross
Phoenix Lake
Phoenix Lake
Gertrude
Pod Trail
Southern
Grade
Marin
Filter
Line
Plant
Fire Road
Allen
Goodhill Rd.
To Lagunitas Picnic Area
Pilot Knob
Road
Road
Eldridge
Bill
Williams
Crown Rd.
Kentfield
Marin Municipal Water District
Pilot Knob
Trail
Tucker Trail
Phoenix Rd.
To Lagunitas Picnic Area
Grade
Bill Williams Trail
N
Lakeview
Fire Road
Eldridge Grade
Indian Fire Road
0   Kilometers   0.5
0   Miles   0.5
Tucker
Trail
To Eldridge Grade
To East Peak Mount Tamalpais

ranches off from Ross Station so that milk had to be taken on the more tedious trip over the hill to Fairfax. Legend has it that, in resistance, one of the ranchers threatened the builders with a gun. In compromise, the Marin County Water Company built a road over the dam and up the canyon. This is the road that starts your hike on the right side of Phoenix Lake.

The Marin Municipal Water District (MMWD) now maintains the little twenty-five-acre lake and its surrounding trails, a gem for local hikers, joggers, horseback riders, bicyclists, and fishermen (for more on the MMWD, see page 83,

Kent Trail along Alpine Lake). It is equally beautiful wearing the oranges, yellows, and reds of autumn or the pastels of spring wildflowers; the dusted, green leaves and budding berry bushes of summer, or the artfully twisted branches of manzanita and buckeye trees against dewy ferns in winter.

The first part of this hike takes you to see a redwood log cabin erected around 1893 by estate owner Janet Porteous and her husband, James, for their coachman, Martin Grant. It predated the reservoir by twelve years. The Queen Anne–style turret over the front porch, the window frames made of an uncommon ribbon burl of wavy grain, and a pieced wood design on the front door seem out of place on a simple cabin. In the 1920s it was the only building spared in a fire that destroyed the rest of the Porteous estate. The cabin has been without full-time occupants for over sixty years, but it was restored to its original condition in 1989.

Looking out over the lake, you see pied-billed grebes bobbing and mallard ducks, wings spread for landing, breaking the glassy surface with a splash. Cormorants dive into the water after fish. Ospreys and hawks hunt from the trees, swooping over their reflections on the water. Fishermen compete with the birds, shore fishing for black bass and trout. The Marin Rod and Gun Club's Fish Restoration Committee, in cooperation with the MMWD, has made the reservoir a self-sustaining bass fishery.

Phoenix Lake from Phoenix Lake Fire Road, looking past a sycamore and a bay tree in autumn

The single-track Allen Trail takes you into a small ravine with oak, bay, and buckeye trees. In spring, pink shooting star, blue hound's tongue, and white zigadene color the trail. In early summer, white modesty, blue dicks, and wood rose border the trail. Late fall, maple leaves turn golden and paprika red, and the buckeye trees drop their leaves, leaving round buckeyes hanging like Christmas ornaments from bare branches. Manzanitas add striking color on gray days, with their burgundy-stained, gnarled branches. The creek below the hillside trail gurgles after rains. There is a wonderful cool, green smell of woodland that gets even better on the Bill Williams Trail.

In the 1860s, Bill Williams lived in a cabin upstream from the dam in the gulch that now bears his name. No one knows much about him, though some say he was a Confederate Army deserter. The biggest mystery, however, is where in the gulch he hid his buried treasure. Story goes that laborers building the Phoenix Dam spent more time looking for Bill Williams's gold than working. When the lake was drained in the mid-1980s, workers attempted another fruitless treasure hunt. The legend persists that Bill's hidden treasure remains buried here to this day.

But you can easily find this treasure of a trail, snaking into the canyon basin, following the Bill Williams Creek into the seclusion of redwoods. Maidenhair and woodwardia ferns, trilliums, huckleberry, creeping mint, and yerba buena make up the understory.

It breaks your heart to think that the MMWD, strapped for money, almost sold Phoenix Lake for development in 1982. The Phoenix, reborn as its name implies, took on heroic proportions when it was tapped during the 1986–1989 drought (it is only a backup water supply).

A pleasant single-track trail returns you to your car in Natalie Greene Park. District land begins up the fire road by the park residence.

Miles/Directions

0.0 START in the parking lot of Natalie Greene Park. Take the gravel road to the right.

0.2 Phoenix Reservoir dam is on the left, park residence to the right. Continue straight on the road to visit the old Queen Anne-style coachman's log cabin. **Option:** Take trail (1.9 miles) to Lake Lagunitas for longer hike.

0.5 The coachman's log cabin on right. Turn around and head back to the dam.

0.8 Back at the park residence, turn right to cross Phoenix Reservoir Dam. On the other side of the dam, to the right of the road, is Tucker Trail.

1.2 Trailhead to Allen Trail (also to Crown Road). Turn left on Allen Trail. Harry S. Allen built the trail that bears his name as a shortcut from his summerhouse in Larkspur over the top of Kent Woodlands to Phoenix. The founder of Allen Newspaper Clipping Company, he was at one time president of the Tamalpais Conservation Club (TCC).

Hike Information

○ Trail Contacts:
Mount Tamalpais Interpretive Association, P.O. Box 3318, San Rafael, CA 94901 (415) 258–2410; www.mttam.net/index.html
Mount Tamalpais State Park, 801 Panoramic Highway, Mill Valley, CA 94941 (415) 388–2070
Marin Municipal Water District, 220 Nellen Avenue, Corte Madera, CA (415) 945–1455

○ Schedule:
Open year-round sunrise to sunset unless otherwise posted

○ Fees/Permits:
None

○ Local Information:
Marin Market, P.O. Box 1408, Mill Valley, CA 94941 (415) 388–9433; www.marinmarket.com
Marin Directory, www.marindirect.com or www.inmarin.net
Town of Ross, P.O. Box 320, Ross, CA 94957 (415) 453–1453; www.digitalcity.com/sanfrancisco/towns/town.adp?city=Ross&state=CA

○ Local Events/Attractions:
Fairfax Theatre, 9 Broadway Fairfax, CA (415) 453–5444; www.cinema-west.com/info.html
Marin County Fair (June/July), Marin Center, Avenue of the Flags, San Rafael, CA (415) 472–3500

○ Accommodations:
Camping: Steep Ravine or Alice Eastwood Camps, Mount Tamalpais State Park (415) 388–2070; www.reserveamerica.com/usa/ca/mtta/index.html

Casa Madrona Hotel and Mikayla Restaurant, 801 Bridgeway, Sausalito, CA (800) 567–9524
Courtyard Larkspur, 2500 Larkspur Landing Circle, Larkspur, CA (415) 925–1800
Panama Hotel Restaurant and Inn, 4 Bayview Street, San Rafael, CA (800) 899–3993

○ Restaurants:
Half Day Cafe, 848 College Avenue, Kentfield, CA (415) 459–0291
Fresco Trattoria, 13 Ross Common Ross, CA (415) 464–0915
Kin Wah Restaurant, 937 Sir Francis Drake Boulevard, Kentfield, CA (415) 457–2900
Marin Brewing Company, 1809 Larkspur Landing Circle, Larkspur, CA (415) 461–4677
Pacific Cafe, 850 College Avenue, Kentfield, CA (415) 456–3898
Willie's Cafe, 799 College Avenue, Kentfield, CA (415) 455–9455

○ Local Outdoor Retailers:
Marin Outdoors, 935 Andersen Drive, San Rafael, CA (415) 453–3400
REI—Corte Madera, 213 Corte Madera Town Center, Corte Madera, CA (415) 927–1938

○ Hike Tours:
Mount Tamalpais Interpretive Association, P.O. Box 3318, San Rafael, CA 94901 (415) 258–2410; www.mttam.net/index.html

○ Maps:
Mount Tamalpais Interpretive Association, P.O. Box 3318, San Rafael, CA 94901 (415) 258–2410; www.mttam.net/index.html
USGS maps: San Rafael, CA

1.4 Trailhead and fork in the road. Bear right onto Tucker Trail to Eldridge Grade. The trail passes over seasonal springs and through a small grove of redwoods. Tucker Trail runs south into Williams Gulch.

2.1 Trailhead for Bill Williams Trail. Stay to your right on trail. Stairs help as you head downhill, still single-track dirt. Around a hairpin turn at the end of the canyon, a bridge built by local Boy Scout Troop 101 in 2001 crosses the creek. This leads to the canyon floor, following Bill Williams Ravine, one of three feeder streams to Phoenix Lake. (*Note:* A good rain on Fish Gulch watershed, the main feeder, can fill Phoenix Lake in a day).

2.2 Stay right on Bill Williams Trail past a small 1886 dam. (*Note:* Trailhead warns that path to the left is not a trail.) Eventually, a trailhead in middle of trail leads to Phoenix Lake. Take this trail, which becomes double-track dirt. (*Note:* Trail can be muddy in winter.)

2.8 Back onto Phoenix Lake Road, dirt and gravel. Continue by the lake until just before dam.

3.3 Trailhead on right reads TO ROSS. Turn right onto single-track dirt trail. Parking lot ahead and below; take one of two trails to lot. (*Note:* Steeper trail comes out near pit toilets; second trail is less steep and enters lot 20 feet away.)

3.5 Back at parking lot.

9   Steep Ravine Loop to Stinson Beach

Overview: *This loop, which includes Steep Ravine Trail, is considered by many the best hike in the North Bay. Though opinions may vary depending on weather, season, mood, and company, the Steep Ravine–Matt Davis–Dipsea Loop with a stop at Stinson Beach is up there at the top of the list. You can start the loop at Stinson Beach, leaving a picnic stowed in the trunk or after spending the night at the Redwood Haus in town. Steep Ravine is your starting point if you are camping or staying in one of the rustic cabins. The featured hike starts at Pantoll Station in Mount Tamalpais State Park. Downhill, you go through the dappled shade of mixed forest and over grassy slopes soaking in the sunlight. Weaving down the trail past rock outcroppings and trickling creeks with western views of sand and surf, you're suddenly in downtown Stinson Beach. Dipsea takes you through meadow and marsh to Steep Ravine Trail, the pride of Mount Tamalpais State Park. In the deep-crested canyon, you follow the rushing Webb Creek under a canopy of tall redwoods. Ferns hang over moist banks, and a rich, earthy smell invites you to take it all in. Up farther you are rewarded with a 15-foot waterfall. Beside it is the 10-foot ladder, beloved by locals, that you must clamber up to make your way back to the starting point, where there are full facilities.*

County: Marin
Start: From Pantoll parking lot, cross the main road to trailhead for Matt Davis Trail.
Length: 7.2 miles
Approximate Hiking Time: 4 hours
Difficulty Rating: Moderate with a sturdy 10-foot ladder to climb
Trail Surface: Single-track dirt trail descends through forest, grassland, chaparral and forest

again, with many stairs ascents on similar terrain. A short stint walking beside the highway is also required.
Land Status: State park and national recreation area
Nearest Town: Stinson Beach/Mill Valley
Other Trail Users: Hikers only except at Stinson Beach
Canine Compatibility: No dogs

Getting There

By Car: From San Francisco, take Highway 101 north. From the Richmond/San Rafael Bridge, exit at Sir Francis Drake Boulevard. Get on Highway 101 south. Exit at the Stinson Beach/Highway 1 exit. At the stop sign, turn left. Turn left onto the Shoreline Highway. Where Highway 1 and the Panoramic Highway split, turn left into the parking lot of Pantoll Station, the Mount Tamalpais headquarters.

By Public Transportation: Take Golden Gate #10, #20, or #50 from Transbay Transit Terminal, Civic Center, or Golden Gate Bridge Toll Plaza to Marin City Transfer Center (frequency: ten to fifteen minutes). Transfer to Golden Gate bus #63 (frequency: about 60 minutes). Deboard bus at Pantoll if you need to get map. Return same way, catching bus at Pantoll, Stinson Beach, or on Panoramic Highway at Mountain Home. For more information, call Golden Gate Transit (415–455–2000; www.transitinfo.org).

Hike Description

Being a loop, you can start on either the Matt Davis or the Steep Ravine Trail from the Pantoll Station. Both ways are fantastic. Matt Davis and Dipsea Trails have the best views. Sunset at Table Rock would definitely be memorable. Steep Ravine Trail keeps you more entertained, but you want to see it for the first time in more than fading light.

The Matt Davis Trail takes you through Douglas fir forest. Bridges take you over cascading creeks in the canyons. Then a blast of sunlight greets you in the grasslands that roll out in front of you like a carpet, green in late winter and early

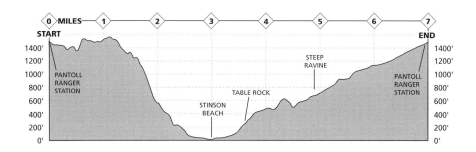

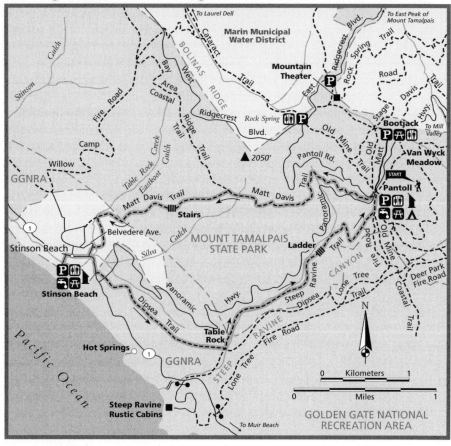

spring, golden the rest of the year. The springtime hills host patchworks of yellow buttercups, orange poppies, and purple lupine. Raptors hover, hunting over the hillsides, talons ready to strike. You might see a bobcat run low to the ground for cover. Rabbits skitter by, their white tails seemingly aglow behind them. Views to the northwest reveal Stinson Beach and Bolinas Mesa. Over your shoulder to the southwest, Montara Mountain juts up beside the sea. Through every ravine is a reprieve into shaded woodland of firs, oaks, and California bay trees, coated with phosphorescent green moss and perfuming the path with their peppery spice. The path serpentines through mixed woodland down the hill. Along the way, Table Rock presents a pleasant vista through the trees that drip with grandfather's beard. The Bischos Steps bring you to Belvedere Avenue and downtown Stinson, along the Shoreline Highway. A short walk past boutiques, galleries, a deli, restaurants, and the local library takes you to the crescent-shaped beach.

With light sand, level at the surf, Stinson Beach is good for wading and swimming. Surfers float on their boards farther out where the big waves break. Lifeguards are on duty May through October. You can also rent boogie boards, wet-suits, surfboards, or kayaks from one of three different surf and beach shops near the park. With 3.5 miles of sand, it is a good running beach as well. Divided into three sections, the main part of the beach by the parking lot is run by the Golden Gate National Recreation Area (GGNRA). North of the parking lot, the county of Marin owns the land and dogs are allowed. Farther north, the Seadrift subdivision, an upscale community of mostly weekend homes (some vacation rentals), owns the beach, but allows public use if it's mellow. South of the Panoramic Highway, nes-tled in a cove, is clothing-optional Red Rock Beach.

Don't be alarmed if you hear the quick bleep of a siren while visiting. The Stin-son Beach Siren is tested twice per day, at noon and 5:00 P.M. When you need to pay attention is if you hear a fifteen-second continuous blast. That indicates that residents should evacuate to higher ground immediately (in the case of a tsunami or other disaster). Two short blasts indicate all clear.

Near where you came into town, a connector trail takes you to Dipsea, which ascends in oak woodland and descends gently into an open marshy meadow past a pond. Around here was an old military site, Hill 640. Up some stairs, the trail climbs moderately, parallel to the California shoreline, until it connects to Steep

Table Rock along the Matt Davis Trail

Ravine Trail. Dipsea is the oldest trail on the mountain, dating back to dairy farm days. In 1905, it became the route of the famous 7.1-mile Dipsea footrace from downtown Mill Valley to Stinson Beach. Each June 1,500 runners race down this trail. It is the second oldest foot race in the United States.

In Steep Ravine, a lush canyon follows Webb Creek through redwoods and bay trees that keep everything beneath them moist, cool, and serene. Rocks are covered with green sheets of fuzzy moss. Blackberry vines hang down from steep banks. Picturesque wood bridges crisscross the flowing stream. On its way, Webb Creek splashes and gurgles, the sound changing over the varied surface of rock and sediment, crescendoing into frothy cascades, then softly lapping in quiet pools. A popular 10-foot ladder takes you to the path above a rock face beside a plummeting waterfall. You climb 1,000 feet in 2 miles. Near the top is the site of an old mining claim. Prospectors dug for gold and silver in 1863. Back at Pantoll Station, you have full facilities.

Miles/Directions

0.0 START in Pantoll parking lot. Take wooden stairs up to road and cross Highway 1 carefully. The trail continues, and you can see the trailhead for Matt Davis Trail.

0.4 Cross upper Webb Creek, continuing on Matt Davis Trail, named for its builder, who worked on it for over fifty years.

1.2 Trail enters grassland open to sunlight and views. To the southwest is Montara Mountain.

1.7 At the junction for Coastal Trail, continue on Matt Davis Trail, the left fork, to Stinson Beach. There are stairs around every switchback down wooded hillside.

3.5 Stop at Table Rock (marked by sign). Continue on Matt Davis Trail. Bischos Steps lead down 1,500 feet from Bolinas Ridge. (*Note:* Beware of rattlesnakes in this area. If you see one, leave it alone and walk away.)

3.9 At the trailhead, go left and cross the bridge over Table Rock Creek. Where the trail splits ahead, go right. (The path to the left takes you to Panoramic Highway.) Table Rock Creek trickles down the Eastkoot Gulch by the trail.

4.1 Trail ends on Belvedere Avenue. Turn left, walking down-slope past the community center to Shoreline Highway (Redwood Haus is on the corner).

4.3 Turn right (north) and walk beside Highway 1 into downtown Stinson Beach.

4.5 Past most of the shops and restaurants on the coast side is the main entrance to Stinson Beach. Return to Highway 1, heading south the way you came. Pass Belvedere Avenue. Look for Arenal Avenue, which goes west off Highway 1.

4.8 Across from Arenal Avenue, on the left (east) side of the street is trailhead for Dipsea Trail. Turn onto double-track dirt trail.

Hike Information

Trail Contacts:
**Mount Tamalpais State Park Pantoll
Station,** 801 Panoramic Highway, Mill Val-
ley, CA (415) 388–2070; cal-parks.ca.gov/
DISTRICTS/marin/mtsp239.htm
**Mount Tamalpais Interpretive Associ-
ation,** (415) 258–2410;
www.mttam.net/index.html

Schedule:
Open year-round 7:00 A.M. to just after sunset unless otherwise posted

Fees/Permits:
$2.00 per car; maps are $1.00

Local Information:
Town of Stinson Beach www.
stinsonbeachonline.com
Mill Valley Chamber of Commerce,
85 Throckmorton Avenue, P.O. Box 5123,
Mill Valley, CA 94941 (415) 388–9700;
www.millvalley.org
Tides Online tidesonline.nos.noaa.gov/

Local Events/Attractions:
Mountain Play Association, P.O. Box
2025, 177 East Blithedale Avenue, Mill Val-
ley, CA 94941 (415) 383–1100
Public Astronomy Programs
(415) 388–2070 or (415) 454–4715
Shakespeare at the Beach, Stinson
Beach, CA (415) 868–9500

Accommodations:
Camping: Steep Ravine, Rocky Point Road
and Highway 1, Stinson Beach, CA 94970
(800) 444–7275
Mount Tamalpais State Park (415)
338–2070

Marin Headlands Hostel, Building 941,
Fort Barry, Sausalito, CA 94965 (415)
331–2777
Redwood Haus Bed and Breakfast,
Belvedere and Highway 1, Stinson Beach, CA
94970 (415) 868–1034

Restaurants:
Beckers' by the Beach, 101 Calle del
Mar, Stinson Beach, CA (415) 868–1923
The Sand Dollar, 3458 Shoreline Highway,
Stinson Beach, CA (415) 868–1272
Stinson Beach Grill, Shoreline Highway,
Stinson Beach, CA (415) 868–2002
Willow Camp Catering, Shoreline High-
way, Stinson Beach, CA (415) 868–1422

Local Outdoor Retailers:
Any Mountain, 71 Tamal Vista Boulevard,
Corte Madera, CA (415) 927–0170
REI—Corte Madera, 213 Corte Madera
Town Center, Corte Madera, CA
(415) 927–1938

Hike Tours:
**Mount Tamalpais Interpretive
Association** (415) 258–2410;
www.mttam.net/index.html
Mount Tamalpais State Park, Pantoll
Station, 801 Panoramic Highway, Mill Valley,
CA (415) 388–2070; cal-parks.ca.gov/
DISTRICTS/marin/mtsp239.htm

Maps:
Mount Tamalpais State Park, Pantoll
Station, 801 Panoramic Highway, Mill Valley,
CA 94941 (415) 388–2070; cal-
parks.ca.gov/DISTRICTS/
marin/mtsp239.htm
USGS maps: San Rafael, CA; Bolinas, CA

5.0 Trail crosses Panoramic Highway; cross carefully. Head toward Steep
Ravine trail.

5.3 Wooden platforms over boggy area. Take stairs up to fire road and cross
road to continue on Dipsea Trail.

5.8 At trailhead for Steep Ravine, go left. (Right turn goes to Highway 1 and
rustic cabins of Steep Ravine.) **Option:** A visit to Steep Ravine cabins will
add approximately 1.8 miles to hike, mostly on pavement. Go 0.4 mile to

Highway 1, and cross highway carefully. Walk past locked gate and down fairly steep paved road 0.5 mile to cabins. Low tide–only natural sulfur hot springs along beach about 0.3 mile north but hard to find. **Option:** To reach springs, from Steep Ravine Trail, walk north on Highway 1 0.2 mile on the coastal side of road to parking area beyond Steep Ravine entrance. Trail is very steep. Recommended for experienced hikers only. Take Steep Ravine Trail back to Pantoll through redwoods along the creek.

6.4 Climb up 10-foot ladder beside waterfall. There is no alternative route.

6.7 Steep Ravine Trail goes between two redwoods joined at the roots. Toward the top, go up stairs around switchbacks.

7.2 Come out onto park service road at Pantoll. Walk up the road about 30 feet and the parking lot is on your left.

10

East Peak Loop

Overview: *The "Sleeping Maiden," or Mount Tam, as she is affectionately called, is a Bay Area treasure, the peak closest to San Francisco, and the heart of Marin parkland and open space. This hike is like the "best of Mount Tamalpais," featuring the diverse habitat of the 6,300-acre park, starting with incredible views of the bay, cities, foothills, lakes, and ocean. Enjoy thick, quiet woodland of coast redwood, Douglas fir, oak, bay, and madrone trees, as well as trickling waterfalls and cascading streams in moist ravines and canyons. Step out in wide, sloping, grass-covered meadows and along hillsides of gnarled manzanita and coyote brush. Pass by statuesque outcroppings of green serpentine and white chert stones and by tall banks of red, sunburnt soil and mossy green growth. These trails also walk you through Mount Tam history, from popular East Peak, down Railroad Grade, where the old steam engines used to run, to the tavern at West Point Inn. Walk right off a trail into an outdoor amphitheater with stone seats built in traditional Greek style. There are camps, picnic areas, and facilities at several locations along the way. The weird aspect of this hike is that you start at the top and hike down and back up again.*

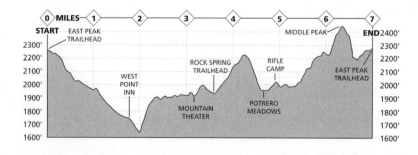

Eldridge Grade

Grade

Wheeler Trail

E. Koo

Hoo-Koo

Grade

Temelpa Trail

Old Railroad Grade

Double Bowknot

Mill Creek

To Mill Valley

Mountain Home

Panoramic

Gravity Car Grade

Fern Creek Trail

East Peak 2571'

Gardner Lookout

Verna Dunshee Trail

Marin Municipal Water District

Camp Eastwood Rd.

Fern Creek

Eldridge Trail

START

Fern Creek Trail

Fern Creek

Old Railroad Grade

E. Koo

Hoo-Koo

Grade

Matt Davis

Sierra Trail

To Muir Woods

East Fork Lagunitas Creek

North Side Trail

Middle Speak Fire Road

Middle Peak 2490'

Lakeview Trail

Old Railroad Grade

West Point Inn

Nora Trail

Matt Davis Trail

Troop 80

Bootjack Trail

Middle Fork Lagunitas Creek

West Fork Trail

North Side Trail

Ridgecrest Blvd.

MOUNT TAMALPAIS

West Peak 2560'

East

Rattlesnake

Panoramic Hwy.

TCC Trail

Lower North Side Trail

International Trail

Rifle Camp

Spring Trail

Davis

Van Wyck Meadow

Pantoll

Lagoon Fire Road

East Fork Swede George Creek

Upper Fire Road

Stage Road

Old Spring Road

Rock Spring

Bootjack

Easy Grade Trail

Old Mine Trail

Pantoll Road

Potrero Meadows

Fire Road

Rock Spring Trail

Benstein Trail

Mountain Theater

Davis

Laurel Dell

Kent Trail

Simmons Trail

Benstein Trail

Rock Spring

MOUNT TAMALPAIS STATE PARK

Laurel Dell

Cataract Trail

Cataract Creek Trail

West Ridgecrest Blvd.

Coastal Trail

Matt Davis Trail

To Stinson Beach

Marin Municipal Water District

N

0 Kilometers 0.5
0 Miles 0.5

County: Marin

Start: From the East Peak parking lot, walk down the parking area exit road (the paved road to the left is for hikers and bicyclists only), and turn left through the gated Old Railroad Grade.

Length: 7 miles

Approximate Hiking Time: 4 hours

Difficulty Rating: Moderate; strenuous section on International Trail

Trail Surface: Some paved road, dirt fire road with easy downhill grade, and single-track dirt trails through woods, chaparral, and grasslands. One trail has short, steep rocky incline

Land Status: State park and municipal water district

Nearest Town: Mill Valley

Other Trail Users: Mountain bikers and equestrians on fire roads

Canine Compatibility: Dogs on leash

Getting There

By Car: From San Francisco, take Highway 101 north. From the Richmond/San Rafael Bridge, exit at Sir Francis Drake Boulevard. Turn on Highway 101 south. Exit at the Stinson Beach/Highway 1 exit. At the stop sign, turn left. Turn left on Shoreline Highway. The road winds its way up. At the split, turn right on Panoramic Highway (signs for Muir Woods and Mount Tamalpais). At the next intersection, continue up the hill toward Mount Tamalpais. At Pantoll Station, turn right uphill toward the East Peak. Where the road splits again, go right toward the East ridgetop, 4 miles to East Peak. (You pass Air Force installation signs on the left.) The road takes you into the East Peak parking lot. Full facilities are available.

By Public Transportation: Take Golden Gate #10, #20, or #50 from Transbay Transit Terminal, Civic Center, or Golden Gate Bridge Toll Plaza to Marin City Transfer Center (frequency: ten to fifteen minutes). Transfer to Golden Gate bus #63 (frequency: about 60 minutes). Deboard bus at Pantoll if you need to get map. Return same way in reverse, catching bus at Pantoll, Stinson Beach or on Panoramic Highway at Mountain Home. For more information, call Golden Gate Transit (415–455–2000; www.transitinfo.org).

Hike Description

"Nevermore, however weary, should one faint by the way who gains the blessings of one mountain day." —John Muir

At 2,571 feet, East Peak is the highest accessible point on the mountain. Before you've even begun hiking, the views are spectacular: On a clear day, you can see the Farallon Islands 25 miles out to sea, the Marin County hills, San Francisco and the bay, the hills and cities of the East Bay, and Mount Diablo. On rare occasions, you can even glimpse the snow-covered Sierra Nevadas, 150 miles away. Most of the land belongs to the Marin Municipal Water District (MMWD). Mount Tamalpais State Park begins officially around the area of the Mountain Theater, although the park service also owns the parking lot and maintains the services on East Peak.

Weekdays or crisp winter days—some of the best on Tam—keep away the majority of the half million people who drive to the top of the mountain each year.

Serpentine rock field along Rock Spring Trail

The mountain used to be full of elk, caribou, and even grizzly bears.

Unlike the weekend tourists, the Miwok Indians rarely climbed the peak. The mountain was the place of "the poison people," or magic practitioners. Instead, they traveled into the foothills from their home in Sausalito to hunt and gather grasses for ceremonies and seeds to eat.

Mount Tam, like Mount Diablo, has many legends surrounding its name. In 1770, two explorers named the mountain La Sierra de Nuestro Padre de San Francisco. In the 1820s the mountain was simply called Table Mountain. The name *Tamalpais* first appeared in 1845, its origin a source of controversy. Spanish soldiers referred to the land as *mal-pais* (bad lands). Others say Tamalpais is a Miwok Indian term—*Tamal*, meaning "bay," *pais* meaning "mountain." Another legend claims that the Spaniards mistook the Miwok for Tamals and added *pais* to the name of the wrongly assumed tribe name, calling the mountain Tamalpais (Tamal country). Another story declares the name originated from an Aztec word for cornmeal dumpling (*tamal*).

The mountain's long ridgeline has been described as the "Sleeping Maiden," from a Miwok legend. It tells how a young Miwok girl was saved from a rival tribe by the shuddering mountain. Afterward, her reclining profile could be seen in the mountain's contour.

That contour drew hikers and outdoor enthusiasts as early as the 1800s. They came first by foot. Then, in the post–gold rush era, visitors rode part way up in stagecoaches. In 1896, Sidney Cushing and other local businessmen bought rights to build a tourist railroad up to the East Peak. As you walk down the Old Railroad Grade, you follow its path (see sidebar below).

In 1925 developers began to subdivide lots for sale. The Tamalpais Conservation Club (TCC), a community group established in 1912 to be the "Guardian of the Mountain," intervened. The TCC raised $30,000 in 1928 to purchase the land to donate it to the state. In 1931 the park officially opened, encompassing over 6,000 acres covering the south slope, the ridgeline, and a portion of the west slope.

Of all the buildings once in operation on the mountain, only the Mountain Theater and West Point Inn are left. This hike visits both.

Built in 1904, West Point Inn was a restaurant and stopover point for passengers taking the stage to Bolinas and Willow Camp (later renamed Stinson Beach). The inn was called West Point because this is the westernmost point of the Old Railroad Grade. Member-maintained, West Point Inn is still in operation. There are rooms and cabins for rent and occasional pancake breakfasts for fun and fund raising.

Down the trail, you walk into the Mountain Theater. In the 1930s, the Civilian Conservation Corps (CCC) constructed the natural-stone Greek amphitheater based on a design by Emerson Knight. It seats 3,750 people, who come to see the Mountain Play each summer and have since 1913, before the stone theater was cre-

The Crookedest Railroad in the World

To reach the peak, a 30-ton engine traversed a double bowknot, where the tracks parallel themselves five times, the shortest radius of the curves at the turns being 75 feet. Locals and tourists alike in the early twentieth century riding the Mill Valley and Mount Tamalpais Scenic Railway delighted in jaw-dropping vistas at the summit, dinner at the Tavern of Tamalpais, and two-stepping in the Dance Pavilion on East Peak. The $1.90 round-trip ticket from San Francisco to the summit attracted some 50,000 people each year. At day's end, the daring would climb aboard the gravity car. The "gravity man" would "turn on the gravity," and down they would coast, around 281 turns on the mountain's 7 percent grade, to the Mill Valley depot or Muir Woods. The line became known as "the crookedest railroad in the world." Sir Arthur Conan Doyle (of Sherlock Holmes fame) was among the passengers. "In all my wanderings, I have never had a more glorious experience," he said. Silent film actor/director Erich von Stroheim worked at the Tamalpais Tavern starting in 1912 and met his first wife there.

In 1929, a great fire burned across the south face of the mountain, destroying 1,000 acres, primarily along the rail route. Already usurped in popularity and practicality by the automobile, the train was not resurrected, and soon thereafter the railway was torn up and sold.

Few remnants of the historic buildings remain. The dance pavilion is now a parking lot. The tavern is the site of two geodesic domes that serve as radio towers.

A fund-raising effort is currently under way to build a gravity car barn on East Peak, a permanent home for a re-created gravity car, and an interpretive display highlighting its time in California and Mount Tamalpais history.

ated. Other features of this hike include manzanita on Old Railroad Grade and banks of "blue goo," the thick clay holding hillsides together on Mount Tam. In the wet season, it turns into a gelatinous mass. On the Rock Spring Trail, you pass numerous streams and small waterfalls. After a small clearing, watch for a large boulder on your right with a dedication to Austin Ramon Pohli and Garnett Holme, founders of the Mountain Theater. Pohli died twenty days after the debut performance. His ashes are scattered on the mountain. Holme fell on Mount Tam and his ashes are embedded in this rock. The Benstein Trail takes you through Douglas fir forest out into the wide Potrero Meadow. The Lakeview Trail gives you just that, with partial views of the watershed lakes through branches.

Miles/Directions

0.0 START in the East Peak parking lot. (**Options:** To get to the true top, take ramped trail 0.3 mile to observation area near seasonal snack bar. Verna Dunshee Trail is a twenty-minute loop around the peak, named for the avid hiker and protector of open space.) Walk down parking area exit road (paved road to left is for hikers and bicyclists only) to Old Railroad Grade, a gated fire road.

0.1 Turn left on Old Railroad Grade, passing entrance gate (sign reads TO WEST POINT AND MILL VALLEY). (*FYI*. This is a popular trail for mountain bikers.)

1.6 West Point Inn. Pass the cabins on your left and proceed to the main lodge. Across the driveway, to the west and slightly north of the inn, is the trailhead for single-track Rock Spring Trail.

2.3 Enter Mountain Theater. Continue along upper tier straight onto paved road that slopes down to Ridgecrest Boulevard.

2.4 Cross Ridgecrest Boulevard, and turn right, walking about 40 feet. Turn left onto single-track dirt Simmons Trail.

2.5 Turn right on Simmons Trail (Benstein reroute) to Benstein Trail. Continue through meadow into woods.

2.6 Turn right on the Benstein Trail. A series of hairpin turns lead uphill.

4.6 Benstein Trail comes out on Lagunitas Fire Road. Turn left and go about 20 yards to where the Benstein Trail continues to the left. Turn left back onto Benstein Trail at the trailhead.

5.1 Benstein Trail dead-ends on Laurel Dell Fire Road. Cross fire road and continue straight on single-track dirt trail through a small grove of trees to Potrero Camp and Laurel Dell, so named for the once dominant bay laurel trees.

5.2 At Potrero Camp, turn right onto single-track trail marked TO RIFLE CAMP. Located here was one of five ranches established on Mount Tam after the gold rush.

5.5 Trail ends at Lagunitas Fire Road. Turn left on fire road and walk

Hike Information

🕿 Trail Contacts:
Mount Tam State Park, 801 Panoramic Highway, Mill Valley, CA 94941 (415) 388–2070; cal-parks.ca.gov/DISTRICTS/marin/mtsp239.htm
Mount Tamalpais Interpretive Association, (415) 258–2410; www.mttam.net/index.html
Pantoll Ranger Station, 801 Panoramic Highway, Mill Valley, CA (415) 388–2070

🕑 Schedule:
Open year-round 7:00 A.M. to just after sunset unless otherwise posted

💲 Fees/Permits:
None at East Peak

❓ Local Information:
Mill Valley Chamber of Commerce, 85 Throckmorton Avenue, P.O. Box 5123, Mill Valley, CA 94941 (415) 388–9700; www.millvalley.org

💡 Local Events/Attractions:
Marin Theatre Company, 397 Miller Avenue, Mill Valley, CA (415) 388–5200
Mountain Play Association, P.O. Box 2025, 177 East Blithedale Avenue, Mill Valley, CA (415) 383–1100
Public Astronomy Programs (415) 388–2070 or (415) 454–4715
Sweetwater Saloon and Music Club, 153 Throckmorton Avenue, Mill Valley, CA (415) 388–2820; www.sweetwatersaloon.com

🛏 Accommodations:
Camping: Mount Tamalpais State Park (415) 338–2070
Alpine Lodge, 730 Panoramic Highway, Mill Valley, CA (415) 381–4975
Mountain Home Inn, 810 Panoramic Highway, Mill Valley, CA (415) 381–9000; www.mtnhomeinn.com
Tam Valley Bed and Breakfast, 508 Shasta Way, Mill Valley, CA (415) 383–8716
West Point Inn, 1000 Panoramic Highway, Mill Valley, CA (415) 388–9955

🍴 Restaurants:
Buckeye Roadhouse, 15 Shoreline Highway, Mill Valley, CA (415) 331–2600; www.buckeyeroadhouse.com
Dipsea Cafe, 200 Shoreline Highway, Mill Valley, CA (415) 381–0298
Stefano's Pizzeria, 8 East Blithedale Avenue, Mill Valley, CA (415) 383–9666

🌿 Local Outdoor Retailers:
Any Mountain, 71 Tamal Vista Boulevard, Corte Madera, CA (415) 927–0170
REI—Corte Madera, 213 Corte Madera Town Center, Corte Madera, CA (415) 927–1938

👥 Hike Tours:
Mount Tamalpais Interpretive Association (415) 258–2410; www.mttam.net/index.html

🗺 Maps:
Muir Woods National Monument (415) 388–2596; www.nps.gov/muwo
USGS maps: San Rafael, CA

---

another 20 yards down the hill. Rifle Camp is on the right. Walk into Rifle Camp, down the stairs. On the other side of the camp is the trailhead. Cross over the bridge and go straight (trail to the left) on Northside Trail (sign also reads TO ELDRIDGE GRADE). Follow it about 0.5 mile. Pass a rockslide before reaching the International Trailhead.

6.0 Turn right on International Trail.

6.5 Trail ends at Ridgecrest Boulevard. Do not cross the street. Turn left and walk on the paved road 36 yards to Lakeview Trailhead. Turn left on Lakeview Trail (to East Peak).

6.7 Turn left on Middle Peak Fire Road.

6.9 Fire road meets Ridgecrest Boulevard. Cross the road and turn left onto paved road marked FOR HIKERS AND BICYCLISTS ONLY up to East Peak parking lot.

7.0 Back in parking lot.

11 Marin Headlands: Miwok Trail to Point Bonita

Overview: *The Marin Headlands features 15 square miles of beaches, marsh, lagoon, grass-covered valleys, and coastal hills with magnificent views. There is a large population of wild animals, including bobcats, mountain lions, and lots of hunting raptors. You'll see about 150 years of military history, with batteries, bunkers, cannons, and missile launching sites all along the hike, adding an eerie contrast to the natural beauty. The walk also includes a tour of Point Bonita lighthouse that takes you through a hand-chiseled tunnel and across a suspension bridge to the little lighthouse sitting dramatically on a deteriorating cliff. The area has many other hikes of shorter and longer length and all kinds of other fun sights for after the hike or another day of exploration. On a tip of land, isolated by hills from Marin traffic, it feels like a small town up the coast rather than just across the bridge from the big city. You also get a good glimpse of what the area was like a hundred years ago.*

County: Marin
Start: Marin Headlands Visitor Center
Length: 8.5 miles
Approximate Hiking Time: 4 hours
Difficulty Rating: Moderate, a few strenuous hills
Trail Surface: Double-track and single-track dirt trails up and down grassy coastal foothills with views; a stretch of walking the beach and a sandy trail along the cliffs; a paved path to the lighthouse and some walking beside the road
Land Status: National recreation area
Nearest Town: Sausalito
Other Trail Users: Mountain bikers and equestrians; hikers only on Wolf Ridge, Rodeo Beach, and Point Bonita Trail
Canine Compatibility: Dogs on leash

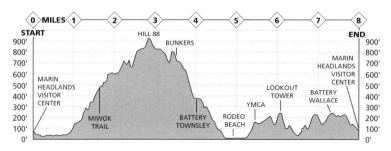

Marin Headlands

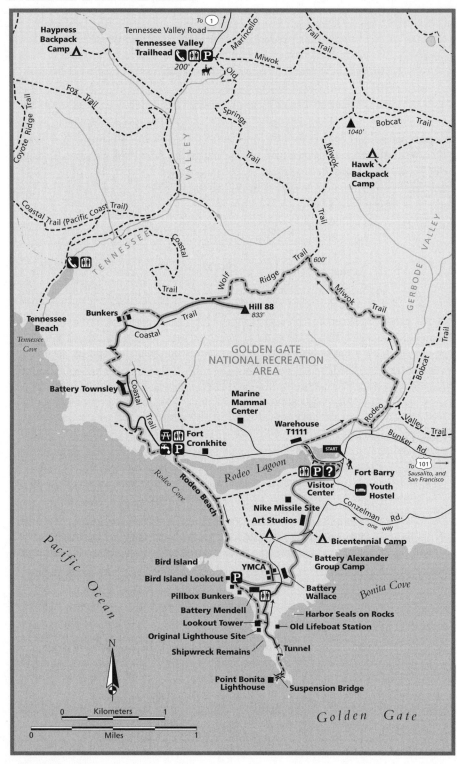

Haypress Backpack Camp

Tennessee Valley Road
To 1

Tennessee Valley Trailhead
200'

Marincello
Miwok Trail
Trail

Fox Trail
Old

Coyote Ridge Trail
Springs

1040'
Bobcat Trail

VALLEY
Trail

Hawk Backpack Camp

Coastal Trail (Pacific Coast Trail)

Coastal

Miwok Trail

GERBODE VALLEY

TENNESSEE

Coastal

Trail

Ridge
Trail
600'

Wolf
Trail
Miwok Trail

Bunkers
Trail
Hill 88
833'

Tennessee Beach
Tennessee Cove
Coastal

GOLDEN GATE
NATIONAL RECREATION
AREA

Bobcat Trail

Battery Townsley
Coastal Trail

Marine Mammal Center

Rodeo

Warehouse T1111

Valley Trail

Bunker Rd.

Fort Cronkhite
START

To 101
Sausalito, and
San Francisco

Rodeo Cove
Rodeo Beach
Rodeo Lagoon

Fort Barry

Visitor Center
Youth Hostel

Nike Missile Site
Art Studios

Conzelman Rd.
one way

Bicentennial Camp

Pacific Ocean

Bird Island
Bird Island Lookout
YMCA

Battery Alexander Group Camp

Pillbox Bunkers
Battery Wallace

Bonita Cove

Battery Mendell
Lookout Tower
Original Lighthouse Site
Shipwreck Remains

— **Harbor Seals on Rocks**
Old Lifeboat Station

Tunnel

N

Point Bonita Lighthouse
Suspension Bridge

Golden Gate

Kilometers
0 _____ 1

Miles
0 _____ 1

Getting There

By Car: From San Francisco, take Highway 101 north across the Golden Gate Bridge to Alexander Avenue exit. Take an immediate left (sign reads TO SAN FRANCISCO), and go under the freeway. Turn right up the hill toward Marin Headlands—do not get back on Highway 101. This is Conzelman Road. From the Richmond/San Rafael Bridge or North Bay, take Highway 101 south through the Waldo Tunnel. Take the last Sausalito exit before the Golden Gate Bridge (Alexander Avenue). Road dead-ends; turn left, then right up the hill on Conzelman Road. Be careful of bicyclists. Conzelman will become a one-way road and drop you into the Marin Headlands. Follow the signs to the beach and Marin Headlands Visitor Information Center. (The center is open daily from 9:30 A.M. to 4:30 P.M.)

Leaving the park: Out of the visitor center parking lot, turn left on Field Road. At the yield sign, it becomes Bunker Road. Follow this out to the freeway. You go through a one-way tunnel with a five-minute traffic light. Follow signs to Highway 101, San Francisco to go north or south.

By Public Transportation: On weekends, take Muni bus #76 from Caltrain (4th and Townsend), Transbay Transit Terminal, Montgomery BART, or the Golden Gate Bridge Toll Plaza. (frequency: every sixty minutes). For the hike that comes out at Spencer Bus Pad, take any Golden Gate bus that comes along for return to Transbay Transit Terminal (frequency: every thirty minutes). On weekdays, take GG bus #20, #30, #60, #70, or #80 from Transbay Transit Terminal, or Golden Gate Bridge Toll Plaza to Spencer Bus Pad; return on any southbound Golden Gate bus. For more information, call Golden Gate Transit (415–455–2000; www.transitinfo.org).

Hike Description

The experience of this hike actually starts on the drive in. The view of San Francisco and the Golden Gate and Bay Bridges from Hawk Hill (Battery 129) at the top of Conzelman Road is postcard perfect. After that point, Conzelman becomes a one-way street winding down to the headlands on death-defying cliffs. People afraid of heights should take the alternative route in on Bunker Road.

Where the hike starts, you have already stepped back in time, surrounded by whitewashed wooden buildings with red roofs. The visitor center was the old Fort Barry chapel; the youth hostel up the hill (two buildings) was the army hospital, dating back to 1907.

The Marin Headlands served as a military base until the late 1960s, designed, along with the Presidio, to protect San Francisco Bay from invasion from the Civil War through the Cold War. Sadly, each of the five installations constructed among the rolling hills was obsolete upon or before completion. Happily, none of them ever fired a gun.

The lagoon you pass by—like the beach—may have been named for the Rodier family, who settled nearby in the mid-1800s. Ducks, gulls, herons, and egrets are almost always present, bobbing on the water or resting in the reeds.

View from lighthouse station of the Golden Gate Bridge and the San Francisco Bay

The Miwok Trail, starting at the historic military warehouse building T1111, takes you above the Gerbode Valley into windswept hills. There are also patches of tight-knit scrub, colorful rock outcrops, and the marshy part of the lagoon, hidden in tall reeds and skinny trees. In late winter and spring the valley and hills are covered with nearly fifty species of wildflowers. A pamphlet describing them is available at the visitor center. As the trail ascends into the hills, you are entertained by hunting raptors, hovering and diving at prey in the grassland. The headlands are home to the Golden Gate Raptor Observatory's hawk watch site. Any time of year you can see the soaring birds of prey. Depending on the season, use your binoculars to spot markings of ospreys, red-shouldered hawks, rough-legged hawks, ferruginous hawks, golden eagles, American kestrels, merlins, and peregrine falcons.

In 1966, the Gerbode Valley and surrounding hillsides were slated for an 18,000-person residential community called Marincello. A group of concerned citizens helped to stop the development, but remnants of it are still visible: the Rodeo Avenue highway exit-to-nowhere on Highway 101 north and the Marincello trailhead out of Tennessee Valley. The preservation of this open space so near the city led to legislation that established the Golden Gate National Recreation Area (1972), the largest urban parkland in the world.

From Wolf Ridge Trail, you can look down at a farmhouse, barn, windbreak, and pond in the Tennessee Valley, a reminder of the area's ranching days. In the early 1800s, when the headlands became a grazing land for cattle, vaqueros (Spanish for cowboys) ruled these lands. Mostly Native Americans, they learned to rope and ride from the Spanish and tended the herds for the Spanish missions, then for wealthy ranch owners. By 1850, the headlands changed from vast ranches to smaller dairies, started by immigrants from the Azores Islands off Portugal. These hard-working settlers and their descendants kept the farms going for 100 years.

Up at the top of Wolf Ridge Trail is Hill 88, a former radar installation for guiding Nike missiles. Wander through the abandoned Cold War buildings and enjoy 360-degree views of Marin towns and foothills, the metropolis east and west of the bay, beautiful coastland, and the Pacific Ocean.

Down the Coastal Trail, you pass World War II–era bunkers and batteries to wander in and explore. The massive slabs of cement that make the fortifications are slowly being taken over by nature. You can see where long-range cannons pointed out to the sea, protecting the Golden Gate from possible attack.

Rodeo Beach is popular with weekend sun worshipers and surfers. Because of its strong currents and deadly undertows, it is not recommended for swimming, but it's pleasant to wet your feet in the cold Pacific waters on warm days, hang out for a while, and make a sandcastle in the chocolate brown sand.

A highlight of the hike is a tour of Point Bonita Lighthouse (open Saturday, Sunday, and Monday from 12:30 to 3:30 P.M.). On the hike in, you can see the remains of a shipwreck, the bobbing black heads of sea lions in the water, and harbor seals lounging on rock islands. The lighthouse, built in 1855, was moved to its current location in 1877. It sits at the headlands' outermost tip. With the cliff slowly melting into the sea, someday the lighthouse will sit on an isolated sea stack.

The Fresnel lens is the oldest still in use on the West Coast. The light shines 18 miles out to sea. By 1979, all California lighthouses but Point Bonita had modern lights that no longer required full-time keepers. In 1980 the Coast Guard automated Point Bonita's light and foghorn.

You will pass the Nike Missile Site, with missiles on the premises. Even unarmed, they look spooky. The Nike Historical Society has displays on the missile site. It's open Wednesday to Friday and the first Sunday of each month from 12:30 to 3:30 P.M. From there, return to the visitor center, where there are full facilities.

Miles/Directions

0.0 START at visitor center. Dirt fire road leads down hill to Bunker Road.

0.1 Turn right on Bunker Road and walk beside the paved road over lagoon bridge to the old warehouse on right side of road.

0.2 On side of warehouse is trailhead for Miwok Trail (1.6 miles to Wolf Ridge Trail).

0.6 Stay on Miwok Trail to the left as it passes the trailhead for Bobcat Trail.

2.0 Trailhead for Wolf Ridge Trail. Turn left on single-track, hikers-only trail. (*Note*. Stay on the trail to avoid poison oak.) To the northwest is one of the few remaining old ranch buildings in the Tennessee Valley. The valley and the cove were named for the 1853 wreck of the SS Tennessee.

2.7 At the junction with paved Coastal Trail, turn left to the top of Hill 88.

2.9 Top of Hill 88. The buildings for the Nike Missile IFC (Fire Control) are still here, but are in a state of disrepair. At only 833 feet, the coastal view is amazing, north past Tennessee Point to the Point Reyes Peninsula, south past Point Bonitas to Ocean Beach, west to Farallon Islands. Head back down on Coastal Trail.

3.1 Continue down paved Coastal Trail toward Rodeo Beach (2.3 miles). Notice remains of gun batteries. Below and ahead is Rodeo Beach and old military buildings.

4.1 Where the road ahead has eroded away due to landslide, take the established dirt trail to the right to an abandoned bunker. Continue on dirt trail to the left of bunker until you see the trailhead for Pacific Coast Trail. **Option:** Take a quick detour west about 40 feet toward the cliff and trees. There's a great spot for contemplation. Head back and take the single-track dirt Pacific Coast Trail down 106 steps.

4.2 Back to the paved Coastal Trail. Turn right. Listen for the foghorn of Point Bonita lighthouse.

4.4 On the right side of trail, look for a painted arrow on the pavement. It points to an otherwise unmarked dirt trail that veers left down the hill. Take that trail. Where trail splits, stay left. You can see the paved Coastal Trail below you.

4.6 Back on paved Coastal Trail. Turn right to Battery Townsley (World War II defense station). Turn left into battery. On the ocean side of the gun station, follow dirt trail to the left.

4.7 Another gun station of Battery Townsley. Head through the second tunnel of Battery Townsley to its entrance. Turn right onto paved Coastal Trail.

5.1 At a curve in the road—near an inviting grassy hillside—there is a double-track dirt trail right of the road toward Rodeo Beach. Take this trail to Rodeo Beach. When it splits, bear left toward the beach on the path with the wooden railing.

5.3 Trail again meets paved Coastal Trail. Turn right and walk the remaining short distance to the beach.

5.4 Rodeo Beach. Walk along the beach, heading south, toward the bluffs on the other side. The sea stack beyond the point is Bird Island. Beyond it, west, is a shallow sandbar called the Potato Patch. (*Note*. Surf is dangerous here.)

5.7 Head up the bluff on the steep, single-track sand trail nearest the water.

Hike Information

📞 Trail Contacts:
Marin Headlands Visitor Information Center, Field Road, Marin Headlands, Sausalito, CA 94965 (415) 331–1540; www.nps.gov/goga
Golden Gate National Recreation Area (415) 556–0560

🕐 Schedule:
The park is open 24 hours a day

💲 Fees/Permits:
None

❓ Local Information:
City of Sausalito
www.ci.sausalito.ca.us/vis-info/index.htm
Sausalito Chamber of Commerce
www.sausalito.org

💡 Local Events/Attractions:
Bay Area Discovery Museum, Building 557, East Fort Baker, Sausalito, CA (415) 487–4398
Golden Gate Raptor Observatory, Building 201, Fort Mason, San Francisco, CA (415) 331–0731; www.ggro.org
Headlands Center for the Arts, Building 944, Fort Barry, Sausalito, CA (415) 331–2787
Marine Mammal Center, Marin Headlands, 1065 Fort Cronkhite, Sausalito, CA (415) 289–7325
Nike Historical Society, 879 Walnut Street, Alameda, CA www.nikemissile.org
Miwok Livery Stables, 701 Tennessee Valley Road, Mill Valley, CA (415) 383–8048; www.miwokstables.com

🛏 Accommodations:
Marin Headlands Camping (415) 331–1540 or (415) 561–4304; www.nps.gov/gaga/camping

Marin Headlands Hostel, Building 941, Fort Barry, Sausalito, CA (415) 331–2777
YMCA Point Bonita Outdoor and Conference Center, Building 981, Fort Barry, CA (415) 331–YMCA (331–9622)
B & B Exchange of Marin, 45 Entrata, San Anselmo, CA (415) 485–1971
San Francisco As You Like It (houseboats), P.O. Box 735, Sausalito, CA (415) 389–1250; www.sausalito-lodging.com

🍴 Restaurants:
Horizons, 558 Bridgeway, Sausalito, CA (415) 331–3232; www.calcafe.com/horizons
Sausalito Gourmet Deli, 209 Caledonia Street, Sausalito, CA (415) 332–4880
Scoma's Seafood Restaurant, 588 Bridgeway, Sausalito, CA (415) 332–9551; www.scomas.com

🎣 Local Outdoor Retailers:
Any Mountain, 71 Tamal Vista Boulevard, Corte Madera, CA (415) 927–0170
REI—Corte Madera, 213 Corte Madera Town Center, Corte Madera, CA (415) 927–1938

🚶 Hike Tours:
Marin Headlands Visitor Information Center, Field Road, Marin Headlands, Sausalito, CA (415) 331–1540; www.nps.gov/goga
Golden Gate National Recreation Area (415) 556–0560

Ⓝ Maps:
Muir Woods National Monument (415) 388–2596; www.nps.gov/muwo
USGS maps: Point Bonita, CA

The unmarked path goes toward Point Bonita Lighthouse. Bear right on double-track dirt trail toward the YMCA Conference Center.

5.9 Enter YMCA center area and walk toward the Resident Staff Building.

At the end of the building, turn right for single-track dirt path that heads toward Battery Mendell.

6.1 Go right on paved road past Battery Mendell to Bird Island overlook parking lot.

6.3 Take dirt path left along cliff, passing two World War II–era pillboxes.

6.5 At the far end of Battery Mendell, continue along cliff.

6.6 Trail passes through the split trunks of a tree. Up ahead is old Coast Guard radar tower. **Option:** If you're not afraid of heights, you can climb up the tower and take a look down for a frightening adrenaline rush. Continue along the cliff. The trail curves left. Take it out to parking lot.

6.7 Turn right onto main paved trail to Point Bonita Lighthouse. Look down and to the right to an isolated beach and rusty remains of a wrecked ship. Watch to the left for old pier and remains of Life Saving Station, established in 1899.

6.9 On the right side of trail is a square cement foundation. This is where fog signal was located before it was moved to its current location next to the lighthouse visitor center. The trail takes you through a tunnel when the lighthouse is open.

7.0 On the other side of the tunnel are interpretive signs and view of San Francisco. After crossing the suspension bridge, look up at the bluff from the right side of the lighthouse building to see its original 1855 location. After touring the lighthouse, go back out the main path to the Point Bonita parking lot.

7.3 From the parking area, take the main road right.

7.4 On the left of the road, just beyond the stop sign, is a single-track dirt trail going up the hill to Battery Wallace. Take this trail.

7.7 Battery Wallace (1942). Go through battery tunnel to main road. Turn left and walk beside road.

7.8 To the left is the last Nike missile site. Follow the signs TO BEACH, SAUSALITO, SAN FRANCISCO, turning right at the stop sign. On the left beside the missile site is the Marin Headlands Center for the Arts studio building.

8.2 Back to the visitor center and parking lot.

<table>
<tr><td>

12

</td><td>

Marin Municipal Water District: Kent Trail along Alpine Lake

</td></tr>
</table>

Overview: *A little bit of everything and a hike that takes you away from it all: This is an exhilarating hike along the conifer shores of Alpine Lake, up through a dark red-wood forest, emerging onto a manzanita-covered ridge with good views. Along the way, you can pick huckleberries in the early fall, and admire many water-loving flowers among the ferns and mosses along the banks. This is treasured watershed land in Marin, for both its consumer and recreational value.*

County: Marin
Start: Bon Tempe Dam in Marin Municipal Water District. Start at the parking area below Bon Tempe Dam and head uphill to the spillway
Length: 5.2 miles
Approximate Hiking Time: 3 hours
Difficulty Rating: Moderate
Trail Surface: Starting on a gravel and dirt road, crossing a dam, you will proceed onto a narrow

dirt path, mostly shaded, that winds around the lake, then climbs rather steeply about 800 feet. It is a bit rocky in places. A double-track fire road takes you back down to the dam
Land Status: Municipal water district
Nearest Town: Fairfax
Other Trail Users: Equestrians on all; mountain bikers on Rocky Ridge Road
Canine Compatibility: Dogs on leash

A peaceful Alpine Lake from Bon Tempe dam

Getting There

By Car: From the Golden Gate Bridge, take Highway 101 north and turn west on Sir Francis Drake Boulevard. From the San Rafael Bridge (Interstate 580), take Sir Francis Drake Boulevard exit. Stay on Sir Francis Drake into Fairfax. Turn left on Claus, left on Broadway, right on Bolinas Road, then left on Sky Oaks Road. You will see a sign: LAKE LAGUNITAS, BON TEMPE AND WATER TREATMENT PLANT PARK GATE. Turn right on road to Bon Tempe.

By Public Transportation: For bus schedule information, call Golden Gate Transit (415) 257–4563; www.goldengate.org.

Marin Watershed Weather

The greatest seasonal rainfall recorded is 112 inches in 1889–1890.

Maximum twenty-four-hour rainfall is 10.45 inches on March 4, 1879.

Twenty-five days of nonstop rainfall were recorded in December 1889, January 1916, and March 1983.

The longest period of subnormal rainfall occurred from 1927 to 1934.

The statistical relative improbability of two winters as dry as 1975–1976 and 1976–1977 is about 1 in 300.

Hike Description

Leaders of the ninety-year-old Marin Municipal Water District (MMWD) would tell you that managing the 24,000-acre watershed comes first, recreation is second. But both seem a passion and a pride.

Around the watershed's five lakes, and through the numerous forests, the MMWD maintains 130 miles of trails. The beginning of Kent Trail, skirting Alpine Lake, is magical for hikers, with the lake shimmering through mature Douglas firs and skinny, peeling madrones stretching into patches of sun like a Sierra scene. Inlets near the trail expose hundreds of minnows squirming about the shore, feeding on algae.

The water district has stocked Alpine and Bon Tempe Lakes with rainbow trout. Bass, bluegill, crappie, and catfish are also here. Anglers pick key spots along the shore; the Bon Tempe Dam seems to be a favorite. They report that the trout in Alpine tend to be larger—12 to 15 inches—but harder to catch than in Bon Tempe. Catch and release is encouraged.

Along Kent Trail in spring, elegant white and lavender iris show off their blooms. Hound's tongue, pink shooting stars, and delicate white milkmaids decorate the forest floor. Farther along, there are patches of grassland with orange pop-

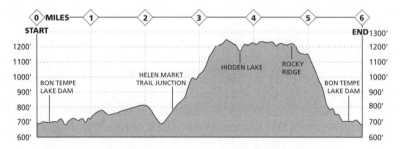

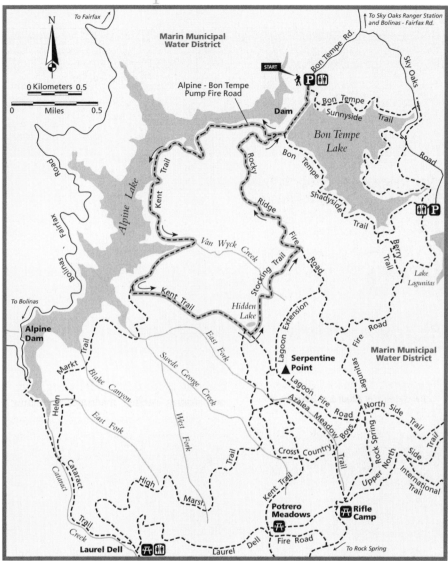

pies and yellow buttercups. Deer like to graze on the wild oats and Spanish grass during morning and late afternoon hours. Jackrabbits are also numerous, but are more often heard as a startling rustle in the scrub than seen. Butterflies flutter at the base of oaks in summer.

Turning inland from the lake, the sunlight dims as you enter a grove of redwoods. The sound of your footfall changes on the needle-blanketed ground. Sword and maidenhair ferns fawn onto the moist earth. The canopy muffles noises outside as your eyes adjust to the darkness in the grove, which may feel both secluded and strange. But in a short time, the trees thin, the light brightens, and the trail warms in the sun.

On the sun-drenched Stocking Trail, the scenery takes a dramatic change, opening up into manzanita barrens, hillsides full of red snarled branches and green-penny leaves. The uphill trek to Rocky Ridge Fire Road rewards you with views.

In an area plagued by drought every ten years or so—California is, after all, mostly desert—the priority of the water district makes a lot of sense. In drought years, expect the lake levels to go down, like they did during the dry years of 1976–77, when MMWD gained recognition for its innovative conservation program that resulted in a 67 percent reduction in community water usage; or in 1986–89, when Marin County experienced the driest 32 months in 110 years and Lake Lagunitas, usually kept in reserve, had to be tapped as a water supply. The oldest water district in the state, it supplies 61 million gallons of water a day to 170,000 inhabitants in southern and central Marin County.

The Mount Tamalpais area makes an ideal watershed. Storms from the coast climb up the steep ridge. The rapid lifting of clouds causes warming. They wring out over the range, and the rainwater "runoff" drains into Lagunitas, Ross, Redwood, and Old Mill Creeks and the seven reservoirs. From these are some 791 miles of pipelines, 134 storage tanks, 103 pump stations, and two treatment plants. Erosion control, whether through controlled burns, combating nonnative plant species, or limited road development, is very important. The quality of the water is directly related to the quality of the watershed, a good thing for us hikers.

Rest rooms and maps are available at the Sky Oaks Ranger Station when it's open; drinking water is available there anytime (close to the source too).

Miles/Directions

0.0 START at parking lot below Bon Tempe Dam, then head uphill to spillway. Cross 94-foot high dam overlooking Bon Tempe Lake on your left.

0.3 Continue right to Alpine Lake. Soon, at a trailhead, the trail splits; take Kent Trail by turning right, downhill on the double-track trail above Alpine Lake. (Trail is also known as Alpine–Bon Tempe Pump Fire Road.)

0.8 Road ends at pump house where water from Alpine is pumped to Bon Tempe Lake and on to a treatment plant. Kent Trail becomes single track and follows curves of Alpine Lake.

1.8 Kent Trail continues through a conifer forest. Following the shoreline, the trail winds around the lake. Just ahead, the trail enters Van Wyck Canyon, with two small waterfalls and a bridge. The trail then enters into a silted canyon with a narrow streambed.

2.3 About 100 yards past the trailhead for Helen Markt Trail (to Cataract Gulch), take the Kent Trail left, away from the lake. After skirting Foul Pool on the right, the trail follows the Swede George Creek into a redwood grove.

3.1 Junction with multiple trails. Go straight on Stocking Trail to Hidden Lake. Trail soon heads downhill about 200 yards, passing Hidden Lake. Trail follows ridge; to the left is Van Wyck Creek.

Hike Information

🕐 Trail Contacts:
Sky Oaks Ranger Station, Fairfax-Bolinas Road, Fairfax, CA 94930 (415) 945–1181
Mount Tamalpais Interpretive Association, P.O. Box 3318, San Rafael, CA 94912 (415) 258–2410; www.mttam.net/index.html
Mount Tamalpais State Park, 801 Panoramic Highway, Mill Valley, CA (415) 388–2070
Marin Municipal Water District, 220 Nellen Avenue, Corte Madera, CA (415) 945–1455

🕐 Schedule:
Open year-round sunrise to sunset unless otherwise posted; gates close at 9:00 PM.

💲 Fees/Permits:
$5.00 per vehicle. Annual pass $40 (out-of-county residents, $50, seniors, $20)

❓ Local Information:
Town of Fairfax, 142 Bolinas Road, Fairfax, CA (415) 453–1584; www.mo.com/fairfax
Marin Directory, www.marindirect.com
Fairfax Historical Society, P.O. Box 622, Fairfax, CA 94978; www.marindirect.com/fxhistory

📍 Local Events/Attractions:
Annual Fairfax Festival, early June (415) 453–1584
Marin Shakespeare Company, Forest Meadows Amphitheatre, Dominican University, San Rafael, CA (415) 499–1108; www.marinshakespeare.org

Peri's Music Bar, 25 Broadway Avenue, Fairfax, CA (415) 459–1190

➖ Accommodations:
Camping: Steep Ravine or Alice Eastwood Camps, Mount Tamalpais State Park (415) 388–2070; www.reserveamerica.com/usa/ca/mtta/index.html
Fairfax Inn Bed and Breakfast, 15 Broadway Boulevard, Fairfax, CA (415) 455–8702
Gerstle Park Inn, 34 Grove Street, San Rafael, CA (415) 721–7611 (800) 726–7611

🍴 Restaurants:
Ghiringhelli's Pizzeria, 45 Broadway Boulevard, Fairfax, CA (415) 453–7472
Ross Valley Brewing Company, 765 Center Boulevard, Fairfax, CA (415) 485–1005

🎿 Local Outdoor Retailers:
Marin Outdoors, 935 Andersen Drive, San Rafael, CA (415) 453–3400
REI—Corte Madera, 213 Corte Madera Town Center, Corte Madera, CA (415) 927–1938

🚶 Hike Tours:
Mount Tamalpais Interpretive Association, P.O. Box 3318, San Rafael, CA 94930 (415) 258–2410; www.mttam.net/index.html

Ⓝ Maps:
Mount Tamalpais Interpretive Association, P.O. Box 3318, San Rafael, CA 94912 (415) 258–2410; www.mttam.net/index.html
USGS maps: Bolinas, CA; San Rafael, CA

3.5 Cross bridge and continue on Stocking Trail away from creek. This leads to a heavily wooded area, then manzanita barren and open prairies.

3.7 Stocking Trail dead-ends at Rocky Ridge Fire Road. Turn left. About 200 feet ahead is a great view of the bay: Angel Island, Marin foothills and homes, and Richmond refineries across the bay. Road then heads downhill. (*Note*: Watch for loose rock.)

4.9 Back at Bon Tempe Lake. Cross spillway, and return the way you came.

5.2 Back at parking lot.

13

Mount Burdell Open Space Preserve

Overview: *It's understandable why the Miwok Indians chose to keep a village at the base of this mountain for 6,000 years. The rise they called Olompali had oaks shedding acorns, their main food source, and grasslands that supported plenty of animals to hunt for food. Fresh water for drinking (not anymore) ran down the ravine. You can imagine them making special tribute to the great rock spirits, black volcanic, green serpentine, and pale yellow sandstone on the hillsides. Starting in Novato's backyard, this hike ascends the mountain, past the quarry sites that provided cobblestones for the streets of San Francisco. It takes you over great expanses of grassland: golden and flowing in summer, green like English countryside in winter, and sprinkled with a rainbow of wildflowers and fluttering butterflies in spring. It dips under the dappled shade of bay and oak trees, along gurgling seasonal creeks, then back onto open hillsides before you finally reach the ridge of this extinct volcano and Novato's highest hill. A low stone wall invites you to sit for a while before the descent, though it is hardly wilderness, with a repeater station and satellite nearby. But the views are rewarding. On the northwest side is Bowl Meadow, a pastoral delight with scampering gray squirrels and maybe black-tailed deer, voles, raccoons, foxes, and badgers. Western meadowlarks and savanna sparrows nest in the grassy meadow. In the sky, which seems larger over the meadow, red-shouldered hawks and American kestrels circle. There are no facilities in this open space preserve.*

County: Marin
Start: Open Space Preserve gate near the end of San Andreas Drive
Length: 5-mile loop
Approximate Hiking Time: 2.5 hours
Difficulty Rating: Strenuous because of elevation change
Trail Surface: The dirt trail is rocky in places. It climbs through oak savanna and drops 1,400

feet in elevation. Much of the trail is in shade. Hike ends on gravel fire road.
Land Status: Open space preserve
Nearest Town: Novato
Other Trail Users: Mountain bikers and equestrians on fire roads
Canine Compatibility: Dogs on leash

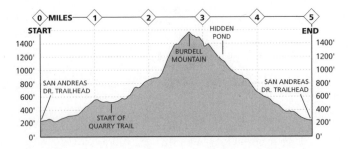

Mount Burdell Open Space Preserve

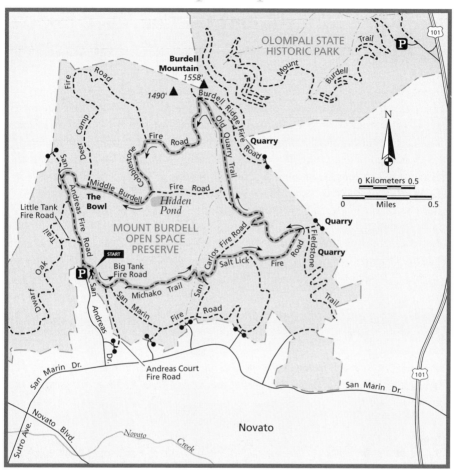

Getting There

By Car: From San Francisco or San Rafael/Richmond Bridge, take Highway 101 north past San Rafael. Take the Atherton/San Marin exit in Novato. At the light, turn left on San Marin Drive, which takes you through a neighborhood. Turn right on San Andreas Drive. Near the end, look for the Open Space Preserve gate on the right side of the road. If you go too far, there is a cul-de-sac to turn around. Park on San Andreas Drive and proceed to the gate.

By Public Transportation: From Transbay Terminal or Civic Center BART, take Golden Gate bus #50 to the stop on San Carlos Way at San Marin Drive (these streets cross in two places). Returning, bus stop is on opposite side of the street. For a boat ride (weekdays only), take Golden Gate Ferry (frequency: every one or two hours) to Larkspur from San Francisco Ferry Building, and transfer to GG bus #30. From El Cerrito del Norte BART, take GG bus #40 (frequency: every thirty to ninety minutes). Transfer from GG buses #30 and #40 to northbound GG bus #50 at the San Rafael Transit Center. For more information, call Golden Gate Transit (415-455-2000; www.transitinfo.org).

Hike Description

Around twelve million years ago, long after the ocean had receded and the coastline here (15 miles farther out then) had sprouted life and animals settled into the new habitat, molten rocks worked their way through the jumbled oceanic rocks. They erupted to create a rise of lava over the Franciscan sandstone and serpentine. This disturbance became Mount Burdell. Landslides over the years continued to shape the mountain, until bunch grass and native scrub, oak and bay trees took their place, growing in and over the rocky mixture.

Long ago, its name was Mount Olompali (Miwok for "southern village" or "southern people"), the hunting grounds and acorn-gathering site for the Miwok Indians, who had a village at its base. Sir Francis Drake reported in his 1579 journals that the people were friendly and contented, blessed with an abundant food supply and an excellent climate. In 1776, an exploring party from the Presidio in San Francisco arrived at the village of Olompali. The villagers welcomed them warmly. According to the old story, the explorers repaid their hosts by showing them how to

A tree with acorns resembling Christmas tree ornaments in the meadow

make adobe bricks and to use them to create a building. The natives built two adobe houses, modernizing their village. Historians doubting this story say the Native Americans may have built them under the tutelage of the priests at Mission San Rafael Archangel as late as 1830 or 1840. And then Olompali was taken away. The Spanish, Mexican, and later American governments gave the land to settlers, encouraging them to ranch and farm the area. In some ways, it still feels like old ranch land, as you pass through meadows, through canyons and up the side of the mountain. Patches of oak and bays shade small sections of the trail. This oak savannah, so typical of the Bay Area, was once part of the 8,877-acre Olompali Rancho, a wedding gift to Dr. Galen Burdell and his wife Mary Black from her father.

Now the park is bordered by houses and horse stables. The mountain that you climb has been returned to the birds, squirrels, deer, and mountain lions. But steep-cut hills and deep depressions in the earth that you see from the trails are reminders of the busy quarries that in 1888 produced the cobblestones to pave the streets of San Francisco. The southeast spur was quarried for asphalt as late as 1954.

Mount Burdell is now part of the Marin County Open Space District, which, since 1972, has preserved nearly 14,000 acres of land in thirty preserves. Mount Burdell was acquired in parcels starting in 1978, with the last addition in 1994, totaling 1,558 acres, most of it on the south-facing slopes above the city of Novato. Parcels were bought from a private owner, development companies, and Exxon Corporation.

Burdell is now an entirely new place, from the Spanish grasses that turn golden every summer, to the old roads and exposed patches of ancient rock in the quarry sites. Oak trees now feed the many birds and mammals that make the mountain home. Views on the ridge reveal the pattern of suburban streets and a busy Highway 101 corridor, but between each neighborhood there are other hillsides, preserved and treasured by the communities. Mount Tamalpais rises high and quiet to the southwest, the rivers of the delta snake through the valley to the northwest. And there is new growth in the renewal of the Bowl Meadow (Hidden Pond).

Miles/Directions

0.0 Go through Open Space gate and turn right onto double-track flat dirt trail. After about 350 feet, turn right onto San Marin Fire Road. It starts up hill. It passes Andreas Court Fire Road.

0.2 Bear left onto Big Tank Fire Road.

0.4 Turn right onto signed, hikers-only Michako Trail. Pass over a seasonal creek that has the potential of mud after rain. Pass through cattle gate.

0.8 Michako Trail bears right at the water trough.

0.9 Turn left onto San Carlos Fire Road. It loops around a curve. Stay on San Carlos past Salt Lick Fire Road.

1.3 Turn left on Old Quarry Trail. Cross through a gate. It starts out flat, curves under a few trees, with hillside views and starts to ascend.

1.5 Take a short jog left onto Middle Burdell Fire Road and then turn right on Old Quarry Trail where it resumes. For a while this trail gets steep and rocky.

2.2 Old Quarry Trail ends at a junction with Cobblestone Fire Road and paved and gravel Burdell Mountain Ridge Fire Road, which is also part of the Bay Area Ridge Trail. Go straight, crossing over the Burdell Mountain Ridge Fire Road up the hill. A stone wall is ahead, built by Chinese laborers in the 1870s. At the fence, enjoy views to the north. Head back down to the trailhead on the fire road. **Option 1:** Go left (west) on Burdell Mountain Ridge Fire Road. An unsigned trail to the left enters Olompali State Park. Continue hike in Olompoli. **Option 2:** Turn right (southeast) on Burdell Mountain Ridge Fire Road to reach the old cobblestone quarry.

2.3 Take the double-track dirt Cobblestone Fire Road that heads at a 45-degree angle right of the Old Quarry Trail. It is also part of the Bay Area Ridge Trail. Watch your footing in loose rocks on the trail. Trail moves into partial shade and becomes smooth and moderately sloped.

2.9 At the junction with Deer Camp Fire Road, continue straight on Cobblestone Fire Road away from summit. **Option:** Go right on Deer Camp Fire Road, also the Bay Area Ridge Trail, which is a loop.

3.3 Turn right onto Middle Burdell Fire Road. To your left is Hidden Pond, beyond it The Bowl, a lovely meadow in fall and summer under restoration.

3.8 Stay left on Middle Burdell Fire Road. Deer Camp Fire Road goes off right.

4.2 Turn left onto San Andreas Fire Road, also part of the Bay Area Ridge Trail, a gravel road.

4.8 Stay on San Andreas Fire Road past the Dwarf Oak Trailhead and Little Tank Fire Road Trailhead.

5.0 Back at the gate on San Andreas Drive.

Hike Information

🖀 Trail Contacts:
Marin Open Space Preserve Field Office (415) 499–6405
Marin Open Space Preserve Main Office, 3501 Civic Center Drive, Room 415, San Rafael, CA 94903 (415) 499–6387; www.marin.org/mc/parks/open.htm

🕐 Schedule:
Sunrise to sunset unless otherwise posted

💲 Fees/Permits:
None

❓ Local Information:
Novato Chamber of Commerce, 807 DeLong Avenue, Novato, CA (415) 897–1164; www.Tourism.novato.org or www.ci.novato.ca.us

📍 Local Events/Attractions:
Northern Marin Artists Open Studios Tour, May (415) 499–8350
Miwok Park/Marin Museum of the American Indian, 2200 Novato Boulevard, Novato, CA (415) 897–4064
Novato Art, Wine and Music Festival, June, Grant Avenue, Old Town Novato, CA (415) 897–1164
Novato History Museum, 815 DeLong Avenue, Novato, CA (415) 897–4320
Olompali State Historic Park, off U.S. Route 101, Novato, CA (415) 892–3383
Public Astronomy Programs (415) 388–2070 or (415) 454–4715
Pacheco Ranch Winery, 235 Alameda del Prado, Novato, CA (415) 883–5583

🛌 Accommodations:
Camping: China Camp State Park (415) 456–0766 or Mount Tamalpais State Park (415) 388–2720 or (800) 444–7275
Marin Headlands Hostel, Building 941,

Fort Barry, Sausalito, CA (415) 331–2777
Casa Mia, 1116 Elm Drive, Novato, CA (415) 892–0900
Inn Marin, 250 Entrada Drive, Novato, CA (415) 883–5952

🍴 Restaurants:
California Grill, 1531 A South Novato Boulevard, Novato, CA (415) 893–1540
Maya Palenqeu Restaurant, 349 Enfrente Drive, Novato, CA (415) 883–6292
Moylan's Brewing Company, 15 Roland Way, Novato, CA (415) 898–4677

🌲 Local Outdoor Retailers:
Any Mountain, 71 Tamal Vista Boulevard, Corte Madera, CA (415) 927–0170
Orca Outdoor Products, 3060 Kerner Boulevard, Suite Y, San Rafael, CA (415) 459–4437
REI—Corte Madera, 213 Corte Madera Town Center, Corte Madera, CA (415) 927–1938

👥 Hike Tours:
Marin Open Space Preserve Field Office (415) 499–6405
Marin Open Space Preserve Main Office, 3501 Civic Center Drive, Room 415, San Rafael, CA 94903 (415) 499–6387; www.marin.org/mc/parks/open.htm

Ⓝ Maps:
Marin Open Space Preserve Field Office (415) 499–6405
Marin Open Space Preserve Main Office, 3501 Civic Center Drive, Room 415, San Rafael, CA 94903 (415) 499–6387; www.marin.org/mc/parks/open.htm
USGS maps: Petaluma River, CA; Novato, CA

14

Ring Mountain

Overview: *A ridge top between the towns of Tiburon and Corte Madera, Ring Mountain is surprisingly enjoyable to hike and explore, although mountain is a misnomer. Still, the hike includes a moderate 600-foot climb that invigorates. On the way up, enjoy expanses of native grasslands, a compact bay, oak, and buckeye woodland, sculptural rock outcrops, trickling seasonal springs, and colorful wildflowers. Miwok Indians left signs of their inhabitance from 2,000 years ago, and environmentalists left traces of the strong spirit in which they fought to protect these precious 377 acres for us hikers and nature lovers.*

County: Marin
Start: On Paradise Drive in Corte Madera, just past Westward Drive
Length: 2.3 miles
Approximate Hiking Time: 1.5 hours
Difficulty Rating: Moderate
Trail Surface: A mostly sunny dirt trail that

climbs and descends 600 feet; some rocky and rutted areas, one short stretch in woodland
Land Status: County open space preserve
Nearest Town: Corte Madera
Other Trail Users: Mountain bikers and equestrians on fire roads
Canine Compatibility: Dogs on leash

Getting There

By Car: From San Francisco, go over the Golden Gate Bridge on Highway 101 north. From the Richmond/San Rafael Bridge, take the Sir Francis Drake Boulevard exit to Highway 101 south. Take the Paradise Drive/Tamalpais Drive turnoff. Turn left off freeway. Make first right on San Clemente Drive, which becomes Paradise Drive. Park on Paradise Drive just past Westward Drive, and keep walking along the street toward the Marin Country Day School. Look for the Nature Preserve sign and gate.

By Public Transportation: Take the #20 bus from San Rafael or San Francisco or take your bicycle on the ferry to either Larkspur or Tiburon and ride the remaining few miles. For more information, call Golden Gate Transit (415–455–2000; www.goldengatetransit.org).

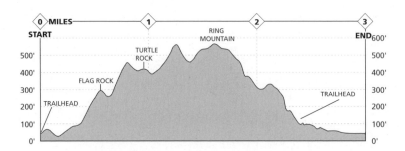

Ring Mountain

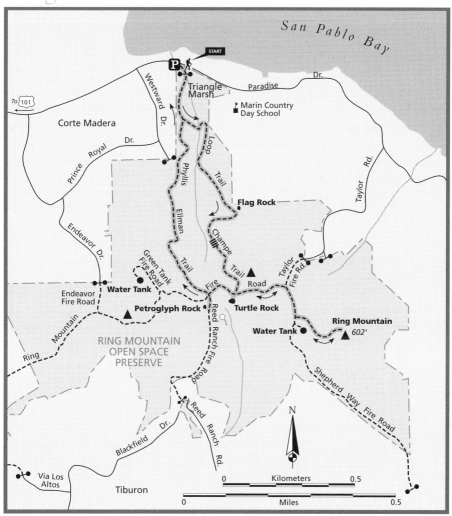

San Pablo Bay

START

Triangle Marsh

Paradise Dr.

Westward Dr.

To 101

Corte Madera

Prince Royal Dr.

Marin Country Day School

Loop Trail

Phyllis

Taylor Rd.

Flag Rock

Ellman Trail

Champe Trail

Endeavor Dr.

Green Tank Fire Road

Taylor Fire Rd.

Endeavor Fire Road

Water Tank

Fire Road

Petroglyph Rock

Reed Ranch Fire Road

Turtle Rock

Ring Mountain
▲ 602'

Water Tank

Mountain

RING MOUNTAIN OPEN SPACE PRESERVE

Ring

Shepherd Way Fire Road

N

Reed Ranch Dr.

Blackfield Dr.

Reed Ranch Rd.

Via Los Altos

Tiburon

0   Kilometers   0.5

0   Miles   0.5

Hike Description

At the start of the hike, the single-track Loop Trail crosses a bridge in Triangle Marsh, full of sticky gum plant, salt grass, salty pickle weed, and cordgrass, that reaches to the bay. In the rainy season, the muddy fill is like solidified Jell-O underfoot. In the fall, the ground is dry; the leaves on certain scrub turn golden and orange behind clumps of toyon berries, and the grasses, thin and sun-tanned, sway in the slightest breeze.

Across the bridge, a plaque dedicates this preserve "in loving memory of Patricia Bucko-Stormer . . . at the Nature Conservancy." To a nature lover, it is like a memorial in a church. Before the international, nonprofit membership organization bought the land as part of their mission to "preserve plants, animals and natural communities that represent the diversity of life on earth," Ring Mountain was threatened. Local groups, charged by the Marin Branch of the California Native Plant Society, battled to save it. And there's a whole lot to save.

Of greatest pride is the Tiburon mariposa lily *(Calochortus tiburonesis)*. Its long, shiny bronze leaves and yellow-green flowers can be seen nowhere but Ring Mountain. In 1973 Dr. Robert West, a physician and amateur photographer and botanist, identified the plant as a new species.

Other rare plants include Marin dwarf flax, Tiburon buckwheat, Tiburon paintbrush, and Oakland star tulip.

The springs and watercourses in the rocks along the trail provide for many resident animals and insects. The most unique is the rare and endangered blind harvestman spider, a type of daddy longlegs. While most of its kind are cave dwellers, this species resides under rocks on an exposed hillside, a true anomaly.

Though the spider may be blind, the three mice that commonly dwell here are not. Meadow mice move through tunnels in the valley to reach seed. Harvest mice, nocturnal omnivores, make birdlike nests in the marshes. Deer mice, a rather cuddly cinnamon brown with white underbellies, hide in burrows in the forest and feed at night on berries and insects.

Humans used to live here too. Miwok Indians ground acorns in bedrock mortars along one of the seasonal streams. They left a midden site, basically a refuge heap, and a temporary occupation site on the mountain. They made petroglyphs, or rock carvings, in thirty sites on the mountain, the only ones recorded in Marin County. The meaning of these prehistoric rock symbols, some dating back 2,000 years, is unknown. Some archeologists believe they are fertility symbols. Years of vandalism have destroyed the integrity of the petroglyphs, which should be treated with great care. (If you see any sign of tampering, report it to the rangers, and please refrain from adding your mark.)

Until 1965, cattle grazed the land here. In the 1970s, it became a favorite run for motorcyclists. In the 1980s grassroots effort, Phyllis Ellman (for whom a trail is named), saved Ring Mountain. In 1995 the California Nature Conservancy transferred ownership of the nature preserve to the Marin County Open Space District.

So even on this short circuit, there's a lot to see. Ring Mountain is a small island for nature and hiking with Corte Madera, Sausalito and the bay at its base. Climbing up, you see the ominous San Quentin Prison and ferries and freighters skidding through the water. The serpentine soil that you walk on is a truly unique mixture, which includes a rare mineral called lawsonite. Looking closely you may see miniscule garnets and watermelon tourmaline sparkling in the dirt.

Through clumps of hobbit trees and up the hills with grass rippling, you reach Turtle Rock. Only 602 feet above sea level, it still offers expansive views of bayside towns and the San Francisco skyline. To the west are the Marin headlands, the towers of the Golden Gate Bridge and shapely Mount Tamalpais. The loop back is equally entertaining with flora, fauna and more views ending back at the bridge over the marsh.

The "Statue of Man" rock outcropping

Miles/Directions

0.0 START at Paradise Drive in Corte Madera, just past Westward Drive. Look for Nature Preserve sign and gate. Go through gate. The trail crosses a small bridge to an information display. (*FYI:* Pick up a nature guide if available—lately it hasn't been. You can call the Open Space District Field Office to order one before your hike, 415–499–6387.)

0.2 Just past the information display, the trail splits. Take the trail to the left through a stand of blackberry bushes and onto Loop Trail. There are sixteen numbered signposts on the self-guided nature trail. Turn right at marker #2 for nature walk. Trail heads up moderately past some boulders.

0.3 At marker #4, there are several unofficial crossing trails. Continue right on the main trail. It parallels a stand of oak and bay trees on the right.

0.4 At marker #5, turn left. Pass through grassland.

Hike Information

📞 Trail Contacts:
Marin County Open Space District
3501 Civic Center Drive, Room 415, San
Rafael, CA 94901 (415) 499–6387; ranger's
office (415) 499–6405;
www.co.marin.ca.us/
depts/PK/main/index.cfm
Marin Open Space Council www.
openspacecouncil.org

🕐 Schedule:
Open year-round sunrise to sunset unless
otherwise posted

💲 Fees/Permits:
None

❓ Local Information:
**Corte Madera Chamber of Com-
merce,** 129 Corte Madera Town Center,
Corte Madera, CA (415) 924–0441;
www.cortemadera.org
County of Marin, www.visitmarin.org
Marin Directory, www.marindirect.com

💡 Local Events/Attractions:
San Anselmo
www.sananselmo.com/tourism/#SUMMARY
Bay Model Visitor Center, 2100 Bridge-
way, Sausalito, CA (415) 332–3871
Dragon Fly Cafe and Jazz Bar, 1546
Redwood Highway, Corte Madera, CA
(415) 927–8889
Windsor Vineyards Tasting Room, 72 Main
Street, Tiburon, CA (415) 435–3113

🛏 Accommodations:
Camping: Steep Ravine or Alice Eastwood
Camps, Mount Tamalpais State Park (415)
388–2070; www.reserveamerica.com/
usa/ca/mtta/index.html

**Casa Madrona Hotel and Mikayla
Restaurant,** 801 Bridgeway, Sausalito, CA
(800) 567–9524;
www.casamadronahotel.com
Corte Madera Inn, 56 Madera Boulevard,
Corte Madera, CA (415) 924–1502;
www.renesonhotels.com/Corte/Corte_home.
html
Green Gulch Farm and Zen Center,
1601 Shoreline Highway, Sausalito, CA (415)
383–3134

🍴 Restaurants:
Atrium, 1546 Redwood Highway, Corte
Madera, CA (415) 927–8889
Sam's Anchor Cafe, 27 Main Street,
Tiburon, CA (415) 435–4527

🎣 Local Outdoor Retailers:
Marin Outdoors, 935 Andersen Drive, San
Rafael, CA (415) 453–3400
REI—Corte Madera, 213 Corte Madera
Town Center, Corte Madera, CA (415)
927–1938

👥 Hike Tours:
Marin County Open Space District,
Naturalist-led interpretive walks (415)
499–6405;
www.co.marin.ca.us/depts/PK/Main/os/
osdnature.cfm
**Mount Tamalpais Interpretive Associ-
ation,** P.O. Box 3318, San Rafael, CA 94930
(415) 258–2410; www.mttam.net/index.html

Ⓝ Maps:
**Marin County Department of Open
Space,** 3501 Civic Center Drive, Room
415, San Rafael, CA (415) 499–6405;
www.co.marin.ca.us/depts/PK/main/index.
cfm
USGS maps: San Quentin, CA; San Rafael,
CA

0.5 Rock maze left of marker #6. The biggest rock is named Flag Rock.
Years ago, Marin Country Day School children used to play "Capture
the Flag" near it.

0.7 Post #7. Look left up the hill to see the "guarding man" rocks set in a
clump of juniper trees. Cross two bridges; follow the trail that goes

straight up about 20 feet, then take the trail right across the mountain and slightly downhill (parallel to the bay). The trail flattens out, curves, and heads toward the bay. Railroad ties protect trail edges. Stay to the left going uphill. At marker #8 there's a little shady grove. You can see the next marker ahead. On the railroad ties TRAIL and an arrow are carved into the wood to assure you that you are on the right trail. Looking back down toward the street, you can see part of Marin Country Day School.

0.8 At a trail post, with more railroad ties to mark your way, turn right into the grove of bay trees. Though not signposted, this is Champe Trail, named for the Nature Conservancy intern who laid out this part of the trail. The main trail takes you through the woods. Bear left to marker #10 where you can view Mount Tamalpais. The trail again splits, but you can see the next marker. The single-track trail opens up at marker #11.

0.9 Cross over the gravel and dirt ridge road to Turtle Rock. Walk east on the fire road along the hilltop.

1.1 Road becomes paved. Turn around and head back to Turtle Rock.

1.3 Back at Turtle Rock, head west on Ring Mountain Fire Road.

1.5 Trailhead for Phyllis Ellman Trail. Turn left. At marker #13, to the left, is where the Tiburon mariposa lily grows. Stay on path. **Option:** Before heading down the hill, turn left on Phyllis Ellman Trail and head up and over the hill and back. To add another 2 miles to this hike, take the dirt road off the Ring Mountain Fire Road up the hill to the west along the ridge and back.

2.3 Back at gate and Paradise Drive.

Honorable Mention:
Mount Tamalpais and Its Foothills

C. Cataract Trail

One trail and a dozen waterfalls—that's the wonderful ratio on the Cataract Trail. Above Alpine Lake in the Mount Tamalpais watershed, the trail follows Cataract Creek uphill steeply. The first waterfall is less than a 100 yards up. And they get bigger and louder as you climb.

The trailhead is on Bolinas Road (limited parking). About a mile up the trail, a wooden bridge crosses Cataract Creek. Take the fork to the right beyond it, following the creek until it levels out into a wide meadow and the Laurel Dell picnic area. The trail, though short, is of fairly sharp grade. Give yourself plenty of time before dark, and stay on assigned trails.

From the Laurel Dell picnic area, you can connect to many trails on Mount Tamalpais. For a pleasant loop, take Laurel Dell Fire Road to the Potrero picnic area. Cross the bridge and make a left on Kent Trail. This connects to the Helen Markt Trail around the edge of Alpine Lake. You can take it back to the Cataract Trail Bridge. Or you can turn around at the top and go back down the hill, admiring the falls from the top down for a round trip of 2 miles. Either way, be sure to take a look at Alpine Dam before you go.

To get there, take Highway 101 to Sir Francis Drake Boulevard. Follow Sir Francis Drake Boulevard west to the town of Fairfax. Veer right to Broadway, and turn left onto Bolinas-Fairfax Road. Go about 5 miles. Beyond Alpine Dam, the parking area is located near the hairpin turn and the trailhead. For more information, call the Sky Oaks Ranger Station at (415) 459–5267.

San Francisco and the Bay

San Francisco is an incredible city, one of the most visited in the world, with top-notch restaurants, museums, theaters, professional sports teams, music venues, and unique stores. But what many people don't know is that it also boasts the largest urban park system in the world, extending far north and south of the city. A short distance from this great metropolis, you could spend every weekend exploring some new trail or outdoor adventure. The coastal range and valleys support all kinds of plant and wildlife, in water and on land. And there's great hiking right in the city.

A hike in Golden Gate Park goes through botanical gardens and memorial groves, past lakes, a rose garden, grazing bison, and Dutch windmills. At Land's End, 4 miles of Ocean Beach and Fort Funston offer good running or strolling, and from the historical Cliff House, with its vintage arcade museum, a trail follows the bluff under Monterey cypress and eucalyptus trees with views of the Golden Gate. This path leads to China Beach and Baker Beach. The Coast Trail can take you all the way to Fort Point and across the bridge to Sausalito if you want. It also takes you to the Presidio, the oldest continuously operated military post in the nation only recently opened to the public. Lover's Lane, a forest of trees and military history, is there to explore. Crissy Field, once an airstrip, has lawns for picnicking near newly restored wetlands.

A ferry ride on the bay starts a memorable day of hiking on Angel Island. Past the infamous Alcatraz Island, its prison buildings still intact, the boat docks at Ayala Cove. Hiking or camping up on Mount Livermore, the island is yours for a precious moment. Trails take you through history from the Civil War to an immigration station to a World War II army hospital.

To check out native plants more closely, consider the pleasant loop through chaparral to the peak of San Bruno Mountain. Fog may hamper the view, but that's the nature of the city by the bay.

15

Angel Island State Park

Overview: *You have to love a hike that you can only reach by ferry. But the Angel Island hike does not take you away from it all. Instead, you take in gobs of civilization from a lofty and isolated plateau. On a clear day from Mount Livermore, you can see all four major bridges on the Bay. You can watch the fog roll over the city, like a slow-moving avalanche. Even with limited visibility, you can admire landmarks of the unique San Francisco skyline and the street-faire towns of Sausalito and Tiburon in Marin County. Looking at it a different way, you have a prison-to-prison view atop Angel Island: San Quentin to Alcatraz, both with their fascinating histories. That's the keyword here: history.*

Angel Island, the largest island in San Francisco Bay, spans a microcosm of U.S. history. It served as hunting ground for the Miwok Indians before becoming a Spanish cattle ranch, a quarry during the war between Mexico and the U.S., and a Civil War post for the Union. It was a quarantine station during the Spanish-American War, then a detention camp during the Philippine Insurrection. It was once the largest Army discharge depot and processing center on the West Coast, a World War I immigration station, a POW camp during World War II, a Nike missile site (1955 to 1962), and finally, a public park. Today, a few rangers and a small army of dedicated volunteers—mostly retired persons—take care of this rich historic island.

Bring a picnic lunch and carry water. Binoculars and a Bay Area map are recommended.

County: San Francisco
Start: From Ayala Cove on Angel Island
Length: 6.2–mile loop
Approximate Hiking Time: 3 hours
Difficulty Rating: Moderate; uphill to Mount Livermore, then downhill and fairly flat the rest of the way
Trail Surface: A single-track, well-maintained footpath leads to Mount Livermore. A less main-

tained path leads down to a double-track dirt road, then the paved road around the perimeter of the island.
Land Status: State park
Nearest Town: San Francisco and Tiburon
Other Trail Users: Roads accessible by mountain bikers
Canine Compatibility: No dogs permitted

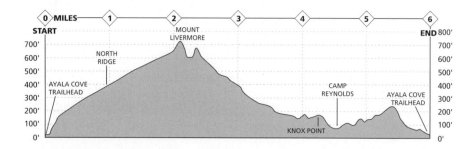

Angel Island State Park

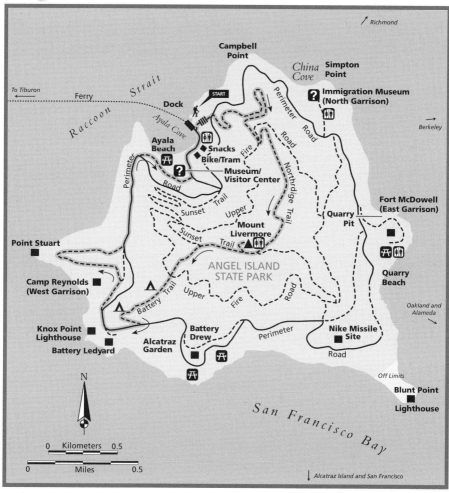

Getting There

By Car: From the San Francisco–Oakland Bay Bridge, take the first San Francisco exit on the left off the Bay Bridge, Embarcadero exit. At the stoplight, turn right on Harrison. At the end, turn left onto The Embarcadero. Follow The Embarcadero about 2 miles to Pier 39 and the Fisherman's Wharf area. You can find expensive but ample parking in the Pier 39 parking garage. Otherwise, continue down Bay Street to look for unmetered street parking. Catch a Blue and Gold ferry at Pier 41. Check the current schedule and prices at www.blueandgoldfleet.com, or call (800) 229-2784. Book by phone (415) 773-1188. The ferry will take you to Ayala Cove on Angel Island. You may want to take a quick stroll through the visitor center. The trailhead is to your right as you face inland from the ferry dock.

Other ferry service:

From downtown Tiburon: Tiburon–Angel Island Ferry Company terminal (415) 435–2131

From Vallejo: Vallejo Baylink Information Line (707) 643–3779

From Oakland/Alameda: (510) 522–3300

By Public Transportation: Take BART to Embarcadero Station. Catch the F line Muni on Market Street or at the Ferry Plaza across The Embarcadero. Take the F line to Fisherman's Wharf Terminal at Beach and Jones. It's a short walk to Pier 41. **Option:** Take BART to the Powell Street exit. Take the cable car to the end of the line at Hyde and Beach near Fisherman's Wharf; www.sfcablecar.com. For more information, call (415) 673–6864 or 673–MUNI, or visit www.sfmuni. com or www.transitinfo.org.

Hike Description

When you disembark from the Blue and Gold ferry at Ayala Cove on Angel Island, you are already steeped in history. For nearly two thousand years, when the weather was good and the salmon were spawning through Raccoon Strait, the Miwok landed here to camp, hunt, fish, and gather acorns. They rowed across the bay from their Marin homeland in narrow canoes made of tule. But the arrival of the Spanish saw the end of the Miwok presence on the island.

In August 1775 Juan Manuel de Ayala, whose mission was to complete the first accurate survey of the area for future Spanish conquest, christened this little island Isla de Los Angeles.

View of Marin County from Mount Livermore—Tiburon, Belvedere, and Sausalito

In 1892, a quarantine station was opened at Ayala Cove (known as Hospital Cove). Here, U.S. Immigration officials fumigated foreign ships and isolated immigrants that might be carrying diseases. The forty buildings at the cove included a 400-bed detention barracks, a disinfection plant, and laboratories. When the U.S. Public Health Service took over, this bleak facility was shut down. Once state parkland, the quarantine buildings were torn down, except for the bachelor officers' quarters (now the park museum) and the surgeons' homes, used as park offices. Take a brief detour to visit the tree-shaded museum behind the sandy beach of the cove before the hike. When you double back to the trailhead, purchase an Angel Island map brochure. It's only $1.00, and it covers a lot of great history.

Serpentining up the steep but well-maintained Northridge Trail, you pass native island trees and shrubs: oak, bay, and madrone trees, sagebrush, chamise, manzanita, toyon, elderberry, and coyote brush. This island was totally covered with trees and clearcut in the 1850s to accommodate the growth of San Francisco. The Youth Conservation Corps built this trail in 1975. Turn around to admire terrific views of Marin County.

Deer and raccoons live on the island, but you don't see them much anymore. In the 1970s, the deer overpopulated the island. They were so tame, you could pet them, and they hovered over picnickers on Ayala Beach. After efforts to export the deer became too expensive, many were killed to protect the ecology of the island.

Mount Livermore (781 feet) is named for Marin County conservationist Caroline Livermore, who led the campaign to create Angel Island State Park in 1958. If you can stand the sunshine, the peak is a great place for a picnic. On a clear day, you have fabulous views of the Transamerica Building, Fisherman's Wharf, Sutro Tower up on Twin Peaks, and the Golden Gate Bridge. Follow the Golden Gate north to spot the Marin Headlands all the way to San Rafael. Look east to the Bay Bridge, Treasure Island, and the East Bay with the Campanili of UC–Berkeley and the castle-like Mormon Temple.

Heading down the unmarked Battery Trail, you pass spectacular campsites. (There are nine campsites, only $12 per night, but you'll need to make reservations six months in advance.) Suddenly, you'll see a massive block of cement. This is Battery Wallace. In 1886, a report critical of Pacific Coast harbor defenses led to the development of these gun batteries facing the Golden Gate. You can't miss another massive slab, Battery Ledyard, once on Perimeter Road. Five years after they were built, these artillery units became obsolete and were decommissioned.

In just a few minutes' walk on Perimeter Road, you come to Angel Island's Civil War site, Camp Reynolds. The Civil War in California? Mare Island, near Martinez, was an important naval installation for the Union, and the Benicia Arsenal stocked valuable arms. Fearing that Confederate sympathizers might slip into the bay and attack these resources, the federal government established Camp Reynolds in 1863. Rebel troops never did invade. Accounts of soldiers stationed here reveal that their biggest challenge was fighting boredom.

After the Civil War, it became a busy infantry camp, with over 200 soldiers preparing to fight Apache and Sioux in the westward expansion. Isolated from the mainland, a village sprouted to support the troops. The buildings along the parade area are some of the oldest wooden structures on the West Coast. Docents can show you the restored Victorian officers' quarters and bake house. If you time it right, volunteers fire an 1800s replica cannon on weekends.

After a pleasant loop to Point Stuart, it's about 25 minutes back to the Ayala Cove ferry terminal.

On the ferry ride back, you can sometimes spot seals and sea lions playing in the bay. Blue herons, egrets, grebes, kingfishers, pelicans, seagulls, and ducks feed near Angel Island. Salmon and striped bass still migrate between the ocean and the Sacramento River Delta through Raccoon Strait.

This is a good time to plan your next visit to tour the other side of Angel Island, with Fort McDowell and the immigration station.

Miles/Directions

0.0 START at ferry dock in Ayala Cove. Facing inland, turn left. Northridge Trailhead is clearly marked and starts with wooden steps.

0.1 Cross over Perimeter Road. Northridge Trail continues up across road to the right.

1.2 Cross over dirt Fire Road. Northridge Trail continues on other side of road.

2.4 Sunset Trail. Follow trail to top of Mount Livermore.

2.7 Mount Livermore. Return to Sunset Trail.

3.0 Turn right on Sunset Trail.

3.3 Well-defined but unmarked trail to the left. Turn left onto unsigned Battery Trail. (*Note:* Watch for poison oak.)

3.5 Pass over Fire Road, continuing on Battery Trail.

3.8 Battery Wallace to the right.

3.9 Perimeter Road. Turn right to head toward Camp Reynolds.

4.1 Battery Ledyard on left.

4.3 Path heads down to the left of Perimeter Road to chapel.

4.5 Camp Reynolds (West Garrison). At the top of the slope are the officers' quarters, gardens, and bake house. Walk the grassy parade yard down toward the bay to see the cannon fired. Facing the officers' quarters, go left on the small road that curves west toward Point Stuart.

4.7 Rest rooms on the left.

4.9 Point Stuart. Continue as the road turns to hiker-only footpath going east toward the Perimeter Road.

5.3 Back on Perimeter Road, turn left.

5.7 Take the footpath on the left to Ayala Cove. The signs reads TO THE FERRY DOCK.

6.0 Back at visitor center, picnic area, and Ayala Beach.

6.2 Ferry dock.

Hike Information

Trail Contacts:
Angel Island Association, P.O. Box 866, Tiburon CA 94920 (415) 435–3522; park information: (415) 435–1915; www.angelisland.org
California State Parks Information Office, P.O. Box 942896, Sacramento, CA 94296-0001 (916) 653–6995; www.cal-parks.ca.gov
Groups tours/docent tours (415) 435–3522
Camping reservations: (800) 444–PARK

Schedule:
Open year-round 8:00 A.M. to sunset unless otherwise posted

Fees/Permits:
Ferry fare round trip: Adult (ages 13+), $12.00; children (ages 6–12), $6.50. Children 5 and under are free. If coming by boat, slips are available from 8:00 A.M. to sunset for $2.00. Mooring buoys are $3.00 per night, first come, first served.

Local Information:
Angel Island Tram Tours and Catered Events (415) 897–0715; www.angelisland.com
Angel Island Immigration Station Tours and information (415) 435–3522
General information for San Francisco: San Francisco Convention and Visitors Bureau, Visitor Information Center, 900 Market Street, San Francisco (415) 974–6900; www.ci.sf.ca.us/infovis.htm
Online: bayarea.citysearch.com

Local Events/Attractions:
Angel Island Immigration Station (415) 435–3522
Fort McDowell, East Garrison, Angel Island (415) 435–1915 or (415) 435–5390; www.angelisland.org
Aquatic Park, Hyde Street Pier Beach at Polk Street, San Francisco (415) 556–3002
Pier 39 and Fisherman's Wharf, Embarcadero and Powell Street, San Francisco (415) 981–7437
The Cannery, 2801 Leavenworth Street, San Francisco (415) 771–3112
San Francisco Museum of Modern Art, 151 Third Street (between Mission and Howard Streets), San Francisco (415) 357–4000

Accommodations:
Bed & Breakfasts:
www.ibbp.com/ca/sf.html or www.bbsf.com
Edward II Inn, 3155 Scott Street, San Francisco, CA (415) 922–3000 or (800) 473–2846; citisearch.com/sfo/edwardiiinn
Hostels: www.hostels.com/us.ca.sf.html
Pacific Tradewinds Hostel, 680 Sacramento Street, San Francisco, CA (415) 433–7970; www.hostels.com/pt/
Hotels:
sfbay.yahoo.com/external/fodors/lodging.html#fisherman_s_wharf_north_beach
Hyatt at Fisherman's Wharf, 555 North Point Street, San Francisco, CA (415) 563–1234 or (800) 233–1234
San Remo Hotel, 2237 Mason Street, San Francisco, CA (415) 776–8688 or (800) 352–7366

Restaurants:
Online: bayarea.citysearch.com
Albona Ristorante Istriano, 545 Francisco Street, San Francisco, CA (415) 441–1040
Hornblower Pier 33, San Francisco, CA (415) 788–8866
Lou's Blues Club Pier 47, 300 Jefferson Street, San Francisco, CA (415) 771–5687

Local Outdoor Retailers:
Any Mountain, 2598 Taylor Street, San Francisco, CA (415) 345–8080
Big 5 Sporting Goods, 2159 Chestnut, San Francisco, CA (415) 474–8670
Patagonia, 770 North Point, San Francisco, CA (415) 771–2050
Sullivan's Sport Shop, 5323 Geary Boulevard, San Francisco, CA (415) 751–7070

Hike Tours:
Angel Island Association, P.O. Box 866, Tiburon, CA 94920 (415) 435–3522; park information: (415) 435–1915; www.angelisland.org

Maps:
USGS maps: San Francisco North, CA

16   Cliff House Walk at Land's End

Overview: *A popular family trail, the wide and pleasant dirt path follows the cliffs above the bay. It occasionally heads inland through scrub and eucalyptus trees, just often enough to make the next open view of the Golden Gate Bridge and San Francisco stunning all over again. If you're making a day of it, check out the California Palace of the Legion of Honor museum, across from the Lincoln Park Golf Course. A short stint on city sidewalks takes you past the mansions of upscale Sea Cliff. The hike next heads to historical China Beach, where you can talk to surfers returning from a morning at Land's End, the popular surfing spot you can see from Eagle's Point. An option is to continue to Baker's Beach—along more city sidewalks—to the end of the beach, where you can catch the Coast Trail all the way to the Golden Gate Bridge, Fort Point, and the Marina District.*

County: San Francisco
Start: Trailhead at the end of the parking lot on Merrie Way off Point Lobos Avenue
Length: 4.3+ miles round trip
Approximate Hiking Time: 3 hours (with stops at Sutro Baths, Musée Mécanique, Camera Obscura, and Ocean Beach)
Difficulty Rating: Easy
Trail Surface: A double-track dirt trail narrows to a single-track, rising and falling on the bluff in

scrub, eucalyptus, and cypress trees, with coastal and city views. One short stint is on city sidewalks. There are beaches and viewing platforms along the way.
Land Status: Golden Gate Park and Recreation Association
Nearest Town: San Francisco
Other Trail Users: Mountain bikers
Canine Compatibility: Dogs on leash; no dogs allowed on China Beach

Getting There

By Car: From the Bay Bridge, exit Fell Street, turn right on Masonic Avenue, left on Geary Boulevard heading west. Geary turns into Point Lobos Avenue. Turn right onto Merrie Way, which is a parking lot. The Cliff House is about 200 yards ahead. From Highway 1 or 280, take Skyline Drive (Highway 35) north to the Great

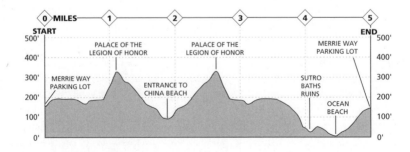

Cliff House Walk at Land's End

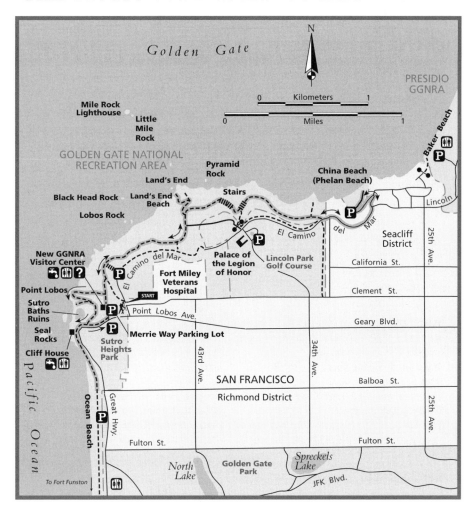

Highway. There are two other large parking areas available across the street on Point Lobos Avenue and just up the hill on Seal Rock Drive.

By Public Transportation: Take an outbound Route 38L: Richmond District or 38 Geary or 31 Balboa bus and ride to the end. Call Bay Area Transit at (415) 923–2000 or (415) 673–MUNI (6864); www.transitinfo.org.

Hike Description

As you walk along Land's End, you may hear five or ten different languages. It is a tourist destination, and as such is crowded on weekends, more tolerable and pristine on weekdays and in inclement weather. Mountain bikers are also allowed, so this is not a getaway trail; however, it's well worth the views and fits the bill if you want a short, scenic hike. From the parking lot on Merrie Way, you can look to

Looking down at Sutro Baths ruins from Merrie Way parking lot, with seal rocks beyond

your left at the foundations of the famous Sutro Baths and the nondescript Cliff House paused over the vast Pacific Ocean. Leave time to explore these San Francisco landmarks after your walk.

The walk along the cliffs immediately offers you breathtaking views of the Marin Headlands across the bay, with Point Bonita Lighthouse on the westernmost tip.

As the trail starts heading east, suspended there in front of you is the copper-stained Golden Gate Bridge. San Francisco stands proud over the water in shades of seagull white and fog gray, the glass of city windows gleaming in sunlight. Get out a city map and see how many neighborhoods and famous buildings you can identify. The bridge gets closer and closer as you walk the dirt trail, which starts out roadwide and only narrows when you climb wooden stairs, and then sink into a gully that curves slightly inland and out again among tall scrub and sharp-scented eucalyptus.

The manicured lawns to the right are part of the Lincoln Park Golf Course. According to local players, with the beautiful Legion of Honor museum located smack-dab in the center of the course and with the spectacular views of the bay, it can be a challenge to focus on your golf game. Nonetheless, Lincoln Park Golf

Course hosts the San Francisco City Golf Championship, the oldest and largest continuous event in U.S. golf history.

The California Palace of the Legion of Honor (closed Monday; admission) hosts an impressive collection of mostly European art, featuring an early cast of *The Thinker* by Rodin. Rodin himself gave it the museum's founder, Alma Spreckels, in 1915. Some of the golfers passing by on the Lincoln course claim that Rodin conceived of *The Thinker* after an especially difficult day of golf.

The only way to China Beach if you don't have a boat is on city sidewalks, but the short walk through the prestigious Sea Cliff neighborhood takes you past beautifully designed, multimillion-dollar homes. Many of these homes went up soon after the 1906 earthquake. While homesteaders around Market Street slapped together inventive structures, developer Mark Daniels laid out this rarified enclave. Sea Cliff and the Cliff House are all part of San Francisco's Richmond District. The name came as a suggestion from early settler George Turner Marsh, so the story goes. He thought the sand dunes that used to dominate the northwest corner of the city looked like Richmond, Australia.

China Beach, just off 25th Avenue, is a small, secluded beach sheltered by steep, rocky cliffs on both sides that tend to keep the howling winds at bay. The beach was a small camp, a shrimping and abalone gathering spot, and safe anchorage by the 1880s for Chinese fishermen, who made up 50 percent of all fishing crews in the Bay Area. In 1979, the National Park Service took over protection of the historic location. Lincoln Park Golf Course fairways used to be a Chinese cemetery. A monument still stands there (on the cart path northwest of the Lincoln clubhouse).

Back at the trailhead, you head down by the water in a small inlet near Seal Rocks to visit the ruins of the grand old Sutro Baths. Erected by philanthropist Adolph Sutro in 1886, the baths, six in all, sprawled across three acres. Sutro Baths also had three restaurants that could accommodate 1,000 people, as well as exhibits of sculptures, paintings, tapestries, and artifacts from Mexico, Egypt, Syria, and East Asia. A large amphitheater offered stage shows. Up to 25,000 people visited each day, arriving on one of three 5-cent railroads connecting to the city, and paying 10 cents for entry (25 cents for swimming).

Nothing but the photos in the Cliff House Visitor Center would suggest the grand public park and statuary that San Franciscans visited in the 1880s and 1890s. In 1966, land developers bought the Sutro Baths site to build high-rise apartments and began demolition. A fire destroyed what was left. In 1980, the remains became part of the Golden Gate National Recreation Area.

Next door is the historic Cliff House. The original was built in 1858, with the current structure from 1909. (The mansion had survived the 1906 earthquake, only to burn to the ground in a fire the next year.) George K. Whitney, owner of Playland-at-the-Beach, a popular amusement park for fifty years across from Ocean Beach, purchased, renovated, and reopened the Cliff House in 1937. The fifth and current Cliff House opened in 1950 with several dining rooms and the Sequoia Cocktail Lounge. It is undergoing a retrofit through 2004. From the lounge or the observation deck below, you can watch the hundreds of sea lions, pelicans, gulls, and cormorants that gather on Seal Rocks.

On the lower terrace is the Musée Mécanique (free admission), which houses a working collection of 160 antique arcade games dating back to 1880. Slip in a quarter and enjoy Love Testers, Strength Testers, Fortune Tellers, Fortune Scales, MutoScopes, and a variety of mechanical displays and games of chance and skill. Sometime during the retrofit, the Musée will move temporarily to Pier 45 near Fisherman's Wharf.

The Camera Obscura (admission: $1.00), a tourist attraction dating from 1948, is on the National Register of Historic Places. Inside, you stand in a darkened room and watch as a rotating lens and mirror (based on a design by Leonardo da Vinci) project a panoramic view of Cliff House, the Sutro Baths, Seal Rocks, and the Golden Gate Bridge.

Looking south from the Cliff House, you see the greenbelt of Golden Gate Park, ending with its windmills (see page 133). Condominiums have taken the place of Playland-at-the-Beach since 1972. Surfers and dog walkers claim Ocean Beach, which offers a wonderful extension of your hike if you enjoy a sandy stroll. Because of the presence of the endangered western snowy plover, hikers with hounds need to keep their pets under voice control or on a leash. Ocean Beach is the longest beach in the San Francisco area, stretching 4 miles along the Great Highway, terminating at Fort Funston. It is known for its cold, windy conditions and ferocious waves (nor for swimming), though you can sometimes find fantastic sunbathing days in the fall. The Beach Chalet Brewery and Restaurant at the end of Golden Gate Park might make a good destination and turnaround point.

Mile Rocks Lighthouse

In 1904, it was one of the great lighthouse engineering feats of all time. Now Mile Rocks is a pair of stones about a half mile north of Point Lobos in San Francisco. The larger of the two rocks is 40 feet by 30 feet, and rises about 20 feet above sea level. Mariners considered these to be a serious hazard due to fog and strong currents in the area. In 1901, when the *Rio de Janeiro* was wrecked near Fort Point and 140 lives were lost, engineers went to work to protect ships from the dangerous rocks. The first construction crew refused to work on the isolated, sea-swept rock, so the contractor hired deep-water sailors to do the work. They had only a few hours each day at low tide, and workers were constantly being knocked into the cold water. But they managed to erect a steel tower of three tiers and a lantern room. They painted the lighthouse tower white, the caisson below it black. Keepers had to commute by boat during low tide and climb a ladder to the lighthouse to do their isolated job. They had to wear earplugs for the loud fog signal. In powerful waves and high winds, a keeper could literally be blown from one of the tower's catwalks. Despite these hazards, some keepers enjoyed the assignment. Keeper Lyman Woodruff served on Mile Rocks for eighteen years. In the 1960s, despite protests from the general public, the tower of Mile Rocks was dismantled in the name of progress. The U.S. Coast Guard had deemed the station difficult to access and best suited to automation.

Hike Information

🕐 Trail Contact:
Golden Gate National Recreation Area, (415) 556–0560; www.nps.gov/goga

🕐 Schedule:
Park grounds open 24 hours a day

💲 Fees/Permits:
None

❓ Local Information:
San Francisco Convention and Visitor Center, 900 Market Street, Lower Level, Hallidie Plaza, San Francisco, CA 94103 (415) 283–0177; www.sfvisitor.org

📍 Local Events/Attractions:
Balboa Movie Theatre, 3630 Balboa Street (at 37th Avenue), San Francisco, CA (415) 221–8184
California Place of the Legion of Honor, 100 34th Avenue, San Francisco, CA (415) 863–3330; www.thinker.org
Camera Obscura, 1090 Point Lobos Road, San Francisco, CA (415) 750–0415
Lincoln Park Golf Course, 34th Avenue & Clement Street, San Francisco, CA (415) 221–9911
Musée Mécanique, 1090 Point Lobos Road, San Francisco, CA (415) 386–1170

🛏 Accommodations:
Camping: Rob Hill Campground (in the Presidio) (415) 561–5444; www.nps.gov/goga/camping/robhill.htm
Hostel: Fort Mason International Hostel, Fort Mason's Building #240. Marina Boulevard at Laguna Street, San Francisco, CA (415) 771–7277
Casa Arguello, 225 Arguello Street at California, San Francisco, CA (415) 752–9482
Edward II B&B (Marina District), 3155 Scott Street, San Francisco, CA (415) 922–3000

Red Victorian B&B, (near Golden Gate Park) 1665 Haight Street, San Francisco, CA (415) 864–1978
The Seal Rock Motor Inn & Restaurant, 545 Point Lobos Avenue at 48th Avenue, San Francisco, CA (415) 752–8000 or (888) SEALROCK (732–5762)

🍴 Restaurants:
The Beach Chalet Brewery and Restaurant, 1000 Great Highway (at Ocean Beach) San Francisco, (415) 386–8439; www.beachchalet.com
Cliff House, 1090 Point Lobos Avenue, San Francisco, CA (415) 386–3330; www.cliffhouse.com
Garden House Cafe, 3117 Clement Street (at 32nd Avenue), (415) 668–1640.
Louis', 902 Point Lobos Avenue, San Francisco, CA (415) 387–6330
Seakor Polish Delicatessen, 5957 Geary Boulevard (at 24th Avenue), San Francisco, CA (415) 387–8660
Ton Kiang, 5821 Geary Boulevard, San Francisco, CA (415) 387–8273

🛍 Local Outdoor Retailers:
Any Mountain, 2598 Taylor Street, San Francisco, CA (415) 345–8080
Play It Again Sports, 45 West Portal Avenue, San Francisco, CA (415) 753–3049
Sullivan's Sport Shop, 5323 Geary Boulevard, San Francisco, CA (415) 751–7070

🚶 Hike Tours:
Cliffhouse Visitor Center, (415) 556–8642
Golden Gate National Recreation Area, (415) 556–0560
City Guides, (415) 557–4266

🅝 Maps:
USGS maps: San Francisco North, CA

Miles/Directions

0.0 START at trailhead at end of parking lot on Merrie Way. Once on the double-track dirt trail, follow it to the right, going east. Look for an orange-and-white caisson beyond Land's End. This is Mile Rocks Lighthouse, the modern version.

1.2 Trail goes up wooden stairs and slightly inland, where it narrows.

1.7 Eagle's Point and Lincoln Park Golf Course. From the observation platform at Eagle's Point, descend stairs and look west to the tip of Land's End. Return to observation platform, then continue on the trail to its end and on to the sidewalk beside El Camino del Mar.

2.0 China Beach. Head back the way you came to Coast Trail. **Option:** Continue to Baker Beach and catch the Coast Trail on the other side of the beach all the way to the Presidio and Golden Gate Bridge, about 4 miles.

4.0 Back at Merrie Way parking lot. Walk on western sidewalk, then turn right down paved path to Sutro Bath ruins.

4.1 From the rise above the baths on the northwestern corner, enjoy view of Seal Rocks. Continue on paved path up to Point Lobos Avenue and Cliff House.

4.2 Cliff House. Follow signs right down stairs to museum and observation deck. Exit back up to sidewalk and go right downhill past Cliff House to Ocean Beach. Otherwise, turn around and take sidewalk back to Merrie Way.

4.3 Parking lot at Merrie Way.

17

Sweeney Ridge: The Portolá Discovery Site

Overview: *The small, open space area on scrub-covered moors is for locals an oasis in an urban desert, which includes the San Francisco International Airport and the busy Highway 280/101 corridors. Protected as Golden Gate National Recreation Area in 1984, the ridge (at about 1,250 feet) offers 360-degree views up to 30 miles on clear days. You'll need a jacket on this hike (daytime temperatures can range from the upper 20s (°F) in January to 100°F in September). The north ridge is home to an abandoned Nike missile site. The south ridge offers short, single-track trails that leave civilization behind for a time. There are no facilities.*

County: San Mateo
Start: At the gate at the end of Sneath Lane
Length: 5.8 miles round trip
Approximate Hiking Time: 3 hours
Difficulty Rating: Moderate with elevation gain
Trail Surface: A paved path takes you up to the ridge. A double-track dirt trail, rutted from rain and horse hoofs, goes the length of the ridge, with very narrow single-track dirt trails cre-ating a loop on the south end.
Land Status: Golden Gate National Recreation area
Nearest Town: San Bruno
Other Trail Users: Equestrians and mountain bikers
Canine Compatibility: Dogs on leash

Getting There

By Car: From San Francisco Bay Bridge, take Highway 101 south to Highway 280 south. Take the Pacifica/Highway 1 exit. Get off at Skyline Boulevard south, Highway 35. Go about 4 miles, past Skyline College entrance, and turn right on Sneath Lane. Take it to the end through a residential area. Parking area is on the right past the entrance gate.

By Public Transportation: Take SamTrans bus #110 from Daly City BART (frequency: every one to two hours), or SamTrans bus #112 from Colma BART (hourly service), to Highway 1 at Reina Del Mar Avenue. From Colma BART, take either SamTrans bus #121 (frequency: every thirty to sixty minutes) to stop at Skyline College or, on weekdays only, SamTrans bus #123 (frequency: every hour) to the first stop at Skyline College (southeast campus). Weekdays only, take SamTrans bus #294 (frequency: every eighty minutes to two hours) from Hillsdale Caltrain to Linda Mar Shopping Center and transfer to either SamTrans bus #110 or #112. Deboard at Highway 1 and Reina Del Mar Avenue. At end of hike, catch SamTrans bus #14 on Fassler Avenue to Linda Mar Shopping Center (frequency: every thirty minutes, weekdays only), then transfer to SamTrans bus #110 or #112 back to Daly City BART or Colma BART, respectively; or, at end of hike, walk west on Fassler Avenue to Highway 1 (about 1 mile) and SamTrans buses #110 or #112 (about seventy minutes total). SamTrans info: (800) 660–4287 or (650) 817–1717.

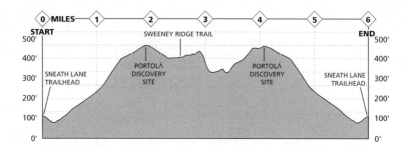

Hike Description

In 1769, an expedition led by Don Gaspar de Portolá was ordered to find a land route to Monterey Bay, a "fine harbor, sheltered from winds." Leaving from the tip of Baja California in July of that year with 64 men and 200 horses, Portolá was guided by only scant reports of the place, vague descriptions as seen from the sea, and a mariner's navigation handbook of the California coastline. When Portolá and his men saw the mouth of the Salinas River, they were greeted by stinging winds and rough seas. Concluding this could not possibly be the place, they continued north.

Food and supplies were running short when they reached the peaceful San Pedro Valley (the Linda Mar area of Pacifica today; see page 170, San Pedro Valley County Park). The gentle Ohlone Indians, who lived in the valley, befriended the strangers and helped them regain their strength. (Ironically, most of them would die twenty-three years later from an epidemic contracted from the new settlers.)

One of Portolá's scouts, Jose Francisco Ortega, climbed a nearby ridge. To his surprise, there to the east was, in his own words, "an enormous area of the sea or estuary, which shot inland as far as the eye could see." He became the first European to see the San Francisco Bay.

On November 4, 1769, Captain Portolá and the entire party followed Ortega up to the ridge to see this view for themselves. Portolá, a military man and really not an explorer at heart, was unaware of the discovery's great significance. Perhaps focused on the goal of the mission, he was anxious by then to get back to the Monterey Bay. Nevertheless, he named the body of water San Francisco Bay and claimed it as part of New Spain.

You can stand in the spot where Ortega took in this vista for the first time. A monument on the site is dedicated to Carl McCarthy, who was among those that assured the public ownership of this open space. It illustrates the peaks you are seeing all around you: Mount Diablo, Mount Hamilton (the highest peak in the region), Montara Mountain, Point San Pedro, Mount Tamalpais and San Bruno Mountain.

There are several ways of getting there. The hike from Skyline College perhaps offers the most exercise, going up the ridge and down into a lush ravine before climbing again to the Portolá site. The Baquiano (Spanish for *scout*) Trail may be

Sweeney Ridge

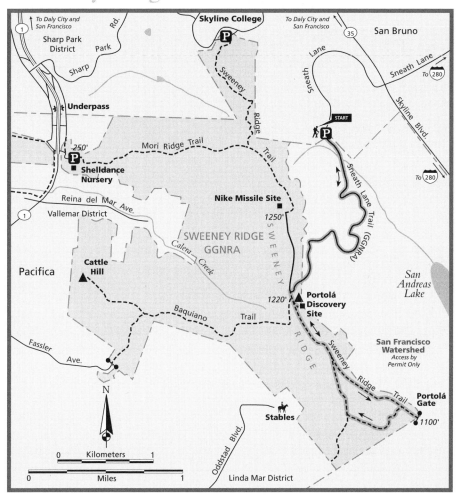

the closest to the route Ortega took up what is now called Sweeney Ridge. The main entrance to the park is at the end of Sneath Lane, where the featured hike begins.

A paved path and hearty cardiovascular climb take you up the hill, with pretty San Andreas Lake to your left. The active right-slip San Andreas Fault line runs beneath it and Crystal Springs Reservoir to the southeast.

A short stint north brings you to the decaying structures of the U.S. Army Nike Missile Radar Station, which was in operation here between 1957 and 1974. It was rendered obsolete by the Anti-Ballistic Missile Treaty that year. Northwest on Milagra Ridge, silos housed the deadly rockets in a manned battery.

In contrast, the loop going south offers a peaceful stroll on narrow paths—

muddy after rains—showing off the vegetation and wildlife on the ridge in quiet detail. Someday, you will be able to continue your hike south past the reservoir on the Bay Area Ridge Trail. A group of volunteers called Friends of Sweeney Ridge, in cooperation with the Pacific Trust, is doing what it can to preserve the space that is open and accessible to the public. The City of Pacifica owns 9.2 of the park acres bordering the entrance gate and, strapped for cash, are selling it off. Rather than impacting the watershed with the construction of luxury homes here, the Pacific Trust is collecting funds to purchase the acreage to remain as parkland. They could always use help.

If you end up hiking in the fog, you won't see much beyond the white-tailed rabbits and wildflowers. Sometimes it gets so thick you can barely see 20 feet ahead. It is isolating and disorienting, so stay on the trails. The yellow line down Sneath Lane is a fogline painted to keep bikers and hikers from going off the edge. When you actually see it in fog, you totally understand.

Miles/Directions

0.0 START at gate at main entrance to Sweeney Ridge. Go to double-track, paved Sneath Lane. To the south is San Andreas Lake.

1.0 Fogline begins on trail; road gets steeper. A stand of eucalyptus grows near top of trail to the south.

1.7 Top of ridge, with ocean views to the west on clear days. Double-track dirt trail is Sweeney Ridge Trail heading south; to the north, it goes to Skyline College. The whole circuit is part of Bay Area Ridge Trail. Turning south (left facing the ocean), walk a short way to the Portolá monument on the left side of the trail. Return to main trail and continue south on Sweeney Ridge Trail. Pass Baquiano Trailhead.

2.3 Bay Area Ridge Trail sign. Stay on Sweeney Ridge Trail past this single-track dirt trail, which goes to horse stables at the end of Linda Mar Valley; you will be returning on this trail on the southwestern loop.

2.8 At the junction with another unmarked dirt trail, turn right. Ahead, south on Sweeney Ridge, is gate to San Francisco Watershed area, warning no trespassing. Trail narrows. (*Note:* Long pants are recommended here. Also, trail gets muddy after rains.) Trail rises and falls in scrub.

3.2 Junction. Take fork to the right, which heads back to Sweeney Ridge Trail (left to horse stables). (*Note:* Watch out for horse droppings. More equestrians than hikers use this trail.)

3.6 Back on Sweeney Ridge Trail, turn left.

4.1 Turn right on Sneath Lane back down the hill. **Option:** To extend round-trip hike to 7.4 miles, go straight past the junction with Sneath Lane to the Sweeney Ridge Trail to Skyline College to see abandoned Nike missile radar site, which is less than a mile from here.

5.8 Back at trailhead and parking lot.

Hike Information

🕿 Trail Contact:
Golden Gate National Recreation Area, Ocean District at (415) 556–8371

🕒 Schedule:
Open daily 8:00 A.M. to dusk

💲 Fees/Permits:
None

❓ Local Information:
San Bruno Chamber of Commerce, 357 Angus Avenue West, San Bruno, CA 94066 (650) 588–0180; www.ci.sanbruno.ca.us

Pacifica Visitor Center, 225 Rockaway Beach #1, Pacifica, CA (650) 355–4122; www.ci.pacifica.ca.us

San Francisco Convention and Visitor Center, 900 Market Street, Lower Level, Hallidie Plaza, San Francisco, CA (415) 283–0177; www.sfvisitor.org

💡 Local Events/Attractions:
Coyote Point Museum for Environmental Education, 1651 Coyote Point Drive, San Mateo, CA (650) 342–7755

Plymire Schwarz Museum and Center Fire Museum, 519 Grand Avenue, South San Francisco, CA (650) 875–6988

San Mateo County Historical Museum, 777 Hamilton Street, Redwood City, CA (650) 574–6441

⊟ Accommodations:
Camping: Rob Hill Campground (in the Presidio) (415) 561–5444; www.nps.gov/goga/camping/robhill.htm

Hostel: Fort Mason International Hostel Fort Mason's Building #240. Marina Boulevard at Laguna Street, San Francisco, CA (415) 771–7277

Courtyard San Francisco Airport, 1050 Bayhill Drive, San Bruno, CA (415) 952–3333

🍴 Restaurants:
Green Valley Organic Vegetarian Restaurant, 422 San Mateo Avenue (at El Camino), San Bruno, CA (650) 873–6677

Gabriana's Pizza, 120 Skycrest Center, San Bruno, CA (650) 873–0144

🌳 Local Outdoor Retailers:
Big 5 Sporting Goods, 314 Gellert Boulevard, Daly City, CA (650) 994–3688

REI, 1119 Industrial Road, Suite 1–B, San Carlos, CA (650) 508–2330

Sportmart, 301 Gellert Boulevard. Daly City, CA (650) 301–9000

👥 Hike Tours:
Golden Gate National Recreation Area, Ocean District (415) 556–8371

Friends of Sweeney Ridge and Pacifica Land Trust, P.O. Box 988, Pacifica, CA 94045 (650) 871–9478; www.pacificalandtrust.org/sweeneyridge/sweeneyridge.htm

🗺 Maps:
USGS maps: San Francisco South, CA

18

The Presidio: Lovers' Lane and the Ecology Trail

Overview: *With the closing of military bases all over the West Coast in the 1990s, San Francisco's Presidio, one of the oldest of them all, dating back to 1776, is yours to wander. This hike takes you through military and social history, through scenic forests and lawn area, and along the path of lovers. Besides some interesting history and ecology, the trail covers most stages of a relationship: strolling down Lovers' Lane, passing a proven well of fertility, reaching Inspiration Point, cruising by the chapel, and walking along by the old officer family homes, ending with the post hospital, where babes were born and loved ones said good-bye. As a bonus, there's a bowling alley near the start of the hike to take a date to afterwards.*

County: San Francisco
Start: William Penn Mott Jr. Visitor Center
Length: 2.7–mile loop
Approximate Hiking Time: 2 hours
Difficulty Rating: Easy
Trail Surface: Single- and double-track dirt trail through forest and on paved pathways

Land Status: Golden Gate National Recreation Area
Nearest Town: San Francisco
Other Trail Users: Bicyclists on paved pathways
Canine Compatibility: Dogs on leash

Getting There

By Car: From the north, take Highway 101/Highway 1 across the Golden Gate Bridge. Take the U.S. 101 south ramp toward Downtown/Lombard Street. Merge on Route 101. Route 101 becomes Route 101/Richardson Avenue. Route 101/Richardson Avenue becomes Route 101/Lombard St. Enter the Presidio at the Lombard Street entrance, and follow signs to the visitor center. In the Presidio, turn right on Lincoln Boulevard. Turn left on Montgomery Street, and park near the William Penn Mott Jr. visitor center, which is in one of the red brick buildings on the right-hand side, clearly marked.

From the east, take I–80 west ramp toward San Francisco. I–80 W becomes I–80 West/Bay Bridge. Take the Embarcadero exit. At the light turn right on

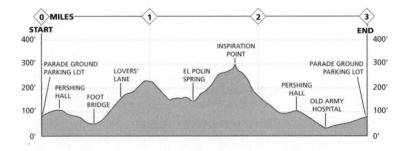

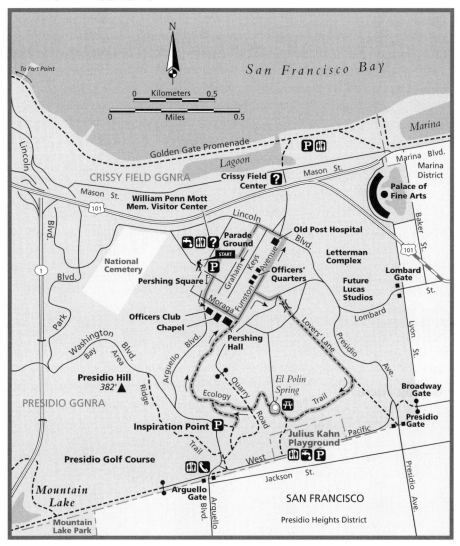

Harrison. At the end, turn left on the Embarcadero. Turn left on Bay Street. Cross Van Ness, and after a few blocks, turn right on Laguna. Laguna becomes Marina Boulevard. Continue straight into the entrance of the Presidio (Careful: veering left will take you onto the Golden Gate Bridge and Highway 101 N.). Marina Boulevard becomes Mason. At a stop sign, turn left on Halleck. At the next stop sign, turn right on Lincoln Blvd. Turn left on Montgomery Street, and park near the William Penn Mott Jr. visitor center.

Public Transportation: San Francisco Municipal Railway (MUNI) buses serve the Presidio via the 28, 29, 43, and 82X lines. Bus service from the North Bay to the Golden Gate Bridge toll plaza is available through Golden Gate Transit. Commercial cable car buses are available from Fisherman's Wharf. For more information call (415) 673–6864, www.transitinfo.org/.

Hike Description

First stop is the William Penn Mott Jr. Visitor Center to pick up a free brochure called the "Main Post Walk: 200 Years of History and Architecture." It covers the fascinating architectural mile of this hike. The rest is among trees and parkland.

In the Presidio Woods—the ground is sand.

Maps of this unmarked but well-worn trail are also available. Have a volunteer ranger show you the Ecology Trail on the map.

At Pershing Square, where the hike begins, you can lay your hands on two of the oldest known cannons in North America. The bronze "San Francisco" (1679) and the "Virgin of Barbaneda" (1693) once guarded the Spanish fort here.

Pass the chapel (built in 1864, but greatly modified in the 1950s), where many a soldier tied the knot while doing duty in the Presidio. But before they took that leap, many took a long walk through the forest, down Lovers' Lane.

Notice that this paved, lamp-lit pathway is absolutely straight. It leads directly to the Presidio Boulevard Gate (1896), a main entrance for the U.S. Presidio grounds. By foot, this is still the quickest way out of the fort and into town. Probably the oldest travel corridor in San Francisco, this trail has witnessed the passing of Spanish soldiers, Mexican missionaries, and American soldiers of two centuries. In the early 1800s this path connected the Presidio to the Mission District, 3 miles to the southeast, where most of the civilian population moved for better weather. It was part of Mexico then. You can still find some of the oldest Victorian houses in the city there.

From Lovers' Lane, you turn to wander in the woods. When the Spanish arrived, this area was low dunes, scattered shrubs, and bunch grass, all of it swept by the Pacific winds. Along the shore were extensive marshes that hosted seagulls, pelicans, a few deer, and sometimes a hungry mountain lion or grizzly bear. The Ohlone Indians lived well with what was here for about 5,000 years, in temporary villages constructed of reeds and moving about with the seasons. In 1848, the U.S. government decided to tame the wind and sand. In a beautifying effort starting in 1883, Major William A. Jones and his crew planted 400,000 seedlings of 200 tree species on the slopes around the Presidio, most of them in orderly rows like soldiers in formation. It was the most ambitious landscaping effort the army had ever undertaken. The idea, Jones said, was to, "crown the ridges, border boundary fences, cover areas of sand and marsh waste with forest that would generally seem continuous and thus immensely larger than it really is." He succeeded. Eucalyptus, cypress, and pine trees thrived the best, altering the landscape forever. With the trees so abundant, mature and healthy, it's hard to imagine that they are immigrants to the area, a military garden.

Just when you thought it was safe to drink the water, beware El Polin. Now a cement fixture surrounded by paved pathways and lawn, it's not much to look at. But it is a "proven" fertility fountain. The legend says if a woman drinks the water of the well on a full moon, she will be very fertile and likely to have many children. Although the Spanish wrote of the legend, it is possible that it goes back to the Ohlone people. The wives of the first Spanish officers at the Presidio drank regularly from this spring and proceeded to have twelve, fifteen, and twenty children.

To the left of the fountain on the fenced hillside, you see birth of another kind, a restoration effort to bring back native plants that have all but disappeared. These serpentine grasslands are one of the most threatened natural ecosystems in North

America. The Presidio *clarkia franciscana* and the Marin dwarf flax are coming back on these few acres, a landscape that used to be common in San Francisco.

Where else do you take a hot date in San Francisco but Inspiration Point? It's probably a better visit parked in a Cadillac with some appropriate music on the radio to accompany a Golden Gate sunset. It's mostly a parking lot up here, which is not terribly inspiring, but it's still worth the detour for the memorable vista and interpretive signs about the area. You can look down and admire one of the oldest continually operating posts in North America as well as the immediate Golden Gate Recreational Area, with its 1,480 acres of historic buildings, grasslands, dense forests, coastal fortifications, and hiking trails. Golden Gate Bridge never gets to be an old sight either. The name Inspiration Point dates back to the mid-1800s, when the trees did not block part of the view.

The Ecology Trail brings you back to Funston Avenue and Officers' Row. For more than 140 years this street was home to commissioned officers and their families. Despite the military setting, life here in the 1800s was typical of middle-class America. Wives cooked meals and tended the garden, children played in the yards, and husbands went off to work. Outside, there were chicken coops and flower gardens.

Inside, the homes were spacious, with two or four bedrooms, a living and dining room, and a study. Running water arrived in the 1880s, electricity in 1912. Currently, they are park offices. By around 2003, these houses will be open to the public for overnight accommodations.

Recording the family relations of the past is the Funston Avenue Archeological Research Project. During summer, you may find archeologists here labeling the remains in open digs around the grounds. They have uncovered fragments of butchered animals bones, wrought iron tools, English-made China, children's toys, beads, construction materials, and, most importantly, a stone foundation from the original Spanish presidio. They welcome questions and visitors to the sites.

Turning the corner onto Lincoln, you come to the post hospital, built in 1863, rounding out the Lovers' hike "in sickness and in health." Go around back to check out the 1906 fire and earthquake refugee camp exhibit. There is an example of two of the tent cottages the army provided for quake survivors. Photos show hundreds of them set up on the Presidio and give you a chance to imagine the postquake homelessness.

Most of the officers' and enlisted family housing quarters have been modernized by the Presidio Trust to rent to the public. Other housing is subsidized and provides needed student apartments for overflow from San Francisco State, San Francisco University, and UC–Berkeley. Some businesses have moved in too. The grandest new resident of the Presidio is film producer and director George Lucas. His new twenty-three–acre studio (the Letterman Complex, near the Lombard Street entrance) will encompass many buildings where he will create romance for the screen.

To top off the Lovers' hike, take a picnic to recently renovated Crissy Fields or stroll through the pillars of the unforgettable Palace of Fine Arts, tour the tactile room in the Exploratorium, then head to Chestnut Avenue in the trendy Marina District for an intimate dinner for two.

Miles/Directions

0.0 START from parking lot on Montgomery in front of visitor center. Walk southwest (away from bay) toward white flagpole in Pershing Square.

0.1 Pershing Square. Walk up sidewalk between cannons and cross Moraga Avenue.

0.2 Pass Officers' Club and continue on Moraga Avenue, past chapel to Funston Avenue.

0.3 Cross Moraga Avenue, and walk downhill to the Alameda. Trail behind Pershing Hall is return route on this loop. Site of Funston Avenue Archeological Research Project and officers family housing (1862). Halfway down Funston Avenue, the Alameda (Spanish for *avenue*) served as the post's official entrance from the 1860s until 1895.

0.5 Turn right onto the Alameda. Complete the rest of Main Post Historic Walk at the end of this loop trail.

0.6 Where Presidio Boulevard meets Barnard Avenue you'll see a footpath. (Leashed pets welcome.) Turn right onto paved pathway with wild blackberries on either side of trail (ready to eat in fall months). Cross over brick footbridge dating to 1885, and proceed onto Lovers' Lane.

1.0 Five hundred feet before West Pacific Boulevard, turn right onto an unmarked but well-worn dirt and sand trail that leads to Presidio woods. This is Ecology Trail.

1.3 Bear right to Paul Goode baseball and recreation field. Head around left of the field; take the path left of the white houses. (*Note:* If you need a rest room, you can detour up the hill to your left to the Julius Khan Playground.)

1.4 Walk down the stairs to El Polin and lawn area. Walk to the left of fountain to view native plant restoration on hillside.

1.5 Cross over trail leading to Quarry Road; continue straight.

1.7 Take single-track dirt trail up hill to the left to take in the vista at Inspiration Point. Head back down to Ecology Trail, turning left to continue.

2.0 Trail runs along Barnard Street. Follow path to Pershing Hall.

2.1 Walk beside Pershing Hall back onto Funston Avenue. Continue Main Post Walk, heading down Funston Avenue toward corner of Lincoln Boulevard.

2.3 Victorian-era houses. Continue toward Lincoln Boulevard.

2.4 Turn left at Lincoln Boulevard; look for fire station. Cottages (1906) around the back. Continue west on Lincoln to Graham Street. Barracks (1886) on the left.

2.5 Cross to other side of Graham Street, turn left, and begin walk on street.

Enlisted barracks (1862) on the right. Continue uphill to Owen Street.

2.6 Take Owen Street back to parking lot (parade ground) and Montgomery Street.

2.7 Back at visitor center.

Hike Information

📞 Trail Contacts:
William Penn Mott Jr. Visitor Center, Building 102, Montgomery Street, San Francisco, CA 94129 (415) 561–4323 (temporarily at 50 Moraga Avenue in 2003) **Golden Gate National Recreation Area—Presidio, Fort Mason,** Building 201, San Francisco, CA 94129 (415) 705–5555, www.nps.gov/prsf/index.htm www.nps.gov/prsf/prsfphot/cultureh.htm

🕐 Schedule:
Open year-round sunrise to sunset; visitor center is open from 9:00 A.M. to 5:00 P.M.

💲 Fees/Permits:
None

❓ Local Information:
Bay Area City Search: bayarea. citysearch.com/ **The California Welcome Center,** Pier 39, Second Level Unit Q5, (Beach Street and Embarcadero), San Francisco, CA (415) 956–3493; www.visitcalifornia.com **San Francisco Convention and Visitors Bureau,** 201 Third Street, Suite 900, San Francisco, CA (415) 283–0177; www.srd.yahoo.com/srst/7430584/San+ Francisco+Convention+and+Visitors+Bureau +/1/2/*http://www.sfvisitor.org/ **Outdoors Unlimited,** 500 Parnassus Avenue, San Francisco, CA (415) 476–2078

💡 Local Events/Attractions:
William Penn Mott Jr. Visitor Center, Building 102, Montgomery Street, San Francisco, CA 94129 (415) 561–4323 **Crissy Fields,** (the corner of Mason and Halleck Streets), the Presidio, San Francisco, CA (415) 561–3000 www.crissyfield.org/

Exploratorium, 3601 Lyon Street, San Francisco, CA (415) EXP-LORE (397–5673); www.exploratorium.edu/ **Fort Point National Historic Site,** Long Avenue, San Francisco, CA (415) 561–4395 or (415) 673–5642, www.nps.gov/fopo/ **Presidio Bowl** (corner of Moraga and Montgomery Streets), the Presidio, San Francisco, CA (415) 561–BOWL (2695); www.yahoo.com/goo/Presidio+Bowl/1/* www.hvm64.tripod.com/presidiobowl/ **Presidio Golf Course,** 300 Finley Road, P.O. Box 29063, San Francisco, CA (415) 561–GOLF (4653), www.presidiogolf.com/

🛏 Accommodations:
Camping: Rob Hill Campground (in the Presidio) (415) 561–5444; www.nps.gov/goga/camping/robhill.htm **Hostels:** **HI—San Francisco—Fisherman's Wharf,** Fort Mason, Building 240 San Francisco, CA (415) 703–9988; www. norcalhostels.org **Pacific Tradewinds Hostel,** 680 Sacramento Street, San Francisco, CA (415) 433–7970, www.hostels.com/pt/ **Hotels and B&Bs:** **Bed and Breakfast Inn,** 4 Charlton Court, San Francisco, CA (415) 921–9784; www.BedandBreakfast.com/ **B&B channel:** www.bbchannel.com/USA/California/ San%20Francisco.asp **Bed and Breakfast San Francisco,** www.bbsf.com/ **Phoenix Hotel,** 601 Eddy Street, San Francisco, CA (415) 776–1380 **Stanyan Park Hotel,** 750 Stanyan Street San Francisco, CA (415) 751–1000

Restaurants:
Ace Wasabi's Rock-N-Roll Sushi,
3339 Steiner Street, San Francisco, CA
(415) 567–4903
Andale Taqueria, 2150 Chestnut Street,
San Francisco, CA (415) 749–0506
Bistro Aix (American/Mediterranean),
3340 Steiner Street, San Francisco, CA
(415) 202–0100
Faultline Brewing Co., 2001 Chestnut
Street, San Francisco, CA (415) 922–7397
Greens Restaurant (Vegetarian), Fort
Mason, Building A, San Francisco, CA (415)
771–6222 (reservations); (415) 771–6330
(take out); www.greensrestaurant.com/
Pizza Orgasmica, 3157 Fillmore Street,
San Francisco, CA (415) 931–5300
For more, check out bayarea.citysearch.com/
(search by Marina) or www.activediner.com

Local Outdoor Retailers:
Any Mountain, 2598 Taylor Street, San
Francisco, CA (415) 345–8080

Hike Tours:
William Penn Mott Jr. Visitor Center,
Building 102, Montgomery Street, San Fran-
cisco, CA (415) 561–4323
**Golden Gate National Recreation
Area**—Presidio, Fort Mason, Building 201,
San Francisco, CA www.nps.gov/prsf/
home.htm

Maps:
USGS maps: Point Bonita, CA; San Fan-
cisco North, CA

19

San Bruno State Park: Summit Loop Trail

Overview: *San Bruno Mountain doesn't look like much at first glance, with cars on the Guadalupe Parkway speeding past. But though the sounds of combustion engines and urban white noise are unavoidable on lower trails, this can be a highly enjoyable hike with incredible detail and stunning vistas. The mountain's ridgeline runs in an east-west configuration, with considerable slopes and elevations ranging from 250 feet to 1,314 feet at the summit. A protected zone in Golden Gate National Recreation Area since 1983, the 2,326 acres also serve as a model plan for conserving natural habitats in an ever-spreading metropolis. Full facilities make the start easy going. Dress in layers.*

County: San Mateo
Start: Picnic area parking lot near park entrance
Length: 3.8-mile loop
Approximate Hiking Time: 2 hours
Difficulty Rating: Moderate, with elevation gain
Trail Surface: A short stint on a paved path to single-track dirt trails that ascend the mountain

at a mostly moderate grade, crossing over paved service road before descending on dirt paths
Land Status: State and county park
Nearest Town: Daly City
Other Trail Users: Equestrians
Canine Compatibility: No dogs allowed

Getting There

By Car: From San Francisco, heading south on Highway 101, take the Bayshore/ Brisbane exit (Cow Palace). Drive south on Bayshore Boulevard to Guadalupe Canyon Parkway. Turn right (west) on Guadalupe Canyon Parkway, and drive uphill about 2 miles to the park entrance on the right side of the road.

From San Mateo County, heading north on Highway 101, take the Bayshore/ Brisbane exit (Cow Palace). Turn north on Bayshore Boulevard, and drive about 2 miles to the intersection with Guadalupe Canyon Parkway. Turn left and drive uphill about 2 miles to the park entrance on the right side of the road. From Highway 280, take the Mission Street exit. Go east on San Pedro Road, which crosses over Mission and becomes East Market Street. It will become Guadalupe Canyon Parkway. Drive east on the parkway to the park entrance, about 3 miles from Highway 280.

By Public Transportation: Nothing directly to the park. Take BART to the Daly City terminal. At Location #7, catch bus #130 and disembark at the corner of Orange Street and East Market Street. You have to walk or bike the remaining 2.2 miles. SamTrans info: (800) 660–4287 or (650) 817–1717.

Hike Description

When you look around San Bruno Mountain, you are seeing a slice of an ancient Bay Area, long before European settlement. The land formed 130 million years ago in the Cretaceous period when all this was under water. The earth's crust buckled in the region creating fault blocks. One of the fault blocks was elevated, becoming San Bruno Mountain. For perhaps a thousand years, until the 1800s, Costonoan Indian tribes camped here seasonally, gathering seeds and plants for food and materials for basketry, and hunting small game in the scrub. Tule elk and antelope fed on the grasses. Every few years, the Indians set fire to the mountain in controlled burns to encourage new growth of grasses and to keep the scrub community under control. A lot of the scrub you see has replaced grasslands in the last twenty or so years.

Captain Bruno Heceta explored the western shore of the San Francisco Bay in 1775 for Spain. He named the largest land mass on that side of the peninsula Mount San Bruno after his patron saint. With the arrival of the mission system, the Spanish/Mexican government relocated the natives for conversion and granted this

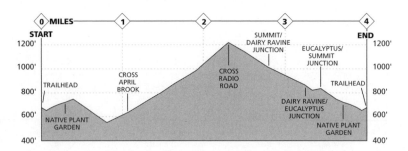

area as Rancho Canada de Guadalupe la Visitation y Rancho Viejo to Jacob Leese in 1839. Leese's cattle and sheep grazed on San Bruno Mountain, but he settled on its flanks. As late as 1869, the mountain was surrounded by civilization, as it is today, but no settlements were on it. This was a saving factor for the original coyote brush, yarrow, and snowberries.

In the 1870s, railroad baron and banker Charlie Crocker acquired the property. The Crocker Land Company after his death leased or sold parcels of land for light industrial uses and mineral resources recovery. This continued into the twentieth century.

San Bruno State Park

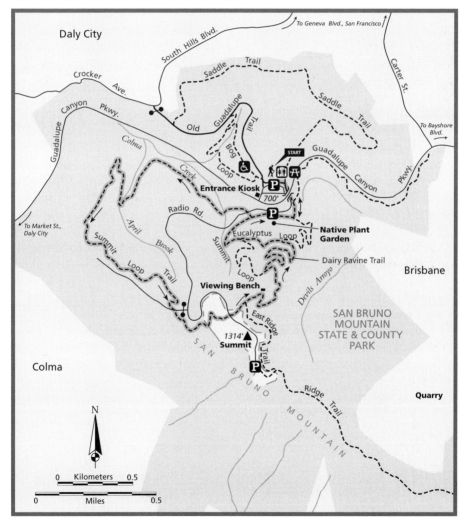

View from Summit Trail looking west

During the cold war in the 1950s, the summit became home to a Nike missile early warning radar site. Ruins mark the site.

In the 1960s, the urban tide reached the edge of the mountain. Housing developers and industrialists started slugging it out with conservation groups, individual citizens and government agencies for the land.

Then in 1982, a hero of the mountain emerged. Fourth-generation San Franciscan Edward J. Bacciocco, Jr. (1935–1991), a member of the San Mateo County Board of Supervisors, mediated the feud. Showing consideration for both sides, he created, in his own words, "a forum of trust so builders and environmentalists could meet to explore avenues of reasonable compromise." This resulted in the San Bruno Mountain Habitat Conservation Plan (HCP). The Edward Bacciocco, Jr. Day Camp, nestled in the Colma Creek watershed, memorializes him.

Some areas around the mountain are designated for housing, but according to the HCP, construction and grading must occur at a time and in a way that protects endangered butterfly habitats, including those of the rare Mission blue butterfly, the San Bruno elfin butterfly, the Callippe silver spot butterfly, and the Bay checkerspot. Also, fourteen endangered plants survive here, including San Bruno Mountain manzanita (*Arctostaphylos imbricata*), coast rock cress (*Arabis blepharophylla*), Pacifica manzanita (*Arctostaphylos pacifica*), and Franciscan wallflower (*Erysimum franciscanum*). Along with the more sensitive species, the common raven and red-winged hawk, deer, and bush rabbits are pretty happy to have a home too.

A grassroots group called Friends of San Bruno Mountain maintains a native plant nursery. A meander through the gardens prepares you for a fun little hike to the peak (1,314 feet).

To get the best out of this trail, stop now and then to see the movement of towhees and wrentits darting through the blackberry brambles. Listen to the song sparrows and meadowlarks. Examine the plants along the way, differentiating the coffeeberry, with its round, little fruits in shades of maroon, from red alderberries, some growing into trees, with bunches of bright red berries. Enjoy the wonderful wildflower display in spring that starts as early as late January with wild coastal iris, ranging in color from white to deep purple, orange California poppies, clumps of blue, cream, and lavender lupines and pink checkerbloom. From February to April, start looking for those very special moths and butterflies.

The changes in plant community are subtle, except for the groves of eucalyptus and Monterey cypress, offering you occasional shade on both uphill and downhill segments of the hike. After rains, a creek gurgles past on the western end of Summit Trail. Marsh life supports bog rushes, sword ferns, and hearty water-loving plants and animals.

Though you don't get a 360-degree view all in one place, you do see all directions from different parts of the trail. The magnificent vistas distract you from the unsightly antennae, satellite dishes, and service vehicles at the top of the mountain. Add the 0.8-mile Bog Trail (starting from the picnic area) for bird-watching. A grassy slope with tables and barbecues provides a great place for a posthike picnic. Bird and wildflower lists are available at the park kiosk, where you find full facilities. When planning your hike, check the weather for fog. When it comes in, between 3:00 and 4:00 P.M. in winter, a little later in summer, it can get chilly fast.

Miles/Directions

0.0 START at picnic area parking lot near park entrance. Facing the rest rooms, turn right on paved path and right again at end, following signs to Summit Trail. Pass under the overpass of the parkway onto a gravel path through the native plant nursery to main trailhead.

0.2 Native plant garden and trailhead. Facing the sign, turn right to start the Summit Loop Trail. At Summit Loop Trailhead, start the loop by taking the trail to the right. Cross Radio Road (service road for vehicles to the summit), staying on the single-track, hikers-only Summit Loop Trail. Pass coffeeberry and red alderberry before heading into eucalyptus grove. A wooden bridge passes over April Brook.

0.5 Trail heads away from street and begins moderate-grade climb on northeast side of mountain.

Hike Information

Trail Contact:
San Bruno Mountain State and County Park, 555 Guadalupe Canyon Parkway, Brisbane/Daly City, CA (650) 992-6770 or (415) 587-7511 (gatehouse)

Schedule:
Open daily 8:00 A.M. to dusk

Fees/Permits:
$3.00 per car

Local Information:
Daly City–Colma Chamber of Commerce, www.dalycity-colmachamber.org
San Francisco Convention and Visitor Center, 900 Market Street, Lower Level, Hallidie Plaza, San Francisco, CA (415) 283-0177; www.sfvisitor.org

Local Events/Attractions:
Mission Dolores, 3321 Sixteenth Street, San Francisco, CA (415) 621-8203

Accommodations:
Camping: Rob Hill Campground (in the Presidio) (415) 561-5444; www.nps.gov/goga/camping/robhill.htm
Hostel: Fort Mason International Hostel, Fort Mason's Building #240, Marina Boulevard at Laguna Street, San Francisco, CA (415) 771-7277
Alpine Inn, 560 Carter Street, Daly City, CA (650) 854-4004

El Camino Inn, 7525 Mission Street, Daly City, CA (650) 755-8667; www.sftravel.com

Restaurants:
Brick Oven Pizza, 160 Visitacion Avenue, Brisbane, CA (415) 468-6633
House of Catfish and Ribs (BBQ), 270 San Pedro Road, Daly City, CA (650) 997-3700
Mom Is Cooking (Mexican), 1166 Geneva Avenue, San Francisco, CA (415) 586-7000

Local Outdoor Retailers:
Copeland's Sports, Serramonte Center, Daly City, CA (650) 991-3063
Sportmart, 301 Gellert Boulevard, Daly City, CA (650) 301-9000

Hike Tours:
San Bruno Mountain State and County Park, 555 Guadalupe Canyon Parkway, Brisbane/Daly City, CA (650) 992-6770 or (415) 587-7511 (gatehouse)
Friends of San Bruno Mountain, 824 Templeton Avenue, Daly City, CA (415) 584-7320

Maps:
USGS maps: San Francisco South, CA

2.1 Cross over Radio Road again, continuing on dirt Summit Trail on the other side. To the southwest, Montara and San Pedro Mountains; to the northwest, Ocean Beach. Beyond this is Rodeo Beach and Tennessee Point in the Marin Headlands and Mount Tamalpais. Nearby are San Bruno, Daly City, Colma, and South San Francisco.

2.4 Pass green building, cross service road once more, to continue on Summit Loop Trail. At junction with East Ridge Trail, continue on Summit Loop Trail. **Option:** The 2.43-mile Ridge Trail is a one-way path that leads to eastern end of San Bruno; will extend hike by up to 4.9 miles. Views of Mount Hamilton, Mount Diablo and the Oakland Hills, cities of Alameda, Oakland, and Berkeley. Also, Candlestick Park (home of San

Francisco 49ers). Abandoned gravel quarry on north base of main ridge.

2.5 Take the short trail to your right for great viewing point. Continue on Summit Loop Trail.

2.8 At trailhead with Dairy Ravine Trail, turn right on Dairy Ravine Trail.

3.2 At trailhead for Eucalyptus Trail, take leg to the left, to pass through another grove.

3.5 Summit Trailhead. Stay right, heading back to native plant garden.

3.6 Back at garden and upper parking lot. Go back the way you came on the sidewalk and paved trail under the Guadalupe Parkway to picnic area.

3.8 Back at parking lot and picnic area.

Honorable Mention: San Francisco and the Bay

D. Golden Gate Park

Golden Gate Park is green, lush, varied, and utterly man-made. In fact, it is one of the largest man-made parks in the world. The park runs from the Haight-Ashbury area to Ocean Beach, past the Sunset District. It's hard to get a map of the park, but with exploration, you can find lots of trails that take you off the beaten track.

Near Kezar Stadium is the AIDS Memorial Grove, a short walk of remembrance for those in San Francisco who have died in the continuing epidemic. Just west of the California Academy of Sciences are the Shakespeare Gardens, with flora chosen from lines in the bard's plays. Nearby are well-tended rose gardens. Across Martin Luther King Jr. Drive from the Shakespeare Gardens is the Strybing Arboretum. Some paved and some dirt trails take you through native plant life from around the world. You can stroll around Stow Lake, while people paddle across on rented boats, and even cross a bridge onto Strawberry Island. West of the Highway 1 Cross-Over are numerous small lakes. At Spreckels, you can watch model yacht sailing and at Lloyd Lake walk through the "Portals of the Past." Elk Glen Lake and North Lake have trails leading to them too. Ocean Beach makes a great destination point on a walk or run through the park. In the spring, visit the Queen Wilhelmina Tulip Garden, famous for its 10,000 tulips and two windmills.

To get to Golden Gate Park, from the Bay Bridge or the Peninsula, take Highway 101 north (Golden Gate Bridge). Exit at Fell Street. Take Fell Street to the park (where Fell crosses Stanyan Street and becomes John F. Kennedy Jr. Drive). The Recreation and Park Department Administrative Offices (McLaren Lodge) will be on your right as you enter the park.

From Marin County, cross Golden Gate Bridge (southbound, Highway 1), take the Golden Gate Park/19th Avenue exit. Eventually, this will become Park Presidio Boulevard. Follow the signs to Golden Gate Park (if you don't, you will end up on a road going through the park; you will not be able to get off this road to get into the park).

Parking can be a nightmare. Try the lot between the deYoung Museum and Steinhart Aquarium.

For information, call City of San Francisco Parks and Recreation (415) 666–7200; picnicking reservations for large groups (415) 831–2790. Other useful numbers: Guided walks (415) 263–0991; Japanese Tea Garden (415) 752–4227; National AIDS Memorial Grove (415) 750–8340; Strybing Arboretum and Botanical Gardens (415) 661–1316; M. H. de Young Memorial Museum (415) 863–3330; Asian Art Museum (415) 379–8800; California Academy of Sciences (415) 750–7145; Bicycle rentals (415) 668–6699; Roller skate rentals (415) 752–8375; Fly casting (415) 386–2630; Boating at Stow Lake (415) 752–0347.

San Mateo County Coastline

California boasts one of the most accessible coastlines in the world, and San Mateo County has a lot of it to explore. You can walk the dunes, coastal bluffs full of lemon-yellow lupine, and trails under windblown cypress trees.

In Pacifica, San Pedro Valley County Park offers rolling coastal hills and wildflowers, a seasonal waterfall, and mellow picnicking in an area that was once the winter camp for the Coast Miwok Indians. Above it, Montara Mountain invites a climb. Walking on a wide path of Montara granite through manzanita and Monterey pines, you enjoy almost continuous ocean views. The James V. Fitzgerald Marine Reserve at Moss Beach has the longest intertidal reef in California. Hundreds of marine animals hang out in the pools, and you can see them all. Combined with a walk on the bluffs, where rum was smuggled during Prohibition, it forms a great loop hike. Along the Coast Trail through Half Moon Beach, hikers can access more than five separate beaches and swim on hot summer days.

The little town of Pescadero, besides its artichoke and strawberry fields, has several great hikes nearby. Pescadero Marsh is host to migrating seabirds in the Pacific flyway. Egrets, geese, ducks, and loons rest in the lagoon among the rushes and feast on fish and insects, readying to continue their journey. Across from the wetlands, harbor seals lounge on rocks by Pescadero Beach. Just inland, Butano State Park, the coast's best kept secret, has creeks and alder trees, redwoods and oaks, wildflowers in spring, mushrooms in winter. A little farther down the coast at Año Nuevo, visitors gawk at the hundreds of snorting elephant seals gathered to give birth, mate, and molt on the beach. In March and September, gray whales cruise by the coast on their semiannual migration. It is quite a sight to see one breach.

And all the way down the coast for after hiking, there are little coastal towns with friendly bed-and-breakfasts and great fresh fish restaurants with Pacific views. Can't beat that.

Pescadero Marsh Trail

Overview: *Pescadero Marsh, 360 acres of protected wetland on the San Mateo Coast south of Half Moon Bay and north of Año Nuevo, offers hikers a memorable opportunity to witness the best of nature. The trails are short but rich with life if you take the time to stop along the way, stay very quiet, and watch. Add a walk on the dunes of Pescadero State Beach, and you have a nice circuit of shoreline and wetland to explore. This is not a hike for stretching out the legs and working up a sweat, but it is a memorable, meandering tour of nature. Of the three short trails, the flat Sequoia Audubon Trail is best for a family hike and the one to take if you are short on time. Dress in layers with long pants; there's a lot of poison oak, and the lack of funds have reduced trail maintenance. Bring water and binoculars. With 250 species of birds out here, a bird identification book would also come in handy.*

County: San Mateo
Start: Parking lot for Pescadero State Beach, just north of the Highway 1 bridge over the lagoon
Length: Up to 6.0 miles round trip for all three hikes
Approximate Hiking Time: 3 hours
Difficulty Rating: Moderate because of invading scrub on path

Trail Surface: Sand, dirt, bridges and undoubtedly some mud (it is marshland, after all); flat narrow trails with scrub hitting legs, blackberry bushes with their prickly vines beside the trail require pants and not your good pair.
Land Status: Natural preserve
Nearest Town: Pescadero
Other Trail Users: Hikers only
Canine Compatibility: No dogs

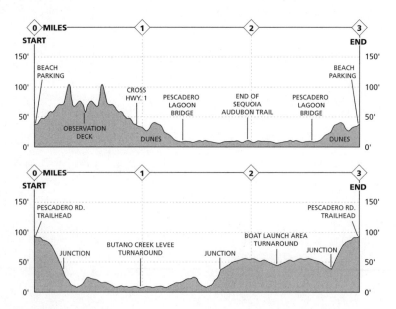

Pescadero Marsh Trail

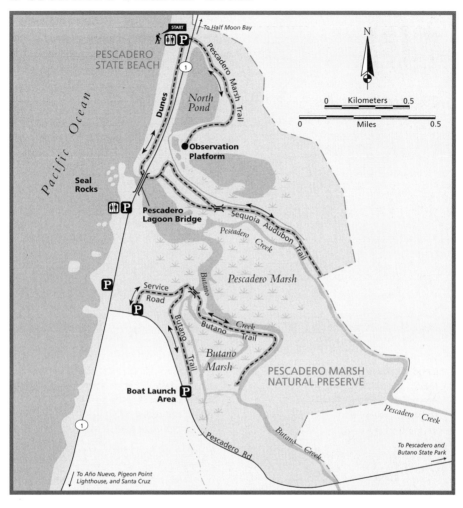

Getting There

By Car: From San Francisco/Oakland and North Bay, take Highway 101 south to 280 toward Daly City. Exit onto Highway 1 south toward Pacifica. Drive on Highway 1 (Cabrillo Highway) past Half Moon Bay. From the San Mateo Bridge, stay on Highway 92 west past the bridge all the way to Half Moon Bay. Highway 92 ends at Highway 1. Turn left and take Highway 1 south 15 miles from the 92 turnoff. Watch on your left for the sign for Pescadero State Beach. Turn left into the first parking lot. If you miss it, you can turn around at one of the two other parking areas for the beach or at Pescadero Road.

By Public Transportation: From the Hillsdale CalTrain, take bus #294 to Half Moon Bay. Route 15 takes you from Half Moon Bay to Pescadero. If the driver won't stop at the beach, you can stop at the corner of Pescadero Road and

Highway 1 and do the hikes in reverse order. SamTrans info: (800) 660–4BUS; www.transitinfo.org.

Hike Description

Historically, wetlands like this have been viewed as wastelands. According to the old adage, being sold a piece of old swampland meant you were robbed. Agriculturally minded humans looked upon marshes like this, with their dry, coarse plants, muddy, unmanageable earth, and strong smell of methane, as nothing but acres of wasting decay. But consider that it was in mud and slime like this that life was born. And those microscopic one-celled organisms, our evolutionary ancestors, are still here, coexisting with complex creatures evolved over hundreds of millions of years. The marsh is home to 250 species of birds, more than 50 species of mammals, 13 kinds of reptiles and amphibians, and 300 varieties of plant life. Many of them can survive nowhere else but in wetland areas, and those areas have been rapidly shrinking for over a century.

Currently, California has 450,000 acres of wetland. There used to be four million. Of the coastal wetlands surviving, 90 percent are around the San Francisco Bay and estuary. But 90 to 95 percent of the salt marshes around the San Francisco Bay have been filled in (50 percent around the United States). Groups like North American Waterfowl Management Plan (NAWMP), the Audubon Society, and Nature Conservancy are doing what they can to restore and maintain wetlands in North America. The waterfowl hunting group Ducks Unlimited has improved or preserved seven million acres of wildlife in the United States, Canada, and Mexico. Here in California, the Trust for Public Land (415–495–4014) and the State Coastal Conservancy (510–268–1015) have been buying up and preserving as much prime habitat along the Pacific flyway as they can. It's a battle. Yet the wetlands provide even more than vital nesting and feeding areas for wildlife. They act as giant sponges that help regulate winter flood waters, refill underwater aquifers, filter pollutants from runoff, and improve water quality. Pescadero Marsh is indeed special in what it can teach. And the experience of being among all this interdependent life, listening to all the whistling, squawking, croaking, and chattering of the birds, the movement of the water and wind and animals in the sky, brush, grasslands, and water, is unforgettable.

The marshland includes not just marsh but sand dunes, tidal flats, and rolling hills. The freshwater streams—Pescadero Creek and Butano Creek—meet in the lagoon and flow into the sea. As you hike, you go from salt to freshwater and back again, a bit like the Steelhead trout that spawn here.

First, you walk on nearly 40-foot high Pescadero sand dunes, formed from 5,000 to 3,000 years ago by drifting sand. The protruding headland south of Pescadero Beach trapped the sand as it blew down the coastline, and it accumulated into these dunes. Plants here have grown tough, impervious to the strong sun and salty air. Low to the ground, they avoid the harsh winds and keep the hillsides together. Sea fig and Hottentot fig have evolved thick fleshy stems to store water.

North Pond and dunes

Silver beach weed and California sagebrush have silvery or light foliage to reflect sunlight. Dwarf lupine have tiny hairs to protect the leaves from the damaging effect of blowing salt and sand. Out here by the ocean, you may see brown pelicans gliding inches above the water in lines of up to twenty birds, following schools of squid and small fish. Surf scoters crush bottom-dwelling shellfish with their thick beaks. Sanderlings scurry after the waves searching the wet sand for small bits of food. Marbled godwits use their long beaks to probe the sand for small shellfish. Western gulls, the most common coast bird, eat almost anything and may stand near you and squawk for food. If you get to close to a killdeer nest, it may put on a broken wing act. It does this to lead predators toward it instead of its eggs. The endangered snowy plover also nests on this beach, laying its eggs in low depressions in the sand that blend in so well you may not see them until you almost step on them, so be careful. Even passing nearby causes birds to leave their nests, exposing eggs to sun, wind, and predators. On the rocks offshore parallel to the bridge, a crowd of lazy harbor seals lie against the contours of rocks, basking in the sun.

Under the bridge past an overwhelming array of driftwood, you come to the marsh, lagoon, and the divide in the creeks. In geologic terms, the brackish here is a baby (the word *brackish* refers to a blend of fresh and salt waters). Fifteen thousand years ago, neither it nor the beach was here. The ocean was 300 feet lower, the coastline 15 miles farther west. Glacial melting later caused the sea level to rise, flooding the depression at Pescadero Valley and forming a marsh about 6,500 years ago. The Ohlone Indians, over generations, saw this transformation. They were here at least 10,000 years ago. They valued the marsh, finding diverse food sources here, from wild herbs to clams, shellfish, elk, and sea mammals. Diseases that came with the Spanish explorers in 1774 wiped them out. The old ways and names forgotten, the Spaniards gave the area a new name: Pescadero, Spanish for "fisherman."

In or near the marsh are several other endangered animals, including the red-legged frog, salt marsh harvest mouse, and San Francisco garter snake. On land you may see raccoons, long-tail weasels, meadow moles, wood rats, western fence lizards, and great-horned owls. There are many songbirds and raptors, some migratory, some not. Among the many in the water are American coots, ducks of all sorts, hooded mergansers, cinnamon teal ducks, kingfishers, royal terns, herring gulls, and all kinds of other migrant waterfowl. The western aquatic garter snake and the elusive western pond turtle keep the waterfowl company. (For more information on the saltwater marsh, check out the San Francisco Wildlife Preserve at Coyote Point east of the Dumbarton Bridge.)

Miles/Directions

0.0 START from northernmost parking lot for Pescadero State Beach. Cross highway to single-track dirt North Pond Trail. Trail ascends up ridge.

0.1 Interpretive sign with pictures of some of the animals in the area; continue on.

0.8 Observation platform. Head back the way you came.

1.5 Cross highway back to parking lot (pit toilet available), and take trail out toward beach, turning left on roped, wooden walkway that goes over dunes. **Option:** Drive to the next Pescadero State Beach Parking Area south, and start from there, walking on path along highway to the trailhead.

1.9 Interpretive sign and trail marker for Pescadero Marsh Natural Reserve. Follow trail, turn left under bridge. Continue to sign with international hiker icon (about 0.2 mile east).

2.1 Sequoia Audubon Trail. Follow single-track sandy path.

2.3 At bridge, continue straight on Sequoia Audubon Trail. (*Note.* Some of the trail on the narrow levee between creeks (Pescadero north, Butano south) is eroding but still passable.)

Hike Information

🌿 Trail Contacts:
Pescadero State Beach (and Pescadero Marsh Natural Preserve), P.O. Box 370, Pescadero, CA 94060 (650) 879–2170
California Department of Parks and Recreation, San Francisco, CA (415) 330–6300

🕐 Schedule:
Open daily 8:00 A.M. to dusk

💲 Fees/Permits:
$2.00 per car; free when kiosk unattended

❓ Local Information:
Half Moon Bay Coastside Chamber of Commerce and Visitors' Bureau, 520 Kelly Avenue, Half Moon Bay, CA 94019 (650) 726–8380; www.halfmoonbay chamber.org

💡 Local Events/Attractions:
Aerial Sightseeing: Coast Flight (650) 520–4559
Fishing and Whale Watching: Riptide Sportfishing (888) RIP–TIDE or (415) 469–8433
Phipps Ranch (petting zoo/pick-your-own farm), 2700 Pescadero Road, Pescadero, CA (650) 879–0787

🏕 Accommodations:
Camping: Butano Campground (800) 444–7275
Hostel: Pidgeon Point Lighthouse, 210 Pigeon Point Road, Pescadero, CA (650) 879–0633; www.norcalhostels.org

Costanoa Coastal Lodge and Camp, 2001 Rossi Road, Pescadero, CA (650) 879–1100
The Goose & Turrets B&B, 835 George Street, Montara, CA (650) 728–5451; www.goose.montara.com/index.html
Pescadero Creekside Barn, 248 Stage Road, Pescadero, CA (650) 879–0868; www.pescaderolodging.com

🍴 Restaurants:
Arcangeli Grocery, 287 Stage Road, Pescadero, CA (650) 879–0147; www.arcangeligrocery.com
Duarte's Tavern and Grill, 202 Stage Road, Pescadero, CA (650) 879–0464
Three Amigos Mexican Restaurant, 1999 Pescadero Road, Pescadero, CA (650) 879–0232

🏕 Local Outdoor Retailers:
Outdoor World, 136 River Street, Santa Cruz, CA (831) 423–9555
REI, 1119 Industrial Road, Suite 1-B, San Carlos, CA (650) 508–2330; www.rei.com

🥾 Hike Tours:
Pescadero State Beach (and Pescadero Marsh Natural Preserve) (650) 879–2170
California Department of Parks and Recreation, San Francisco, CA (415) 330–6300

Ⓝ Maps:
USGS maps: Franklin Point, CA

2.4 Blue gum eucalyptus by the path on right. Continue on trail.

2.6 Take side trail to the right to two viewing benches. Return to main trail and continue east.

2.8 Stop at sign that warns about poison oak. (*Note*: Trail is overgrown beyond this point, and a bridge over the creek is down. These conditions may change.) Turn around and head back the way you came, stopping at bridge.

3.3 Turn right over bridge. Take North Pond Trail to end. Boat launch off Pescadero Road.

3.5 Bench and trailhead. Turn left for double-track Sequoia Audubon Trail.

3.6 Sandbank beside stream. Turn right and head back under bridge. Once under bridge, walk to the southwesternmost corner next to creek to view harbor seals. (*FYI*: If you can cross the water safely, the view from the bluffs is great.)

3.7 Viewing point of seal rocks. Turn right, heading north either along the beach or back along the dunes.

4.1 Back at car, drive south to Pescadero Road, then turn left and park in gravel area beside road (you can also park at southernmost parking area for Pescadero Beach and cross the highway). Just east is a dirt service road. To start third hike, turn left onto service road. Destination is bridge with view of marsh. (*Bail-out*: Call it a day and go hang out on the beach or in Pescadero.)

4.3 Service road ends; single-track dirt trail begins at end of road and heads through grassland. Continue on Butano Trail along the levee.

4.4 Trail splits. Turn left.

4.5 Bridge for view of marsh. Continue on Butano Trail along the levee. (*Note*: Trail is overgrown with prickly blackberries. Wear long pants and stay on trail.) Cross bridge to narrow levee between creeks.

4.8 The levee bends, turning south. Turn around here and return the way you came. (*Note:* Continue on to end, another 0.3 mile. Trail ends at water, where part of levee was removed to relieve flooding.)

5.1 At the split in the trail, continue straight onto the unmarked Butano Trail. Follow trail to end at boat launch. (*Bail-out:* Head back to service road and the car.)

5.4 Boat launch area with interpretive sign. Head back the way you came.

5.7 Back at the split in trail. Turn left up-slope to return to service road.

5.8 Service road begins. Take it out of beach area and preserve.

6.0 Back at car.

21 Butano State Park

Overview: *In the secluded wilderness of 3,560-acre Butano State Park you have the opportunity to walk miles under pillared groves of coastal redwoods. As a matter of fact, most of this hike is under the shade of trees that insulate you from the outside world. Stop on numerous wooden bridges to admire cascading and gurgling creeks. Take in views from the contrasting high ridges among dry manzanita and knobcone pines. There you see an unforgettable picture of the densely wooded Santa Cruz Mountains before the sweeping Pacific Ocean. The camping here is great, the crowds minimal.*

County: San Mateo
Start: Six Bridges Trailhead
Length: 8.3-mile loop
Approximate Hiking Time: 4.5 hours
Difficulty Rating: Moderate
Trail Surface: Single- and double-track dirt trails mostly shaded through mixed woodland, featuring many wooden bridges crossing creeks

Land Status: State park
Nearest Town: Pescadero
Other Trail Users: Equestrians and mountain bikers on Butano Fire Road only
Canine Compatibility: Dogs on leash allowed only on fire roads and developed areas

Getting There

By Car: From San Francisco, take Highway 101 south to Highway 280 south to Highway 1 toward Half Moon Bay. From the East Bay, take Highway 880 south to the San Mateo Bridge (Highway 92). Continue on Highway 92 until it ends in Half Moon Bay. Turn left, heading south. Take Highway 1 (Cabrillo Highway) south 16 miles to Pescadero Road and turn left, going inland. Stay on this road past the town of Pescadero, about 5 miles. Turn right on Cloverdale Road. Watch for a sign for Butano, and take a left into the main entrance. Go past the kiosk to the next parking area you see on your right, where there are picnic tables, barbecues, and rest rooms. From Santa Cruz, drive north on Highway 1 for 20 miles to Gazos Creek Road, and turn right, going inland. Turn left on Cloverdale Road, and follow the rest of the directions above.

By Public Transportation: From the Hillsdale CalTrain, take bus #294 to Half Moon Bay. Route 15 takes you from Half Moon Bay to Pescadero. You would have to ride a bike, walk, or catch a ride from there to the park entrance (5 miles). SamTrans info: (800) 660–4BUS; www.transitinfo.org.

Hike Description

Driving into the park from Highway 1 on the ocean, past the sleepy town of Pescadero, past workers leaning over the artichoke fields and horses whisking away flies with their tails as they graze on grassy hillsides of little ranches, it's hard to believe you will soon be hiking in thick, mysterious woodland for the day. Butano's

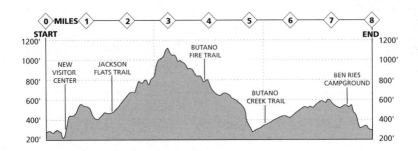

second-generation redwoods and mature Douglas fir trees survived because of the canyons that protect them. The mother redwoods, some 500 or even 1,000 years old, were not so lucky. They provided good revenue for families during the post–gold rush growth spurt of Northern California. But before their demise, the towering redwoods ruled these ravines.

Native Americans who lived in the valley rarely ventured into the forest of giants. They had spiritual and practical reasons to avoid it. They felt a "presence" among the trees, concluding that the redwoods hosted powerful spirits and were not to be disturbed. Had there been valuable commodities in the dark woodland, they might have reached a different conclusion. But the canopy's shadow does not allow for the growth of many eatable and usable plants, so they had little motivation to go into the woods. Hikers today say they feel that presence too when surrounded by a community of redwood trees.

The tribal names of these people were lost after the Portolá expedition of 1769 came through, claiming the land for Spain. The "Butanoans" were removed to the missions as European and Mexican ranchers, farmers, and loggers settled in the countryside.

In the 1860s, when this became American territory, several families settled in what is now Butano State Park. The Jackson family occupied the north side of the canyon, where it became known as Jackson Flats. An abandoned landing field sits on top of the Butano Fire Road. The county used it for fire suppression. Descendants of the European settlers continued to live in the canyon until the State of California purchased the land and dedicated the park in 1961.

Forged by nature and the presence of man, Butano contains a diverse range of habitats, each with its own community of plant life and wildlife. This loop hike, recommended by frequent Butano hiker and retired physician John Salzer, gives you a taste of all the different environments and a great introduction to the park.

Starting on Six Bridges Trail from the picnic area, you crisscross a feeder creek, lined with chalky-barked alder trees. They shade you with a thick canopy in summer and let the sun in with bare branches, like an old man's arms, in winter. Beneath them are stinging nettles, dogwood, willow, and lots of different berry bushes providing shelter for insects, reptiles, small mammals, and migrant songbirds, though birds are not always particularly plentiful in Butano.

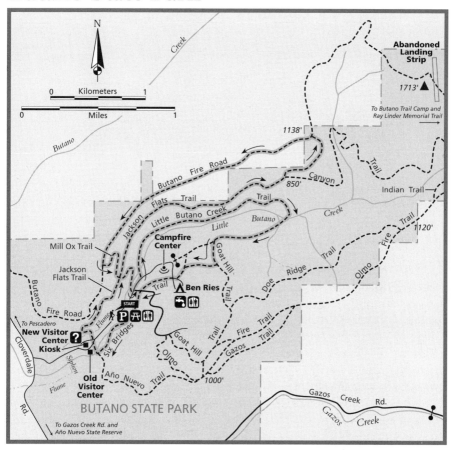

Around the entrance station is open grassland, dominated by coyote brush and bush lupine, with purple flowers in spring. Blue-eyed grass and yellow coastal sun-cups grow among them. This is where you are most likely to spot the larger mammals in the park: black-tailed deer, bobcats, coyotes, rabbits and other rodents. This area and the chaparral on the upper slopes are the most popular hunting grounds for peregrine falcons and other birds of prey. During summer and off-season weekends, the nature center offers insight on what you see along the trail.

It doesn't take long on the Jackson Flats Trail before you find yourself in and around redwood groves. Some of the trees damaged by fire over the last 150 years have caves in their wide base, providing homes for bats. Huckleberries top the wide stumps of fallen trees. Be careful, as you share the trail with slow-moving banana slugs and California newts making their way to breeding ponds in late winter. In winter, check out but don't pick the bright yellow witch's hat (*Hygrocybe conica*), toothed jelly fungus (*Pseudohydnum gelitinosum*), or bleeding milky cap mushrooms (*Lactarius rubrilacteus*). Blooming February to April is the park's star attraction, the purple calypso orchid. The Little Butano Creek Trail shows off the redwoods the best, with ferns and clover around the pretty cascading creek.

When you reach the north side of Jackson Flats, you see the mountainside marshes, surrounded by giant skunk cabbages and seasonal cattails. This is primarily where the newts are coming to breed. Listen for the chirping of the frogs. Earthquakes on the San Gregorio fault, which runs past the entrance to the park, caused landslides long ago. The marshes lie at the heads of those slides. The wetlands disappear in the dry summer months.

You encounter a surprising change in environment at the top of Jackson Flats and Butano Fire Road. Suddenly, bathed in sunlight, you are walking on sandstone. The chaparral up here consists of long-needled knobcone pines, scrub oaks, and manzanita. If you see a rattlesnake bathing in the sun, just don't approach it. Probably it will make its way into the chinquapin scrub and orange monkey flow-

Knobcone sky—a western scene at the top of Jackson Flats Trail

ers to avoid you. Indian paintbrush provides dabs of red-orange in the springtime landscape.

On Goat Hill, you go through a section of oak woodland, mostly tan bark oak. Stay on the path to avoid poison oak. Enjoy the sight of bright orange chanterelles—thick fluted gourmet mushrooms—and honeysuckle among the berry bushes. Listen in the branches for the songs of chickadees and warblers, which sound like their names.

Butano, according to Native American lore, means "drinking cup" or "a gathering place for friendly visits." The park lends itself to just that.

Miles/Directions

0.0 START at Six Bridges Trailhead in picnic area, about 20 yards east of rest rooms. Single-track dirt trail leads back to park entrance, crossing over one of the six bridges on trail. (*Note*: Be careful of poison oak.) Trail splits. Take fork to right.

0.1 Bat habitat. Turn left for a quick detour to see it. Return to Six Bridges Trail.

0.2 Turn left, continuing on Six Bridges Trail. Cross first two bridges.

0.3 At the trailhead for Año Nuevo Trail, turn right and cross creek to stay on Six Bridges Trail. (*Note*: When creek is really flowing, a wooden board helps you across, but be careful—it's a little slippery.)

0.4 At the park entrance, kiosk and Nature Center. Even when unattended, help yourself to map in wooden box on side of kiosk building. (*FYI*. In 2002, the Nature Center is being moved to the new building near the Jackson Flats Trailhead. When completed, it will greet visitors with a relief map of the park, a stuffed bobcat, and many interactive exhibits (open in summer only).) Cross road to Jackson Flats Trail through redwood groves. Narrow, single-track trail serpentines moderately uphill. Moderate gain in elevation.

1.2 At trailhead for Mill Ox Trail, stay on Jackson Flats Trail.

1.4 Marsh on left. (*Note*: Watch out for newts in this area, especially in February and March.) Trail goes over and under fallen trees (trail volunteers have cut gaps in more obtrusive logs).

2.7 At trailhead for Canyon Trail, stay on Jackson Flats Trail, bearing left. One steep grade toward top. **Option:** For a backpacking camp, take Canyon Trail to Indian Trail.

3.0 Top of ridge. Views open up to Pacific Ocean beyond densely wooded Santa Cruz foothills.

3.2 Trailhead for Butano Fire Road. Dead-end onto double-track, multiuse fire road. Turn left onto Butano Fire Road.

3.7 Ruins of old cabin on right. Land to the north along Big Butano Creek is still privately owned.

Hike Information

🕯 Trail Contacts:
Butano State Park, 1500 Cloverdale Road, Pescadero, CA 94060 (650) 879–2040; www.parks.ca.gov
San Mateo Coast District—California Department of Parks and Recreation, P.O. Box 2390, Sacramento, CA (415) 726–6203

🕐 Schedule:
Open daily from dawn to dusk

💲 Fees/Permits:
$2.00 per car; free when kiosk unattended

❓ Local Information:
Half Moon Bay Coastside Chamber of Commerce and Visitors' Bureau, 520 Kelly Avenue, Half Moon Bay, CA 94019 (650) 726–8380; www.halfmoonbay chamber.org

💡 Local Events/Attractions:
Phipps Ranch (petting zoo/pick-your-own farm), 2700 Pescadero Road, Pescadero, CA (650) 879–0787

🛏 Accommodations:
Camping: Butano Campground (800) 444–7275
Hostel: Pidgeon Point Lighthouse, 210 Pigeon Point Road, Pescadero, CA (650) 879–0633; www.norcalhostels.org
Davenport Inn Bed & Breakfast, (22 miles south on Highway 1), 31 Davenport Avenue, Davenport, CA (800) 870–1817;

www.swanton.com
Pescadero Creekside Barn, 248 Stage Road, Pescadero, CA (650) 879–0868; www.pescaderolodging.com
Zaballa House B&B, 324 Main Street, Half Moon Bay, CA (650) 726–9123 zaballa@zaballahouse.com

🍴 Restaurants:
Beach House, 5720 Cabrillo Highway, Pescadero, CA (650) 879–1290
Duarte's Tavern and Grill, 202 Stage Road, Pescadero, CA (650) 879–0464
Muzzi's Market and Deli, 251 Stage Road, Pescadero, CA (650) 879–0410
Tony's Place (Greek and American), 1956 Pescadero Creek Road, Pescadero, CA (650) 879–0106

🌲 Local Outdoor Retailers:
Outdoor World, 136 River Street, Santa Cruz, CA (831) 423–9555
REI, 1119 Industrial Road, Suite 1-B, San Carlos, CA (650) 508–2330; www.rei.com

🚻 Hike Tours:
Butano State Park, 1500 Cloverdale Road, Pescadero, CA 94060 (650) 879–2040; www.parks.ca.gov
San Mateo Coast District—California Department of Parks and Recreation, Sacramento, CA (415) 726–6203

🅝 Maps:
USGS maps: Franklin Point, CA

4.7 Trailhead for Mill Ox Trail. Turn left onto single-track dirt trail going downhill. (*Note.* Trail is steep in some sections.) Route follows old logging skid trail.

4.9 Cross over Jackson Flats Trail, staying on Mill Ox Trail, still heading downhill. Back in redwoods, passing by dedicated groves.

5.2 Little Butano Creek and picnic table. Take bridge across creek to paved main park road. Stay on same side of street, turning left, and walk about 150 yards to trailhead for Little Butano Creek Trail to the left. Turn left onto hikers-only, single-track dirt trail. Creek on left. Cross bridge again, trail widens to double-track. Cross over several more bridges, including an arched one, following creek.

6.0 Social trail to left follows feeder creek with 5-foot cascade during wet season just off the main trail. Continue on Little Butano Creek Trail. Trail soon starts to climb to pump house, above creek to left.

6.7 Little Butano Creek Trail merges into dirt Pump House Road, which intersects with main park road (gravel and dirt here). Go up hill on Pump House Road.

7.0 Turn left onto single-track Goat Hill Trail.

7.2 Trailhead. Turn right onto Trail to Ben Reis Campground.

7.4 When trail splits, continue left to campground. Pass the walk-in camp-sites. Take steps up to campground loop road. Turn left, past campsite 16, 15, and counting down. Continue downhill on paved campground road.

7.6 Pass sign for campground host; watch for sign TO THE CAMPFIRE CENTER. Turn left onto trail.

7.7 Campfire Center. Before reaching campfire stage, look for Six Bridges Trailhead. Take Six Bridges Trail. This section of double-track dirt trail passes through mixed woodland. Watch for another seasonal pond. After one bridge, cross gravel and dirt fire road and continue on now single-track Six Bridges Trail on other side. Cross over two more bridges. The creek separates you from paved main park road on the right. Pass by employee residence, continuing on Six Bridges Trail.

8.3 Trail splits. Go right to picnic area and parking lot.

22

Año Nuevo State Park

Overview: *Come here to watch the elephant seals in their yearly rituals. From April through November, you can hike the trail yourself, but you must obtain a hiking permit to enter the Wildlife Protection Area at Año Nuevo Point. Molting elephant seals bask on beaches that are visible from viewpoints along a designated trail. During the December 15 to March 31 breeding season, you can see the reserve only on one of the regularly scheduled guided walks. These highly informative walks have been designed to minimize disturbance to the animals and their natural habitat. Advance reservations are recommended and can be made as early as October (800–444–4445). Beyond the seals are another 4,500 acres to explore.*

County: San Mateo
Start: Parking lot of Año Nuevo State Park
Length: 3 miles
Approximate Hiking Time: 2.5 hours
Difficulty Rating: Easy
Trail Surface: Loose sand and some rocks
Land Status: State reserve

Nearest Town: Pescadero
Other Trail Users: Hikers only
Canine Compatibility: No dogs allowed (dogs cannot be left inside parked vehicles in the parking lot either)

Getting There

By Car: From the San Francisco Bay Bridge, take Highway 101 south to Highway 280 south to Scenic Highway 1 south. Año Nuevo State Reserve is located on State Highway 1 between Santa Cruz and Half Moon Bay, about 1.5 hours south of San Francisco. Reserve signs are located on the highway in both directions. (Some people miss the brown signs. Be alert about 27 miles south of Half Moon Bay and 20 miles north of Santa Cruz.) Turn right into the parking lot of Año Nuevo State Park where you will find rest rooms and drinking water. Signs direct you to the visitor center where you begin your hike. Driving time is about 1 hour 39 minutes.

  By Public Transportation: On weekends in January and February, you can take the special Seal Line bus that departs from the Hillsdale Shopping Center in

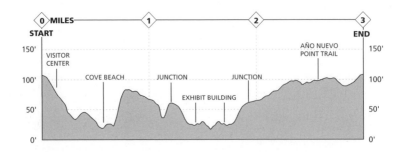

Año Nuevo State Park

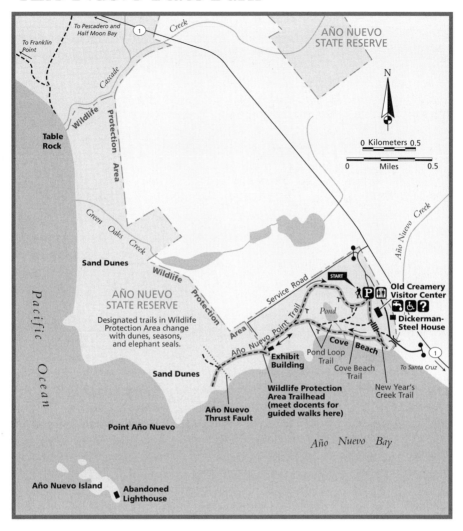

San Mateo and The Albertson's Shopping Center in Half Moon Bay. Price ($12 per person) includes round-trip fare and the guided walk. The 6.5-hour adventure starts at 9:00 and 10:00 A.M. Call in advance, (650–508–6441).

The rest of the year, direct public transit isn't available. If you have time, you can take BART to Colma Station, Daly City end of the line. Catch bus #112 to Linda Mar in Pacifica. Take bus #294 to Half Moon Bay, and catch bus #15 to Pescadero, then ride your bike, take a taxi, or ask a local for a ride. SamTrans: (800) 660–4287; www.SamTrans.com. CalTrans Road Information: (800) 427–7623; www.dot.ca.gov/hq/roadinfo.

Hike Description

Ah, the sound of the surf crashing against rocks, the squawk of seagulls, the wind whistling in the dunes, burps, gurgles, farts, and growls. No, it's not a fraternity beach party. These are the sounds of the Point of the New Year: Año Nuevo, the most popular beach on the West Coast, that is, for elephant seals. Here, the blubbery animals breed and molt as they cruise the Pacific. And a peculiar sight they are, lying around on pretty Northern California beaches, bluffs, and dunes. They even have their own Victorian house on a private island where they do more lying around.

How much fun can you have watching apathetic 3,000-ton creatures lusting, sleeping, losing skin, and flipping sand over themselves? You might be surprised. Their story is fascinating. For your first time, take a docent-led tour, available from December 15 through the end of March. Inside the wildlife protection area, you may also see harbor seals, California sea otters, and Stellar sea lions. Experienced and enthusiastic volunteer docents have a wealth of information about the seals, birds, and geology of the area.

Before you get to the seals, you start on the bluffs where you find the visitor center, built within the old Dickerman barn. There you can look at maps of the area to learn more about Año Nuevo's coastal beaches and bluffs, plenty to explore after your elephant seal tour if you wish. During low tide, you can also find good tide pools.

Behind the barn is an old farmhouse and ranching equipment that date back to the early 1860s, when the Steele family owned most of Año Nuevo and ran dairy operations here. By 1870, they had the second-largest herd of milk cows in California, with several additional dairies in San Mateo and San Luis Obispo counties. They produced mostly cheese, but also transported beef to San Francisco. A daughter, Flora Steele, lived here until 1963.

The Point of the New Year was seen and named unimaginatively by Father Antonio de la Ascension, chaplain for the Spanish maritime explorer Don Sebastian Viscaino on January 3, 1603, while sailing to Mexico. Before they cruised by, the native Quroste people, a group of Ohlone Indians, lived and fished on this shore for 10,000 to 12,000 years. On the beaches, you can still see remnants of their ancient shell mounds that served as both dumping grounds and graveyards.

Take a good look at the landscape. The elephant seals chose a

Elephant Seals' Annual Schedule

Breeding season: Males show up in late November and start fighting; females start arriving in late December and continue arriving until the end of February to give birth. By mid-March, the adults have mated and wean their pups by leaving. Weaners remain until late April to bask in the sun and learn to swim. A pup nurses for twenty-eight days, a diet equivalent to seventy-five milkshakes a day.

Molting season: Juveniles and females come home to molt March through May; in early summer, subadult males show up to molt; in late summer, July and August, adult males arrive to change skins.

During the December 15 to March 31 breeding season, you can see the reserve only on one of the regularly scheduled guided walks. These highly informative walks have been designed to minimize disturbance to the animals and their natural habitat. Advance reservations are recommended and can be made as early as October (800–444–4445).

Elephant seals—mostly weaners—on the beach

dramatic setting: sandy, flowered bluffs with scurrying rabbits and songbirds, smooth cresting dunes, beaches that sparkle with mica, and fields of coastal plants like sand lupine and arroyo willow. Look closely also because this place will be different the next time you visit. The dunes are constantly changing.

On the other side of a channel, you can see Año Nuevo Island, where today the seals live communally in a lovely old Victorian house with sea lions and seabirds. There used to be a five-story lighthouse there. Between 1880 and 1920, 235 woodenhold steam schooners appeared on the West Coast, operating under dangerous conditions to haul lumber, farm products, and passengers between growing coastal towns. The federal government bought the island in 1870 and built the lighthouse to put an end to shipwrecks in the area. But still, the schooner *Catalina* went aground at Point Arena in 1887. The Schooner *Point Arena* wrecked at Pidgeon Point in 1913. Some of the wreckage drifted to the beach at Año Nuevo and was uncovered by storm waves in 1983. You can see part of the bow near the Año Nuevo Point Trail.

The house out on the island was built in 1904 for a resident lightkeeper. It had a garden and fence, and the owners brought rabbits onto the island that ate all the vegetation. Then the California sea lions started visiting in large numbers. One lightkeeper's wife complained that the sea lions kept knocking down the front door. In 1948, an automated system was installed, and the keeper's residence was abandoned. The sea lions hang out in the house today, as do seabirds, but the elephant seals have a hard time walking on land with their five-digit flippers, and can't hoist their mounds of fat over the door jambs. Yet elephant seals still dominate the area.

Bulls live to battle. They start arriving at Año Nuevo late in November and immediately start fighting to determine the dominant bulls. Only 10 percent of the males actually get to mate, and all the mating is based on the dominance hierarchy, so they learn even as pups how to chest butt on the beach. Size is everything for the male elephant seal. Mature males can weigh up to 5,000 pounds.

In December, the females start to arrive. They don't come in all at once, but stagger in a few at a time. Within three to five days of arriving, each female will give birth to a single pup. The mother vocalizes to the pup soon after it is born, so the baby will know her voice and identify his mother among the hundreds of seals on the beach. If they are separated, there is a chance they won't come back together and the pup will starve.

The elephant seals were almost all wiped out by hunting and disease. Genetically, the seals you see here today are almost identical, indicating they derive from the same few, the Adams and Eves of modern-day elephant seals, but slowly, their population has been growing. At the end of the day, you will have had a good laugh at their socially unacceptable sounds and probably feel lucky to have walked among these white-bellied, snorting creatures on their home beaches of Año Nuevo.

Miles/Directions

0.0 START from parking lot. Follow signs to visitor center. (*FYI*: Center features live video cameras of seal activity on beaches, information about other wildlife, geology, and plant life, with interactive exhibits.) If taking the guided hike, meet on deck in front of the barn. Ranger will direct you to Año Nuevo Point Trail that goes back toward parking lot and bends left at trailhead.

0.7 Junction with Pond Loop Trail. Turn right, staying on Año Nuevo Point Trail to exhibit building.

1.0 Exhibit building (with information on seals and sea lions). This is entrance to Wildlife Protection Area. If taking the guided walk, meet docent here. Otherwise, you must have permit to enter area. The next 0.5 mile, hike dunes and beach among elephant seals. (*Note*: Stay 25 feet away from the animals.)

1.2 Lawrence of Arabia Dune, the largest in Año Nuevo.

1.5 Cross Año Nuevo Thrust Fault, a branch of the San Gregorio Fault Zone. View of Año Nuevo Island and abandoned lighthouse cottage. Keep a lookout for bow of shipwrecked schooner *Point Arena*. There are several branches of trail here, only a few hundred feet long, providing different views of seals' beach. Go back the way you came to exit.

2.0 Back at exhibit building. Retrace your steps on Año Nuevo Point Trail to junction with Pond Loop Trail.

2.3 Turn right on Pond Loop Trail.

2.4 Turn right on Cove Beach Trail to Cove Beach. Continue on Cove Beach. Pass over New Year's Creek.

2.7 Turn inland to New Year's Creek Trail.

3.0 Back at Dickerman Barn and visitor center.

Hike Information

🖉 Trail Contact:
Año Nuevo State Reserve (650) 879–2025; recorded information: (650) 879–0227; parks.ca.gov/central/bayarea/ansr228.htm

🕐 Schedule:
Open year-round from 8:00 A.M. to sunset

Ⓢ Fees/Permits:
Parking: $2.00 per car. Visitors must obtain a hiking permit (free) to enter Wildlife Protection Area at Año Nuevo Point (8:30 A.M. to 3:30 P.M. only). Docent-led tour: $4.00 per person

❓ Local Information:
Año Nuevo State Reserve, (650) 879–2025; parks.ca.gov/central/ bayarea/ansr228.htm
SouthCoast.net, www.southcoast.net/
South Coast Business Directory, www.tool-makers.com/bizdir/bizdir.htm

💡 Local Events/Attractions:
Bean Hollow Beach, 40 miles south of San Francisco, 31 miles north of Santa Cruz, (415) 726–6238; bonita.mbnms.nos.noaa. gov/Visitor/Access/bean.html
Butano State Park, 5 miles south of Pescadero on Cloverdale Road, off Highway 1 from Gazos Creek Road, (650) 879–2040; parks.ca.gov/central/bayarea/bsp423.htm
Made In Pescadero, 216 Stage Road, Pescadero, CA (650) 879–9128; www.madeinpescadero.com/
Pigeon Point Light Station State Historic Park, 210 Pigeon Point Road, Pescadero, CA (650) 879–2120; www.virtual cities.com/ons/ca/h/as/cah79a22.htm

🍴 Accommodations:
Camping: Butano State Park, 5 miles south of Pescadero on Cloverdale Road, off Highway 1 from Gazos Creek Road, (650)

879–2040; www.reserveamerica.com/usa/ ca/buta/index.html
The Davenport Inn, 31 Davenport Avenue, Davenport, CA (831) 425–1818; www.davenportinn.com
Estancia del Mar, 460 Pigeon Point Road, Pescadero, CA (650) 879–1500
Hostelling International Pigeon Point Lighthouse, 210 Pigeon Point Road, Pescadero, CA (650) 879–0633; www.norcalhostels.org
Costanoa Coastal Lodge and Camp, 2001 Rossi Road (at Highway 1), Pescadero CA (650) 879–1100.

🍽 Restaurants:
Beach House, 5720 Cabrillo Highway, Pescadero, CA (408) 685–4213
Merry Prankster Cafe, 8865 La Honda Road, La Honda, CA (650) 747–0660
Muzzi's Market and Deli, 251 Stage Road, Pescadero, CA (650) 879–0410
New Davenport Cash Store, Highway 1, Davenport, CA (831) 423–1160

🥾 Local Outdoor Retailers:
REI—San Carlos, 1119 Industrial Road, Suite 1-B, San Carlos, CA (650) 508–2330
The Runner's High, 895 Santa Cruz Avenue, Menlo Park, CA (888) DO-U-RUN-2; www.runnershigh.com/

👥 Hike Tours:
Año Nuevo State Reserve, (650) 879–2025; recorded information: (650) 879–0227; reservations: (800) 444–4445; parks.ca.gov/central/bayarea/ansr228.htm

Ⓝ Maps:
Año Nuevo State Reserve, parks.ca. gov/central/bayarea/an228/map228.htm
USGS maps: Año Nuevo, CA; Franklin Point, CA

23 McNee Ranch State Park and Montara State Beach

Overview: *McNee Ranch State Park (625 acres), adjacent to Montara Beach State Park, Gray Whale Cove State Beach, and Montara Mountain, offers a hillside climb with views and two short walks to caramel-colored beaches with wild, seething surfs. A stroll on the bluffs above the Cabrillo Highway with glorious Pacific views, the sound of tide and traffic fighting it out, takes you to historic McNee Ranch in the shade of Monterey cypress and Monterey pine trees. Then prepare to use those calves as you ascend up both moderate and strenuous grades to the top of Montara Mountain (1,898 feet). Dressing in layers is important to compensate for lots of direct sunlight and sudden cold fog. Bring plenty of water too, as there are virtually no facilities.*

County: San Mateo
Start: Parking lot on the west side of Highway 1 across from Gray Whale Cove
Length: 8.1 miles round trip
Approximate Hiking Time: 4.5 hours
Difficulty Rating: Mostly moderate, but strenuous in steep uphill sections
Trail Surface: Sand and stairs lead to beach across Highway 1. Single-track dirt trail in

McNee starts off relatively flat, then rises on dirt fire road and broken pavement with some steep portions. Trail floor becomes granite rock, then dirt and gravel at the top.
Land Status: State park
Nearest Town: Montara, CA
Other Trail Users: Equestrians and mountain bikes
Canine Compatibility: Dogs on leash

Getting There

By Car: From San Francisco/Oakland and North Bay, take Highway 101 south to 280 toward Daly City. Exit onto Highway 1 south toward Pacifica. Drive on Highway 1 (Cabrillo Highway) past Pacifica. The Gray Whale Cove parking lot is 3 miles past the last stoplight in Pacifica (Linda del Mar). Parking is on the left-hand side of the road (east). Signs read MCNEE RANCH. There is more parking ½ mile down Highway 1 at Montara State Beach. From the South Bay or the San Mateo Bridge, stay on Highway 92 west past the bridge all the way to Half Moon Bay. Highway 92 ends at Highway 1. Turn right, heading north on Highway 1. Go through Half Moon Bay, Moss Beach, and Montara, about 8 miles.

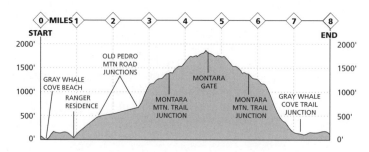

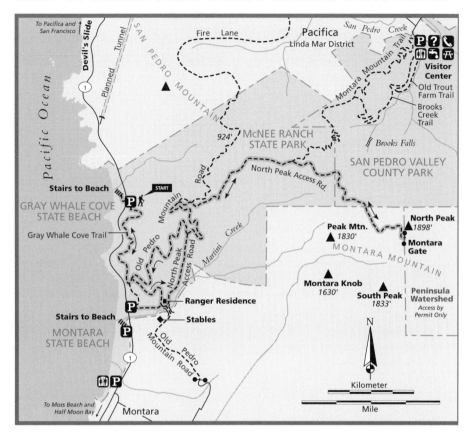

By Public Transportation: The SamTrans 1C and 1L lines run past the park but do not stop there. You can get off at Second and Main in Montara and walk back to the park, about 1/3 mile. Or ask the driver to stop at the Montara State Beach parking lot. SamTrans info: (800) 660-4BUS.

Hike Description

This hike starts with an optional venture down the wooden-railed steps to the small but dramatic Gray Whale Cove. But be forewarned: This beach is clothing optional. You don't have to wear your birthday suit to enjoy the crashing surf and secluded, sandy enclave, but gawkers are not welcome. The surfers and sunbathers that come here are generally very respectful. In winter, you probably have the beach to yourself. Until 2001, this beach, known then as Devil's Slide Beach, though state-owned, was privately run. The green, dilapidated building on the way to the stairs used to be the office of the cove's caretaker. As a private entity, he charged $6.50 or $7.50 per car for beachgoers. During the transition between management, the place was evidently a mess. Now operated by the state, there is no garbage, clean rest rooms are in place, and the entrance is free. Eventually it will have the $2.00 day-use fee required of California state parks.

Between the two state beaches is People's Beach, considered part of Montara. Traditionally also a nude beach, it is not safely accessible due to the frequent landslides in this area, but you can see it as you gain elevation up the mountain.

Slides are one thing this part of the coast is famous for. McNee Ranch State Park has been involved in a controversy for many years as the alternative route for Highway 1, where the treacherous landslides of Devil's Slide have covered the road with dirt and rock, closing it down many times. More than a few drivers have wound up swimming with their Volvos. One alternative plan—called the Martini Creek bypass—was to plow right through McNee for a 4.5-mile two-lane highway, requiring seven cuts into the mountains. But after much legislation and lobbying by environmental groups and locals, finally a measure was passed to dig a tunnel under the northern Montara foothills, avoiding Devil's Slide and the impact on the parkland.

You can see the reason for the slides in the beach cliffs and the banks along the North Peak Access Road—a combination of the Pacific wearing away the land's edge and the geological nature of the place. The sparkling, camel-colored Montara Mountain Granite, which makes up part of the floor and walls of the North Peak Trail, meets Paleocene sediments, causing a crumbling effect. The main contact zone of these two rocks occurs at Devil's Slide.

Pampas grass in front of Montara Mountain

The drought-tolerant natural grasses and chaparral on Montara Mountain act like superglue, holding the slopes together against erosion. The plant community changes subtly as you gain elevation. At the lower elevations, you find coastal scrub consisting of coyote bush, coast sagebrush, seaside daisy, Pacific blackberry, and coast buckwheat. Next up is coastal chaparral. At different times of the year, lowland brush and sage give way to pink- and white-flowered manzanita (including the unique Montara manzanita), blue ceanothus, fuchsia, coffee berry, and chinquapin, changing the rugged green and gray mountainside to soft colors and textures. The marine chaparral at the highest elevation, consisting of manzanita, salal, and lupine, grows only in this location on the San Mateo Coast. Native vegetation includes the endangered Hickman's cinquefoil, as well as San Francisco gum plant, Montara bush lupine, coast and San Francisco wallflowers, and coast rock cress.

In the late winter, bring binoculars to spot gray whales on their migration north. Watch for Anna's and ruby-throated hummingbirds hovering to feed from sticky monkeyflowers in summer and berry blossoms anytime of year. Besides a healthy raptor population, large black ravens add a Poe-eeriness on foggy days. Look for tracks of coyotes, fox, bobcats, deer, raccoons, and brush rabbits. Mountain lions, though present, are rarely sighted.

Gray Whale Cove Trail skirts the ridge above Highway 1. The traffic noise can be distracting, but you have constant, lovely views of the beaches and surf and in the spring a colorful and fragrant wildflower show, all along an easy, mostly flat, single-track trail. It connects Gray Whale Cove parking lot with the small lot at Martini Creek.

You are welcomed to the flat valley of McNee Ranch by a shaded road between rows of mature cypress and Monterey pines. The bridge to the stables stretches over Martini Creek. Before ranch days, Native Americans hunted and picked berries here. Then in 1769, Don Gaspar de Portolá's scouting party camped here as they trekked north to discover the San Francisco Bay by land.

Claiming the area under a Mexican land grant, prominent San Franciscans Francisco Guerrero, one of the early mayors of San Francisco, and rancher Tiburcio Velasquez brought cattle to graze the hillsides. That land grant still exists today, the only one left in the state and one of the largest undeveloped properties on the San Francisco Peninsula: Rancho Corral de Tierra. In 1996, its three principal private owners sought permits to develop ranchettes and homes on the property. Public and procedural resistance halted this, and they put the 4,262 acres up for sale at a price of $52 million. In 2000, the Peninsula Open Space Trust (POST) reached an agreement to purchase the land for $30 million. The plan for this rich land of mountain, watershed, and farmland is to give the open space over to the Golden Gate National Recreation Area to manage. Already the largest urban national park in the world, Rancho Corral de Tierra will increase its size by over 5 percent. Then we hikers can venture into all those lovely foothills you can see south of the mountain, 6,700 glorious continuous acres.

After California entered the Union in 1848, the first of many roads and railroads, which traversed McNee Ranch, including the Ocean Shore Railroad, opened up the coast to development. McNee Ranch became part of the empire of Duncan McNee, an early California land baron. During World War II, the U.S. Army moved onto the ranch, using it as a training ground. You can still see two of the bunkers.

The broken pavement on Old San Pedro Road comes from pre–Highway 1 days when it used to be the only winding connector for auto traffic over the hills between Montara Mountain and San Pedro Mountain, from Montara to Pacifica. According to local naturalist and area expert Barbara VanderWerf, "Within the boundaries of McNee Ranch State Park, you can trace all the human crossings of

Montara Mountain, from a Native American Costanoa trail to the Ocean Shore Railroad to present-day Highway 1."

During or after your hike, carefully cross Highway 1 for a rest or stroll on mile-long Montara Beach.

A great option: With two cars, park one at Montara Beach with lunch, and drive back to the San Pedro Valley County Park (see page 170). Take the Brooks Creek Trail to Montara Mountain Trail to the peak, then descend on North Peak Access Road, Old Pedro Mountain Road, and come out at the Martini Creek entrance to McNee Ranch State Park. Cross the street to your car and picnic on Montara Beach.

Miles/Directions

0.0 START in parking lot across the street from Gray Whale Cove State Beach. Cross the street carefully to visit cove. *(Note:* Gray Whale Cove Beach is clothing optional.) Turn right past green shack and rest rooms to staircase that leads to beach. *(Note:* If swimming, watch for dangerous surf, recurring riptides, and sleeper waves.)

0.3 Gray Whale Cove Beach. Come back up stairs, retracing steps. Cross highway carefully.

0.6 Trailhead at south end of parking lot for McNee Ranch, across from Gray Whale Cove State Beach. Interpretive sign with park map marks start of single-track Gray Whale Cove Trail. *(Note:* Trail can get flooded after rain.)

1.2 Viewing bench on bluff.

1.5 Veer right on connector to North Peak Access Road (toward McNee Ranch) at Old Pedro Mountain Road junction. This is a multiuse trail.

1.8 Trail winds down and meets paved North Peak Access Road. Turn left.

1.9 Pass ranger residence on left and bridge to stables on right. Go through gate, starting up hill on double-track, dirt North Peak Access Road.

2.1 Trail (formerly Old Pedro Mountain Road).

2.4 Trail splits; stay right on the North Peak Access Road, past unmarked Old Pedro Mountain Road to San Pedro Mountain. North Peak Trail becomes maintained dirt fire road.

3.3 Stay right, continuing on North Peak Access Road to top of Montara Mountain. Trail left is Montara Mountain Trail to San Pedro Valley County Park.

4.4 North Peak of Montara Mountain (1,898 feet). Beyond this point, gate blocks fire road, which continues on permit-only San Francisco Water Department Peninsula Watershed. *(FYI:* When this area becomes part of the Golden Gate National Recreation Area, it will probably become more accessible to hikers, an exciting prospect.) Note repeater stations on the peak (used for relaying signals from cellular phones, radios, etc.). Return the same way down North Peak Access Road.

5.5 Pass Montara Mountain Trail again, staying on North Peak Access Road.

6.4 After about 0.1 mile of broken paved trail, turn right, due west, onto single-track, dirt trail marked by two wooden posts on either side of path. This is Old Pedro Mountain Road Trail. Path widens, then becomes single-track again. There are steep downhill sections. Follow trail to Gray Whale Cove Trail.

7.2 Junction with Gray Whale Cove Trail. Turn right to head to the parking lot across from Gray Whale Cove State Beach.

8.1 Back at parking lot. **Option:** Drive 1 mile to Montara State Beach.

Hike Information

Trail Contacts:
Half Moon Bay State Beach (ranger station for McNee Ranch) (650) 726–8819
San Mateo Coast District—California Department of Parks and Recreation, P.O. Box 2390, Sacramento, CA 94296 (415) 726–6203

Schedule:
Open year-round daily 8:00 A.M. to dusk

Fees/Permits:
None

Local Information:
Half Moon Bay Coastside Chamber of Commerce and Visitors' Bureau, 520 Kelly Avenue, Half Moon Bay, CA 94019 (650) 726–8380; www.halfmoonbay chamber.org
Tide Information: www.co-ops.nos.noaa.gov/tides/westSF.html

Local Events/Attractions:
Day Spa: Beach House, 4100 North Cabrillo Highway, Half Moon Bay, CA (650) 712–0220
Horseback Riding: Friendly Acres Ranch and Sea Horse Ranch, 1828 North Cabrillo Highway, Half Moon Bay, CA (650) 726–8550 or (650) 726–2362
Pumpkin Patches: Andreotti Family Farm, 329 Kelly Avenue, Half Moon Bay, CA (650) 726–9151; festival: (650) 726–9652; www.miramarevents.com
Theater: This Side of the Hill Players, 1167 Main Street, Half Moon Bay, CA (650) 569–3266

Accommodations:
Camping: Half Moon Bay State Beach, 95 Kelly Avenue, Half Moon Bay, CA (650) 726–8820
Hostel: Point Montara Lighthouse, Sixteenth Street at Highway 1, Montara, CA (650) 726–8819; www.norcalhostels.org/pointmontaralighthouse.html
The Goose & Turrets B&B, 835 George Street, Montara, CA (650) 728–5451; www.goose.montara.com/index.html

Restaurants:
Cafe Gibralter (Mediterranean), 171 Seventh Street, Montara, CA (650) 728–9030
Two Fools Cafe and Market, 408 Main Street, Half Moon Bay, CA (650) 712–1222

Local Outdoor Retailers:
Play It Again Sports, 1111 El Camino Real, Millbrae CA (650) 952–6882
REI, 1119 Industrial Road, Suite 1-B, San Carlos, CA (650) 508–2330; www.rei.com

Hike Tours:
McNee State Park Office, Half Moon Bay, CA (650) 726–8819
Hike sponsored by Save Our Shores (415) 726–3123; (415) 726–9525; (415) 949–0708

Maps:
McNee State Park Office Half Moon Bay, CA (650) 726–8819
USGS maps: Montara Mountain, CA

24

James V. Fitzgerald Marine Reserve: The Tide Pool Loop

Overview: *The time of the low tide determines whether you walk along coastal bluffs first, with terrific Pacific views, or along sandy shores, with the longest intertidal reef in California to explore. On the high road, you pass over a creek and up through a grove of old, tall cypress trees, shaped by the salty winds. A short stint past the coastal wood-framed homes on Beach Way and Ocean Street and the haunted favorite haunt, Moss Beach Distillery, take you to a trail through seaside scrub and grassland along the cliffs. The trail is slowly moving inland as the sandstone bluffs fall away into the sea to be reformed into sand under crashing surf. Over the ridge to the east is the fishing harbor of Pillar Point and a trail through a bird watcher's paradise. The walk on the beach through the tide pools is unforgettable.*

County: San Mateo
Start: James V. Fitzgerald Marine Reserve Information Center, corner of California and North Lake Street
Length: 3-mile loop
Approximate Hiking Time: 2 hours
Difficulty Rating: Moderate
Trail Surface: Single-track, dirt trail along bluffs to walking roadside, back to dirt trail along

cliffs, mostly level; paved trail down marsh; a couple of miles on sandy and rocky beach
Land Status: Marine reserve
Nearest Town: Moss Beach
Other Trail Users: Hikers only on beach (no restrictions on bluffs)
Canine Compatibility: No dogs on beach or in the marsh

Getting There

By Car: From San Francisco/Oakland and North Bay, take Highway 101 south to 280 toward Daly City. Exit onto Highway 1 south toward Pacifica. Drive on Highway 1 (Cabrillo Highway) to Moss Beach. Turn right (west) on California Street (signs for the Marine Reserve). Turn right at the end of California Street on North Lake Avenue and immediately right into the parking lot there on the corner. From the San Mateo Bridge, stay on Highway 92 west past the bridge all the way to Half Moon Bay. Highway 92 ends at Highway 1. Turn right, heading north on Highway 1. Go through Half Moon Bay to Moss Beach. Turn left (west) on California Street

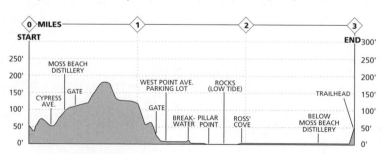

James V. Fitzgerald Marine Reserve

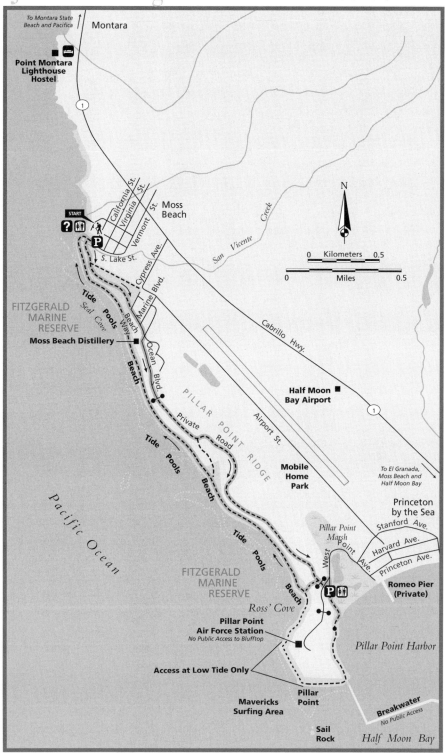

To Montara State
Beach and Pacifica

Montara

Point Montara
Lighthouse
Hostel

California St.
Virginia St.
Vermont St.

Moss
Beach

START

S. Lake St.

Cypress Ave.

San Vicente Creek

N

Kilometers 0.5

Miles 0.5

Tide

Seal Cove

Pools

FITZGERALD
MARINE
RESERVE

Beach Way

Marine Blvd.

Moss Beach Distillery

Ocean Blvd.

Beach

Cabrillo Hwy.

Half Moon
Bay Airport

PILLAR POINT RIDGE

Tide

Private Road

Pools

Airport St.

Beach

Mobile
Home
Park

To El Granada,
Moss Beach and
Half Moon Bay

Princeton
by the Sea

Pacific Ocean

Tide

Pools

Beach

FITZGERALD
MARINE
RESERVE

Ross' Cove

Pillar Point
Air Force Station
No Public Access to Blufftop

Access at Low Tide Only

Mavericks
Surfing Area

Pillar Point
Marsh

Stanford Ave.

West Point Ave.

Harvard Ave.

Princeton Ave.

Romeo Pier
(Private)

Pillar Point Harbor

Pillar
Point

Breakwater
No Public Access

Sail
Rock

Half Moon Bay

(signs for the Marine Reserve). Turn right at the end of California Street on North Lake Avenue and immediately right into the parking lot there on the corner.

By Public Transportation: You can take CalTrain to Hillsdale and take Route 294 Pacifica–Half Moon Bay. The SamTrans 1C and 1L lines run from Half Moon Bay to Moss Beach. SamTrans info: (800) 660–4BUS; www.transitinfo.org.

Hike Description

This stretch of coastline was officially protected as a reserve in 1969 and named James V. Fitzgerald Marine Reserve for a San Mateo County board member involved in the process. Some 100,000 people explore the tide pools and stare back at the harbor seals each year, most of them schoolchildren on field trips. With thirty acres of marine habitat, more than 400 species of animals, and 150 plant species revealed by the low tides, it makes a fantastic classroom. Docents (adults and high school students) teach kids about tides and offer guided tours on the weekends to the public. Scientists studying the shallow marine shelf have discovered twenty-five new plant and invertebrate species, as well as a few endemic ones, living nowhere else but here. They include a worm, a type of seaweed, and a shrimp that lives in the gut of a sea anemone. Species are still being catalogued, there are so many. The best time to see the tide pools is at minus tide, on the days following a full moon, but any low tide will do. Because a reef about a hundred yards out to sea breaks the waves, you don't have to worry about sneaky waves while you lean entranced over a crevice full of anemones, black turban snails, purple sea urchins, chitons, and starfish. But a good rule is to always keep an eye on the ocean.

Besides the jellyfish and flatworms in the pools, you might see an octopus or a sun star with up to twenty-four arms. On the sand are the shed shells of crabs, dry coral, and sand dollars, also called cake urchins or sea biscuits. Black mussels and white barnacles stick to the rocks. Bullwhip kelp and other seaweed wash to shore. Maps at the information kiosk show where the main reefs are on the beach. You may notice in the brochure that fishing for abalone, rockfish, halibut, and a few other species is legal with a license.

The featured hike starts first on the bluffs above all this, where you can watch the tide roll out, exposing the complex life in the stone. Harbor seals take a rest on the quiet beaches before people arrive. Seagulls pry at mussels on the rocks. Willets scamper in tight flocks on their toothpick legs away from the surf. A rare sight on the beach is the penguin-like common murre, and sadly, if you see one, it's probably injured. Thousands live off shore, mostly around the Farallon Islands. But forty years ago, they were threatened with extinction. Development encroached on their habitats and chronic oil spills killed many. Fortunately, starting in 1969, the U.S. Fish and Wildlife and Point Reyes Bird Observatory started protected nesting murres on the Farallons, helping the population to rebound to approximately 60,000 in 2001.

There are also some interesting landmarks on the land above the water. The cypress forest, trees neatly lined in rows, were planted as windbreaks by coastal

Walking through the cypress grove

farmers and ranchers around World War I. Cypress and eucalyptus trees were the most popular trees for this purpose on the Northern California coast, both fast-growing and able to withstand extreme weather conditions.

A strange little oasis appears after the main grove: three fat and healthy palm trees in a patch of grassland. These, along with exposed foundation, were once part of a large Victorian estate owned by the Reverend Arthur Smith of Oakland. He had a main house and a cottage, marked by periwinkle, which he and his family used as a summer home. Later owners tore it down.

The lore of the Moss Beach Distillery gives you some insight into the colorful past of the San Mateo Coast. A plaque below the entrance tells much of its story.

During prohibition, the San Mateo Coast was an ideal spot for rum running, bootleggers and speakeasies, establishments that sold illegal booze to thirsty clients. One of the most successful speakeasies of this era was Frank's Place on the cliffs by Moss Beach built by Frank Torres in 1927. Frank's Place became a popular nightspot for silent film stars and politicians from the city. Mystery writer Dashiell Hammett frequented the place and used it as a setting for one of his detective stories. The restaurant located on the cliffs above a secluded beach was in the perfect location to benefit from the clandestine activities of the Canadian rum-runners. Under cover of darkness and fog, illegal whiskey was landed on the beach, dragged up the steep cliffs, and loaded into waiting vehicles for transport to San Francisco. Some of the booze always found its way into the garage beneath Frank's Place.

With the repeal of Prohibition in 1933, Torres turned the place into a successful, legal restaurant. The distillery is also famous for its resident ghost, the Blue Lady, one of Torres's old customers from the speakeasy days. She was evidently drowned, and the culprit never caught, though a jilted lover was suspect.

Within a few blocks of the distillery, look for an old foundation on the cliffs. It is all that remains of the posh Moss Beach Hotel, built by wealthy landowner J. F. Wienke. Wienke, an immigrant from Germany, bought the whole coastline down to Half Moon Bay. At the time, the town was called Blenheim. Wienke called his new hotel the Moss Beach Hotel after the green seaweed he saw on the beach below, and eventually, the town took its name. As the largest landowner in the area, people called Wienke "The Mayor of Moss Beach." The hotel burned down before World War I and was not rebuilt.

Pillar Point looks dramatic as you near it, with water visible on both sides of its 175-foot crown. According to local historian Barbara VanderWerf, long ago, Pillar Point was called Snake's Head for its unique shape. The Costanoans used to gather shellfish at its base. They lived by this bay as long as 5,800 years ago. Their middens, old shell piles, are buried in the marsh. Spaniards, then Mexicans and Americans, grazed cattle on the hillsides from 1790 through the 1890s. Portuguese whalers used the high point as a lookout for humpback whales and launched their whaling boats from Whaler's Cove (Ross' Cove today). Farmers grew artichokes and peas on the ridge in the 1920s and 1930s. Not until World War II did buildings appear on the point, when it became an observation post linked to the harbor defenses of San Francisco. The military also built the landing strip you see inland, which is now the Half Moon Bay Airport. Today Pillar Point is still an active U.S. Air Force base, with soldiers stationed in the 120-foot tower and its giant dish, 80 feet in diameter, still tracking military activity over long distances.

On the eastside of the point is the town of Princeton-by-the-Sea and the Pillar Point Harbor. You can watch local fishing boats rock into port after long hours on the water. There are great fish restaurants like Barbara's Fish Trap, a favorite of day-tripping aviators, and Ketch Joanne's Restaurant, an icon here for twenty-seven years. Take the trail from West Point Avenue through the Pillar Point Marsh, home to 151 species of birds, as recorded by the Audubon Society. Also from this trail, you can watch—with binoculars—the surfers at Mavericks, where its famous 100-foot waves curl to the

Mavericks has some of the highest waves on the coast. Every year, the Men Who Ride Mountains competition is held here (with a female chemist competing in 2002, the name doesn't fully describe all the contestants).

Taking Care of Tide Pools

Twice a day, retreating tides leave seashore life clinging to the rocks. Intertidal plants and animals are well adapted to this changing world of surf and sand but have no defense against humans. Therefore, whenever you are tide pooling, observe the following guidelines:

1. The best way to observe tide pools is to sit quietly until animals emerge from their hiding places and resume their activities. Watch out for rising tide.
2. You may touch marine life, but DO NOT pick it up or place it in a container. If you do, it will die. Examine it in the place that you find it.
3. Watch your step! Walk carefully around the tide pools for your own safety and to spare the marine life underfoot.
4. Any rocks that get moved should be replaced with the seaweed side up. Life on the bottom of the rocks will die when exposed to sun and air. Avoid moving the rocks whenever possible.
5. Shells and rocks are a natural part of the areas. Many serve as future homes for creatures such as hermit crabs. DO NOT COLLECT SHELLS, VEGETATION, ROCKS OR MARINE LIFE IN THE RESERVE.

delight of professional surfers. It is located about 200 yards southwest of Bird Rocks beyond Pillar Point. During low tide, you can walk around the base of the point for up to 3$^{1}/_{2}$ miles of lovely beach and tide pools, taking you back to the start.

Miles/Directions

0.0 START from the parking lot at marine reserve information kiosk. Turn left (south) on North Lake Street. Just past parking lot, on the right, watch for dirt trail that leads over creek (going west). There are several trails heading up to bluff. Take well-worn trail on right that curves up to top of bluff.

0.1 Single-track dirt trail beside split-wood safety fence heads south along cliffs. Looking along the line of the bluffs south, you can see the Moss Beach Distillery out on short point.

0.3 Pass palm trees and back into some woods. (**Option:** Stairs down to the beach create a 0.5-mile loop.)

0.4 At the corner of Beach and Cypress, continue south, walking on side of Beach Way past coastal houses. Seal Cove Inn on left. Stay on Beach Way straight, past stop sign at Marine Boulevard. Follow signs to Moss Beach Distillery.

0.5 Moss Beach Distillery, where Beach Way meets Ocean Boulevard. Continue south past parking lot on Ocean Boulevard. Small paved road leads uphill. Views of Pillar Point. The cement pillar in the water is a sighting to range artillery from Pillar Point, one of eighty including landmarks and lighthouses.

0.9 Ocean Boulevard dead ends at field. Two dirt trails begin here through grasslands. Stay to the right on bluff trail. There are many social paths.

Hike Information

📞 Trail Contacts:
James V. Fitzgerald Marine Reserve,
P.O. Box 451, Moss Beach, CA 94038
(650) 728–3584
Coyote Point Museum, 1651 Coyote
Point Drive, San Mateo, CA (650) 340–7598
San Mateo Coast District—California
Department of Parks and Recreation,
P.O. Box 2390, Sacramento, CA 94296
(415) 726–6203

🕐 Schedule:
Open daily from dawn to dusk

💲 Fees/Permits:
None

❓ Local Information:
Half Moon Bay Coastside Chamber of
Commerce and Visitors' Bureau, 520
Kelly Avenue, Half Moon Bay, CA 94019
(650) 726–8380; www.halfmoonbaycham
ber.org
Tide Information: www.co-
ops.nos.noaa.gov/tides/westSF.html

💡 Local Events/Attractions:
Fishing and whale watching: Riptide
Sportfishing (888) RIP–TIDE or (415)
469–8433
Surfing: Maverick's Surf Shop and Cafe,
460 Capistrano Road, Princeton-by-the-Sea,
CA (650) 728–1233
Wine tasting: Obester Winery, San Mateo
Road (Highway 92), Half Moon Bay, CA
(650) 726–9463; Thomas Fogarty Winery,
19501 Skyline Boulevard, Half Moon Bay, CA
(650) 851–6777

🛏 Accommodations:
Camping: Half Moon Bay State Beach, 95
Kelly Avenue, Half Moon Bay, CA
(650) 726–8820

Hostel: Point Montara Lighthouse, Sixteenth Street at Highway 1, Montara, CA
(650) 726–8819; www.norcalhostels.org/
pointmontaralighthouse.html
Seal Cove Inn, 221 Cypress Avenue,
Moss Beach, CA (800) 995–9987 or (650)
728–4114; www.sealcoveinn.com
Zaballa House B&B, 324 Main Street,
Half Moon Bay, CA (650) 726–9123;
zaballa@zaballahouse.com

🍴 Restaurants:
Barbara's Fish Trap, 281 Capistrano
Road, Princeton-by-the-Sea, CA
(650) 728–7049
Half Moon Bay Brewing Co., 390 Capis-
trano Road, Princeton-by-the-Sea, CA
(650) 728–2739
Ketch Joanne's, 17 Johnson Pier, Pillar
Point Harbor, Princeton-by-the-Sea, CA
(650) 728–3747
Moss Beach Distillery, 140 Beach Way,
Moss Beach, CA (650) 728–5595

🔧 Local Outdoor Retailers:
REI, 1119 Industrial Road, Suite 1-B, San
Carlos, CA (650) 508–2330; www.rei.com

👥 Hike Tours:
James V. Fitzgerald Marine Reserve,
P.O. Box 451, Moss Beach, CA 94038
(650) 728–3584
Coyote Point Museum, 1651 Coyote
Point Drive, San Mateo, CA (650) 340–7598

🅝 Maps:
James V. Fitzgerald Marine Reserve,
P.O. Box 451, Moss Beach, CA 94038
(650) 728–3584
USGS maps: Montara Mountain, CA; Half
Moon Bay, CA

Follow the cliffs toward Pillar Point. You can see several areas where the
cliffs have fallen away so do not stand right on the edge. Views of Montara Mountain and Half Moon Bay beyond Pillar Point.

1.4 Turn right onto dirt path down to beach. Watch footing. **Option:** Take
trail left (east) down to parking lot. Then turn right onto paved pathway, right again on West Point Avenue and out onto trail to visit marsh-

land and the piers of Pillar Point Harbor. Adds 1 mile roundtrip. In very low tide only, it is possible to walk the beach around Pillar Point. Proceed with caution.

1.5 Ross' Cove (formerly Whalers' Cove) on north side of point, a favorite surfing spot. To the southwest beyond Bird Rocks is the famous Mavericks surfing spot (named for a surfer's dog). Best viewed from south side of Pillar Point, but hard to see in general. Turn north up the beach to enjoy the tide pools.

2.0 Frenchman's Reef. Continue along beach.

2.5 Seal Cove.

3.0 San Vicente Creek, which runs into ocean. Carefully cross creek and climb up rocks on other side. *(Note:* This is the most strenuous part of the hike when the tide is in. Alternate route is path up to cypress grove.) Turn inland for a brief walk to the parking lot, where there is a rest room and information kiosk, which is sporadically attended. **Option:** The marine reserve continues north all the way to Montara Lighthouse, another 0.9 mile, if you want a longer hike on the beach and a look at the lighthouse, which now houses an International Youth Hostel. Montara State Beach starts beyond it.

The Marine Mammal Center often uses the reserve as a place to reintroduce nursed harbor seals, sea lions and other ocean creatures to the wilds of the Pacific, and this is usually the spot where they make the release. Call the Marine Mammal Center (415–289–7325) to find out scheduled releases; it's a great thing for kids to see.

25 San Pedro Valley County Park

Overview: *San Pedro Valley County Park has been a place to breathe easy for a long time. Nestled between the northernmost Santa Cruz Mountains and foothills of Pacifica, the valley is protected from harsh coastal winds and weather. Three freshwater creeks flow under the shade of willows, oaks, and dogwood with fish and riparian flora and fauna. Eight different trails offer chaparral and views, meadows of deer and wildflowers, hillside grasslands, herbal eucalyptus groves, and a waterfall. People have enjoyed the peaceful scenery here for thousands of years. With the addition of picnic areas and an interesting weekend visitor center, you can spend the day doing the same.*

County: San Mateo
Start: In the parking lots by the San Pedro Valley County Park Visitor Center
Length: 6.1-mile loop
Approximate Hiking Time: 3 hours
Difficulty Rating: Moderate
Trail Surface: Single- and double-track dirt

trails, a couple of wooden bridges, and some paved path
Land Status: County park
Nearest Town: Pacifica
Other Trail Users: Bikers on Weiler Ranch Road
Canine Compatibility: No pets

Getting There

By Car: From San Francisco/Oakland and North Bay, take Highway 101 south to Route 280 toward Daly City. Exit on Highway 1 south driving toward Pacifica. Turn east on Linda Mar Boulevard (there's a stoplight). Follow Linda Mar Boulevard until it ends at Oddstad Boulevard. Turn right on Oddstad Boulevard and proceed 1 block to the park entrance. Turn right up the hill into the park, pay at the kiosk, and park in either lot. (You have to pay admission even when the kiosk is unattended, so bring $4.00 in change.)

By Public Transportation: Take SamTrans bus #110 from Daly City BART (weekday frequency: every thirty minutes), or SamTrans bus #112 (hourly service) from Colma BART, to Linda Mar Shopping Center in Pacifica. Transfer to SamTrans bus #14 for a short ride to the bus stop on Terra Nova Boulevard near Odd-

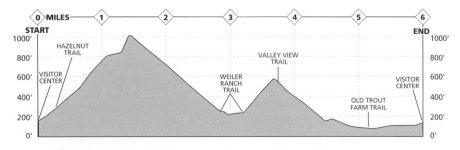

San Pedro Valley County Park

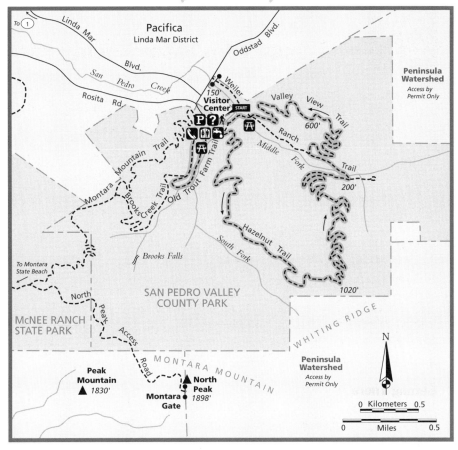

stadt Boulevard (weekday bus frequency: every thirty to sixty minutes; no weekend service). Return the same way in reverse. If hiking to McNee Ranch State Park, return by catching northbound SamTrans bus #294 on Highway 1 (frequency: approximately every 70 to 120 minutes, weekdays; every two hours on Saturdays; every three hours on Sundays (limited to three buses). SamTrans info: (800) 660–4BUS; www.transitinfo.org.

Hike Description

It's easy to see why people have gathered in this valley for centuries. The south and middle forks of San Pedro Creek flow here year-round and provide safe spawning areas for migratory steelhead trout. Few of these habitats remain undeveloped. Brooks Creek during the rainy winter months puts on a show with Brooks Falls, splashing down 175 feet in three tiers. The Middle Valley is an artist's palette with springtime wildflowers. California poppies, suncups, buttercups, wild mustard, and wild radish make a heavenly bed. At dusk, as picnickers pack up for home, or on

Weiler Ranch Road Trail from Hazelnut Trail

quiet weekday afternoons, it becomes a playground for wildlife. Brush rabbits cautiously hop out of hiding to feed. Black-tailed does and fawns munch contentedly on flowers. Bobcats, mountain lions, owls, and hawks keep the field mice, moles, snakes, and small birds constantly aware. At these times, the cycle of life continues undisturbed right before your eyes.

The Costanoan Indians were the first humans that we know of to enjoy the valley. They had a seasonal camp here for possibly thousands of years. In 1769, Spanish explorer Captain Gaspar de Portolá and his men arrived here sick and exhausted. Their expedition, which was supposed to end at Monterey, had missed the target, and they had walked on. They stumbled into this valley and set up camp. It was so peaceful and rejuvenating, they stayed a while, and it was from this camp that Portolá's scout, Sergeant Jose Francisco Ortega, set out to explore the area and, climbing Sweeney Ridge, saw the San Francisco Bay for the first time.

As part of Mexico in 1839, the area merged into a land grant. Don Francisco Sanchez, *alcalde*, or mayor, of San Francisco, claimed it and built the adobe home that you pass coming through the Linda Mar community on your way to the park. It is the oldest building in San Mateo County, open to the public daily. General Edward Kirkpatrick acquired the adobe for $17,500 in 1879. Between 1900 and

1946, it was used at various times as a hotel, bordello, speakeasy, bootleg saloon, hunting lodge, and artichoke packing shed.

The first Americans to build homes here around the turn of the twentieth century were wealthy San Franciscans, who constructed palatial summer homes on the coast side. Not long ago, cattle still ruminated on the hillsides, and commercial farmers harvested crops of pumpkins and artichokes in the meadow. A fellow named John Gay operated a trout farm on the south fork of San Pedro Creek until 1962, when rainstorms washed out his operation.

In the early 1950s, developer Andres Oddstad in one weekend bought up seven of the ranches in the San Pedro Valley and soon started construction on tract homes in Linda Mar. By 1957, nine hamlets along 6 miles of coastline incorporated as the city of Pacifica, Spanish for "peace" (the name was chosen in a contest). The new community found the natural meadows and hillsides a backyard paradise. With a citywide vote, the citizens donated as much open space as possible to the National Park Service and the county. As a result, Pacifica's population hasn't grown significantly in thirty years, and back at the end of Oddstad Boulevard are 1,150 acres of serene valley, hillsides, and cascading streams.

Of course nothing is perfect. Hiking here today, you still have the feeling of entering an oasis, but there are factors of reality to consider. Poison oak grows heartily along with everything else in the park. Fog can roll in, blocking views and chilling the bones when you're in the hills. And the valley just can't protect from big storms. The park has great group picnic sites, but that means there are often large groups of people here on the weekends. Pooches have to stay home. Small portions of Hazelnut Trail, though under repair, are rutted by rain runoff, and deer paths on the Valley View Loop require that a hiker pay attention to stick to the main trail.

These considerations are slight, however, compared with the hiking possibilities. If hiking with young children, the nature trail and a tour of the visitor center make a nice outing. The Brooks Fall Loop is a short 2 miles. With two cars, a wonderful option is hiking Montara Trail through McNee Ranch and ending at Montara Beach for a picnic. The featured hike takes in a little bit of everything for a satisfying 6-mile loop.

Miles/Directions

0.0 START at visitor center in San Pedro Valley County Park and walk toward trailhead for Plaskon Nature Trail. Cross bridge. After about 30 yards, turn right on signed Hazelnut Trail. Trail ascends hill on switchbacks.

1.2 Higher up trail you enter the drier sandstone area where rare Montara manzanita and giant golden chinaquapin grow beside coyote brush, toyon, and coffeeberry. Continue on Hazelnut Trail, which eventually starts east on switchbacks down to valley.

3.3 Turn right on Weiler Ranch Road.

Hike Information

Trail Contacts:
San Pedro Valley Park, 600 Oddstad Boulevard, Pacifica, CA (650) 355–8289
San Mateo County Parks and Recreation, 455 County Center, 4th floor, Redwood City, CA (650) 363–4020; group picnic reservations: (650) 363–4021

Schedule:
Open daily from 8:00 A.M. to dusk

Fees/Permits:
None

Local Information:
Pacifica Chamber of Commerce and Visitor Center, 225 Rockaway Beach, #1, Pacifica, CA (650) 355–4122 or (650) 355–6949; www.pacificachamber.com

Local Events/Attractions:
Milagra Ridge (protected habitat hiking), College Drive, Pacifica, CA
Fort Funston Ranger Station (415) 239–2366
Pacifica Performances (650) 355–1882
Sanchez Adobe Historic Site, 1000 Linda Mar Boulevard, Pacifica, CA (650) 359–1462
Sea Bowl Entertainment Center, 4625 Coast Highway, Pacifica, CA (650) 738–8190; www.seabowl.com

Accommodations:
Camping: Half Moon Bay State Beach, 95 Kelly Avenue, Half Moon Bay, CA (650) 726–8820

Hostel: Point Montara Lighthouse, Sixteenth Street at Highway 1, P.O. Box 737, Montara, CA (650) 726–8819; www. norcalhostels.org/pointmontaralighthouse. html
The Goose & Turrets B&B, 835 George Street, P.O. Box 370937, Montara, CA (650) 728–5451; www.goose.montara. com/index.html
Nick's Sea Breeze Motel, 100 Rockaway Beach Avenue, Pacifica, CA (650) 359–3903

Restaurants:
Colombo's Delicatessen, 484 Manor Plaza, Pacifica, CA (650) 355–5023
Moonraker Restaurant, 105 Rockaway Beach Avenue, Pacifica, CA (650) 359–0303
Ristorante Mare, 404 San Pedro Avenue, Pacifica, CA (650) 355–5980

Local Outdoor Retailers:
REI, 1119 Industrial Road, Suite 1-B, San Carlos, CA (650) 508–2330; www.rei.com

Hike Tours:
San Pedro Valley Park, 600 Oddstad Boulevard, Pacifica, CA (650) 355–8289
San Mateo County Parks and Recreation, 455 County Center, 4th floor, Redwood City, CA (650) 363–4020

Maps:
San Pedro Valley Park, 600 Oddstad Boulevard, Pacifica, CA (650) 355–8289
San Mateo County Parks and Recreation, 455 County Center, 4th Floor, Redwood City, CA (650) 363–4020**USGS maps:** Montara Mountain, CA

3.6 Turn right on Valley View Trail. (**Option:** Continue on Weiler Ranch Road back to visitor center for a 4.3-mile loop.) Valley View traverses south-facing slopes above valley. Be careful of rocks on the trail and watch for scat and footprints of coyotes and other critters. The trail rises, then descends.

5.0 Valley View Trail ends. Turn right on Weiler Ranch Road, then left on park service road, heading toward visitor center. Road crosses over Middle Fork of San Pedro Creek and passes by Walnut Grove Group Picnic Area. Continue on service road to north parking lot.

5.2 Continue on sidewalk past visitor center to end of south parking lot. Take Old Trout Farm signed trail for 0.8 mile.

5.3 On Old Trout Farm Trail, pass by picnic area on left and, near beginning of trail, remains of John Gay's Trout Farm, a couple of tanks.

5.5 At hairpin turn, trail looks up ravine at Brooks Falls.

5.6 At junction with Brooks Creek Trail, stay right on Brooks Falls Overlook Trail. **Option:** For a different view of the falls, turn left and head to a bench another 0.3 mile.

6.1 Back at the parking lots and visitor center.

The Northern
Santa Cruz Mountains

You're up on Highway 35, Skyline Boulevard, sun shining through the windshield. Motorcyclists ride in posses on Sunday mornings on their way to the famous Alice's Restaurant at the Saratoga Gap. They have one destination, but for you, the hiker, your quest could take years, to explore all the parkland and open space accessible from this one road. Skyline Boulevard follows the ridge of the northern Santa Cruz Mountains. Sloping down to valleys and coastline on either side are tens of thousands of acres and hundreds of miles of trails through thick forests, scrub, and grassland. You can follow trails into the heart of Silicon Valley to the east and to the Pacific Ocean to the west.

The Midpeninsula Regional Open Space District alone has saved 46,500 acres in twenty-six preserves where sawmills once stood. Soda Gulch Trail in Purisima Creek Redwoods Open Space Preserve provides a meditative stroll through giant redwoods. Portola Redwoods has its Old Tree Trail and out-of-the-way campgrounds. Castle Rock State Park, besides its groves of madrones and black oak trees, has amazing rock outcroppings. Rock climbers gather around Goat Rock to practice maneuvers. In reptilian poses, they grasp to the faces of vertical stone with chalky hands.

Sawmills made their first appearance in these vast forests, dominated by coast redwoods, back in 1849. But the steep mountains and tight gullies that keep the redwoods protected from wind and sun also protected a lot of them from becoming timber. The mills only operated when prices were high enough to compensate for the cost of hauling the lumber out of here. Cutting is still happening on private land today, but the happy consequence of the delay is that much of the forest has been saved. Big Basin State Park has the largest continuous stand of ancient coast redwoods south of San Francisco, some up to 2,000 years old. The waterfalls on Berry Creek Falls Trail are some of the most memorable in the whole Bay Area.

California's coastal mountain range formed when the North America Plate, supporting the continent, and the Pacific Plate, under the Pacific Ocean, collided and began rubbing past each other along the San Andreas fault line, which follows Stevens Creek east of the Santa Cruz Mountains. The pressure caused the folding of the sea floor and formed an almost continuous series of ranges and valleys the length of California, separating the coast from the Great Central Valley and the deserts of the interior. The mountainous barrier here is what causes the weather pattern most important to the redwoods: fog. The line where thick forests end and primarily scrub and grasslands begin marks the fog line. Where the fog comes in you have green mixed forest up to the top of the ridge and slightly over the top where the fog spills, but then, suddenly, grasslands and scattered drought-resistant live oaks take over. You can find all of these habitats in the parks off Skyline Boulevard.

26

Big Basin State Park: Berry Creek Falls Trail Loop

Overview: *This 11-mile loop is a satisfying jaunt through the largest continuous stand of ancient coast redwoods south of San Francisco. Following the contours of the hillside, the Sunset Trail brings you over several deep canyons and cascading creeks. Berry Creek Falls Trail takes you past a series of waterfalls and through a deep basin. The Golden Cascade and Silver Falls feature just that: manes of silver water against golden earth. Berry Creek Falls is a 60-foot vertical sheet of white water falling down dark glistening rocks. Out of the canyon, the Skyline to the Sea Trail takes you back to the start through lush canyons past downed trees and more red giants. The park has 148 campsites and several backpacking camps.*

County: Santa Cruz
Start: Main parking lot across from Big Basin Redwoods Park headquarters
Length: 11.6 miles
Approximate Hiking Time: 6 hours
Difficulty Rating: Strenuous for the distance; moderate trail
Trail Surface: Single- and double-track dirt trail

that, with a few rises, descends into dense woodland, by creeks and waterfalls, then ascends back to trailhead
Land Status: State park
Nearest Town: Boulder Creek
Other Trail Users: Hikers only
Canine Compatibility: No dogs

Getting There

By Car: From the San Jose, Oakland, Fremont area, take Highway 880 south, which becomes Highway 17. As you head toward Santa Cruz and come down from the summit, you will see a sign on the freeway for Big Basin. The actual road name is Mount Hermon Road. Exit the freeway here and stay right on Mount Hermon Road. Stay on this road as it goes through the city of Scotts Valley. Mount Hermon Road ends at an intersection with a signal (Graham Hill Road). Turn right at this light. You will immediately come to another lighted intersection (Highway 9); turn right again. Stay on Highway 9 north for 15 miles. You will be traveling through several mountain towns. You will eventually come to the town of Boulder Creek. In

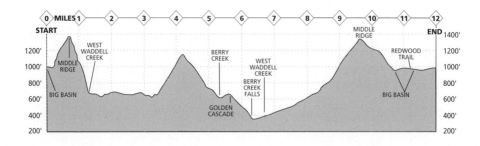

Big Basin State Park: Berry Creek Falls Trail Loop

To Waterman Gap and 9

Sempervirens Creek

Sempervirens Falls

Huckleberry

Wastahi

236

Sempervirens
To Boulder
Creek

Store

Jay

BIG BASIN 1000'

Nature Lodge

236

Blooms
Creek

N

Blooms Creek

Sequoia Trail

North Escape Rd

Skyline - to-the-Sea Trail

Opal Creek

Rogers Creek

Redwood
Trail

Maddock Creek

Waddell Creek

Forest Trail

Creeping

Road

Sunset Trail

Meteor Trail

To Waterman Gap and
Castle Rock State Park

Creek

START

Dool

Road

Fire

Trail

to the Sea

Ridge

Middle

Gazos

Skyline

To Butano State Park

Ocean View
Summit
1685'

BIG BASIN
REDWOODS
STATE PARK

Sunset

Road

Creek

Gazos

Sunset

Trail

Trail

Kelly Creek

Skyline to the Sea Trail

King

Trail

Howard

Fire

Road

Mount McAbee Overlook
1730'

Hihn Hammond

Timms Creek

West Waddell

Timms Creek Trail

Berry

Creek

Trail

Berry Creek
Falls

400'

East Fork

To Backpack Camps

Gazos Creek Rd.

Johansen

Road

Gazos

Creek

Road

Berry Creek

Sunset

Trail

Berry Silver Falls

Creek Falls Trail

Howard King Trail

To Backpack Camps,
Rancho del Oso, and 1

West Waddell Creek

Sandy Point
Guard Station

West Berry Creek

Sunset Trail Camp
900'

Golden Cascade

Henry Creek Trail

Whitehouse

Canyon Road

Chalks Road

Chalks Mountain
1609'

To Año Nuevo
State Reserve
(Cascade Ranch)

Gazos Creek

Kilometers

Miles

0 1

Boulder Creek, there is one stop sign. At this stop sign, turn left on Highway 236/Big Basin Way. Stay on this highway for 9 miles to Big Basin State Park. Proceed to park headquarters.

From San Francisco or Palo Alto, take either Highway 101 or 280 south. From there, take Highway 85 south. Take exit 85 at Saratoga Road. Turn right and head west on Saratoga Road. This road goes through Saratoga, then begins to climb into the mountains. At this point, the road becomes Highway 9. Stay on 9 as it winds through the mountains for 12 miles. You will then see a sign for Highway 236/Big Basin. Turn right on Highway 236 and continue on this road for 9 miles until you come to park headquarters.

By Public Transportation: Contact BART Information (www.transitinfo.org); SamTrans: (800) 660–4BUS; or Santa Clara Valley Transportation Authority (408) 321–2300; www.vta.org.

Hike Description

"These trees because of their size and antiquity, are among the natural wonders of the world and should be saved for posterity." —Photographer Andrew P. Hill, Savior of Big Basin, circa 1900

Beside the visitor center, a slice of an ancient redwood tree tells the first story of many on this hike. It sprouted in the year 544 during the Byzantine Empire and was already 1392 years old when the park opened in 1902, the first state park in California. This early conservation effort came from photographer Andrew P. Hill, who started the Sempervirens Club to protect these redwoods. Today, the club is still hard at work protecting forests for future generations.

The Ohlone Indians lived around Big Basin for nearly 10,000 years. They believed the trees to be spirit beings, part of a divine race that existed before humans, who taught people the proper way to live among the redwoods. Even their houses, made out of planks split from fallen redwoods over pits, were understood to be living bodies. Grizzlies, whom the natives respected and feared, lived in the dense ravines. Other than mushrooms, there wasn't a lot the Ohlones needed in the shadowy woods, so they pretty much left them alone. Sometimes their controlled burns in the grasslands reached the forest, but the redwoods always withstood the flames.

When Portolá's Spanish expedition came through in 1769, the men, sick with scurvy, camped at the mouth of Waddell Creek and gorged themselves on berries. With their miraculous recovery, they named the valley Cañada de la Salud or Canyon of Health. But their presence was not good for the health of the natives. The U.S. government was even more ruthless, paying posses to kill remaining tribes.

Logging of the redwoods happened at a frantic pace after the gold rush as new settlers in the Bay Area built homes, churches, and post offices. Cities rose. The resources seemed endless. Frustrated miners and other men seeking a new life in

Logger Legends and Big Basin Place Names

Waddell and West Waddell Creek—William White Waddell (b. Kentucky, 1818) arrived in Santa Cruz County in 1851 and built sawmills. One, along with a tramway and a wharf, was along the creek that now bears his name. They burned down. Waddell died in 1875 from complications to injuries resulting from a bear attack that ripped one of his arms off. Every Halloween there's a special night hike in Big Basin, "The Missing Arm of William Waddell."

Berry Creek—The Berry Creek flowing southward into Waddell Creek, was named for old lumberman, Tilford George Berry, probably an employee of old Waddell. Tilford, from Indiana, built a cabin at the base of the lower Berry Creek Falls in the mid-1860s. He mysteriously disappeared during the next decade and finally in 1890, his bones were found in the chaparral above Boulder Creek.

Dool Trail—William H. "Billy" Dool served as warden of Big Basin from 1911 until 1932. A Canadian, naturalized in Santa Cruz County in 1888, he was also a butcher, with a shop on what is now Central Avenue near Big Basin Way.

Hihn Hammond Road—Originally built in 1917 by the Hihn Hammond Lumber Company, it is a retired logging road.

Timms Creek—George Timms was a squatter and a timber claimant who had a cabin in an opening in the woods near the present Gazos Creek Road. Like many of the mountain men around here, Timms was a hard drinker and occasionally had delirium tremens (the DTs). Around 1884 he disappeared, leaving the basin's greatest mystery behind him. Three different stories pointed to murder, but none had sufficient factual evidence to make an accusation.

Kelly Creek—This short creek is named for Dr. Thomas Kelly, a surgeon in the Civil War who took up a timber claim in the area in the 1870s. The Kelly Cabin became a well-known rendezvous for hunters. He died in his bed in 1906 at the age of seventy.

the west became lumbermen, living and working in the forests in a rough and isolated existence. Their stories still live on in Big Basin. Trail names on this hike memorialize them (see sidebar above).

Single-track and double-track trails take you through cool canyons, following the contours of the hills. They meander by fern-lined creeks and immense tangled roots of fallen trees. This vast stand of giant redwoods, with their orangutan fur and citrus-scented needles, is overwhelming in scale. The mixed woodland also features very mature Douglas fir and tan bark oak trees, their trunks covered with soft, hairy moss. This landscape is uninterrupted for miles, except for the occasional orange monkeyflower, yellow banana slug, wild strawberry, and colorful mushroom that grow beside the trail. Bridges take you over gurgling streams. Natural sulphur in a couple of the creeks causes some sharp smells. In the rainy season, marshes serve as breeding ground to California newts.

After the Berry Creek crossing, the trail climbs to the edge of the forest, where startling afternoon sun blanches the scene for a tenth of mile. Here you find knobcone pines, manzanita and soft, dry sandstone. Most of the animals in the park live in chaparral like this, the coastal valleys or oak groves. Foxes, coyotes, bobcats, opossums and the rare mountain lion share this area with hunting raptors, brush rabbits, lizards and western rattlesnakes.

The Mother of the Forest

Back in endless woodland, you eventually reach the Berry Creek Falls Trail, the discovery and the prize for this long hike. It features almost continuous waterfalls. Golden Cascade, so named for the gold sandstone earth that forms the 20-foot slide beneath the falls, is followed by the two cascades of Silver Falls. A wire railing helps hikers down rock steps right beside the roaring water. A meditative walk beside Berry Creek and its moss-covered logs, thick ferns and dark, moist earth, brings you to 60-foot Berry Creek Falls, splashing bridal veil–fashion into the creek below.

The lush Skyline to the Sea Trail, following Kelly and Timms Creeks, takes you back to the Redwood Trail Loop, a great finale to the day. A 25–cent guide from the visitor center leads you to redwood fairy circles and burls, the Chimney Tree, and the largest redwoods in the park. Chipmunks, gray squirrels, and dark-eyed junkos dart through oak scrub.

Miles/Directions

0.0   START at parking lot outside park headquarters. *(Note:* Before starting hike, check out the visitor center and the redwood tree display beside it. Maps cost $1.00, self-guiding nature guides for the Redwood Trail 25 cents.) Look for trailhead for Redwood Nature Trail on side of parking lot opposite the park headquarters. Go straight *(Note:* You will take Redwood Nature Trail as a cooldown on way back.)

0.1   Past rest rooms is start of Skyline to the Sea Trail, connecting to most other trails. Cross bridge over Opal Creek to trailhead. Turn right on Skyline to Sea Trail to Sunset Trail. It becomes single-track dirt trail following creek.

0.3   Stay to the left on Skyline to Sea Trail toward Dool Trail.

0.4   Trailhead for Dool Trail. Turn left on Dool 0.1 mile to Sunset Trail. Redwood Creek is on the right.

0.5   Trail splits. Turn left on Sunset Trail toward Middle Ridge Fire Road.

1.1   Up a small rise, pass over gravel-and-dirt Gazos Creek Road (which meets Middle Ridge Fire Road) and continue on Sunset Trail on other side.

1.3   Trailhead for connector trail. Continue straight on Sunset Trail toward Timms Creek Trail. Trail goes through redwood groves and over hills. Cross several bridges, one of them over West Waddell Creek.

3.9   At trailhead for Timms Creek Trail, make sharp turn right uphill, continuing on Sunset Trail (sign reads TO THE SUNSET TRAIL CAMP). *(FYI:* Just before crossing Berry Creek, notice the face in the redwood stump to the right of the trail.)

5.4   Cross Berry Creek. Trail begins to climb, then crosses ridge.

5.5   At turnoff to Sunset backpacking camp, continue straight on Sunset Trail to Berry Creek Falls Trail. Trail to the right leads to Sunset backpacking camp, not far from end of Gazos Creek Road, an access point off Highway 1.

5.6   Around a bend, you are now on Berry Creek Falls Trail. This is Golden Cascade (so named for gold sandstone earth that forms 20-foot slide beneath the falls). This is followed by the two cascades of Silver Falls, so that you have 0.1 mile of continuous waterfall. Follow trail down rock stairs right beside falls.

6.4   Berry Creek Falls.

6.5   Trailhead at bridge. Turn left over bridge toward Big Basin headquarters.

Hike Information

📞 Trail Contact:
Big Basin Redwoods State Park and California Department of Parks and Recreation, 21600 Big Basin Way, Boulder Creek, CA 95006 (831) 338–8860 or (831) 338–8861; www.bigbasin.org or www.parks.ca.gov

🕐 Schedule:
Open daily from 6:00 A.M. to 10:00 P.M.

💲 Fees/Permits:
$3.00 parking

❓ Local Information:
Santa Cruz County Conference and Visitors Council, 1211 Ocean Street, Santa Cruz, CA 95060 (831) 425–1234 or (800) 833–3494; www.santacruzca.org
San Lorenzo Valley Information, P.O. Box 31, Boulder Creek, CA; www.sanlorenzovalley.com

📍 Local Events/Attractions:
Santa Cruz Beach Boardwalk, 400 Beach Street, Santa Cruz, CA (831) 423–5590; www.beachboardwalk.com
Natural Bridges State Park, West Cliff Drive, Santa Cruz, CA (831) 423–4609
Seymour Marine Discovery Center, 100 Shaffer Road, Santa Cruz, CA (831) 459–3800

🛏️ Accommodations:
Camping in Big Basin: ReserveAmerica (Park-Net)(800) 444–7275; tent cabins: (800) 874–8368
Hostelling International Santa Cruz, Carmelita Cottages Beach Hill, 321 Main Street, Santa Cruz, CA (831) 423–8304
Chateau des Fleurs, 7995 Highway 9, Ben Lomond, CA (831) 336–8943 or (800)

291–9966; www.chateaudesfleurs.com
Merrybrook Lodge, 13420 Big Basin Way, Boulder Creek, CA (831) 338–6813; www.showhotel.com
Villa Montagne, 28495 Big Basin Way, Boulder Creek, CA (831) 338–2174

🍴 Restaurants:
Boulder Creek Brewery and Cafe, 13040 Highway 9, Boulder Creek, CA (831) 338–7882; www.bouldercreekbrewery.com
Scopazzi's Restaurant, 13300 Big Basin Highway, Boulder Creek, CA (831) 338–6441

🌲 Local Outdoor Retailers:
Bugaboo Mountain Sports, 1521 Pacific Avenue, Santa Cruz, CA (831) 429–6300
Outdoor World, 136 River Street, Santa Cruz, CA (831) 423–9555
REI, 1119 Industrial Road, Suite 1-B, San Carlos, CA (650) 508–2330; www.rei.com

👥 Hike Tours:
Big Basin Redwoods State Park and California Department of Parks and Recreation, 21600 Big Basin Way, Boulder Creek, CA (831) 338–8860 or (831) 338–8861; www.bigbasin.org or www.parks.ca.gov

Ⓝ Maps:
Big Basin Redwoods State Park and California Department of Parks and Recreation, 21600 Big Basin Way, Boulder Creek, CA 95006 (831) 338–8860 or (831) 338–8861; www.bigbasin.org or www.parks.ca.gov
USGS maps: Big Basin, CA

Now on Skyline to Sea Trail (uphill, with some flat areas and short descents all the way back to the start).

6.6 Trail passes over West Waddell Creek and follows creek uphill. (*FYI:* There are several old-growth trees on this trail.)

7.5 Continue straight on Skyline to Sea Trail as you pass trailhead for Timms Creek Trail. Trail now follows Kelly Creek.

8.1 Trail splits; take either one. Lower trail passes over creek and back; upper trail goes along ridge and passes through burned out base of tree.

8.3 Two trails rejoin. Continue east on Skyline to Sea Trail.

9.2 At trailhead, turn right to stay on Skyline to Sea Trail. This is also connector to Hihn Hammond Road. Other leg goes to Sunset Trail.

9.6 Turn left and pass over Middle Ridge Fire Road, continuing on Skyline to Sea Trail, downhill.

10.7 Take bridge, continuing straight back to park headquarters (right is Skyline–Hihn Hammond Connector).

11.0 Turn right back over bridge to start of hike. Past rest rooms, turn right between split-rail fencing to take Redwood Trail Loop, a great finale to the day. You pass great examples of a redwood circle (or fairy circle), redwood burls, the burned out Chimney Tree, the Father of the Forest, and the Mother of the Forest. (*FYI:* On Redwood Trail, notice the memorial to Andrew Hill, who helped to preserve these redwoods as parkland.)

11.6 Back at parking lot.

27 Castle Rock State Park

Overview: *Castle Rock Park is on one of the highest ridges in the Santa Cruz Mountains. The hike features great variety: cool, dark mixed forests, creeks and a seasonal waterfall, dry, manzanita-lined ridges, grassy hills, oak savannah and above all rock formations. The boulders come in amazing shapes with curves, crevices and caves. On weekends you will see climbers navigate their way up 90-degree rock faces with chalky fingers. The giant boulder that gives the park its name sits in high woodland toward the end of the hike. There are interpretive exhibits and scenic overlooks that show off the park's 3,661 acres and over 50 miles of hiking paths. Bring water (limited facilities) and dress in layers. If you are looking for a rewarding backpacking trip, try the three-day, 30-mile Skyline to the Sea Trail that starts at the trailhead for Saratoga Gap through Castle Rock and Big Basin redwoods ending at the sea by Año Nuevo, mostly downhill.*

County: Santa Cruz
Start: From the Saratoga Gap Trailhead in the Castle Rock main parking lot on Highway 35 (Skyline Boulevard)
Length: 6.1 miles
Approximate Hiking Time: 3 hours
Difficulty Rating: Moderate, with strenuous (but safe) passes over rock near sheer cliff

Trail Surface: Single- and some double-track dirt trail descending and ascending through woodland, scrub, and grassland to rocky paths, passing between giant boulders
Land Status: State park
Nearest Town: Los Gatos
Other Trail Users: Hikers only
Canine Compatibility: No dogs

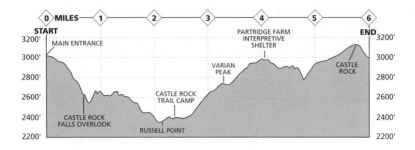

Getting There

By Car: From San Francisco, take Highway 280 south to Highway 92 west. Turn south on Skyline Boulevard (Highway 35). Travel approximately 25 miles to the junction of Highways 35 and 9 (Saratoga Gap). Continue on Highway 35 another 2.5 miles south past this junction. Look for the brown sign on the right to Castle Rock State Park. Turn right onto dirt and into the packed dirt parking lot.

By Public Transportation: There's no direct way to the park. Contact BART for more information (www.transitinfo.org). SamTrans info: (800) 660–4BUS; Santa Clara Valley Transportation Authority (408) 321–2300; www.vta.org.

Hike Description

The trail starts creekside in shady redwood, oak and bay woodland, with lichen-covered rocks against hillsides. Costanoan Indians used to hike this trail from their coastal villages to gather acorns produced by the park's plentiful oak trees. Rangers have found arrowheads and other faint traces of their travels through Castle Rock. After the Civil War, farmers and dairy cattle ranchers settled in the hills around Castle Rock.

Just over a wooden bridge on the Saratoga Gap Trail, the sound of running water crescendos. An observation platform allows you to stand at the top of Castle Rock Falls and watch the water drop approximately 60 feet down onto the rocks below. This seasonal waterfall is best after storms. The trail descends through oak scrub, with sticky monkey flowers and wild strawberries. In spring, the park offers a surprising display of wildflowers. Coral bells, chickweed, hedge wood rose, and California fuchsia decorate the banks of the creek. Dryer areas host lots of orange California poppies and Indian paintbrush, with blossoms like red sparklers that stay around through most of summer, providing perches for cabbage butterflies.

The trail rises again onto rocky ridges high above wooded ravines with spectacular views of the park and Pacific waters. A safety cable helps hikers climb a set of narrow stone steps on the cliff. This rite-of-passage brings you to Goat Rock. The pockets, patterns and protrusions of Goat Rock look like part of an alien landscape. The intricate patterns of thin ridges and small cavities in the sandstone called stone lace and honeycomb are the result of what geologists call "chemical weathering."

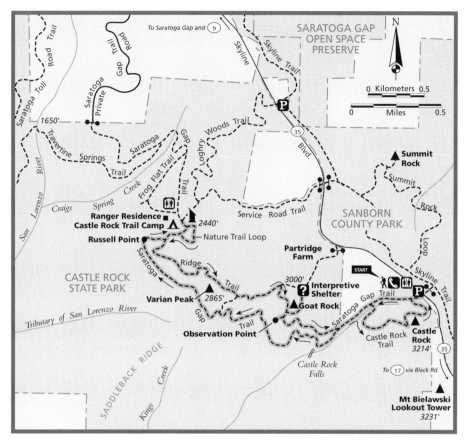

The rock formations are an intriguing sight in the park. Climbers often compare the Castle Rock boulders to those in Fontainebleau, France, though the Santa Cruz rocks, mostly less than 12 feet tall, are small in comparison. They use them to boulder, practice low-altitude maneuvers without the protection of a rope. If the boulder is high, the climbers place a landing pad on the ground below the rock. They have christened the rocks here with wonderful names like Duct Tape, the Domino, the Ecoterrorist, Parking Lot Rock, Ten Arrows, Deforestation, Lost Keys Boulder, and the Beak.

Continuing past Goat Rock, an interpretive shelter, though in disrepair, shares interesting information about park life and history. Back in the woods, you walk through the largest stand of black oak left in the Bay Area, which hosts a score of animals. Blanched boulders sit in groves of orange-red madrones against blue sky. The popular climbing rock, Castle Rock sits near the park entrance amongst trees at 3,214 feet on the highest rise.

Castle Rock became a park thanks to a boy named Russell Varian. Young Russell fell in love with the big boulders. He hatched the dream to preserve the land

Climbing Ethics

These are the Castle Rock Climbers Committee guidelines for conduct in the park for low-impact fun:

The tafone formations found on this sandstone are unique and must not be damaged. Avoid fragile formations.

Prevent erosion. Use only existing access trails, and avoid damaged or eroding slopes. Avoid dragging crashpads while bouldering.

Do not climb when the rock is wet, such as after a rainstorm. The rock, especially small features or footholds, will break when the rock is wet. A minimum three-day drying time is required after it rains.

Do not remove vegetation such as moss, trees, plants, or branches.

Do not tamper with the rock. Chipping, sculpting, gluing, "comfortizing," or otherwise defacing the rock is not accepted. Wire brushes are not acceptable for brushing holds.

Consider visual impact when using chalk. (Avoid long marks, unnecessary marks, and chalk graffiti.)

Avoid overcrowding rocks.

Observe all park rules and closures.

around them as a public park for all to enjoy. As an adult he took steps to buy the land himself and donate it to the state park system. But just as he was about to buy the land in 1959, he died. His friends finished the process, purchasing 27 acres. The state officially opened it in 1968 with 513 acres. Castle Rock continues to grow. The Sempervirens Fund bought acres connected to the southwest side of the park in 2000. When the state takes it over, Castle Rock State Park will increase by 50 percent with new trails and attractions on the Highway 9 side along the San Lorenzo River.

Miles/Directions

0.0 START at Castle Rock main parking lot on Skyline Boulevard. Follow Saratoga Gap Trail. Trail follows creek (flow is seasonal) and passes over wooden bridge.

0.2 Pass by trailhead to Castle Rock. (*Note:* End of the hike brings you back here and to the stone chateau for the hike's finale.) Continue on Saratoga Gap Trail. Pass memorial grove.

0.6 At split in trail, stay left, continuing on Saratoga Gap Trail. Fork on the right is return route on Ridge Trail.

0.8 Castle Rock Falls and observation platform. Trail descends through oak scrub. (*Note:* Poison oak bushes add color in the fall—and winter too, with bare red branches. Don't touch!) Then you find yourself climbing a moderate grade into sunshine where coyote brush, coffeeberry and manzanita plants grow healthy beside the trail. You get your first views of the lush hillsides and canyons. The trail follows the edge of the cliff. Back by the creek, another bridge takes you across where there is a resting bench. You go through some oak and madrone woodland and grassland. If you hear gunfire, do not be alarmed. The shots are echoing through the canyon from the Los Altos Rod and Gun Club. This noise, audible from the campground, has been a source of controversy since at least 1998.

1.3 Continue straight on Saratoga Gap Trail past the trailhead for connector path to Ridge Trail. **Option:** Turning on this path reduces hike to 3.1 miles.

1.5 There's a flat rock with a rocky shelf above it hanging over the cliff by the trail that would make a quiet place to drink water, admire the view, and dangle your feet.

2.0 Trail crosses over cliff (a cable gets you safely across). After 2.3-mile trailhead, trail heads west through madrone grove.

2.5 Pass posts 13 and 14 of nature trail, then come to trailhead for Ridge Trail. Before heading uphill, bear right, crossing over bridge toward picnic area. Follow trail to post 20. (*FYI:* Contact the park for the brochure on the self-guided nature trail, the Danny Hannavan Trail, memorializing a Boy Scout.)

2.6 At trailhead for Saratoga Gap Trail, turn left to campground and park office. Return to this spot, heading in the opposite direction on the self-guided nature trail loop.

2.7 Back at split for Ridge Trail and Saratoga Gap Trail. Bear left, ascending the Ridge Trail.

3.0 Trail leads to ridge (rock-climbing boulder to right).

3.8 Pass trailhead for connector trail, staying on Ridge Trail.

3.9 Emily Smith Bird Observation Point to the right. (**Side-trip:** Detour to the observation point to spot raptors, ravens, and vultures, stellar and western scrub jays, chestnut-backed chickadees, and wrentits, dark-eyed juncos, and sparrows. Be sure to bring binoculars.) Return to Ridge Trail to continue hike.

4.0 Continue on Ridge Trail.

4.1 Take trail 0.2 mile to Goat Rock.

4.3 Goat Rock. This is the backside of rock. Turn right and detour to scenic overlook. Return to Goat Rock.

4.4 At Goat Rock, continue on Ridge Trail toward parking lot. In about 0.1 mile, reach trailhead for interpretive shelter; turn left on path to shelter. Rock cave on right.

4.5 Interpretive shelter. Return 0.1 mile to Ridge Trail.

4.6 Turn left on Ridge Trail to parking lot. Take stairs down to watch climbers challenge face of Goat Rock. Pass other boulders. Trail once again opens up to views before heading back into woodland.

Hike Information

🕐 Trail Contacts:
Castle Rock State Park, 15000 Skyline Boulevard, Los Gatos, CA 95033 (408) 867–2952
Big Basin Redwoods State Park and California Department of Parks and Recreation, 21600 Big Basin Way, Boulder Creek, CA 95006 (831) 338–8861
Friends of Castle Rock State Park, (408) 621–8779; www.FoCRSP.org

🕐 Schedule:
Open daily from 8:00 A.M. to dusk

💲 Fees/Permits:
Parking $2.00 when kiosk attended; $5.00 for camping

❓ Local Information:
Los Gatos Chamber of Commerce, 349 North Santa Cruz Avenue, Los Gatos, CA 95033 (408) 354–9300; www.losgatosweb.com
Town of Woodside, 2955 Woodside Road, Woodside, CA 94062 (650) 851–6790; www.ci.woodside.ca.us

💡 Local Events/Attractions:
Thomas Fogarty Winery, 19501 Skyline Boulevard, Half Moon Bay, CA (650) 851–6777

🛏 Accommodations:
Camping (walk-ins): Castle Rock State Park, 15000 Skyline Boulevard, Los Gatos, CA (831) 338–8861
Hostel: Hidden Villa Hostel, 26870 Moody Road, Los Altos Hills, CA (650) 949–8648; www.hiddenvilla.org/
The Laurel Mill Lodge, 16770 Redwood Lodge Road, Los Gatos, CA (408) 353–5851

🍴 Restaurants:
Alice's Restaurant, 17288 Skyline Boulevard, Woodside, CA (650) 851–0303
Bella Vista Restaurant, 13451 Skyline Boulevard, San Mateo, CA (650) 851–1229
Bentleys, 2991 Woodside Road, Woodside, CA (650) 851–4988
Delizioso Delicatessen, 133 North Santa Cruz Avenue, Los Gatos, CA (408) 395–7737
The Mountain House Dinner and Cocktails, 13808 Skyline, Woodside, CA (650) 851–8541

🌱 Local Outdoor Retailers:
Outdoor World, 136 River Street, Santa Cruz, CA (831) 423–9555
REI, 1119 Industrial Road, Suite 1-B, San Carlos, CA (650) 508–2330; www.rei.com

👥 Hike Tours:
Castle Rock State Park, 15000 Skyline Boulevard, Los Gatos, CA 95033 (408) 867–2952
Big Basin Redwoods State Park and California Department of Parks and Recreation, 21600 Big Basin Way, Boulder Creek, CA 95006 (831) 338–8861

🅝 Maps:
Castle Rock State Park, 15000 Skyline Boulevard, Los Gatos, CA (408) 867–2952
Big Basin Redwoods State Park and California Department of Parks and Recreation, 21600 Big Basin Way, Boulder Creek, CA (831) 338–8861
USGS maps: Castle Rock Ridge, CA

5.0 At junction with Saratoga Gap Trail, cross bridge heading back toward the parking lot.

5.5 At trailhead for Castle Rock, turn right. Trail heads through thick Douglas fir forest.

5.8 Castle Rock. The trail leads around rock and becomes fire road width.

5.9 Turn left at trailhead for parking lot. Single-track trail heads downhill to starting point.

6.1 Back at parking lot.

28 Portola Redwoods State Park

Overview: *A hike in Portola Redwoods State Park takes you past an ancient 300-foot redwood tree and through first- and second-generation redwood forest and down shady paths under mixed evergreens lined with ferns and western azaleas. The ample creeks support crawdads and steelhead trout and are centerpiece to the stories of the old lumber days in the canyon. A nature trail guides you to details in the forest. Perhaps the best thing about Portola is that the crowds don't seem to gather here, so you may have the 18 miles of trails to yourself.*

County: San Mateo
Start: Parking area on the road to the Campfire Center
Length: 5.4 miles
Approximate Hiking Time: 2.5 hours
Difficulty Rating: Moderate
Trail Surface: Well-maintained dirt canyon trail

up and down the ridge, crossing streams; a nature trail and small stints on service road and main road
Land Status: State park
Nearest Town: La Honda
Other Trail Users: Equestrians
Canine Compatibility: Dogs on leash

Getting There

By Car: From San Francisco and the valley, take Highway 280 toward Redwood City. Take State Route 84 west to Highway 35 (Skyline). Turn left, heading south on Skyline for 7 miles, then turn left (west) onto Alpine Road. Go 3 miles, and turn left on Portola State Park Road. Stop at the park headquarters to pay the day-use fee, then continue past the office. Cross the bridge and take the first right toward the Campfire Center. Immediately on the right is parking. (If full, head back toward the park headquarters, turning right into the Tan Oak picnic area and park there.)

From the San Mateo Bridge, continue on Highway 92 to Highway 35 (Skyline), and turn left. Follow it to Alpine Road, and turn right. Follow directions above. For a long but historical route, following the original road to the Page lumber mill in Portola Park, from Palo Alto, take Page Mill Road up the hill. At the top of the ridge, it becomes Alpine Road. Cross Highway 35, staying on Alpine Road, and follow the directions above. (Note: Do not take the Alpine Road exit on Highway 280. It dead ends east of Skyline Boulevard.)

By Public Transportation: There's no direct way to the park. Contact BART for more information (www.transitinfo.org) SamTrans info: (800) 660–4BUS.

Hike Description

Within Portola's rugged basin, quiet trails cross Peters Creek and Pescadero Creek and curve and climb through the canyons under the foliage of redwoods, Douglas firs, live oak, madrone, and hazelnut trees. Sunlight drifts down through needles,

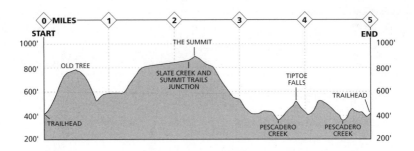

spotlighting the leaf-carpeted forest floor. Spiderwebs glisten after fog. Shelf fungi hang on logs and rocks. Mushrooms push up through the dark soil as banana slugs inch their way across the trails (see sidebar on page 200).

On the Old Tree and Slate Creek Trails, fallen every which way are dead tree trunks in varied states of decay. Stumps are a reminder of logging days, and charred bark tells the story of the many fires to sweep through the canyon, one every sixty years or so. The last blaze to clean up the basin was in 1989. It finally took down the park's Shell Tree on the Sequoia Nature Trail. It was 2,000 years old and had survived some thirty fires during its long life.

The Summit Trail takes you through woodland of mostly live oaks and madrones. False Solomon's seal, trillium and wood fern grace the hillsides. In spring, the huckleberry bushes flower. Reclusive winter's wrens and American robins hop through the brush. Steller's jays and ravens squawk from branches. Gray squirrels scamper up tree trunks. Downhill, it returns you to the redwood basin and the Iverson Trail.

The trail takes the name of the first local settler here, Christian Iverson, a Scandinavian immigrant who worked as a Pony Express rider and shotgun guard. Iverson lived on two parcels of land on Pescadero Creek in the 1860s in a hand-split redwood cabin. The cabin stood here for over 120 years until the Loma Prieta earthquake of 1989 finally brought it down. Planks piled beside the trail now serve as a memorial to the site. Iverson Trail also takes you to seasonal Tiptoe Falls, with water pouring over a six-foot shelf of rock.

On the Slate Creek Trail, you have the option of visiting the Page Mill site. Here, the men made shingles and also cut tan oak for use in the tanneries, where slabs of dried wood were pulverized and boiled in water to make liquid tannic acid. Redwoods now grow through what was once a mill platform or tramway.

The second growth did well in the wet basin, and the beauty of the area attracted San Francisco businessman, John A. Hooper. He bought the property and built himself a two-story summerhouse on Pescadero Creek around the turn of the twentieth century. In 1924, he sold 1,600 acres to his friends in the Islam Temple Shrine of San Francisco. They used it as a summer retreat until 1945 when the state purchased the parcel for a park. The visitor center and park office now occupy the Shriner's Recreation Hall. The Save the Redwood League donated more land to create the park of today, with over 2,800 acres.

Portola Redwoods State Park

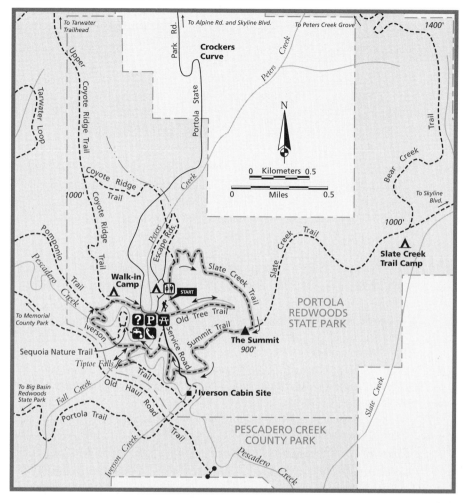

The campgrounds here are a great place to spend the night. If hiking with kids, the Sequoia Nature Loop makes a fun short hike. The $2.00 park map includes the guide for the nature trail and is worth buying. Backpack camps and many longer trails are available. Paths connect to Long Ridge Open Space Preserve and Pescadero Creek County Park. In spring and early summer, repellent to ward off mosquitoes is highly recommended. Before you leave Skyline Boulevard for the valleys below, visit Methuselah, another giant ancient redwood tree. The huge redwood is just off Skyline Boulevard on the east side of the road between King's Mountain Road and Highway 84.

Miles/Directions

0.0 START from parking area, walk toward Campfire Center until you see trailhead on the left. Turn left on Old Tree Trail.

0.3 Old Tree. (*FYI:* The Old Tree is 300 feet tall, 12 feet in diameter, and probably between 1,500 and 2,000 years old. Yet its shallow roots are only about 10 feet below the ground, connected to other trees in the area in a family system. It is among the tallest redwoods on the peninsula.) Turn around and head back the way you came.

0.5 At trailhead for Slate Creek Trail, turn right. The single-track trail goes uphill and over a seasonal creek.

0.9 Stay right on Slate Creek Trail.

1.8 At junction with Summit Trail, turn right on Summit Trail. (**Option:** Continue another 1.4 miles on the Slate Trail to check out the Page Mill Site.) Single-track trail becomes winding, with switchbacks and stairs. Past the water tanks, path widens to double-track and soon ends at service road.

2.6 Turn left on service road. It crosses Iverson Creek and curves past Iverson's Cabin Site.

3.0 At Iverson Trailhead, turn right. Pescadero Creek on the right.

3.6 Turn left to view Tiptoe Falls. Bear left to continue on Iverson Trail. Path follows the curve of the river.

3.9 Continue on Iverson Trail, taking the left fork. (**Option:** To shorten the hike by 1.1 miles, turn right to nature trail, then back to the car.) Cross bridge over Pescadero Creek. (*Note:* If visiting in winter or early spring, look for spawning steelhead trout in the creek.) On the other side, trail continues through redwood grove.

Old Tree Trail

Hike Information

🌿 Trail Contact:
Portola Redwoods State Park, 9000 Portola State Park Road, P.O. Box F, La Honda, CA 94020 (650) 948–9098; www.cal-parks.ca.gov

🕐 Schedule:
Open daily from 8:00 A.M. to dusk

💲 Fees/Permits:
Parking $3.00 per car when kiosk attended; maps $2.00

❓ Local Information:
Half Moon Bay Coastside Chamber of Commerce and Visitors' Bureau, 520 Kelly Avenue, Half Moon Bay, CA 94019 (650) 726–8380; www.halfmoonbay chamber.org
Town of Woodside, 2955 Woodside Road, Woodside, CA 94062 (650) 851–6790; www.ci.woodside.ca.us
La Honda Local Info, www.geocities.com/lahonda94020/listings.html
San Mateo County Convention and Visitors Center, www.sanmateocountycvb.com/

💡 Local Events/Attractions:
Apple Jack's Tavern La Honda, 8790 La Honda Road, La Honda, CA (650) 747–0331
Yerba Buena Nursery, 19500 Skyline Boulevard, Woodside, CA (650) 851–1668; www.yerbabuenanursery.com

🛏 Accommodations:
Camping: Portola Redwoods State Park, 9000 Portola State Park Road, P.O. Box F, La Honda, CA (650) 948–9098;

www.cal-parks.ca.gov or www.reserveamerica.com
Hostel: Hidden Villa Hostel, 26870 Moody Road, Los Altos Hills, CA (650) 949–8648; www.hiddenvilla.org
The Laurel Mill Lodge, 16770 Redwood Lodge Road, Los Gatos, CA (408) 353–5851

🍴 Restaurants:
Alice's Restaurant, 17288 Skyline Boulevard, Woodside, CA (650) 851–0303
Bentleys, 2991 Woodside Road, Woodside, CA (650) 851–4988
Boulevard Bar and Grill, 17285 Skyline Boulevard, Woodside, CA (650) 851–7444
Merry Prankster Cafe, 8865 La Honda Road, La Honda, CA (650) 747–0660

🌴 Local Outdoor Retailers:
Outdoor World, 136 River Street, Santa Cruz, CA (831) 423–9555
REI, 1119 Industrial Road, Suite 1-B, San Carlos, CA (650) 508–2330; www.rei.com

🚶 Hike Tours:
Portola Redwoods State Park, 9000 Portola State Park Road, P.O. Box F, La Honda, CA 94020 (650) 948–9098; www.cal-parks.ca.gov

Ⓝ Maps:
Portola Redwoods State Park, 9000 Portola State Park Road, P.O. Box F, La Honda, CA 94020 (650) 948–9098; www.cal-parks.ca.gov
USGS maps: Woodside, CA; La Honda, CA

4.2 Turn right at junction with Pomponio, staying on Iverson Trail.

4.3 At junction with Old Haul Road and Coyote Ridge Trail, turn right, continuing on Iverson Trail.

4.4 Iverson ends at park road across from Madrone picnic area. Turn right, walking a short distance along park road to park headquarters.

4.5 To the left of park headquarters, follow signs to Sequoia Nature Trail.

4.7 Stay to the right, remaining on Sequoia Nature Trail.

4.8 Cross footbridge and turn left at marker #8 to do the loop. At trailhead for Iverson, bear right toward marker #9.

5.0 Back at marker #8, bear left back the way you came, crossing the bridge and returning to visitor center.

5.3 Turn right on park road and walk beside it, crossing bridge the way you drove in.

5.4 Turn right onto road to Campfire Center, with parking area on the right.

29 Purisima Creek Redwoods Open Space Preserve

Overview: *Purisima is one of the gold nuggets in the bounty of the Midpeninsula Regional Open Space District. The trails in this 3,117-acre westernmost preserve take you through deep canyons under towering redwoods with creeks gurgling and cascading between rich banks of ferns and sorrel. They traverse grassy, oak-scattered hills and ridges with inspiring views. Some of these trails follow the old mill roads of Purisima's logging past. A moderately strenuous climb is an unavoidable part of almost any hike in Purisima, except the wheelchair-accessible Redwood Trail. Bring your own water, though you can find all other basic facilities at the trailhead.*

County: San Mateo
Start: From the North Ridge Trailhead on Skyline Boulevard (can start the same loop at Higgins Purisima Road off Highway 1 just south of Half Moon Bay)
Length: 9.9-mile loop
Approximate Hiking Time: 5 hours
Difficulty Rating: Moderate, with a 1,600-foot gradual ascent

Trail Surface: Well-maintained single- and double-track dirt trails descending into redwood canyons and ascending into mixed forest and to ridges with views
Land Status: Open space preserve
Nearest Town: Woodside/Half Moon Bay
Other Trail Users: Bicyclists and equestrians in summer only (hikers only on Soda Gulch)
Canine Compatibility: No dogs

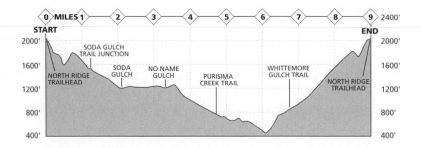

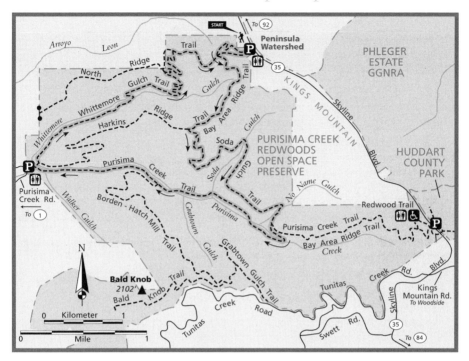

Getting There

By Car: From San Francisco, take Highway 280 south to Highway 92 west. Turn south on Skyline Boulevard (Highway 35). Travel approximately 4.5 miles. Look for the sign for Purisima, and turn right into the parking lot (parking for twenty cars). If you start the hike in Half Moon Bay, take Highway 1 1 mile south of Half Moon Bay, and turn left on Higgins Purisima Road. Drive 4.5 miles just past the short white bridge and before the road horseshoes onto Purisima Creek Road. The parking lot is on the left with room for ten cars.

By Public Transportation: There's no direct way to the park. Contact BART for details (www.transitinfo.org). SamTrans info: (800) 660–4BUS.

Hike Description

In Spanish, *purisima* means "the most pure," and this is one of those hikes that have a purifying quality. The Spanish named the creek and canyon to honor the Virgin Mary, and the park takes its name from the creek. The Purisima Creek and Soda Gulch Trails both have a meditative feel under the shadowy redwoods. Beside the flowing creek, several kinds of ferns prosper: sword fern, with serrated edges on its leaves (called pinnae); western wood fern, with spaced long pinnae; and the lacy bracken fern. The magic of the redwood trees is all around you. These ancient trees once dominated all of the Northern Hemisphere but are now limited to the coastal range between Monterey and southern Oregon, thriving on the cool, foggy sum-

Soda Gulch on the trail

mers and mild winters. Even in drought years, they collect the water they need by catching the moisture of the fog on their needles and letting it drip to the ground like a private shower (10 extra inches of water in summer). This is enough to feed their shallow roots that stretch wide beneath the ground. Walking these meandering trails makes a person grateful for the gift of this place to the people by the Midpeninsula Open Space District.

A grassroots effort by residents of the Portola Valley started the organization in 1972. They wanted to stop the development of million-dollar homes up on the pristine ridge of the Santa Cruz Mountains above them. They were able to purchase the land and secure an initiative on that year's ballot, and the voters of northwestern Santa Clara County and Southern San Mateo County approved the independent district. The movement continued with the acquisition of more properties, mostly along Skyline Boulevard. Today, the district manages over 46,500 acres of public land in twenty-six open-space preserves and continues to grow.

A great deal of the acreage was owned by lumber companies, which had been cutting down redwoods to sell for siding, fencing, and furniture from the gold rush up to 1970. A gift of $2 million from Save the Redwoods League helped the district to secure the land. After early loggers cut down the virgin growth, trees up to 20 feet in diameter and 1,000 years old, a forest of second-generation trees grew in their place. Workers, unknowingly at first, helped them along. They used controlled burns to singe away the undergrowth for easier access to the trees. Ironically the fire discouraged the growth of competition, making it easier for new redwoods to get started. The redwoods standing today are about one hundred years old. As you walk through Soda Gulch, you can see both burn stains on their trunks—redwoods withstand most fires—and painted bluish white lines around the trunks of trees that were marked to be cut but were saved by the acquisition of the park. These ghostly marks are a reminder of how tenuous the public hold on open space is, and that, as times change, we must remain vigilant to protect it.

Purisima's logging past is apparent in the big stumps of ancient redwoods that now host moss, mushrooms, insects, and other redwoods. Around the decay of a mother tree, often a circle of tall, straight, second-generation redwoods grow, sprouted from the roots of the original. These circles are called "fairy rings" or "family circles." There are wonderful ones on the Soda Gulch Trail. Some people consider these circles to be sacred places, spots for inspiration, meditation, or rejuvenation.

It took sixty years to cut down all the virgin growth within Purisima Canyon. Transportation of the lumber was difficult. Logs had to be "gulched out," cut into shingles, and taken over the steep canyon walls to Redwood City to be shipped to San Francisco. (That's how Redwood City got its name.) The easier route was to haul the lumber downhill to Half Moon Bay. The extensive labor it took to run the mills was expensive, so they only operated when the prices were high.

The first boom was after the gold rush, with everybody settling into the new Golden West. Loggers used handsaws and axes to fell trees. One giant redwood took them a week to cut down, according to the park brochure. Once cut, the oxen dragged the logs to the creek side mills down "skid trails," roads with greased logs across them to ease the movement of the giant logs. Mill workers then blasted the logs with dynamite to split them into manageable pieces. Once in the mills, powered by water wheels, they cut them into shingles.

The next big boom occurred after the Great San Francisco Earthquake of 1906. Most of the city burned to the ground from fires after the quake. By then, "donkey engines," machines that pulled a tree down easily to the mill, replaced the tired oxen. Steam power replaced the water wheels. The Borden and Hatch families

The Purchase of Purisima

When acquiring the land to create this park, the Open Space District discovered something odd. In 1900, *Collier's* magazine had a special promotion: buy a subscription and get a parcel of land in the Santa Cruz Mountains. People ordered the magazines and the deeds were handed out. They were mostly forgotten over time. When the district contacted the descendants of the *Collier's* readers, most didn't even know they owned the land. There was good news and bad news. The good news was the land was theirs. The bad news was they were liable for all the back taxes from 1900. Given the choice, most agreed to donate their parcels to the district for a tax break.

owned most of the mills in this area. Their original Borden-Hatch mill was located at the bottom of the canyon, close to the junction of Purisima Creek Trail and Whittemore Gulch Trail. Later it was moved up stream about a half mile. Then the two families went separate ways, forming their own businesses. You can see the clearing where their mills once stood, the Borden mill at the intersection of Grabtown Gulch and Purisima Creek, and the Hatch mill at the junction of No-name and Purisima Creeks.

There was dairy ranching here too, but today's scattered ranches are mostly horse ranches. You can see a couple in the western valley. At one time, there were hog farms as well.

Miles/Directions

0.0 START at parking lot for North Ridge and Harkins Ridge Trailheads. Go through gate to start hike on Harkins Ridge Trail (also Bay Area Ridge Trail). The first 0.5 mile is hikers only.

0.5 Junction with North Ridge Trail. Continue straight on Harkins Ridge Trail downhill on double-track dirt trail through mixed woodland. Views of Half Moon Bay and Pillar Point. *(Note:* Look carefully beyond Pillar Point for the white caps of Mavericks, the famous surfing spot.)

1.4 Trailhead for Soda Gulch Trail. Turn left onto single-track, hikers-only

Banana Slugs *(Ariolimax columbianus dolichophallus)*

Almost any walk through redwood forests includes stepping around these yellow, slimy creatures. Because of the banana slug's associations with the giant redwoods and its unique characteristics, Bay Area hikers have a great affinity for it. UC–Santa Cruz even declared the banana slug its mascot.

Some slug facts:

- The banana slug has few natural enemies.
- Its slime is anesthetic, a bit like novocaine.
- Slug slime can take away the sting from nettles.
- The banana slug has both male and female reproductive organs; in mating banana slugs cross-fertilize.
- It has a tongue with 27,000 teeth and rasps its food.
- A slug goes about .007 miles an hour.
- A slug can stretch out 11 times its normal length.
- Slugs mark their own scent so they can find their way home after dark.
- Banana slugs were a food source for the Yuroks Indians (Yuck!)

A banana slug on Dipsea Trail

Hike Information

Trail Contact:
Midpeninsula Regional Open Space District, 330 Distel Circle, Los Altos, CA 94022 (650) 691–1200; www.openspace.org

Schedule:
Open daily from 8:00 A.M. to dusk

Fees/Permits:
None

Local Information:
Town of Woodside, 2955 Woodside Road, Woodside, CA 94062 (650) 851–6790; www.ci.woodside.ca.us
Half Moon Bay Coastside Chamber of Commerce and Visitors' Bureau, 520 Kelly Avenue, Half Moon Bay, CA 94019 (650) 726–8380; www.halfmoonbay chamber.org

Local Events/Attractions:
King Mountain Art Fair, Labor Day week-end, 13889 Skyline Boulevard, Woodside, CA, www.kmaf.phc.net

Accommodations:
Camping: (walk-ins): Castle Rock State Park, 15000 Skyline Boulevard, Los Gatos, CA (831) 338–8861
Hostel: Hidden Villa Hostel, 26870 Moody Road, Los Altos Hills, CA (650) 949–8648; www.hiddenvilla.org/

The Laurel Mill Lodge, 16770 Redwood Lodge Road, Los Gatos, CA (408) 353–5851

Restaurants:
Bella Vista Restaurant, 13451 Skyline Boulevard, San Mateo, CA (650) 851–1229
Buck's Restaurant, 3062 Woodside Road, Woodside, CA (650) 851–8010
The Mountain House Dinner and Cocktails, 13808 Skyline, Woodside, CA (650) 851–8541

Local Outdoor Retailers:
Outdoor World, 136 River Street, Santa Cruz, CA (831) 423–9555
REI, 1119 Industrial Road, Suite 1-B, San Carlos, CA (650) 508–2330; www.rei.com

Hike Tours:
Midpeninsula Regional Open Space District, 330 Distel Circle, Los Altos, CA 94022 (650) 691–1200; www.openspace.org

Maps:
Midpeninsula Regional Open Space District, 330 Distel Circle, Los Altos, CA (650) 691–1200; www.openspace.org
USGS maps: Woodside, CA

trail, which leads into one of the deepest parts of the redwood forest and more mixed forest.

2.4 As you cross bridge over Soda Gulch, look to the right from the bridge at pile of roots, rocks, and mud (debris washed down into creek during heavy rain in 2000). Continue on Soda Gulch Trail.

4.0 Trailhead for Purisima Creek Trail, which splits. Take fork to the right. (**Option:** If you have two cars, park one at the trailhead for Purisima Creek and the Redwood Trail, and turn left at this junction for a 5-mile hike.) After crossing creek around a bend, you next cross No-name Creek. (Clearing is the site of Hatch Mill.) Cross Purisima Creek several times.

5.3 Pass trailhead for Borden Hatch Mill Trail, continuing on Purisima

Creek Trail. Path continues to follow creek.

6.3 Trailhead on Higgins Purisima Road. Half Moon Bay is about 5.5 miles away. Turn right and cross bridge onto Whittemore Gulch Trail. On the other side of bridge, go left. **Option:** You can shorten the loop to around 7 miles by turning right onto Harkins Ridge Trail. Ascend on Whittemore Gulch Trail, through redwoods, big-leaf maples, red alderberries, and Douglas firs. Trail zigzags uphill through chaparral. *(Note:* Watch out for poison oak. It's beautiful in the fall, but always keep your distance.)

8.5 Continue on Whittemore Gulch Trail straight, pass the bridge (crosses to North Ridge Trail).

9.1 Whittemore Gulch Trail dead ends at North Ridge Trail. Turn right.

9.6 Junction with Harkins Ridge Trail. Continue straight on North Ridge Trail.

9.9 Back at gate and parking lot.

Honorable Mentions:
The Northern Santa Cruz Mountains

E. Huddart County Park and Phleger Estate

The 1,232-acre Phleger Estate feels like a discovery, with no signs to mark the trailhead on Skyline Boulevard. The best access is through Huddart County Park (973 acres), near the town of Woodside. Both parks climb from the foothills up the Northern Santa Cruz Mountains. There are five picnic areas, three covered shelters, day and overnight camps, an amphitheater, and an archery club. Trails are popular with equestrians and runners. You can find family trails like Chickadee or long, expert loops through both parks climbing 1,900 feet and back. A great 9-mile loop starts at the Crystal Springs Trail in Huddart, joins the Richards Road, and turns on the Miramonte Trail to enter Phleger Estate. The Mount Redondo Trail meets Lonely Trail. The Lonely Trail takes you a few hundred feet below the Kings Mountain Fire Department and Skyline Boulevard. Richards Road takes you down quickly to the Skyline Trail and Crystal Springs Trail. Crystal Springs links to the hikers-only Dean Trail. It once more intersects with Crystal Springs Trail and returns you to the start.

To get to Huddart Park from Highway 280 in San Mateo County, turn off at the Woodside Road (Highway 84) exit. Turn west toward the town of Woodside. Drive approximately 1.5 miles through town. Turn right on Kings Mountain Road. Proceed up the hill to the main park entrance. Information: Huddart County Park, 1100 King's Mountain Road, Woodside, CA (650) 851–1210 or (650) 851–0326. Phleger Estate (650) 556–8642.

F. Wunderlich County Park

Meadows, woodlands, flowing creeks, and an early-twentieth-century horse stable are some of the features that make Wunderlich hiking fun. The 942 acres of steep mixed forest and grassland can be explored on a number of well-maintained loop trails, with sections following the old logging and ranch roads. You can combine it with hiking through Huddart Park or cross Skyline on its high ridge into El Corte de Madera Open Space Preserve. No bikes are allowed in the park, but equestrians frequent the trails.

The Alambique Trail passes the fine, large stable built by James A. Folger II (of coffee fame). The stable is still in operation here, though Folgers' elegant summer mansion has been moved. The Alambique Trail passes through redwoods and mixed woodland. At Alambique Flat, turn right onto the Oak Trail under the dappled shade of oak woodland, popular with birds. A left onto the Meadow Trail takes you to "The Meadows," an open grassland with hawks hunting for field mice and moles. With a right on Bear Gulch, you pass through a large-scale Douglas fir grove. Stay to your left at Redwood Flat for a shady, cool walk through second- and third-growth redwoods on the aptly named Redwood Trail. A right on Bear Gulch again brings you back to the start (about 5 miles).

The park takes its name from contractor Martin Wunderlich, who bought the land from the Folgers and deeded the acreage to San Mateo County for use as a park and open space. It is open daily from 8:00 A.M. to sunset.

To get there, use Highway 280. Turn off at the Woodside Road/Highway 84 exit. Turn west toward Woodside and past town about 4 miles. Turn right into the main park entrance. Wunderlich can also be accessed on Highway 35 (Skyline Boulevard). Information: Wunderlich County Park, 4040 Woodside Road, Woodside, CA (650) 851–1210.

G. Windy Hill Open Space Preserve

The first park of the Midpeninsula District is named for its distinctive, breezy, grass-covered hilltop. But within its 1,308 acres, it has a lot more than what you see from Highway 35. Besides its waving grasslands and spectacular views, you can find redwood, fir, and oak forests on the 12 miles of trails. Hamms Gulch, Eagle Razorback Ridge, and Lost Trail make an 8-mile loop. Kite flyers favor the ridge, and occasionally you may see a paraglider or remote control glider soaring above the eastern hills.

Windy Hill Open Space Preserve is located in the Town of Portola Valley. The main parking area is located on Skyline Boulevard (Highway 35), 2.3 miles south of Highway 84 (La Honda Road), or 4.9 miles north of Page Mill Road. Additional roadside parking is available along Skyline Boulevard. For access to the lower portion of the preserve, please park at Portola Valley Town Hall and follow the town trails to the preserve. Information: Midpeninsula Regional Open Space District, 330 Distel Circle, Los Altos, CA (650) 691–1200.

H. Russian Ridge Open Space Preserve

These 1,822 acres provide a wildflower show, one of the best in the area. Its blown-grass hillsides, numerous springs creating the headwaters of Mindego and Alpine Creeks, diverse plant life, and miles of forest edge make it a popular habitat for animals, including the elusive mountain lion. It's also one of the best South Bay parks for watching raptors. Red-trailed hawks, turkey vultures, Cooper's hawks, sharp-shinned hawks, and golden eagles all soar above the 8 miles of trails. You can extend your hike by crossing Highway 35 into little wooded Coal Creek Preserve (493 acres), one of the newest in the district, or cross Alpine Road into Skyline Ridge.

The parking area is located at the intersection of Skyline Boulevard (Route 35) and Alpine Road. Additional parking is located at the Caltrans Vista Point on Skyline Boulevard. You can reach Coal Creek Open Space Preserve from the vista point or further north along Skyline Boulevard at Crazy Petes Road. Coal Creek is also accessible to hikers, bicyclists, and equestrians from Alpine Road. Information: Midpeninsula Regional Open Space District, 330 Distel Circle, Los Altos, CA (650) 691–1200.

I. Skyline Ridge Open Space Preserve

Within 1,807 acres, you find ridge vistas, expansive meadows, a pond for nature study, a quiet lake frequented by migrating birds, and the David C. Daniels Nature Center, open on weekends. Ten miles of trails also offer views of Lambert Creek watershed, Butano Ridge, and Portola State Park. Two 1-mile trails are accessible to wheelchairs and baby strollers, circling Horseshoe Lake and Alpine Pond.

The preserve's entrance is located about one mile south of the intersection of Skyline Boulevard (Route 35) and Alpine Road. Equestrian parking is also available here. For convenient access to the nature center, park in the Russian Ridge Open Space Preserve parking lot, located at the corner of Alpine Road and Skyline Boulevard, and walk through the tunnel to the preserve. Information: Midpeninsula Regional Open Space District, 330 Distel Circle, Los Altos, CA (650) 691–1200.

J. Monte Bello Open Space Preserve

Aptly named, Monte Bello, Italian for "beautiful mountain," is one of the district's richest parks for wildlife and diverse ecosystems. Rolling grasslands, thickly forested canyons, inspiring vistas, and the most impressive riparian habitat in the Santa Cruz Mountains constitute the 2,782 acres. Fifteen miles of trails take you along Monte Bello Ridge and Black Mountain, from which you can view the whole Santa Clara Valley and Mount Hamilton. Through Stevens Creek Canyon, follow the flowing creek along the San Andreas fault, enjoying the shade of Douglas firs. From the Stevens Creek Nature Trail, you can see Mount Umunhum and Loma Prieta, the epicenter of the 1989 earthquake. By crossing Page Mill Road you can extend your earthquake study in Los Trancos Open Space Preserve on the self-guided San Andreas Fault Trail. With a Los Trancos brochure (available at park entrance or district office), this is a fascinating and educational walk, great for families. Trails also connect to Upper Stevens Creek County Park and down into Rancho San Antonio Open Space Preserve. The backpack camp at Black Mountain is a good first stop on a backpack trip from the valley to the coast.

The preserve's main vehicle entrance is on Page Mill Road, 7 miles west of Highway 280 and 1 mile east of Skyline Boulevard. Parking is available for 45 cars. Information: Midpeninsula Regional Open Space District, 330 Distel Circle, Los Altos, CA (650) 691–1200.

K. Upper Stevens Creek County Park

Madrone and Douglas fir forests, sunny south-facing grasslands, mixed chaparral of sage and manzanita, lovely shaded creekbeds, and the peak of Table Mountain (1,852 feet) await the hiker in this 1,095-acre Santa Clara County Park. About 11 miles take you through this wildlife habitat for deer, rabbits, bobcats, and raccoons.

Stevens Creek Park is located along Stevens Canyon Road and Mount Eden Road in the foothills between Saratoga and Cupertino. To access the park from Cupertino, take I–280 to Foothill Expressway. Follow Foothill Boulevard west three miles to the northern park entrance (Foothill Boulevard changes into Stevens Canyon Road as it crosses McClellan Road). From Saratoga, travel north on Highway 9 to Pierce Road. Turn onto Pierce Road and travel 1.8 miles to Mount Eden Road. Turn left onto Mount Eden Road and travel 1.5 miles to the south park entrance. Upper Stevens Creek Park can be accessed from Skyline Boulevard (Highway 35). A parking area is located approximately 3 miles south of Page Mill Road and 3.2 miles north of Highway 9. Upper Stevens Creek Park may also be accessed by foot, horse or bicycle from Stevens Canyon Road or the connecting Mid-Peninsula Open Space lands and trails. Public transit is available to Stevens Creek County Park. Information: The Stevens Creek County Park, 11401 Stevens Canyon Road, Cupertino, CA (408) 867–3654 (Stevens Creek County Park) or (408) 867–9959 (Upper Stevens Creek).

L. Rancho San Antonio Open Space Preserve and County Park

Combined, these two adjacent parks provide 3,965 acres of oak woodland, cool fern-banked ravines beside babbling creeks, soft open meadows full of lupine, poppies, and blue-eyed grass, hillsides of chaparral, and ridge tops that open to views. Along the extensive 23-mile trail system you can create short family loops and longer, more challenging routes, including a climb to the top of Black Mountain (2,800 feet). A great family feature is Deer Hollow Farm, a working farm with pigs, goats, sheep, chickens and other animals housed in turn-of-the-twentieth-century ranch buildings (open Tuesday through Sunday from 8:00 A.M. to 4:00 P.M. (650–903–6331). Rancho San Antonio adjoins Hidden Villa Ranch, a nonprofit environmental education facility that has miles of lovely trails in 1,600 acres open to the public, and a hostel with a lodge and cabins (650–949–8650). The main entrance to Hidden Villa is located on Moody Road in Los Altos Hills. From Highway 35 (Skyline Boulevard), you have to hike through Monte Bello Open Space 2.9 miles. Direct access is on Cristo Rey Drive off Foothill Boulevard, off Highway 280.

The preserve's main vehicle entrance is located in Rancho San Antonio County Park. Take Foothill Boulevard south from I-280, turn immediately right on Cristo Rey Drive and continue for about 1 mile. There are several vehicle parking lots, and an equestrian parking lot. The 85-car parking area in the northwest lot is the trailhead for the preserve. The secondary vehicle access is from Rhus Ridge Road. It can be reached from I-280, taking the El Monte Road exit west and turning left onto Moody Road just past Foothill College. Travel 0.5 miles and turn left on Rhus Ridge Road, then go 0.2 miles to a 5-car parking area adjacent to a gate and equestrian stile. Horse trailers are not allowed to park here. Information: Midpeninsula Regional Open Space District, 330 Distel Circle, Los Altos, CA (650) 691–1200.

M. Long Ridge Open Space Preserve

Ten miles of trails explore canyons of majestic oaks, grassy knolls with sculpture garden-like rock outcroppings, some of the best views in the area, and the rich, cool environment around Peters Creek in the Pescadero watershed. Within the 1,946 acres you also find an old farm site and apple orchard and trails through mixed evergreen forests of madrone and Douglas fir. Part of the Bay Area Ridge Trail, the pathways also connect to Skyline Ridge, making a continuous 13-mile trail from Russian Ridge to the north and south through Saratoga Gap Open Space to Sanborn-Skyline County Park.

For Long Ridge Open Space Preserve, parking is available at the Upper Stevens Creek County Park–Grizzly Flat parking area on Skyline Boulevard, about 3 miles north of Saratoga Gap (Highways 9 and 35). Parking for both preserves is available in the parking area at the intersection of Highway 9 and Skyline Boulevard. Saratoga Gap Open Space Preserve is located at the northern corner of this junction. Information: Midpeninsula Regional Open Space District, 330 Distel Circle, Los Altos, CA (650) 691–1200.

N. Pescadero Creek County Park

In these four adjacent parks, you and your hiking boots pass creeks blackened with natural tar, trek under giant evergreens dedicated to World War I soldiers, meander in peaceful old growth redwood forests, and walk through land donated by Sam McDonald, the descendant of a slave.

This vast parkland of 7,400 acres is comprised of Pescadero Creek, Memorial, Heritage Grove, and Sam McDonald parks. Trails go through old- and new-growth redwood forests and mixed woodland of Douglas fir, California wax myrtle, tan oak, madrone, California bay laurel, big-leaf maple, and oak trees. Pescadero and Alpine Creeks both contain steelhead trout and silver salmon. You can choose from short family loops like the Mount Ellen Nature Trail or many longer loops. In Pescadero Creek Park, many of the trails follow old logging roads. The 5-mile Tarwater Trail Loop gives you a sense of the park's history as the site of natural gas and oil deposits.

Heritage Grove, accessible through Sam McDonald County Park, is thirty-seven glorious acres of towering old-growth redwoods. You can reach it directly through an entrance on Alpine Road.

The entrance to Pescadero Creek is through Memorial Park or Sam McDonald Park. To get to Memorial, take either Highway 101 or 280 (280 is closer) to Highway 84 west toward La Honda. A half mile past the village center in La Honda, turn left on Pescadero Road. Look for the park entrance about 6 miles down the road. From Highway 1, take the coast highway to Pescadero Road (between Highway 84 and Año Nuevo). Go east on Pescadero Road 11 miles to the park entrance. For the entrance to Sam McDonald, turn west on Highway 84 off Skyline Boulevard (Highway 35). Turn left on Pescadero Road to the entrance on the right.

The entrance to Pescadero Creek is through Memorial Park. From 101 or 280: Take Highway 84 west of La Honda. Turn left ½ mile past village center in La Honda on Pescadero Road. The Park entrance is on Pescadero Road about 6 miles from turn off. From Highway 1: Take coast highway to Pescadero Road about 11 miles to the park entrance. Information: San Mateo County Parks and Recreation, 455 County Center, 4th Floor, Redwood City, CA (650) 363–4020.

Mount Diablo and Las Trampas Foothills

What makes this area unique is its mountain and the hillsides that separate each valley into cities and towns. Mount Diablo is a symbol of home for people who live at its base in the San Ramon Valley or along the Antioch/Oakley line and in between.

Coming toward the mountain from Highway 24 at sunset, Mount Diablo turns crimson. In the morning, it seems to rise with the sun. With the subtlety of California seasons, Diablo becomes a meter. In winter, the rolling green slopes reign majestically over the little city of Danville to the west and Clayton Valley to the north. Billowing clouds cover its peak. Revealed after a storm, the crest has turned white for a day or two in the odd cold front that sifted snow down past the 3,849-foot summit. Summertime, the golden mountain under California sunshine shows off its clumps of fine oaks in contrasting green. Fire is a danger in the fall to the dry savanna, and every few years, charred and smoldering hillsides start the process of reseeding and recovery. The Las Trampas hills across the valley present lush eastern slopes crowded with oak trees. Its western hills of rock and nappy chaparral roll on into canyons, separating Contra Costa and Alameda counties.

Twelve million years ago, Mount Diablo and the Las Trampas Ridge were under a vast ocean. As the Earth's plates moved past each other along the San Andreas fault line, the land buckled, and a tough slab of volcanic rock rose up. The softer sediments around it washed away, forming the valleys around what we now call Las Trampas and Mount Diablo. Geologists suspect the mountain is still rising as landslides reshape it from time to time. Seashells are still readily visible among the serpentine and sandstone rocks on Las Trampas ridges.

For the hiker, these ridges offer miles of trails and mountains to climb from numerous directions. On the way up, visitors can see tumbling waterfalls, scamper up huge boulders with caves and contours, and visit historical sites, like the old coal and sand mines at Black Diamond. On Las Trampas, you can visit the home of playwright Eugene O'Neill and walk the hills as he did while writing *Long Day's Journey into Night*.

There are fields of orange poppies. Wild mustard turns whole hillsides yellow. Red Indian paintbrush and lavender lupine add bursts of color, and California sagebrush perfumes the air with herb and spice. Lizards do push-ups on sunny rocks as crickets chirp the rhythm. Despite the cattle grazing that still goes on in parts of the parks, there's a lot of wildlife inhabiting these hills, and spotting them is always a treat. You can picnic in Bollinger Canyon or camp in Rock City. At the peak of Diablo, visit a nature center, stargaze at night, or just admire expansive 360-degree views. Drop a bicycle off at the top, and after hiking to the summit, enjoy a thrilling ride down the twisting main road. At the top of Las Trampas, follow the ridgeline for miles or, with a permit, drop down into watershed land and keep heading west.

30 Las Trampas Regional Wilderness

Overview: *A trek in 3,882-acre Las Trampas Wilderness promises you windswept ridges, rugged jigsaw rock outcroppings, dusty valleys, moist spring-fed ravines, and trails curving through sunny grasslands and under the shade of pungent bay trees. This hike also includes a couple of great calf-burning, heavy-breathing 1,000-foot climbs up Rocky Ridge and the Devil's Bowl. But you are rewarded with breezy, expansive views of the San Francisco Bay, the city skylines, the distant Delta, and majestic Mount Diablo and its valleys. Look carefully around you and see the abundant wildlife of Las Trampas today and remains of animals, plants, and geological features that tell a story that's about twenty-five million years old.*

County: Contra Costa
Start: Bollinger Canyon Staging Area
Length: 6.5-mile loop
Approximate Hiking Time: 3.5 hours
Difficulty Rating: Moderate to difficult due to two long uphill sections
Trail Surface: Paved path to single- and double-track, dirt trails through grassland, some woodland, and along ridge, with two long uphill treks and downhill on a narrow winding dirt path through chaparral
Land Status: Regional wilderness
Nearest Town: San Ramon
Other Trail Users: Equestrians on all but Sycamore Trail; mountain bikers on Upper Trail and Elderberry Trail
Canine Compatibility: Dogs on leash around staging area and in watershed

Getting There

By Car: From the San Francisco–Oakland Bay Bridge, take I–580 east. In Castro Valley, take Crow Canyon Road north to Bollinger Canyon Road. Turn left and drive 4.5 miles to the end of Bollinger Canyon Road and into the Bollinger Canyon Staging Area parking lot on the left. From I–680, take the Crow Canyon Road exit, heading west to Bollinger Canyon Road. Turn right and go to the end.

   By Public Transportation: For more information, contact AC Transit Trav-Info (510–817–1717; www.actransit.org).

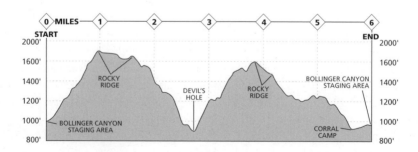

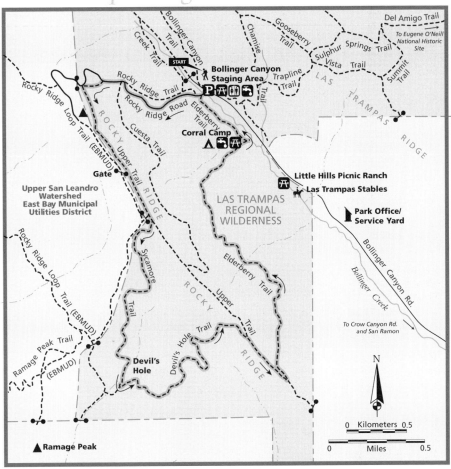

Hike Description

On the upper trail, near the 2,024-foot summit of Las Trampas, you follow the spine of Rocky Ridge and come upon the "Indian" wind caves. Sculptured by the wind and rain and colored by many lichen species, they are ideal for quiet, breezy contemplation and for fossil exploring. You can easily find rocks with seashell fossils. There are literally millions of them embedded in Rocky Ridge, dating back to the Pliocene era some twelve million years ago when Las Trampas was the Pacific Ocean floor.

Scattered and harder to find are the bones and teeth of fossil mammals representing mostly a fauna around nine million years old. Paleontologists say these remains are abundant in these hills. They have found "elephant teeth," from a four-tusked mastodon, primitive camel teeth belonging to four different species of camel, and most commonly the teeth of an extinct three-toed horse. Also here were primitive rabbits, honey badgers, archaic beavers, hyaenoid dogs, and wolverine-like carnivores. Believe it or not there were also rhinoceroses, ground sloths, and mammoths in the Pliocene Las Trampas.

These species disappeared rather suddenly without explanation, like dinosaurs. Blame cold weather? Human overkill? No one knows. Myths in early America told of strange and monstrous creatures that stalked the western forests, but none were found. (Thomas Jefferson, who himself named the ground sloth *Megalonyx*, asked Lewis and Clark to look for them. They had no luck.)

There may be no sloths here anymore (except the ones with you), but there are plenty of modern descendants and new four-legged and feathered residents in the accommodating grassland, chaparral, woodland, and ravine habitats of Las Trampas. On the downhill serpentining Sycamore Trail you may suddenly hear the movement of garter snakes or king snakes slithering into the sagebrush out of your way (kings are efficient rattlesnake killers; neither are dangerous to humans). Western fence lizards may stare at you from rocky perches around the Devil's Hole. You may spot jackrabbits bounding into manzanita scrub, squirrels clinging to the trunk of a big-leaf maple or buckeye tree, or California voles peaking out of burrows in the grassland. Don't be surprised if deer leap through the woods in the afternoon. Overhead, you are bound to see the rare and protected golden eagle, hawks, and turkey vultures soaring and swooping in and around the canyons. Ample rodents are prey to the healthy birds.

In the ravines, especially during wetter months, you are bound to see salamanders and newts, to hear if not see the chirping of Pacific tree frogs, the croaking of endangered red-legged frogs, and the bellow of a western toad.

Though you may not see some of the more elusive and wilder inhabitants here, keep your eyes open for tracks and droppings of cougars, bobcats, badgers, weasels, ringtail cats, opossum, coyote, and red and gray fox, among others. At dusk, Oregon juncos, finches, red-winged blackbirds, and hummingbirds call it a day and bats punch the clock, skittering about the sky hunting for insects along the creeks and springs.

Hunted to extinction were bison, pronghorn antelope, grizzlies, and abundant elk that indirectly contributed to the naming of Las Trampas. Meaning "the traps" in Spanish, the name honored the native Miwok Indians' method of driving elk and deer into the steep box canyons for easier hunting.

Three Spanish brothers tried out that method when they acquired a grant in 1844 for 17,600 acres that included much of Las Trampas. The Romero brothers, Inocencio, Jose, and Mariano, according to tradition symbolized their ownership of the rancho by pulling up grass, breaking branches of trees and shrubs, and throwing stones in four cardinal directions. Inocencio built a home on the land, while the others kept tabs of their landholding from afar.

But the brothers had bad fortune, losing their Rancho San Ramon El Sobrante (El Sobrante means "surplus land") in 1858, when their lawyer, entrusted with the grant documents, left for Georgia and died. Without the documents, they had

View from Upper Trail on the way to Elderberry Trail

trouble proving their claim in the new U.S. courts. The government soon took over the land, and in an 1868 sales transaction, divided it like a giant quilt and sold parcels to families whose names remain familiar in the East Bay: Wm. S. Cull (Canyon), Joshua Bolinger (Canyon), A. Stone (Valley), J. M. Tice (Valley), and Ned Hunsaker (Canyon). The last was sheriff and tax collector.

In the 1970s, a group of kids organized a group called SANE (Save American's Natural Environment) and succeeded in causing the transfer of $26,000 earmarked for "recreational-development" toward acquisition of new lands. The kids, with the help of Jane Helrich, science coordinator for the Mount Diablo School District, forced the limitation of picnic facilities and raised $2,500 to purchase more land for Las Trampas Wilderness. Families started slowly selling off hundreds of acres of ranchland to be protected. Among the parcels purchased was 480 acres in 1966 from the Nordstroms of department store fame.

A geologic feature on Rocky Ridge and down Elderberry Trail worth noticing is the Bollinger fault line. The largest of the many faults traversing Las Trampas Wilderness, it played a crucial role in the uplift of Rocky and Las Trampas ridges. It's probably not active today, say geologists, though some earthquakes have been recorded in its vicinity by the University of California Seismographic Station. You can observe it in the break in the slope near the crest of Rocky Ridge. Also, look for green areas and seeping mountain springs. They are a dead giveaway for the fault. Because of the particular combination of sandstone and mudstone in the area, water collects and drains along the fault contact. In August and September, these areas are very apparent, appearing like oases among the baked golden grasslands, dead thistles, and fall weeds.

Wildflowers are prevalent everywhere in the springtime. One of the best displays is in rocky, steep-walled Sedum Ravine on Sycamore Trail. In mid-April the red delphinium is spectacular there, and a couple of weeks later the yellow-flowered stonecrop forms bright floral mats in the upper part of the ravine. Even in dry late summer, red California fuchsias grow picturesquely around rock outcroppings along Rocky Ridge.

There is no drinking water available until you reach Corral Camp near the end of your hike. Bring plenty!

Miles/Directions

0.0 START at Bollinger Canyon Staging Area. Take paved Rocky Ridge Road by walking through the gate at northwest end of parking lot. **Option:** If you can't stand cement, the Rocky Ridge Trail, a single-track dirt trail, starts to the right of the road and mostly parallels the road.

0.4 Rocky Ridge Trail meets Rocky Ridge Road; junction with Cuesta Trail. Take Rocky Ridge Trail to the right; single-track dirt path through grassland.

0.7 Junction with Upper Trail. Rocky Ridge Trail meets road again (with closed gate ahead). Trailhead for Upper Trail is on the left. Turn left onto single-track trail. It becomes double-track on the ridge.

1.0 Gate to East Bay Municipal Utilities District watershed land. Permit required (see fee information on next page). **Option:** If you have the time and a permit, detour through the gate to the ridge 0.2 mile, where you can see the first series of wind caves. No permit? Don't want to risk it? There are more on upper Sycamore Trail.

1.5 Junction with Sycamore Trail. Turn right on single-track dirt path. Upper San Leandro Reservoir in distance; also San Francisco and Sutro Tower.

1.8 Wind caves up on ridge to the right. *(Note: Beware of poison oak.)*

1.9 Sycamore Trail leads up and over rocky ridge. Sycamore trailhead on west side. Trail heads to the right, and continues with series of hairpin turns. *(Note: If you are susceptible to poison oak, wear long pants and bring Technu; scrub and rinse well at Corral Camp.)*

2.7 Sycamore Trail crosses creek. Cattle path crosses grasslands; stay on trail. Across creek is trailhead marking Sycamore Trail.

2.8 Junction with Devil's Hole Trail. Turn left on double-track dirt path and start climbing. The 1,000-foot ascent is moderate but continual. Opens up to San Ramon Valley view at top.

Hike Information

Trail Contacts:
East Bay Regional Park District Headquarters, 2950 Peralta Oaks Court, P.O. Box 5381, Oakland, CA 94605 (510) 662–PARK or (925) 837–3145; www.ebparks.org/parks/lastram.htm **EBMUD hiking info** (925) 287–0459 **Las Trampas Stables** (925) 838–7546

Schedule:
Open year-round daily from 5:00 A.M. to 10:00 P.M. unless otherwise posted

Fees/Permits:
No fee. EBMUD hiking permit is $2.00 per day or $10.00 per year (925) 287–0459

Local Information:
San Ramon Chamber of Commerce, 2355 San Ramon Valley Boulevard, Suite 101, San Ramon, CA 94583 (925) 831–9500; www.sanramon.org **San Ramon Community Center,** 12501 Alcosta Boulevard, San Ramon, CA (925) 973–3200; www.ci.san-ramon.ca.us

Local Events/Attractions:
Crow Canyon Gardens, 10 Boardwalk, San Ramon, CA (925) 820–7471; www.mudds.com/gardens.htm **Forest Home Farms,** 19953 San Ramon Valley Boulevard, San Ramon, CA (925) 973–3281 **Lindsay Dirkx Brown Art Gallery,** 12501 Alcosta Boulevard, San Ramon, CA (925) 275–2300

Accommodations:
Camping at Corral Camp (510) 562–2267 **Evergreen Bed and Breakfast,** 9104

Longview Drive, Pleasanton, CA (925) 426–0901 **Purple Orchid Inn, Resort and Spa,** 4549 Cross Road, Livermore, CA (925) 606–8855; www.purpleorchid.com **Residence Inn by Marriott,** 1071 Market Place, San Ramon, CA (925) 277–9292

Restaurants:
Hop Yard Alehouse and Grill, 470 Market Place, San Ramon, CA (925) 277–9600; www.hopyard.com **Mudd's Restaurant,** 10 Boardwalk Place, San Ramon, CA (925) 837–9387; www.mudds.com **Pasta Pomodoro,** 146 Sunset Drive, San Ramon, CA (925) 867–1407; www.pasta pomodoro.com **Rolls Deli Cafe,** 3191 Crow Canyon Place, Suite B, San Ramon, CA (925) 866–8440

Local Outdoor Retailers:
Any Mountain, 490 Market Place, San Ramon, CA (925) 275–1010 **The Walking Company,** Stoneridge Shopping Center, 1 Stoneridge Mall, Pleasanton, CA (925) 460–0586

Hike Tours:
East Bay Regional Park District Headquarters, Oakland, CA 94605 (510) 662–PARK; www.ebparks.org/parks/lastram.htm

Maps:
East Bay Regional Park District Headquarters, Oakland, CA 94605 (510) 662–PARK; or www.ebparks.org/parks/lastram.htm **USGS maps:** Las Trampas Ridge, CA

4.0 Trail ends; junction with Upper Trail to Elderberry Trail. Turn right on double-track dirt Upper Trail.

4.4 Upper Trail ends. Turn left on double-track dirt Elderberry Trail.

6.1 Corral Camp. Continue on Elderberry Trail left, northwest to Bollinger Canyon Staging Area.

6.5 Back to Bollinger Canyon Staging Area and parking lot.

31 | Donner Canyon to the Falls Trail

Overview: *Mount Diablo has a forbidding image to many, in part because of its name and the legends it has inspired. While creeks may dry in summer, the reality is that there are always cool canyons, and even on hot days cool breezes cross upper elevations. On the less-traveled north side of Mount Diablo are many shady, wooded canyons, and because they're protected from the sun most of the day, Donner, Back, and Mitchell Canyons have among California's best wildflower shows. The seasonal waterfalls in the upper reaches of Donner Canyon, especially in Wild Oat Canyon along Falls Trail, are spectacular.*

County: Contra Costa
Start: Donner Canyon Road Trailhead at the end of Regency Drive
Length: 5.9 miles
Approximate Hiking Time: 4 hours
Difficulty Rating: Moderate to strenuous
Trail Surface: Double-track, dirt trail creekside through oak woodland and grassland starts off flat and rises steadily into scrubland, turning onto a narrow, single-track trail with some rocks to traverse and waterfalls to view; return trip is downhill on mostly double-track, dirt paths by another narrower stream

Land Status: State park
Nearest Town: Clayton
Other Trail Users: Equestrians and mountain bikers on Donner Canyon and Back Creek trails
Canine Compatibility: No dogs allowed

Getting There

By Car: From the San Francisco Bay Bridge, take Highway 580 to Highway 24. From Highway 24, go north on Highway 680. Take the first exit, Ygnacio Road, to Walnut Creek. Turn right onto Ygnacio at the end of the off-ramp, at light. Stay on Ygnacio 7.5 miles. You will enter the town of Clayton. Turn right on Clayton Road; go 2.5 miles. Turn right onto Marsh Creek Road. Turn right onto Regency Drive and take it until it dead-ends. There is plenty of street parking. Head south down the embankment to the Donner Canyon Road Trailhead.

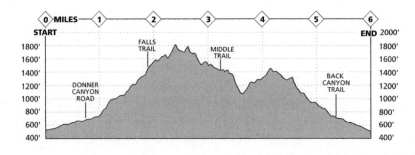

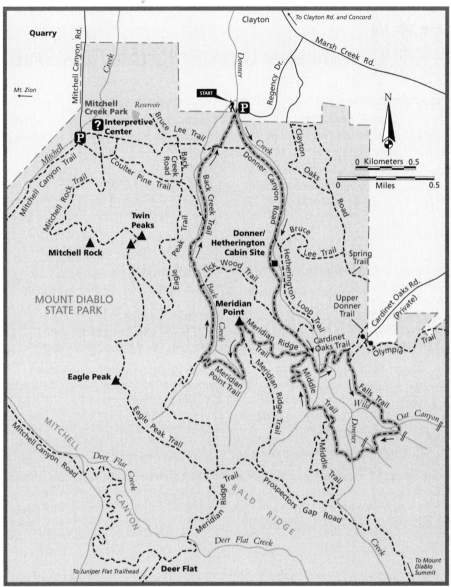

Hike Description

Looking at the dry and golden northeast ridges of the Diablo foothills, it's hard to imagine the glistening tree-lined creek that starts your hike and the lush, cool canyons that exist a few miles up this trail, but they are there. The Cardinet and Falls Trails feature in wet months and after rains a satisfying series of sparkling waterfalls, the largest dropping 25 feet.

It also seems unlikely driving endless Ygnacio Valley Road into the suburbs of Clayton that you can truly get away from it all up here, but parking in the neighborhood at the end of Regency Road, you can say farewell to modern civilization for a couple of hours. When you are feeling more at peace, your heart pumping from the steady uphill, your senses cleansed by the sight of wild mustard in the grasslands, the smell of wild sage, and glimpses of scurrying squirrels and lizards, you can turn around and look down from a reassuring lofty viewpoint upon the town of Clayton and its surroundings, assessing all in a Thoreau-like manner.

This hike is still a little-known treasure, being on the quiet north side of the summit and on land that for many years was in recovery from the raging flames that swept over it in the fire of 1977. Ignited by a lightning strike at 6:30 in the evening on August 1, it burned a total of 6,000 acres of Mount Diablo State Park from Clayton to Blackhawk. One account says that from San Francisco, Mount Diablo looked like a volcano. Along the trail you can still see charred bark on trees and manzanita with young, healthy red branches twining around dead, gray limbs like biomorphic modern art. But nature gave rebirth to these canyons beautifully, with cottonwoods and plants around the creeks more lush, and the coulter forest (especially along Meridian Trail) growing wider and taller than before.

Wildflowers are abundant in upper Donner and Wild Oat Canyons, surrounding you on the narrow Falls Trail in colorful Wizard of Oz clumps. Besides the usual purple California lupine, orange poppies, and fiery, red Indian paintbrush, you see the yellow Mount Diablo daisy, pink mosquito-bills, delicate white milk maids, powder blue grand hound's-tongue, and hundreds of species of herbs, grasses, and shrubs. In the late winter, the pink blossoms of the manzanitas awaken to the approaching spring.

Both Donner Creek and Back Creek flow most of the year, down to a trickle in golden summer. Not long ago, and for hundreds of years, they provided a peaceful hunting camp for Miwok Indians. In the 1860s and 1870s—the area's heyday—the surrounding valley became home to gold rush farmers, miners, and loggers. Joel Clayton, an English immigrant, discovered coal north of Clayton and founded his namesake town in 1857. Men also worked the copper mines on Mount Zion, then called Pyramid Peak, where you see the scars of later quarries. By 1864, the miners had blasted a tunnel 1,100 feet in length, piercing down over 270 feet below ground to the veins of ore. Despite the new commerce, Donner and Back Canyons remained fairly quiet and peaceful. The mines lived a short life, and many of the little cities that formed around them became ghost towns by the 1880s.

Not much else is on the records until well into the twentieth century, except Sunday picnics in nearby Mitchell or Pine Canyons and one hush-hush operation in the hills. The trails above Donner didn't exist then, but during Prohibition days, one path did go as far as Big Spring Trail, where someone operated a successful still; historians don't know who that hearty entrepreneur was. Otherwise, the rest of the north face of the mountain was little used.

The only remains of a structure on your hike are those of the Donner (Hetherington) Cabin along the picturesque creek surrounded by oak savanna that begins your hike. It was built around the 1930s. An eccentric landowner, Mrs. Donner (not related to the Donner Party) bought the land sometime in the 1940s. The creek and canyon take her name. She raised sheep on the land and planted a small grove of fruit trees. Apple, pear, and plum trees still thrive upslope right of the trail. Mrs. Donner sold the building to the local sheriff's department as a hunting lodge, with permission to shoot on her private land. They built the concrete slab you see, most likely as the base of a fire pit for roasting fresh venison.

A waterfall along the Falls Trail in April during a dry spring

The Hetheringtons purchased the land in 1952, changing the focus of the place radically. Members of a horticulture society, the San Francisco couple used the cabin for weekend retreats and spent time planting native species around the area to restore the overgrazed land. In an effort to preserve the canyon, they sold it in 1972 at a reasonable price to the Save Mount Diablo (SMD) organization, who turned Donner, Back, and Mitchell Canyons over to the state park. In 1976, a young ranger and a founder of SMD working his way through college made his isolated home in the pleasantly furnished Donner–Hetherington cabin. With no electricity or phone, Bob Doyle lived happily there for eight years, until the prospect of marriage and other career opportunities pulled him away. Still an active environmentalist today, he says those years in that wild place personified and embedded in him his passion for studying and conserving nature.

In 1939, horse and nature lover George Cardinet moved to Concord from Oakland. George, a life member of the Concord–Mount Diablo Trail Ride Association, immediately fell in love with the north face, finding it more peaceful and rugged than the heavily traveled south side. Wanting to improve the riding and hiking on the mountain, he and his horse began hauling tools up into the canyons to construct new trails. Among them were the Falls and Cardinet trails, dedicated to George around 1986. Mr. Cardinet at ninety-two years old has been maintaining these trails for sixty years and is still at it.

Post–World War II, the Lone Star Co. began quarrying operations up on Mount Zion, removing any resemblance of a pyramid from old Pyramid Peak. Still in operation today, the gravel quarried there, made from imbedded sea floor rock, is the main source of road fill in the Bay Area.

In the 1970s, subdivisions were spreading toward the mountain as the population of the area again grew rapidly. BART opened lines to interior Contra Costa County in 1972, adding to the growth pressure. The open space and the mountain itself were in danger. But thanks to SMD, it's here for us to enjoy. Still in existence, the organization has been instrumental in increasing open space on and around the mountain from the original 6,788 acres to more than 81,000 acres today.

For variations to this hike, double-back on the Donner Canyon Road and have a picnic in the grasslands (cuts a mile off). If hearty and you've got the time, climb another 2 miles up Prospectors Gap Road to North Peak Trail to the Devil's Pulpit, the Devil's Elbow, and the Mount Diablo summit (3,849 feet).

There are no facilities on this hike, so bring plenty of water, and be prepared to make friends with a tree, if need be.

Miles/Directions

0.0 START at end of Regency Drive (it dead-ends at a waterway), and walk south. *(Note:* Be careful going down the embankment.) Donner Canyon Road Trailhead ahead. Trail runs perpendicular to Regency, following Donner Creek.

0.1 Pass trailhead to Bruce Lee and Back Creek Trails to Mitchell Canyon

Hike Information

Trail Contacts:
Mount Diablo State Park Headquarters, (925) 837–2525; ranger's office (925) 837–6119
Mount Diablo Interpretive Association, P.O. Box 346, Walnut Creek, CA 94596 (925) 927–7222; www.mdia.org
Mitchell Canyon Information Center, 96 Mitchell Canyon Road, Clayton, CA 94517 cal-parks.ca.gov

Schedule:
Open daily year-round from dawn to dusk

Fees/Permits:
None

Local Information:
Clayton Business and Community Association (925) 672–2272; www.94517.com
City of Clayton City Hall, 6000 Heritage Trail Clayton, CA 94517 (925) 673–7300; www.ci.clayton.ca.us

Local Events/Attractions:
Chronicle Pavilion at Concord Amphitheatre, 200 Kirker Pass Road, Concord, CA (925) 363–5701; www.chroniclepavilion.com
Dean Lesher Regional Center for the Arts, 1601 Civic Drive, Walnut Creek, CA (925) 943–SHOW; www.dlrca.org
Lindsay Wildlife Museum, 1931 First Avenue, Walnut Creek, CA (925) 935–1978

Accommodations:
The Farm House at Clayton, 7 Alef Court, Clayton, CA (510) 672–8404

Kim Dubois, 15 Malibu Court, Clayton, CA (415) 672–4400
Diablo Mountain Inn, 2079 Mount Diablo Boulevard, Walnut Creek, CA (510) 937–5050; www.diablomountaininn.com
The Secret Garden B&B, 1056 Hacienda Drive, Walnut Creek, CA (925) 945–3600 or (800) 477–7898

Restaurants:
Ed's Mudville Grill, 6200 Center Street, Clayton, CA (925) 673–0333; www.edsmudvillegrill.com
Skipolini's Pizza Garden, 1535 Giammona Drive, Clayton, CA (925) 672–1111

Local Outdoor Retailers:
Big 5 Sporting Goods, 1630 Mount Diablo Boulevard, Walnut Creek, CA (925) 932–4196
Nor-Ski and Sports, 1661 Botelho Drive, Walnut Creek, CA (925) 287–8025
REI, 1975 Diamond Boulevard, Suite B-100 (Willows Shopping Center), Concord, CA (925) 825–9400

Hike Tours:
Mount Diablo State Park Headquarters (925) 837–2525
Mount Diablo Interpretive Association, P.O. Box 346, Walnut Creek, CA 94596 (925) 927–7222; www.mdia.org

Maps:
Mount Diablo Interpretive Association: www.mdia.org/parkmap.htm
USGS maps: Clayton, CA; Diablo, CA

Road; stay on Donner. Ahead above are Mount Diablo foothills. *(Note: Donner Canyon can be very muddy in winter, but that's a good sign for waterfalls.)* Pass Bruce Lee Trail and split at Clayton Oaks Road. Stay right on Donner Canyon Road. *(FYI:* Check out the "Bowl Tree," carved out by fire.)

0.8 Single-track path to Donner Cabin historical site; detour to left by creek. Continue on Donner Canyon Road to Cardinet Oaks Road.

1.2 Pass Tick Wood Trail. Donner Canyon Road starts steady, moderate ascent.

1.4 Top of ridge; views of Clayton, Mount Diablo foothills, northernmost part of San Francisco Bay.

1.5 Trail dead-ends. Go left on Cardinet Oaks Road toward Olympia Trail (though you will be taking Falls Trail before that, around 0.4-mile). Trail crosses creek. Head uphill again after creek; moderate climb.

1.9 Turn right on Falls Trail. *(Note:* Steep, single-track Falls Trail is strenuous climb—narrow ridge sections and some rocks to high-step. Watch for poison oak.) As trail crests, waterfalls become visible. First fall sometimes drops more than 25 feet. Depending on season, you may cross three branches of creek several times. Ridge drops off dramatically to right. Moderate hiking beyond. Trail heads deeper into canyon.

3.1 At Middle Trail, go right (sign reads TO MERIDIAN TRAIL 0.53 MILE)

3.7 Turn left uphill on Meridian Ridge Road.

4.2 Take Meridian Point Trail toward Back Creek Trail, crossing Back Creek.

4.7 Trail dead-ends on double-track Back Creek Trail; turn right, heading north.

5.1 Pass Tick Wood Trail; stay on Back Creek Trail. Trail follows Back Creek.

5.4 Stay right on Back Creek Trail back to where it meets Donner Canyon Road (trail left leads to Mitchell Canyon Visitor Center and Ranger Station).

5.9 Back Creek Trail meets Donner Canyon Road and start of hike on Regency Drive just ahead.

32 | Black Diamond Mines Regional Preserve

Overview: *You have your choice of 65 miles of trails in this 5,036-acre (and growing) preserve that features vegetation and wildlife of all kinds and an amazing history of the people that lived and worked here from the Bay Miwok Indians to the coal miners of the 1850s and the sand miners of the 1940s. This hike will pass through two old mining town sites, Somersville and Nortonville, past many mine openings, and the Rose Hill Cemetery. BRING A FLASHLIGHT. You can explore airshafts for the old coal-mining tunnels and check out "Jim's Place," a mysterious underground dwelling. You hike through areas of grassland and mixed evergreen forest. Black Diamond is the northernmost location of Coulter pine, black sage, and desert olive. Springtime hosts abundant wildflowers. A hundred species of birds have been spotted here too, so you may want to bring binoculars. They'll come in handy for the ridge-top views of the bay and the Central Valley as well. Leave time before or after your hike to tour the underground mining museum and the Hazel-Atlas Mine that supplied sand for the Hazel-Atlas Glass Company of Oakland from the 1920s through the 1940s.*

County: Contra Costa
Start: Parking lot for Black Diamond Mines Regional Preserve
Length: 5.2-mile loop
Approximate Hiking Time: 3 hours (allow 4 to 5 hours if you are taking the tour of the Hazel-Atlas Mine)
Difficulty Rating: Moderate, with a few strenuous uphill sections
Trail Surface: Footpath is dirt and sandstone, widening on Black Diamond Trail and Nortonville

Trail to allow for bicyclists; the end of Black Diamond Trail is paved service road, which becomes dirt footpath again on Coal Canyon Trail
Land Status: Regional preserve
Nearest Town: Antioch
Other Trail Users: Equestrians and mountain bikers allowed on some trails
Canine Compatibility: Leashed dogs permitted (unleashed in open areas okay)

Getting There

By Car: From the San Francisco–Oakland Bay Bridge, take Highway 80 east to Highway 4 (or take Highway 24 to 680 north to Highway 242 to Highway 4 east). Follow Highway 4 to the Somersville Road South exit in Antioch. Drive south on Somersville Road (toward the hills). The first parking lot for the Black Diamond Mines Regional Preserve, just past the kiosk, gives access to the park office and interpretive center. To start the trail, drive to the upper parking lot at the end of the road. Follow the signs to the Hazel-Atlas Mine.

By Public Transportation: Take your bike on BART to the Pittsburg/Bay Point Station. It is an 8- to 9-mile bike ride to the park entrance. Turn right on Bailey Road. Turn left on West Leland Road. Turn right on Somersville Road to the

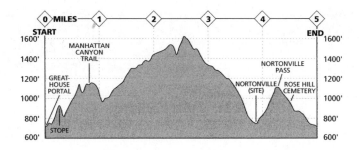

park entrance. For more information, contact BART (510–817–1717; www.transit info.org/BART) or Tri-Delta Transit (925–754–4040; www.trideltatransit.com).

Hike Description

Trail starts at the old Somersville town site, meandering through sandstone towers, manzanita, black sage, and other chaparral. It opens up to grassland with scattered oaks and views. Shaded again through pines and oak woodland, it follows the canyon to the Nortonville town site, opening up again over the hill to the Rose Hill Cemetery and back down to the parking lot.

By hiking in the Black Diamond Mines Regional Preserve, you travel through a time machine. Your first stop is California circa 1772. The Miwok Indians lived in this area for thousands of years. With the arrival of Spanish, Mexican, and American settlers in 1772, the Miwok way of life was rapidly destroyed. Californians have come to associate the East Bay with its golden hillsides in summer. But those grasses are nonnative, brought by the Spanish in hay and seed for cattle. In 1772, an indigenous bunch grass grew on these hills, green year-round (look for original bunch grass in shadier areas).

The next stop on the time travel is circa 1855. This preserve was once the largest coal-mining district in the state, helping to transform its economy. The Mount Diablo coal field, in operation from 1855 to 1902, gave birth to five prospering towns around twelve major mining sites: Nortonville, Somersville, Stewartville, Judsonville, and West Hartley. The Black Diamond Mine produced the weakest grade of coal: lignite (or subbituminous coal), crumbly, dull, and high in sulfur. But it was still cheaper than the stuff bought in Europe that had to travel by ship around South America and up the coast. Taken out of the Antioch Valley by train, the coal was used to run steamships, steam locomotives and to heat post–gold rush homes in the San Francisco Bay Area, Sacramento, and Stockton. Better grade coal found in Washington State eventually put Black Diamond out of business, but not before the area prospered. It is likely that the mines influenced the location of both the seat of Contra Costa County (which at the time included Alameda County) in Martinez and the once capital of California in nearby Benicia.

Below ground are some 100 miles of mining tunnels that produced 4 million tons of coal, amounting to $20 million during its heyday. And all this work was completed

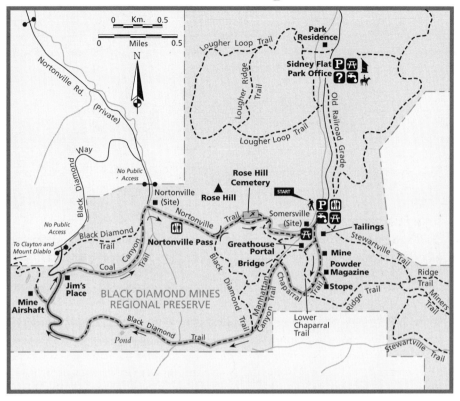

with simple equipment, by hand. Hard-hats weren't yet invented. Men and boys (starting at eight years old) worked twelve-hour days together in the mines.

Conditions in the mines were hard and dangerous. The "rooms" from which the coal was extracted were up to 600 feet long and no higher than the thickness of the coal seam, sometimes as low as 18 inches. And, of course, there were accidents.

Next to what is now the parking lot, you find remains of the Independent Mine (a 710-foot shaft). In 1873, an attached boiler room exploded, killing two men and blowing parts of the boiler a quarter mile away.

Living was tough, too. Babies died in epidemics, women in childbirth, and men of disease from years in the mines. Some were buried in Rose Hill Cemetery.

Despite the hardships, immigrant families flocked to the area. In the 1870s and 1880s, the town of Nortonville was the largest in Contra Costa County, with over 1,000 residents, a hotel, two churches, five general stores, a school, many private homes, and popular saloons. That was until the good church-going folks of Somersville drove the bars back to Sydney Flat, where the park kiosk is today.

The next stop is circa 1922. The ghost towns of Somersville and Nortonville are suddenly active again. Along with coal in the abandoned mines was high-grade silica sand. Marvin Greathouse, owner of the Somersville mine, put it back in oper-

View from Black Diamond Trail

ation in 1922 to supply sand used in glassmaking by the Hazel-Atlas Glass Company in Oakland (later bought out by Kerr). The Nortonville mine supplied the Columbia Steel Works in Pittsburg with foundry (casting) sand. Unlike coal mining, all access to the underground sand mines was through adits, horizontal passages rather than vertical. Some of the mining methods, like the "room and pillar," were the same, but now miners had carbide and electric cap lamps. Silica dust, fatal in high concentrations, still made the work difficult and dangerous. Competition from Belgian glass and the closing of the steel foundry ended the sand mining in 1949. But by that time, more than 1.8 million tons of sand had been mined.

Tour participants take a 400-foot walk back into the mine to see mine workings, the office of the shifter (mine boss), ore chutes, and ancient geological features.

A hike in Black Diamond Regional Preserve today leads you to mine openings, mounds of tailings (residue of the mining process), old dwellings, deserted town sites, railroad beds, and a cemetery, amidst a variety of native and exotic plant life. Notable among the latter are several tree species introduced by the coal miners, including the black locust, pepper tree, almond, eucalyptus, and tree of heaven. Two rare animal species dwell here—the black-shouldered kite and the Alameda striped racer. On the recommended hike, you walk through the sites of Somersville and Nortonville. The buildings are gone, stripped or moved to nearby cities, a couple serving as the park office. But memories haunt the hills.

You are welcome to explore the tailings for treasures such as petrified wood and town artifacts, but anything you find must stay in the park. The visitor center and mining museum in the Greathouse Portal and the Hazel-Atlas Mine tour are must-sees. The museum contains artifacts from the towns as well as examples of petrified wood, different types of coal, and great old photos of the towns and their people. Look for these names again when you reach the Rose Hill Cemetery.

"Don't call it a cave; it's a mine," one of the rangers may tease you during the Hazel-Atlas Mine tour. Hard hats, flashlights, and even jackets are provided. Rangers water down the interior regularly to keep dust down. If you really want to go back in time, look carefully in the sand walls. You can see fifty million-year-old petrified shrimp fecal matter, a reminder that this was once ocean floor. Tours start every hour from noon to 4:00 P.M. on Saturdays and Sundays. You can arrange a tour for an organization on weekdays by calling ahead (925–757–2620).

If you are hiking here on weekdays, don't be surprised to see modern-day miners at work. The Office of the Interior sponsors inspections of abandoned mines all over the country, either to reintroduce coal production or, in the case of Black Diamond, for tourism. Mines are regularly checked and maintained for safety as well.

On the Chaparral Loop, you can see the powder magazine, a small excavation used to store explosives, and the stope, a huge chamber blasted out of sandstone by miners extracting rock for glassmaking. Farther up the Chaparral Trail is a really pretty part of the hike. A narrow footpath is shaded by red-barked manzanita and thicket, oak and short pines. Beware of poison oak. The trail's floor becomes sandstone. Because of its softness, people have carved initials and dates into some of the stones. Call them what you will: graffiti, vandalism, or modern-day petroglyphs. For walking, it grips well except when there's loose sand or leaves.

The Manhattan Canyon Trail, shaded by oaks, may have received its name from the days when the city of Pittsburg was called New York on the Pacific. The post office refused the town permission to use the name (as well as the spelling for the Pennsylvania city). Black Diamond Trail, a wider trail, requires a steady climb into grassland, but rewards you with the sight of gently rolling hills and scattered oaks. At the top, views open north to the valley and west to Martinez, the bay, and the Marin Headlands. On a breezy day, the wind is strong up here.

On Coal Canyon Trail, "Jim's Place" may trigger your imagination. No one knows exactly who lived here, so you can make up your own story. This narrow trail takes you into a wonderful shaded canyon, through a grove of young pines, following a creek bed on your left. Look here for hunks of petrified wood. Mounds of tailings remind you that miners walked here daily to go to work in 1860, and that you are passing by several closed and abandoned mines.

At the bottom of the canyon, the trail is sandwiched between two tall rock faces with a pit at the bottom, site of the Nortonville Mine. The town would have stood just ahead. It's hard to believe, looking at the open space, that here was once the largest town in Contra Costa County.

With a half-mile climb, smelling wild flowers in spring, wild anise in late summer and fall, you pass over a ridge of Rose Hill to the Protestant burial ground. Folks of other religions are buried elsewhere. Go through the gate to explore the supposedly haunted graveyard. Before the park service became caretaker, vandalism took its toll here. There are over two hundred plots; many are missing markers. To keep more from being stolen or broken, descendants and volunteers knocked tombstones down and cemented them into the ground. Rangers are slowly restoring the headstones.

You have a great view here of the Somersville site. Imagine a thriving town in that basin, a stark but serene existence with great comradery born of an isolated community and shared tragedies. Today, you see picnic tables and signs of a well-loved park. Head down the hill back to the parking lot to end this many-faceted hike.

Miles/Directions

0.0 START by park road at parking lot for Black Diamond Mines Regional Preserve. *(Note:* It is the only source on the hike, and it can get hot in the summer.) Follow signs to visitor center and Hazel-Atlas Mine. Pass mound of tailings on the left. At Greathouse Portal, which houses museum and visitor center, take stairs just to the right to begin hike. Turn left toward Hazel-Atlas and Chaparral Loop Trail.

0.1 Hazel-Atlas Mine, where you meet for tour. (Note railway used to haul coal to main railroad that steamed into Antioch, one of three trains that served the mines.)

0.2 Powder magazine, used to store explosives.

0.3 Stope (chamber blasted out of sandstone by miners extracting rock for glassmaking).

0.4 Turn right to continue on Chaparral Loop Trail. **Option:** Ridge Trail to the left leads to Stewartsville, an alternative loop.

0.8 Before bridge, turn left on Manhattan Canyon Trail, which dead-ends at Black Diamond Trail.

1.0 Turn left on Black Diamond Trail, and proceed uphill.

2.1 Pond on left.

2.5 Black Diamond Trail becomes paved Black Diamond Way.

2.9 Take short detour to the left on Cumberland Trail. Go about 0.1 mile to air shaft. (It's on the left before the electric wires tower.) *(FYI:* The air shaft, once 150 feet deep and reached here by a short tunnel, was used to keep a coal mine ventilated and free from dangerous gases. The marks left by miners' picks are still evident on the excavation sides.) Return to Black Diamond Way the same way you came and continue hiking north.

3.1 Look for trailhead to Coal Canyon Trail. Turn right onto narrow dirt footpath.

3.2 Jim's Place. Follow signs to the right of trail. Continue on Coal Canyon Trail.

3.8 Covered hole of old vertical Nortonville Mine. Ahead is Nortonville town site.

3.9 Turn right onto the Nortonville Trail and climb the hill.

4.6 After passing over ridge of Rose Hill bear left to cemetery gate. Go through cemetery and head downhill toward parking lot. Below is what used to be town of Somersville.

5.2 Arrive back at parking lot.

Hike Information

🐾 Trail Contacts:
Black Diamond Regional Preserve, 5175 Somersville Road, Antioch, CA 94509–7807 (925) 757–2620
East Bay Regional Park District Headquarters, 2950 Peralta Oaks Court, P.O. Box 5381, Oakland, CA 94605 (510) 662–PARK; www.ebparks.org/parks/black.htm

🕐 Schedule:
Open daily year-round from 5:00 A.M. to 10:00 P.M. unless otherwise posted

💲 Fees/Permits:
Free on weekdays or when the kiosk is unattended; $4.00 per car on the weekend; $1.00 per dog; $3.00 per person for the Hazel-Atlas Mine tour

❓ Local Information:
Antioch Chamber of Commerce, 301 West Tenth Street, Antioch, CA (925) 757–1800; www.antioch-coc.org/index.htm
City of Antioch/City Hall, Third and H Streets, Antioch, CA; mailing address: P.O. Box 5007, Antioch, CA 94531–5007 (925) 779–7000; www.ci.antioch.ca.us/

💡 Local Events/Attractions:
Black Diamond Regional Preserve concerts, Saturday nights in summer, 7:00 to 9:00 P.M.; parking $7.00 per vehicle
Descendants Day in Black Diamond, third weekend in May; www.ebparks.org/events/byloc/black.htm
Antioch Lynn House Gallery, 809 First Street, Antioch, CA 94509 (925) 779–7018; www.ci.antioch.ca.us/civic_arts/overview.htm
Prewett Family Waterpark and Community Center, 4701 Lone Tree Way, Antioch, CA (925) 776–3070; www.dwetmore@ci.antioch.ca.us

🛏 Accommodations:
Best Western Heritage Inn, 3210 Delta Fair Boulevard, Antioch, CA (925) 778–2000; fax: (925) 778–2000
Brentwood Oaks Bed and Breakfast, 1850 Arabian Lane, Brentwood, CA (925) 634–0378; brentwoodoaks.com/
Camping: Star Mine Group Camp Area or Stewartville Backpack Camp in Black Diamond Mine Preserve ($5.00 per night per person), reservations: (510) 636–1684

🍴 Restaurants:
Humphrey's on the Delta, 1 Marina Plaza, Antioch, CA (925) 778–5800
Schooners Grille & Brewery, 4933 Cougar Peak Way, Antioch, CA (925) 757–6228

🎒 Local Outdoor Retailers:
Foot Locker, County East Mall, 255 Somersville Road, Antioch, CA (925) 757–3537

🚶 Hike Tours:
Hazel-Atlas Mine tours, every hour from noon to 4:00 P.M. on Saturdays and Sundays through November (closed December and January). Tours are strictly limited to ages seven and up. To make weekend reservations, call (510) 562–2267 (Alameda County), (925) 676–0192 (Contra Costa County), or (925) 373–0144 (Livermore); www.ebparks.org/new.htm#MINE

🗺 Maps:
East Bay Regional Park District Headquarters, Oakland, CA 94605 (510) 662–PARK; www.ebparks.org/parks/
USGS maps: Antioch South, CA; Clayton, CA

33

Rock City to the Summit

Overview: *Mount Diablo, the once sacred mountain of the Miwok Indians, continues to be sacred to today's Bay Area hikers, mountain bikers, equestrians, and nature lovers. It is truly the pride of Contra Costa, its silhouette reproduced on local company logos and county stationery. Ask any longtime resident of the area and you'll hear stories of summer camping in Juniper or picnicking near Sentinel Rock, taking a springtime Sunday drive up Mount Diablo Scenic Road, or sledding down sparkling white slopes after one of those rare and wonderful winter snowstorms. The state park and surrounding foothills offer much to see and do year-round. On this hike, you can watch rock climbers, scramble up a few boulders yourself, or search for ancient ocean fossils at Rock City; bird and butterfly watch and enjoy a hearty oak-laurel and gray pine forest on the Juniper Trail; identify wildflowers on the Summit Trail; barbecue at any of a number of picnic areas on the way up (there are fifty in the park); learn about Diablo and Contra Costa history, geology, and wildlife at the Summit Museum; and best of all, take in breathtaking views of the Pacific Ocean and of the snow-crested Sierras from the observatory tower at the 3,849-foot peak (bring binoculars). Exploring Diablo makes for a great day, though be prepared with plenty of drinking water, layered clothing, a hat, and sunscreen. It can be very hot in summer, muddy in winter, and the temperature varies up the mountain.*

County: Contra Costa
Start: Rock City Trailhead north of the Rock City parking and picnic area
Length: 8.5 miles
Approximate Hiking Time: 4 hours
Difficulty Rating: Moderate to strenuous, with a vertical climb of 2,885 feet to the top of Mount Diablo
Trail Surface: Single- and double-track, dirt

trails through grassland and woodland, with one riparian section by Mountain House Creek; trail crosses over paved road several times and includes a short walk over a paved parking lot
Land Status: State park
Nearest Town: Danville
Other Trail Users: Equestrians
Canine Compatibility: Dogs on leash

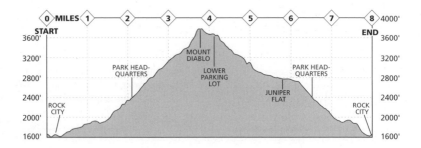

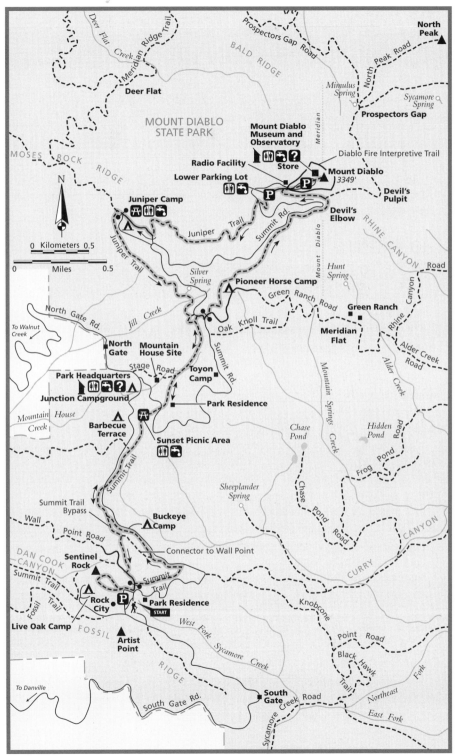

Getting There

By Car: From the San Francisco Bay Bridge, take Highway 580 to Highway 24. From Highway 24, go south on Highway 680. Exit at El Cerro Road. Past a stoplight it becomes Diablo Road. Continue straight on Diablo Road; pass Diablo Country Club. Turn left on Mount Diablo Scenic Boulevard. Signs read TO ATHENIAN SCHOOL (a boarding school on the right-hand side of the street) and TO MT. DIABLO STATE PARK SOUTH GATE ENTRANCE. This becomes the South Gate Road once in the park and winds its way up the mountain. Pay the entrance fee at the kiosk, get a map and information, and proceed to Rock City. Turn left into the Rock City camping and picnic area. Keep going until you see a street veering uphill to your left with a sign that reads TO BIG ROCK, SENTINEL ROCK AND WIND CAVES. Turn left and proceed to parking lot at the end. Walk north to the end of the parking lot to start your hike on the Rock City Trail.

Hike Description

According to Miwok Indian mythology, Mount Diablo was once an island surrounded by water. From this island the creator Coyote and his assistant, Eagleman, made the world. Mol-luk (Condor-man) lived on the north side of Mount Diablo. His wife, the rock on which he roosted, gave birth to Wek-wek (Prairie Falcon-man). With the help of his grandfather, Coyote-man, Wek-wek created the Indian people, providing them with "everything, everywhere so they can live." Though stories vary slightly from tribe to tribe, all felt Mount Diablo was sacred. And you may feel this way too as you trek the 2,000 feet up to the summit over undulating grasslands, by rugged rock outcrops, and through abundant blue oak, valley oak, and coast live oak, from which the Bolbon, the Miwok tribe living closest to Mount Diablo, gathered their main staple of acorns.

Geologically speaking, you go backwards in time as you climb toward the summit. The tan-colored Rock City marine sandstone and shale date back fifty million years to the Eocene epoch. The soft rocks allow for erosion that creates wind caves and great smooth shapes like the modern sculptures of Henry Moore.

The Summit Trail takes you back seventy-five million years to the Cretaceous period. The area around you here was formed from deep-water ocean deposits derived from highlands where the Sierra Nevada Mountains now stand.

The upper part of Mount Diablo is made up of rocks as old as 190 million years from the Jurassic and Cretaceous periods. The dramatic colors of the earth around the summit are made from a combination of shale, basalt, chert, and occasional blocks of schist and green serpentinite. But it is a young mountain geologically and an evolving one, slowly rising and pulling the San Ramon Valley beneath it with earthquakes (every 500 years or so) caused by a thrust fault below. Of course, people caused their own quakes and evolution on Mount Diablo.

When Spanish explorers Pedro Fages and Father Juan Crespi climbed the mountain in 1782, they saw rich lands to claim for their own. Missionaries took most of the Miwoks to the San Jose Mission, founded in 1797 (most died of disease there), and by 1800 the Spanish were using Mount Diablo for winter grazing. They established ranches in the hills until the U.S. government claimed California.

In 1851, during the gold rush, Colonel Leander Ransom, a deputy surveyor-general, and his men ascended Diablo and erected a flagpole on the summit to mark the initial point of the Mount Diablo meridian. Thus began the survey of public lands in California. The base and meridian lines that they established are still referred to today in legal descriptions of real estate throughout two-thirds of California and parts of Nevada and Oregon.

The California Geological Survey Group visited the mountain in 1861, gathering rocks, fossils, and previously unidentified plants on their way up to the peak. William Brewer, part of that expedition, estimated that the view from the summit embraced 80,000 square miles, 60 percent of California, thirty-five counties, and an area equal to the six New England states. Best viewing is often on the day after a winter storm or after summer winds blow off urban smog and haze. Look for 10,466-foot Mount Lassen in the Cascade Range to the north, the Farallon Islands to the west, and Mount Loma Prieta in the Santa Cruz Mountains to the south. To the east beyond California's great Central Valley, with binoculars, you may be able to pick out Half Dome in Yosemite National Park.

When Joseph Seavey Hall, a New Hampshire transplant, climbed the mountain for the view, he saw the flash of tourist dollars. In 1873, he convinced local brethren with bucks to invest in the construction of two roads, like those he had built to the top of Mount Washington in New Hampshire. He himself would build a first-rate hotel on a plateau 2 miles from the summit. You pass the site on the Summit Trail. Completed in only five months, it was immediately popular. Some 800 people traveled the roads to the summit in their first month of operation, paying a 25-cent toll to the Mount Diablo Summit Road Company for each guest.

Later that year, Hall opened the sixteen-room Mountain Hotel and Restaurant on the lofty ridge beside Pulpit Rock. "Lovers of nature and fine mountain scenery" who rode up on the stagecoach could now enjoy a warm bed and a gourmet meal of hot chicken, fresh-baked bread, and molasses cooked by Sarah Jane Hall. For dessert, visitors could hike or ride a horse up the remaining 2 miles to the summit. If they wanted to, they could even camp out there in a wood-floored tent that Hall constructed for the purpose and look through his permanently mounted telescope to spot Mount Whitney to the south, Mount Shasta to the north.

Hall got the idea for his telescope when the United States Coast and Geodetic Survey team climbed the mountain to erect a three-story observatory and signal station on the summit, perfect for housing the telescope. Local papers raved about the Diablo experience. Unfortunately, money troubles forced Hall to sell his hotel, and on July 4, 1891, fire swept up the slopes from Morgan Territory and destroyed the observatory.

Fewer people visited the top of the mountain from then on. This pleased ranchers. They didn't like folks crossing their cattle ranges. They succeeded in getting the Contra Costa County Board of Supervisors to close the Mount Diablo roads and eventually burned down the hotel to prevent it from being used by wandering hikers or campers. Despite this, people were still drawn to the sacred mountain, including prestigious visitors like writer Bret Harte and conservationist John Muir.

In 1912, R. N. Burgess established the Mount Diablo Development Company. His company remodeled an establishment known as Cook's Clubhouse/Casino into the Mount Diablo Country Club and created the community of Diablo. It also built new toll roads accessible to auto traffic all the way to Diablo's summit (North Gate and Mount Diablo Scenic Boulevard—completed 1915).

Burgess had even bigger plans for a tower hotel, Torre de Sol, on the summit, backed and publicized by William Randolph Hearst. But with World War I, Hearst lost interest, and Burgess's company went bankrupt. This allowed for 630 acres on the top to become Mount Diablo State Park in 1921, six years before California established the state park system. In 1927, Frederick Law Olmsted, champion of U.S. parks, prepared a California park survey, recommending acquisition of 6,000 acres at Mount Diablo to "amplify" the small state park at the summit.

Standard Oil crews drove up the mountain in 1928 to construct a 75-foot aviation beacon as a guide for commercial and military planes, visible for 100 miles. Charles Lindbergh came up Diablo to light the beacon for the first time. Now in the Summit Building, it is lit only on Pearl Harbor Day, December 7.

In the 1930s and early 1940s, the Civilian Conservation Corps constructed campgrounds and picnic areas, realigned park roads, marked hiking trails, and built park residences, dams, and the rustic stone Summit Building. The clam, oyster, and other fossil shells you see in the Summit Building stones came from Miocene age rocks near the Fossil Ridge (about twelve million years old). Soldiers scaled Mount Diablo in the 1940s, establishing Camp Diablo, a base at Rock City, to train in mountain warfare and road and bridge construction.

The Alameda Whipsnake

Mount Diablo's rocky, brush-covered slopes provide habitat preferred by both the Alameda whipsnake and its favorite prey, the western fence lizard. Not often seen, this wary snake hibernates in a rock crevice or rodent burrow during the winter months. It also escapes the summer's intense heat underground. Because most of its natural habitat in Alameda and Contra Costa counties has been destroyed by housing, road construction, reservoirs, and other development, only three sizable populations of the Alameda whipsnake still exist. This harmless snake has been listed as a California endangered species and is now protected by law. Habitat preservation is the key to its survival.

The only war affecting the mountain since then has been conservation of the parkland in the face of widespread development. But thanks to the Save Mount Diablo Organization, protected open space has expanded by tens of thousands of acres since the 1970s.

Now it's your turn to ascend this sacred mound, taking in the wildlife, over 400 species of plants, and the expansive views, imagining the stagecoach ride up to the Mountain Hotel, survival training at Rock City, or Miwok hunting and gathering in the woodlands, all the while creating your own experience on Mount Diablo.

Sentinel Rock

Miles/Directions

0.0 START at north end of parking lot for Rock City in Mount Diablo State Park. Start hike on single-track dirt trail to Sentinel Rock. Trail goes through natural-rock Little Rock amphitheater. Take trail behind cave and stay left. *(Note:* For drinking water in the Little Rock picnic area, take trail on the right after Little Rock amphitheater to the picnic tables beyond.)

0.1 Climb a rock to see Sentinel Rock to the west and get your bearings. Take unmarked trail with poison oak warning to head in the right direction. Trail will take you over rocks with stairs carved out in places. It is a moderately strenuous hike. *(Note:* There are numerous trails that lead to Sentinel Rock once you know which direction to go.)

0.2 Sentinel Rock; climb up to top with the help of railings and enjoy the view. Head back toward parking lot for Rock City. Ttrail to the right leads around rocks, staying on soft ground. *(Note:* Beware of poison oak.)

0.4 Take any trail through Rock City toward main road.

0.5 On bend in the road just past Rock City, across from an employee residence, there are two trailheads on the left. Pass the first (Wall Point Road to Macedo Ranch) and take the second one, double-track, multiuse Summit Trail, to summit parking lot (3.7 miles).

0.6 Pass another employee residence and Horseshoe picnic area; road is on the right.

0.8 Make sharp left turn and continue on Summit Trail, with road still on right-hand side. To the southwest is Rocky Ridge of Las Trampas Wilderness.

1.2 Junction of Summit Trail Bypass. Stay right on Summit Trail, which becomes single-track.

1.8 Cross paved Summit Road to stay on Summit Trail, which becomes double-track dirt trail again. State park heliport is along trail. Pass junction to Barbecue Terrace Road, staying on the Summit Trail for moderate climb. To the left is North Gate Road.

2.1 Sunset picnic area on the left. Double-track trail becomes paved road past picnic area. It meets Summit Road, at crosswalk. Cross road and continue on Summit Trail, now paved road (also a driveway for an employee residence). Pass house; Summit Trail once again becomes double-track dirt trail, mostly shady.

2.3 Mountain House Junction. Ranger station to the left 0.2 mile. Fork to the right is Summit Trail (1.9 miles to the top from here). Site of Mountain House is just before junction between the two trails (path leading to the ranger station is part of original stagecoach road). Continue on Summit Trail; Mountain House Creek is on the right (dry in summer).

2.6 Junction with Juniper Trail; stay on Summit Trail. Shortly after, Summit Trail crosses Summit Road again and continues onto paved fire road (#59–8), Green Ranch Road to Frog Pond Road; sign also says Summit Trail. In 0.1 mile, another trailhead heads left to Summit Trail, where it becomes single-track, hikers only.

2.7 Pass water tank, Pioneer Horse Camp, and interpretive sign about Alameda whipsnake. Summit Trail heads up left, becoming double-track dirt again. It ascends into single-track trail in less than 0.2 mile. Summit museum is visible above you.

3.5 Trail meets Summit Road. Follow paved Summit Road about 20 feet, where Summit Trail continues to the right, starting as double-track gravel road.

3.6 Summit Trail to the left becomes single-track dirt path again.

3.7 The Devil's Elbow. Trail meets Summit Road again. There are two trailheads; stay left on Summit Trail (the other is Prospector's Gap, which leads to Donner Canyon and Clayton).

4.0 Trail meets Summit Road again. Lower Summit parking lot to the left. Turn right and stay right on paved road less than 0.1 mile. To the left is trailhead for Summit Trail that leads to single-track trail to Summit parking lot and museum.

4.2 Mount Diablo summit and museum. Return to trailhead for Summit Trail to lower parking lot.

4.4 Trail comes out to the lower parking lot. Walk straight across lot to the end. Trailhead for Juniper Trail to Juniper Camp.

4.6 Cross road on crosswalk, proceed up road to the right about 70 feet to continue on Juniper Trail. Trail heads downhill.

5.6 Juniper Camp. Walk along paved Juniper Campground Road, past campsites, to where road curves. There, take double-track, dirt road. About 100 yards down is gate and trailhead for Deer Flat Creek Road. At gate turn left onto single-track dirt Juniper Trail. About 100 yards later path splits; stay right.

5.8 Stay on Juniper Trail (single-track, hikers only, dirt path). Below are buildings of Diablo Ranch and park headquarters at the junction between North and South Roads. Juniper and chaparral very thick here, then trail opens up into hillside grassland. Cross small wooden bridge over Jill Creek (dry in summer).

6.5 Trailhead. Trail meets gravel parking lot; cross it and restart Juniper Trail on other side. About 20 feet later, stay to the left on trail.

6.7 Junction with Summit Trail. Turn right, going south downhill on double-track, dirt Summit Trail.

7.0 Junction. Mountain House Creek now on the left. Take left fork, Summit Trail.

7.2 Pass employee residence onto paved road, cross road, and pass Sunset picnic area on the right. Back to double-track, dirt trail.

7.3 Cross road on crosswalk and continue on Summit Road. Sign reads TO SOUTHGATE ROAD.

7.9 Junction with Summit Trail Bypass. Take bypass, turning right on single-track trail. Great views of Rock City.

8.1 Junction with connector to Wall Point Road. Turn right on single-track connector trail.

8.3 Deadend at Wall Point Road. Turn left on double-track, dirt Wall Point Road.

Hike Information

● Trail Contacts:
Mount Diablo State Park Headquarters, 96 Mitchell Canyon Road, Clayton, CA 94517 (925) 837–2525; ranger's office (925) 837–6119

Mount Diablo Interpretive Association, P.O. Box 346, Walnut Creek, CA 94517 (925) 927–7222; www.mdia.org

Save Mount Diablo, Walnut Creek, CA (925) 947–3535; www.savemountdiablo.org

● Schedule:
Open daily year-round from 8:00 A.M. to sunset

● Fees/Permits:
$2.00 per car, $12.00 for overnight camping

● Local Information:
www.danville.com
www.diablomag.com
Danville Area Chamber of Commerce, 117-E Town and Country Drive, Danville, CA (925) 837–4400; www.danvillecachamber.com

● Local Events/Attractions:
Blackhawk Museum, 3700 Blackhawk Plaza Circle, Danville, CA (925) 736–2277; www.blackhawkauto.org/home.html
Victoria's Hair on Stage (comedy club), 520 San Ramon Valley Boulevard, Danville, CA (925) 820–8333

● Accommodations:
Camping on Mount Diablo: (800)

444–7275; www.reserveamerica.com
Danville Inn, 803 Camino Ramon, Danville, CA (925) 838–8080

● Restaurants:
Blackhawk Grille, 3540 Blackhawk Plaza Circle, Danville, CA (925) 736–4295
Bridges Restaurant and Bar, 44 Church St., Danville, CA (925) 820–7200
The Crown and Anchor Pub, 331 Hartz Avenue, Danville, CA (925) 855–8663
Father Nature's Shed, 172 East Prospect Avenue, Danville, CA (925) 820–3160

● Local Outdoor Retailers:
Forward Motion Sports, 432 Hartz Avenue, Danville, CA (925) 831–3745
Outside Interests, 422 Hartz Avenue, Danville, CA (925) 837–1230

● Hike Tours:
Mount Diablo State Park Headquarters, (925) 837–2525
Mount Diablo Interpretive Association, P.O. Box 346, Walnut Creek, CA 94597 (925) 927–7222; www.mdia.org
Save Mount Diablo, P.O. Box 5376, Walnut Creek, CA 94596 (925) 947–3535; www.savemountdiablo.org

● Maps:
www.mdia.org/parkmap.htm
USGS maps: Mount Diablo, CA

8.4 Trail meets road right at curve above Rock City where you started on Summit Trail. Head up into Rock City Camp on any trail; turn right on paved road marked LITTLE ROCK PICNIC AREA. At end of gravel turn-around area, take stone steps, climb another set, and pass through the Little Rock amphitheater. Follow rock steps back to parking lot.

8.5 Back to parking lot.

Honorable Mention:
Mount Diablo and Las Trampas Foothills

O. Las Trampas Regional Wilderness: The Eugene O'Neill Loop

This hike is a literary adventure, walking in reflection through the Las Trampas Regional Wilderness focused on the thoughts and property of one man: playwright Eugene O'Neill. The great American playwright moved into the Danville hills with his wife, Carlotta, in 1936. They built a Spanish colonial home, called the Tao House, on 158 acres with the money from the Nobel Prize, awarded him earlier that year.

This hike starts from Danville or Alamo trailhead and heads through the Las Trampas hills to the Tao House to tour the grounds (reservations required; call 925–838–0249). To make the day even more memorable, bring one of his plays and stop now and then in a shady knoll to read some lines aloud. You can also contemplate O'Neill with fellow hikers. This is quite a different way to hike, but remember what O'Neill said: "We all are more or less the slaves of conventions, or of discipline, or of a rigid formula of some sort."

Get a park trail map to plan your route. For a 3.5-mile loop, start at the end of Camille Avenue on the Madrone Trail. Turn left on Virgil Trail and left again on Madrone to get to the Tao House grounds. Make a loop by continuing on Madrone, right on Amigo Trail, right on Williams Trail, left on Madrone, and follow it back to the start.

To get there, take Highway 680 to the Stone Valley exit. Go west on Stone Valley Road. Turn left at the light onto Danville Boulevard. Turn right on Camille Avenue. Follow it to the end, and park on the street. For more information, call East Bay Regional Park District Headquarters (510) 662–PARK or (925) 837–3145; www.ebparks.org/parks/lastram.htm. For Tao House tour reservations, call (925) 838–0249.

Three Ridges: San Pablo, the Oakland/Berkeley Hills, and Sunol Ridge

Like the three tenors, these three ridges have a lot to sing about. Right above bustling cities and dense suburbs are parks and open spaces with an incredible variety of natural beauty and history, punctuated with bodies of water. And in the basins between the ridges a hiker can find solitude exploring areas that are among the East Bay's best kept secrets.

Who would think that above the city "that puts the There in There," Oakland, California, you can find quiet, enchanting hills that were once covered with ancient, giant redwoods. After loggers downed the forest, much of the area gave way to development, but thousands of acres have survived to support native wildlife and remind us of our past. You can find variety as well. Redwood Park and Joaquin Miller Park host gurgling creeks and second-generation redwoods, creating cool, shady trails. Robert Sibley Volcanic Regional Preserve offers geological exploration with dikes, mudflows, and lava flows. Huckleberry Botanic Regional Preserve is an ecological jewel with a native plant population found nowhere else. The ridge also has swimming in Roberts Park and bass fishing and boating at pretty Lake Chabot.

Nearby Briones, above the affluent suburbs of Lafayette and Orinda, offers sweeping grasslands with ridge-top tarns and a view of San Pablo Bay and the Carquinez Straits, where retired warships sit in neat rows in the water.

Water is key to the drama on the Sunol Ridge. In early spring, Little Yosemite splashes down over gray boulders. The wildflower display is unmatched anywhere else in the East Bay. Backpackers can pass by all this into the Ohlone wilderness to spend the night under the stars and finish off with a cool dunk in Lake Del Valle.

On the San Pablo Ridge between Wild Cat Canyon and Claremont Canyon is the family-favorite Tilden Park. A study in combining recreation and preservation,

Tilden offers wooded canyons, view trails, and a nature preserve, along with pony rides, a steam train, a petting zoo, and a beautiful old carousel. It also has Anza Lake, a favorite swimming hole. Just below it all is the UC–Berkeley campus, where pedestrians always have the right of way and almost everything politically is left of center. The free-speech movement started here, with civil rights parades down Telegraph Avenue. It's one of the best places in the world for people watching: eccentrics, hippies, international students, business types, and the homeless inter-mingle in front of bookstores and record shops.

While most of these parks are part of the well-run East Bay Regional Park District, the East Bay Municipal Utilities District (EBMUD) owns a lot of open space around these ridges, too. And here's the secret: To hike on EBMUD, you have to get a permit for a nominal fee. The process is simple, but because of it, few people walk the 55 miles of trails in the watershed, open to the public since 1973. Briones Reservoir offers mixed woodland full of brush rabbits and black-tailed deer. San Pablo Reservoir is a favorite of local anglers.

34

Briones Regional Park

Overview: *Briones Regional Park offers long, ambling walks through grassy, rolling hills spotted with oak trees, some lovely views both of distant towns and landmarks and of neighboring parkland, with the pleasant surprises of lagoons and a contrasting dense, damp woodland. Hawks, eagles, and turkey vultures soar and circle above the canyons. Black-tailed deer love to munch on the brush in the deeper canyons, and mountain lions in turn feast on the deer. There are several small creeks lined with ferns and shrubs, and patches of sun-loving wildflowers grow along most of the trails. Because of the annual grasses, the landscape changes seasonally from summer gold to winter green. Indeed, the largest portion of the 6,002 acres of open space is grassland that has been greatly influenced by 200 years of ranching. In winter months, you share the trail with grazing cows and goats. This park gives you a real taste of California's Spanish ranch past.*

County: Contra Costa
Start: Parking lot of Briones Regional Park
Length: 7.0-mile loop
Approximate Hiking Time: 3.5 hours
Difficulty Rating: Easy valley and ridge trails combined with strenuous uphill and steep downhill sections
Trail Surface: Packed double-track, dirt trail through chaparral, oaks, and mainly grasslands

up to a ridge, down through the valleys, ending with a single-track, dirt trail and one creek crossing
Land Status: Regional park
Nearest Town: Orinda
Other Trail Users: Equestrians and mountain bikers, except Bear Creek Trail, for hikers only
Canine Compatibility: Dogs on leash

Getting There

By Car: From the San Francisco–Oakland Bay Bridge, take Highway 24 through the Caldecott Tunnel. Take the Orinda/Moraga exit, and turn left at the light on Camino Pablo. Two lanes merge into one. About a mile later, turn right on Bear Creek Road. Travel past the Briones Reservoir, past Happy Valley Road (to Lafayette). Turn right into the park. The sign reads BRIONES REGIONAL PARK, BEAR CREEK STAGING AREA. (Note the cement retaining wall on the left. See sidebar, page 246.) Just past the kiosk, turn left into the parking lot. The Abrigo Valley Trailhead is on the right.

By Public Transportation: Start any day from Lafayette BART. Walk east on Deer Hill Road from Lafayette BART 1 mile; left on Elizabeth Street for 200 feet to little used trailhead without sign, a 20-minute walk. Or weekdays, take County Connection bus #206 from Lafayette BART (heading toward Rossmoor, not St. Mary's College) to bus stop at little pergola on Mount Diablo Boulevard next to Third Street in central Lafayette (bus runs every sixty to eighty minutes). It's a ten-

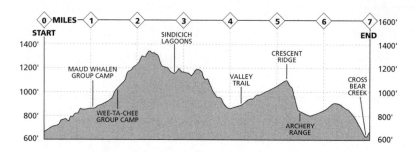

minute bus ride from Lafayette BART. Trail starts across street from pergola, sneaks under freeway to Deer Hill Road, then ⅓ mile to Elizabeth Street. Return either way in reverse.

Hike Description

The land that is now Briones Regional Park has provided grass for grazing cattle for nearly 200 years, replacing the herds of elk and antelope reported by early settlers. Since the land grants of the Spanish in the early 1800s, livestock have shaped this landscape. The annual grasses are Spanish, carried accidentally as seeds by the cattle. The stepped hillsides are a result of cows creating paths to new grass. Also, after the rains, the trails can be badly rutted from hooves, creating an uneven surface for hiking boots. And, of course, watch out for cow pies.

But if you look carefully, you can also see a Georgia O'Keeffe painting in the Briones scenery, long valleys between subtle and smooth rolling hills of grassland and scattered oaks. Those round, grassy hills dominate the park, pastoral green in winter and late spring, like the English countryside, golden in summer and fall, radiating the heat of California sunshine and creating a scene of old western ranchland.

The park is named for Felipe Briones, the original Spanish grant holder of this land, then called Rancho Boca de la Canada del Pinole (Rancho at the mouth of Pinole Canyon). It was popularly known as Rancho San Felipe. In 1829, young Briones fell in love with a waterfall and built a home near what is now the Bear Creek entrance to the park. The retired Spanish soldier cultivated the land and kept a few hundred cattle and horses, supporting a family of eighteen. Before that, the land was home to Native American tribes.

Rejecting the missions set up to "civilize" them, occasionally some of these Native Californians tried to reclaim their land. In the early part of 1839, a group stole nearly all the saddle horses belonging to Captain Ygnacio Martinez, at the Rancho Pinole, Briones's neighbor to the north. The captain's son, Don Jose Martinez, and eight or ten other neighbors went in pursuit of them. They succeeded in recovering the animals, but Felipe Briones was struck by an arrow and killed. The fighting became increasingly severe, forcing the little Spanish posse to retreat with the recovered horses and to leave the body of Felipe Briones where it lay. Some-

Briones Regional Park

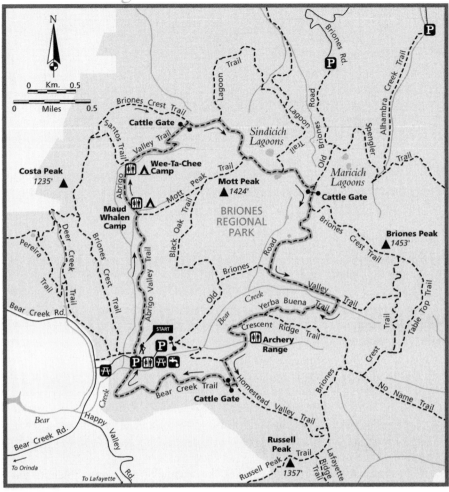

times when the wind from the north washes intently over the hills and down into the canyons, it feels as if Felipe has come back for a visit to his beloved farm.

In 1842, his widow, Maria Manuela Valencia Briones, claimed the grant and continued to ranch here. And so it was for another fifty years, with changes of ownership, the parceling out of smaller farms, and the spreading of orchards from the Alhambra Valley.

In 1906, there was a new kind of battle in these foothills. The People's Water Company began purchasing land in San Pablo and Bear Creek for watershed lands to fight a massive water shortage in the growing Bay Area (watershed is land reserved for rain runoff, collected in reservoirs). The San Pablo Dam and reservoir (1919), Lake Chabot (1875), Upper San Leandro Reservoir (1926), and finally the Briones Reservoir (1964) were built for this purpose. It became parkland in 1957.

The Briones Wall

Look carefully at the retaining wall on the left side of the park road as you drive in. Can you make out the large, abstract California poppies that were once painted there? Faint now, they were bright orange when the Reverend Anthony Bellesorte painted them in 1971. The then thirty-five-year-old Dominican priest took on the part-time job of obliterating ugly graffiti in the East Bay regional parks with outdoor murals. Quite miraculously, vandals seem to leave his art alone.

There is country charm in the clanging green-painted cattle gates you pass through on this hike. Remember to close the gates after you. The first gate on the Abrigo Valley Trail brings you into an area lined with bays, oaks, and maples, hills to the right and a creek far below through the brush to the left. All the trails until you reach Bear Creek Trail are double-track, dirt trails.

You pass by two group camps, both originally established by the Girl Scouts of America. The first, Maud Whalen, is a wide-open grassy area with one large shelter. The second, Wee-Ta-Chee, is across a bridge in a private setting with a wooden covered shelter beside a small amphitheater made of logs.

Abrigo rises steeply in places, making the trek up to the ridge strenuous but over easy terrain. Look for indications of landslides. These sparse hillsides of loose soil are prone to this natural disaster, as is the entire Lamorinda area.

November through February, you share the trail with a lot of cows that will beat you in a staring contest hooves-down. The rule is to just walk on past them; these docile Herefords and Angus are more scared of you than you are of them and will likely move out of your way as you approach. But never stand directly behind a cow, which could kick if frightened. The park leases to three ranchers. The Gnocchio family has kept its cows here in winter for over fifty years.

On the Briones Crest, you are near the elevation of Mott Peak (1,424 feet). Views up here include the top of Mount Tamalpais to the west and the Martinez Valley north and east to Mount Diablo. On an exceptionally clear day, you can see all the way to the Sierras.

An especially noteworthy sight is just north of the Benicia–Carquinez bridge: warships afloat on the bay. This is the mothball fleet, more officially known as the MARAD Reserve Fleet, at Suisun Bay. The fleet is the largest single collection of ships on the Pacific Ocean. The eighty-four cargo ships, tankers, Victory ships, missile cruisers, barges, and tugboats have accumulated more than 2,000 years of total active service. They have sailed every sea, been to thousands of ports, and served in every foreign war and military conflict since World War II.

Notice on the trailhead that the path is dedicated to a man named Ivan Dickson. A member of the Berkeley Hiking Club, Ivan surprised everyone by leaving $427,000, his entire estate, to the East Bay Park District for trail maintenance when he died in 1993. At his official Briones site to the west (see the trail map), officials buried three of Ivan's favorite things in a memorial bench: a can of cheap beer, a pair of wingtips, and junk food.

A well-endowed ram along the Valley Trail

Closer to you on the sunny ridge, in the midst of this scanty grassland, so dry in summer, are two cool surprises: the Sindicich Lagoons, protected pond habitats, fenced to keep out rogue cattle. Named for a farming family that worked this land after Briones, it was probably created as a cattle waterhole and replenishes itself from a natural spring below. The ponds, romantically called lagoons, never seem to dry out. You can enter either one through a gate and go exploring. White egrets and blue herons stop here to rest. In the fall, dragonflies twirl over the water. In the spring, California newts lay their eggs. The larger Sindicich Lagoon is a pleasant place to stop for a rest and a slug of drinking water.

If you are used to lush, single-track trails, the continuous grassland surrounding the wide dirt roads of Briones can get monotonous, especially trekking alone. But let your mind wander, and you have found a great place for quiet, rhythmic reflection. Indeed, you can easily lose yourself without getting lost in Briones. Take a deep breath up on the ridge, and you may have a *Sound of Music* moment.

Old Briones Road is a gradual downhill to the valley below, offering pastoral scenes of glistening grass and grazing cattle. Valley Trail's terrain is obvious by its name, flat, with trees along a creek on your right, the rolling Lamorinda hills to your left. In the fall, you may see herds of goats grazing here, helping the U.S. Park Service to control growth of yellow star thistle, a ground pest that sticks to socks and pokes ankles.

Yerba Buena Trail takes you back into the wooded north-facing hillsides, a nice change from the grasslands. Still double-track and rutted by cow hooves, this trail takes you uphill again with one strenuous steep section.

The Crescent Ridge Trail is a delight for southern views of the wooded hillsides and another valley below, nothing but parkland. The structure you see below you is the Briones Archery Club Range. After a fairly steep downhill, you pass the range, where you find pit toilets, picnic tables, and shelters for rain with places for quivers and bows.

Bear Creek Trail, the only single-track, hikers-only trail in Briones, is a wonderful finale. If you have time for only a short hike, integrate this trail into your loop. It takes you up and down through thick woods and underbrush of fern, moss, and flowering brush. This is the green stuff you were staring at from the sunny ridges. However, poison oak grows right beside the narrow footpath here. If you are susceptible, wear long pants for this section. In winter, when the branches are bare of leaves, it is especially hard to spot, and the branches still contain the poisonous oil of the lovely but annoying plant.

Steps help you down a steep bank to Bear Creek. Not wide, you can jump across it and take the stairs up the opposite bank. A few switchbacks take you back up to the parking lots.

Miles/Directions

0.0 START at Abrigo Valley Trailhead. Take trail past Oak Grove picnic area to cattle gate.

0.1 Go through cattle gate, staying on Abrigo Valley Trail.

1.0 Stay on Abrigo Valley Trail past Mott Peak Trail turnoff. Group Camp Maud Whalen on the right.

1.4 Wee-Ta-Chee Camp is on the right over the bridge. Continue on Abrigo Valley Trail.

2.1 Go through cattle gate, and turn left on Briones Crest Trail.

2.3 Stay on Briones Crest Trail as you pass first trailhead for Lagoon Trail.

3.0 Pass the smaller Sindicich Lagoon on the right. Just past pond on Briones Crest Trail, take a left on Lagoon Trail to see larger Sindicich Lagoon.

3.1 Larger Sindicich Lagoon. Go back the way you came to Briones Crest Trail.

3.2 From Lagoon Trail, take a left back onto Briones Crest Trail to continue along the ridge headed east.

3.4 Turn right on Old Briones Road.

3.5 Stay on Old Briones Road, passing through another cattle gate. It is downhill for a while.

4.1 Take a left on Valley Trail.

4.7 Take a right on Yerba Buena Trail. This leads back up into the wooded hillsides.

Hike Information

Trail Contact:
East Bay Regional Park District Headquarters, 2950 Peralta Oaks Court, P.O. Box 5381, Oakland, CA 94605 (510) 662–PARK; www.ebparks.org/parks/briones.htm

Schedule:
Open daily year-round from 8:00 A.M. to 6:00 P.M. unless otherwise posted

Fees/Permits:
Parking is $4.00 when kiosk is attended, which is mostly on weekends in summer months. Trailered vehicles are $3.00, dogs $1.00

Local Information:
Chamber of Commerce, Orinda, CA 94563 (925) 254–3909; www.orinda chamber.org
Orinda Home Page www.ci.orinda.ca.us/welcome.htm

Local Events/Attractions:
California Shakespeare Festival (May–October), 2531 Ninth Street, Berkeley, CA (510) 548–3422
Orinda Theatre, 2 Orinda Theater Square, Orinda, CA (925) 254–9060
Orinda Farmers' Market, downtown Orinda; open 9:00 A.M. to 1:00 P.M. Saturdays, May through October

Accommodations:
Hillside Inn and Suites, 3748 Mount Diablo Boulevard, Lafayette, CA (925) 283–8200
Lafayette Park Hotel, 3287 Mount Diablo Boulevard, Lafayette, CA (925) 283–3700
Berkeley and Oakland B&B Network, Berkeley and Oakland, CA (510) 547–6380; www.bbonline.com/ca/berkeley-oakland/index.html

Restaurants:
Casa Orinda, 20 Bryant Way, Orinda, CA (925) 254–2981
Niwa Sushi, 1 Camino Sobrante, Orinda, CA (925) 254–1606
Village Pizza, 19 Orinda Way, Orinda, CA (925) 254–1200

Local Outdoor Retailers:
Nor-Ski Sports, 3518 Mount Diablo Boulevard, Lafayette, CA (925) 283–2522
Rossi's Tennis and Running, 1003 Oak Hill Road, Lafayette, CA (925) 284–1222

Hike Tours:
Orinda Hiking Club, P.O. Box 934, Orinda, CA 94563 (925) 254–3689 or (925) 254–1465

Maps:
East Bay Regional Park District Headquarters, Oakland, CA (510) 662–PARK; www.ebparks.org/parks/briones.htm
USGS maps: Oakland East and Briones Valley, CA

5.3 Go right on Crescent Ridge Trail. Steep downhill section brings you to archery club. Continue on Crescent Ridge Trail.

5.9 Turn left on Homestead Valley Trail. You can see next trailhead just ahead 0.1 mile.

6.0 Turn right on Bear Creek Trail. Single-track trail leads through a wildlife-populated woodland habitat. *(Note:* Beware of poison oak.)

7.0 Cross creek. *(Note:* There's no bridge, but it's a short leap over unless you are trekking after unusually heavy rains.) Climb the stairs on the opposite bank, up a couple switchbacks, to parking lot. Starting point is just past kiosk.

35

Redwood Regional Park: East to West Ridge Trails

Overview: *This ridge and canyon hike offers dramatic changes in scenery, light and even temperature. An easy first mile follows a road-wide dirt path among pines, oaks, and eucalyptus, exposed to the sky, with views of the foothills and Mount Diablo. Winding down Prince Road, the scenery changes, shaded by bay and madrone trees. Suddenly, you'll find yourself in the seclusion of a thriving redwood grove, walking beside Redwood Creek, with its banks full of ferns and water-loving plants. The trail heads back up to evergreens and views again. Wear layered clothing to accommodate changes in temperature.*

County: Alameda
Start: From the Skyline Gate Staging Area on Skyline Boulevard
Length: 4.0-mile loop
Approximate Hiking Time: 1.5–2 hours
Difficulty Rating: Moderate due to a few short but steep ascents and downhill sections of the trail
Trail Surface: A wide, dirt road narrows to a footpath in the damp, shaded redwoods, with

several easy creek crossings, then ascends again to sunlight; after a good storm, path may be eroded and muddy in places, but passable
Land Status: Regional park
Nearest Town: Montclair Village of Oakland
Other Trail Users: Partially used by mountain bikers and equestrians
Canine Compatibility: Dogs permitted (must be leashed on the Stream Trail)

Getting There

By Car: From the San Francisco–Oakland Bay Bridge, take the Park Boulevard exit; turn left toward Montclair Village. Turn right on Snake Road. It will wind around through neighborhoods, becoming Shepherd Canyon Road. At the road's end, turn right on Skyline Boulevard. Turn into the parking lot to your left about a half mile away. This is the Skyline Staging Area, one of several entrances to the park.

By Public Transportation: Weekdays only: From Twelfth Street BART, take AC Transit bus #15 and transfer to bus #60 in downtown Montclair, at Moraga and Medau. Bus #60 will take you to Moon Gate, where you turn left on the West

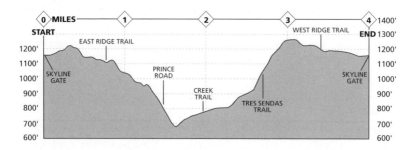

Redwood Regional Park

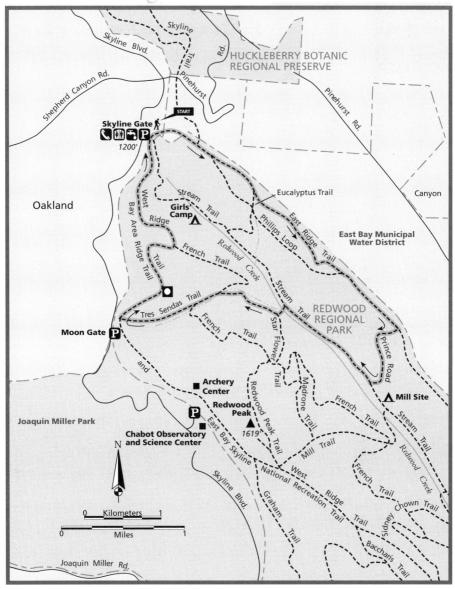

Ridge Trail, until you reach the Skyline Gate. Then follow the directions from the East Ridge Trailhead. For more information, call AC Transit TravInfo (510–817–1717), or visit www.actransit.org.

Hike Description

You might never know as you hike through serene Redwood Regional Park that this was once the background for mass destruction, fires, lynchings, manhunts, and vindictive justice laid down by rifle-toting lumberjacks. Before that, it was a magnificent land of giants. The 2,074-acre, two-county park (Alameda and Contra Costa) also hosted farms, orchards, and ranches for ninety years. It finally became parkland in 1939. Today, a peaceful getaway amid suburban foothills and urban sprawl, the park proves the resilience of nature, with few indications of its dramatic past.

When the Spaniards claimed this area with land grants in the 1800s, it encompassed more than 6,000 acres of virgin redwoods. El Rancho de San Antonio (owned by Luis Maria Peralta) was to the west of the park, El Rancho de la Laguna de Los Palos Colorados (owned by Joaquin Moraga, as in the city of Moraga) inland to the east. Redwood Park is in what was called the "middle redwoods," public domain.

Just how big was the old growth? The 150-foot coastal redwoods you see in the park today are second generation. Their ancient mothers were so tall that sea captains sailing into the San Francisco Bay used them as navigational landmarks 16 miles away, where the Pacific meets the Golden Gate. A report in 1893 measured stumps as wide as 33.5 feet in diameter. If this account is correct, the redwoods here may have been the largest living things on earth.

Peralta put a provision into his 1820 grant (renewed in 1844), allowing neighbors to cut lumber on the ranch for their personal use, but specifically prohibited commercial cutting. He recognized the grand beauty and uniqueness of this forest that was home to grizzly bears, mountain lions, rattlesnakes, and hundreds of California condors, now nearly extinct.

After the gold rush, settlers recognized the profit to be had by lumber. Ten sawmills set up shop in the redwoods. With each mill employing up to 100 men, shantytowns sprang up around them. The loggers, mostly jump-ship sailors, were hard-drinking, oath-swearing, feared men. An awed Bay Area press dubbed them "the redwood boys." Several times, they formed their own retributive posse, emerging from the forest to hang horse and cattle thieves. They once threatened to "lay the town [of Oakland) in ashes" if the mayor didn't convict one suspect. In 1854, they mounted a nighttime manhunt in the woods for twenty-five head-shaved and stripe-wearing felons who had escaped from San Quentin Prison Camp on the Marin Islands. Most prisoners were shot on sight.

By 1860, commercial logging in the canyon had clearcut the entire forest. The wood was used to build the cities of Oakland, San Francisco, Martinez, and Benecia (the old capital of California). The Mission San Jose de Guadalupe was also constructed from East Bay redwood. Less than fifteen years after the gold rush, the giant trees that guided sailors through the Golden Gate were gone. Even the undergrowth was burned away to reach the trees. Left was a charred sea of stumps. Only one old tree still stands today, protected in Oakland's Leona Park.

Ranching, farming, and development followed the logging era. The shantytowns of the mill workers were replaced with homesteads built along the stream. As late as 1940, cattle grazed here. Farm crops and apple orchards—still in evidence

The Stream Trail is darker and damp among the redwood grove; picturesque fences protect riparian life by the creek.

near Roberts Recreation Area—grew in plots. Into the 1920s, the Mahogany Eucalyptus and Land Company planted red gum eucalyptus around here and developed about half of the Montclair townsite. Redwood Park was one of the first purchases by the East Bay Regional Park District after the people voted it into existence in 1934. Because of the redwood tree's amazing system of renewal, the second generation took root and now encompasses a canopied, creekside environment only a fraction of the forest's original size.

Starting your hike on the wide East Ridge Trail, you share the first mile with bicyclists, equestrians, runners, and undoubtedly dogs, romping happily off-leash. This is one of the favorite trails of today's East Bay mutt lovers. With pet restrictions at many city parks, the East Bay Regional Park District offers the most lenient dog rules of almost any park system in the Bay Area. Before new ordinances are put into effect, the district's "dog committee" consults park users. The result is that most dog walkers are respectful of the posted signs and the rest of the community (dogs must be on leash at the staging area and around Redwood Creek's fragile ecosystem). But, like anywhere else, you may run into the occasional vagrant and careless pet owner.

Pines, live coast oaks, and aromatic bluegum eucalyptus border the trail on the ridge. Rabbits, red squirrels, and quail may appear out of the grasses or wild currant. You may see deer or raccoon tracks crossing the trail. Starflowers, lupine, leatherwood, and cleavers grow alongside the path. A half mile in, you can stop at the bench to your right to admire a great view of the rolling hills and dense woodland that make up Chabot Regional Park, the Las Trampas foothills, and Mount Diablo (3,849 feet).

Prince Road was named for Thomas and William Prince, who established a steam-driven sawmill here in 1852. You will pass the exact former location of the mill where the Stream Trail meets Tres Sendas Trail. Today you may hear robins, chickadees, red-tailed hawks, great-horned owls in the evenings, and maybe even the rare golden eagle.

On Prince Road, the landscape darkens in the thicker forest, adding red-barked madrone and California bay trees to the mix. (By the way, those pungent bay leaves are often used for cooking, especially spaghetti sauce.) It feels a bit like falling into Alice's rabbit hole here. Winding down, to your right, you see your first grove of coast redwoods. The temperature changes; the light dims. The sun-lit ridge may suddenly seem distant as you enter the damp, hidden redwood forest in the park's basin, the Redwood Bowl.

As you stroll along the Stream Trail, which runs through the center of the park, the sound of water accompanies you. The wooden fence railing you see protects the replenishing riparian habitat around Redwood Creek. The creek has its place in history as a tributary of San Leandro Creek, where the world-famous rainbow trout was first identified as a distinct species. The water is too low to support the fish now, but you may see a frog or two.

Tres Sendas (Three Paths) Trail continues your journey through the woods, crossing the creek several times and climbing up a short, heart-beater hill. The trail will flatten out for a while among moss-covered rocks. Then the path brightens and narrows. Oaks and grasses take over again. Careful here: Poison oak grows right next to the trail. The West Ridge Trail, a portion of the 31-mile East Bay Skyline National Recreation Trail that runs along the Coast Range, opens once again to sky and expansive views. You can also look down the ridge at the dark forest you just visited.

Back at the Skyline Gate parking lot, you have pit toilets, a water fountain, a hose and silver dog dish, free biodegradable Pick-up Mitts to remove your dog's waste from the trails, a pay phone, trail maps, and a bulletin board that often features an animal in need of a good home.

Miles/Directions

0.0 START at the Skyline Staging Area; take the East Ridge Trail to the far left.

0.5 Enjoy the great view of Mount Diablo.

1.2 Turn right on Prince Road (you will pass Eucalyptus Trail and Phillips Loop first).

1.6 Bear right where the path meets Stream Trail. (*Note:* For rest rooms, water, and picnic tables, turn left and walk 1.0 mile, then double-back.)

2.1 Stream Trail heads up right. Stay left around the bend onto Tres Sendas Trail. *(Note:* If you want picnic tables, water, or rest rooms, proceed up Stream Trail another 0.5 mile to Girls' Camp.)

2.5 Tres Sendas Trail crosses the creek and branches right and left. Bear right. Steep uphill. You will pass Star Flower Trail and French Trail.

2.8 Tres Sendas meets West Ridge Trail. Turn right.

4.0 Arrive back at Skyline Staging Area and parking lot.

Hike Information

☎ Trail Contact:
East Bay Regional Park District Headquarters, 2950 Peralta Oaks Court, P.O. Box 5381, Oakland, CA 94605 (510) 662–PARK; www.ebparks.org/parks/redwood.htm

🕐 Schedule:
Open daily year-round from 5:00 A.M. to 10:00 P.M. unless otherwise posted

💲 Fees/Permits:
Free at Skyline Staging Area. At the Redwood Road entrance, fees are $4.00 per vehicle, $3.00 per trailered vehicle. Buses: $1.00 per person. Dog fee is $1.00 per dog.

❓ Local Information:
Montclair Business Association, 1980 Mountain Boulevard, #205, Oakland, CA 94611 (510) 339–1000; www.montclairvillage.com
Oakland Convention and Visitors Bureau, 475 Fourteenth Street, Suite 120, Oakland, CA 94612 (510) 839–9000; www.oaklandcvb.com
Oakland.com www.oakland.com

💡 Local Events/Attractions:
Chabot Observatory and Science Center, 10902 Skyline Boulevard, Oakland, CA (510) 530–3480; www.chabotspace.org
Crafts fairs and wine tasting, July and late September, Montclair, CA (510) 339–1000; www.montclairvillage.com
General information for Oakland www.oakland.com/arts/index.html; oakland.areaguides.net/; www.sirius.com/~asta/oakland.html

🛏 Accommodations:
Berkeley and Oakland B&B Network, Berkeley and Oakland, CA (510) 547–6380; www.bbonline.com/ca/berkeley-oakland/index.html
Alameda County, San Francisco Bay Area hotels, B&Bs, inns, and resorts pts.placestostay.com/script/node.asp?n=2177&pn=1098

🍽 Restaurants:
Crogan's Montclair Restaurant, 6101 La Salle Avenue, Oakland, CA (510) 339–2098
Flipper's Gourmet Hamburgers, 2060 Mountain Boulevard, Oakland, CA (510) 339–2082
Italian Colors Restaurant, 2220 Mountain Boulevard, #100, Oakland, CA (510) 482–8094

🏕 Local Outdoor Retailers:
Montclair Sports, 1970 Mountain Boulevard, Oakland, CA (510) 339–9313

🚶 Hike Tours:
Crabcove Visitor Center, 1252 McKay Avenue, Alameda, CA 94501 (510) 521–6887; www.ebparks.org/events/byloc/redwood.htm #D25213

Ⓝ Maps:
East Bay Regional Park District Headquarters, 2950 Peralta Oaks Court, P.O. Box 5381, Oakland, CA 94605 (510) 662–PARK; www.ebparks.org/parks/redwood.htm
USGS maps: Oakland East, CA

36 Huckleberry Botanic Regional Preserve

Overview: *The self-guided nature trail guide available at the trailhead provides a chance to stop and notice the details on your walk through the 235-acre preserve. It makes for some fun learning and discovery along this loop trail rich in rare vegetation. Or just walk through the thick brush and breathe. You will descend a canyon under bays and oaks and hear the trickling of San Leandro Creek below. Follow the ridge on a narrow footpath through dense shrubs, mostly huckleberries. Short side trails take you up to bald vistas, home to rare manzanitas and hosting soothing pastoral views of the surrounding foothills.*

County: Alameda
Start: From the staging area on Skyline Boulevard
Length: 2.4-mile loop
Approximate Hiking Time: 1.5 hours
Difficulty Rating: Easy
Trail Surface: Well-maintained, narrow dirt path serpentines into a canyon with one short set of down-slope stairs, then follows the ridge, rising and falling gently
Land Status: Regional preserve
Nearest Town: Oakland
Other Trail Users: Hikers only
Canine Compatibility: Dogs not permitted, except on Skyline National Trail

Getting There

By Car: From the San Francisco–Oakland Bay Bridge, take the Park Boulevard exit; turn left toward Montclair Village. Turn right on Snake Road. It will wind around through neighborhoods, becoming Shepherd Canyon Road. At the road's end, turn left on Skyline Boulevard. Turn into the parking lot to your right where you see the sign HUCKLEBERRY BOTANIC REGIONAL PRESERVE. From Highway 24, take the Fish Ranch Road exit, just east of the Caldecott Tunnel. Continue 0.8 mile on Fish Ranch Road to Grizzly Peak Boulevard. Turn left and go 0.24 mile on Grizzly Peak to Skyline Boulevard. Turn left and drive approximately 0.5 mile to the park entrance, on the left, past Sibley Volcanic Regional Preserve.

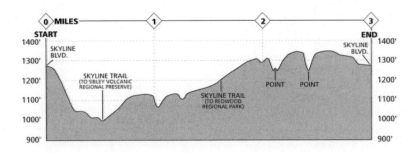

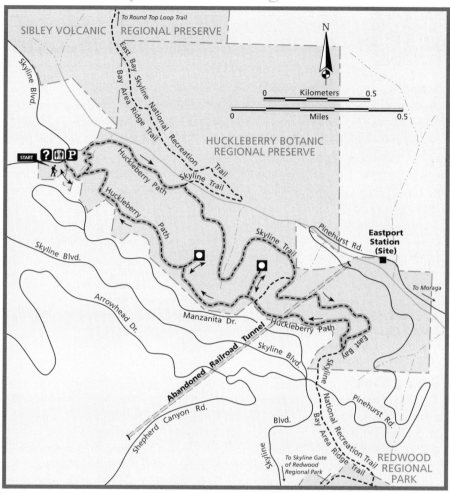

By Public Transportation: From Nineteenth Street BART, take AC Transit bus #59A; from Lake Merritt BART, take AC Transit bus #59 or #59A. These bus lines go to the Montclair Transit Center. From there, transfer to AC Transit bus #5, and exit at the stop on Colton Boulevard and Ridgewood Drive. Walk the short distance from Colton to Skyline Boulevard, turn left, and proceed to the park. It is a mostly level 0.5-mile walk. For times and other details, contact AC Transit Trav-Info (510–817–1717; www.actransit.org).

Hike Description

Looking for a walk to inspire you? A stroll along Huckleberry Botanic Regional Preserve's winding, narrow pathway, surrounded by dense, flowering shrubs, is like a walk through a medieval maze. It provides seclusion, triggers the imagination, and offers a botanical adventure.

Take the short detours up to the two manzanita barrens—a totally different land-scape with sandy, shell rock, rare manzanita and views.

The self-guided nature path guide, available at the bulletin board by the trail-head, describes the plant life you see at the markers along the trail. The information is surprisingly fascinating (even for nongreen thumbs), adding discovery to your walk. Featured are the pliable western leatherwood, the pioneering brittleleaf manzanita, and the sticky-berried pallid manzanita. Extremely rare, you cannot find them anywhere else in the world but these Bay Area foothills.

The park guide calls Huckleberry Preserve "an island of time . . . what's left of a time gone by." Not a part of the Spanish land grant system in the late 1700s, like surrounding areas, this canyon was saved from the grazing cattle that brought so many drastic changes around here. The ancient rock strata below the foliage once lay at the bottom of a deep ocean basin. It contains remains of microscopic diatoms and simple marine life. Subjected to uplift and folding, the bedrock now stands exposed as hard, brittle bands of chert and shale with soil low in nutritional value. Manzanitas like these conditions.

With the complex topography of the area, Huckleberry even has its own Mediterranean-type climate: warm, dry summers and cool, wet winters. This weather pattern used to occur more commonly in the Bay Area of the past. Dense ocean fogs sometimes coat the place in summer, lasting for days. This creates moisture for the local plant life during a time when rainfall is rare. Thus, you can find blooms and birds in the middle of winter. Late summer and fall is berry season, and birds like the golden-crowned sparrow, orange-crowned warbler, purple finch, and California thrasher are abundant. The animals have their pick of juicy berries: thimbleberries, osoberries, California coffeeberries, elderberries, and dwarf snow-berries besides the fruitful huckleberries.

But it's not all peace and love among the plant life here. In the preserve you become witness to botanical warfare. The resilient huckleberry bushes are slowly taking over the manzanita, aided by the shade of live oaks and bay laurels that have moved into the area. You can see indications of this conflict throughout the park.

If hiking with companions, read the guide aloud; it's more fun. If you are feeling playful, you can create some entertaining games out of the tour, like differentiating the types of ferns and manzanita, determining if the coast silktassel is male or female, identifying the "battlefields" where the coast huckleberry is attempting to dominate the disappearing manzanita, and spotting basal burls wherever you can (they are plentiful). You may be a new fan of flora in the next two hours.

Another reason for its preservation is that Huckleberry was among the first lands purchased in 1936 by the newly formed East Bay Park District. Previously owned by the East Bay Municipal Utilities District, the hills still serve as watershed for the San Leandro Creek. In prehistory, this land was used by the Jalquin tribe, members of the Ohlonean language group. Living along the coast or in the canyon mouths below, they probably traveled to this site for hunting and food gathering, sources of stone for toolmaking, and for religious ritual.

The Oakland, Antioch and Eastern Railroad, constructed in the 1850s, passed through here. It connected Oakland with central Contra Costa County. The eastern end of the tunnel (now closed) was located in Huckleberry. It was known as Eastport. In a redwood grove nearby, William Jennings Bryan delivered a campaign speech to the picnicking residents of Canyon and other towns. The line was later reorganized into the Sacramento Northern Electric Railway and abandoned in the mid-1950s. The park became preserve in the 1970s.

Starting from the parking lot, an arrow on the trailhead will show you the way. The loop clockwise offers more of a climax and follows the nature guide. The whole trail is well marked.

You will first descend into a canyon through a mature bay forest. Switchbacks ease the steepness down. Take a whiff of the pungent bays (they are five times more potent than the commercial spice). You will also hear running water from the San Leandro Creek below you (where rainbow trout were first identified as a species). Walking along the ridge in the shade of the trees beside banks of ferns, the narrow path feels secluded and serene, except for the occasional jogger. On the Skyline Trail, oaks dominate and the trail is a bit dryer. The upper

A regional preserve is an area of at least 100 acres with a suitable staging area that must include either a significant historical/cultural resource or a natural feature of scientific importance. This last can be a rare or endangered plant or animal species and its supporting ecosystem, significant fossils or geological features, or unusual topographic features.

Hike Information

● Trail Contact:

East Bay Regional Park District Headquarters, 2950 Peralta Oaks Court, P.O. Box 5381, Oakland, CA 94605 (510) 662–PARK; www.ebparks.org/parks/huck.htm

● Schedule:

Open daily year-round from 5:00 A.M. to 10:00 P.M. unless otherwise posted

● Fees/Permits:

None

● Local Information:

Oakland Convention and Visitors Bureau, 475 Fourteenth Street, Suite 120, Oakland, CA 94612 (510) 839–9000; www.oaklandcvb.com
Oakland.com www.oakland.com

● Local Events/Attractions:

Oakland Zoo, 9777 Golf Links Road, Oakland, CA 94605 (510) 632–9525; www.oaklandzoo.org/services/visitorserv.html
Dunsmuir House and Garden, 2960 Peralta Oaks Park, Oakland, CA (510) 562–7588 or (510) 615–5555
East Bay Gardens www.gardens.com/garden/g_geo.htm
General information for Oakland www.oakland.com/arts/index.html; oakland.areaguides.net; www.sirius.com/~asta/oakland.html

● Accommodations:

Dean's Bed & Breakfast, 5655 Oak Grove Avenue, Oakland, CA 94618 (510)

652–5024; kellyman@pacbell.net
Berkeley and Oakland B&B Network, Berkeley and Oakland, CA (510) 547–6380; www.bbonline.com/ca/berkeley-oakland/index.html
Alameda County, San Francisco Bay Area hotels, B&Bs, inns, and resorts pts.placestostay.com/script/node.asp?n=2177&pn=1098

● Restaurants:

Isobune Sushi, 5897 College Avenue, Oakland, CA (510) 601–1424
La Mediterranee, 2936 College Avenue, Berkeley, CA (510) 540–7773
Zachary's Chicago Pizza, 5801 College Avenue, Oakland, CA (510) 655–6385

● Local Outdoor Retailers:

Any Mountain, 2777 Shattuck Avenue, Berkeley, CA (510) 665–3939
Marmot Mountain Works, 3049 Adeline, Berkeley, CA (510) 849–0735
REI, 1338 San Pablo Avenue, Berkeley, CA (510) 527–4140

● Hike Tours:

Crabcove Visitor Center, Alameda, CA (510) 521–6887; www.ebparks.org

● Maps:

East Bay Regional Park District Headquarters, 2950 Peralta Oaks Court, P.O. Box 5381, Oakland, CA 94605 (510) 662–PARK or 622–7275; www.ebparks.org/parks/huck.htm
USGS maps: Oakland East, CA

Huckleberry Trail, going back toward the trailhead, hosts wonderfully thick plant life, at one point creating a low canopy overhead. You feel like a giant wandering in a dwarfed fairy tale forest. Beware of poison oak that grows right beside the trail.

In sharp contrast, there is one strip of land through the middle of Huckleberry owned by Pacific Gas and Electric. You can't miss it, with the giant steel towers and strung electricity and telephone service lines. A meditation on industry whether you want it or not, it is thankfully only brief in passing.

On the last part of the trail, you will find the .03-mile diversions up to sandy manzanita barrens well worth the short treks. The peaceful, open views include Flicker Ridge, Las Trampas Ridge, and the rise of Mount Diablo.

Miles/Directions

0.0 START at Huckleberry Botanic Regional Preserve trailhead on Skyline Boulevard in the staging area/parking lot.

0.4 Bear right for loop. **Option:** To the left is Skyline Trail heading to Sibley Volcanic Regional Preserve.

0.9 Bear left to extend Huckleberry loop with part of Skyline Trail. *(Note: Turning right would shorten hike to 1.69 miles.)*

1.3 Turn right back onto Huckleberry Path.

1.6 Stay straight. Path heading to the right is the shortcut from where you just came from.

1.7 Take this .03-mile diversion up to manzanita barren for rare California coastal plant life and a good view of Mount Diablo.

1.9 Another .03-mile diversion with three markers for the Huckleberry Self-guided Nature Path.

2.4 Back at parking lot.

37 Robert Sibley Volcanic Regional Preserve

Overview: *What do the Robert Sibley Volcanic Regional Preserve and Mount Saint Helens have in common? The subduction process that caused the explosion here ten million years ago of a great volcanic center eventually moved northward to cause the activity and eruption of Washington's Mount Saint Helens. The park trail guide available at the trailhead includes a self-guided tour of Round Top's fascinating geological journey. Hiking among Monterey pines and on open grassy hills, you will see walls of the caldera left by the ancient blast, old river gravels, basalt lava flows, and varicolored "redbeds," layers of oxidized iron explored worldwide for fossils. Remains have been found of mastodons, hipparions, camels, and prongbucks in the old quarries here. More recently, enthusiastic hikers have built a series of rock mazes in the quarries, complete with altars at their centers. Walking through these formations and admiring the offerings at the altars provide great entertainment. The park is pleasant for walking or jogging. Overall, the hike is easy but with many rising and falling slopes. Those wishing them can find steeper descents up to Round Top and out of the quarries.*

County: Alameda
Start: Robert Sibley Volcanic Regional Preserve entrance on Skyline Boulevard
Length: 3.6-mile loop, with some detours
Approximate Hiking Time: 2 hours

Difficulty Rating: Easy to moderate
Trail Surface: Mostly well-packed dirt trail that varies in width, but with some loose gravel, and finish on a paved path
Land Status: Regional preserve

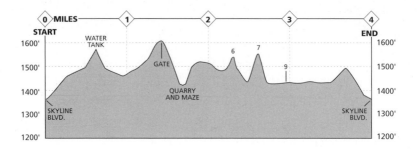

Nearest Town: Oakland and Berkeley
Other Trail Users: Hikers and equestrians only except on the Volcanic Trail and last section of Round Top Loop Trail, where bicycles are also allowed

Canine Compatibility: Dogs on leash

Getting There

By Car: From the San Francisco–Oakland Bay Bridge, take I–580 to I–24. Take the Fish Ranch Road exit just east of the Caldecott Tunnel. Continue 0.8 mile to Grizzly Peak Boulevard. Turn left and go 0.24 mile on Grizzly Peak to Skyline Boulevard. Turn left on Skyline and proceed to the well-marked park entrance on the left.

By Public Transportation: From the Nineteenth Street BART station, take AC Transit bus #59A; from Lade Merritt BART, take AC Transit bus #59 or #59A. These bus lines go to the Montclair Transit Center. From there, transfer to AC Transit bus #5, and exit at the stop on Colton Boulevard and Ridgewood Drive. Walk the short distance from Colton to Skyline Boulevard, turn left, and proceed to the park. It is a mostly level 0.9-mile walk. For more information, contact AC Transit TravInfo (510–817–1717; www.actransit.org).

Hike Description

The Robert Sibley Volcanic Regional Preserve from its beginnings is a story of fire. This greatly loved 660-acre park includes a self-guided geologic tour and an assortment of terrain, views, and trails through Monterey pines, blue gum eucalyptus, and grasslands looping around Round Top Peak. A mere 1,761 feet, people still refer to Round Top as a mountain, perhaps in respect of its eruptive past.

Fire arose from water about ten million years ago. A freshwater lake extended from what is now Tilden Park north to San Leandro Reservoir south and east to Lafayette. Within these waters, a volcano began to thrust itself upward on the western shores. It spewed lava, took a break of a dozen or a few hundred years for sediment to fill in, then gushed again. During its active period, the volcano released at least eleven lava flows with two explosive episodes of epic proportions. One violent eruption likely equaled that of Mount Saint Helens in Washington. This breath of fire helped shaped the area's ridges and formed the mound known as Round Top. Today, you can see the alternating volcanic and sedimentary layers that were folded, tilted, crumpled, and tossed about by millions of years of earthquake activity. Welcome to California.

Sibley Volcanic Regional Preserve

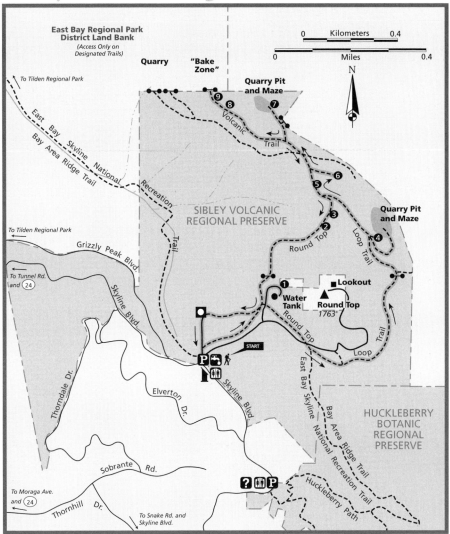

You may see students from nearby UC–Berkeley or teens with high school science assignments taking notes and snapping pictures of red-streaked rock in cut hillsides. Sibley's complex rock formations are enough to make a grown geologist giggle. Rock quarries north of the peak have made features even more visible. Years of commercial gouging by the land's previous owner, the Kaiser Corporation, exposed old lava flows, mudflows, volcanic dikes, vents, cinder piles, and other geologic forms.

Long after the area subdued its volcanic temperament and the land settled, Native Americans of the Ohlonean language group moved in. No doubt, Round

Top was the site of religious rituals, being the highest peak in the vicinity. Instead of modern communication towers up there, imagine wisps of smoke rising from a well-tended bonfire into a western sunset. East Bay rangers have found Indian arrowheads in the little preserve as testimony to their presence.

In the twentieth century, Round Top was witness to fire many times. Author and journalist Herman James Whitaker stood on the peak of Round Top on April 19, 1906, the day after the San Francisco earthquake. He watched flames engulf the city on the bay and described what he saw for *Harper's* magazine. From then on, Round Top became a place to watch fires rage and the landscape change.

In 1910, millionaire Frank Havens founded the Mahogany Eucalyptus and Land Company that forever changed the look of the area, and was eventually the cause of more fire. His ill-conceived idea was to cover the crests of the Oakland–Berkeley Hills with great forests of Australian eucalyptus trees. They are, he proclaimed, "the most valuable tree on the face of the globe. No teak, mahogany, ebony, hickory, or oak was ever tougher, denser, stronger or of more glorious hardness." Havens promised investors quick riches, with saplings that would grow 5 or 6 inches in a single day.

For three years, Havens lured thousands of investors. He set up nine nurseries and an arboretum that employed as many as 200 men at one time. They planted eucalyptus by the millions along the 14-mile stretch from North Berkeley to what is now Redwood Park. Round Top was the center of Havens' new eucalyptus empire, and it is he who built Skyline Boulevard as a scenic drive to connect his various real estate and lumber holdings in the hills.

So vainly self-assured was Havens that he planted the trees without ever verifying his claim. In 1913, he invited a forester to test mill a few of the trees. That's when he learned the terrible truth: The blue gum eucalyptus he had planted was worthless. It turned out that blue gum was never used for lumber in Australia, and the species of eucalyptus that the Australians did use were so slow growing that the trees could not be harvested until they were several hundred years old.

That forester, whoever he was, is an unsung hero. If he had found the trees to be half as valuable as Havens expected, the East Bay Hills today could well be the scene of massive logging operations instead of quiet neighborhoods and scattered parkland. Unfortunately, Haven's hot, oily, and quick-burning eucalyptus led to tragedy in the 1920s, panic in the 1970s, and in 1991, the worst fire involving loss of life and property since the San Francisco earthquake of 1906.

The abandoned eucalyptus trees were never thinned or in any way tended. For decades Round Top was covered with an impenetrable jungle. The year 1923 saw a disastrous fire in Berkeley made worse by the hot-burning eucalyptus out that way. That same year, the East Bay Hills Fire Protection Committee built an official fire lookout on Round Top.

In 1973, loggers downed most of the Australian transplants. This allowed bay trees, Monterey pines, coyote brush, and poison oak to grow. But the resilient eucalyptus made a comeback. Within ten years, the Oakland hills smelled of pungent blue gum once more.

On Sunday, October 20, 1991, winds in excess of 65 miles per hour gusted and swirled through the dangerously dry Oakland hills. Five years of drought had made the brush brittle, and groves of Monterey pines and eucalyptus trees were once again freeze-damaged from the previous winter. An unseen ember found a parched eucalyptus tree. It burst into flames, and fire raced down from the crest of the Oakland–Berkeley Hills toward downtown Oakland on both sides of Highway 24. The East Bay hills firestorm killed twenty-five people and destroyed 3,469 homes, with an estimated loss of $1.537 billion.

An attempt was made to remove more eucalyptus trees from the area after that. But as you'll see, the spunky eucalyptus grove around Round Top is growing back again, despite another brushfire in August 1998.

There is an old story that an ancient Indian cave and burial ground exists somewhere in the park, but contemporary park officials don't know much about it. And then there is the air of mysticism around the mazes in Sibley. There are five of them, with two on marked trails. The rest take wandering to find. The main rock maze in the large quarry was the first, created by Montclair artist Helena Mazzariello in 1989 as a gift to fellow hikers. She modeled it after ancient mazes on the island of Crete in the Mediterranean and uses it as a meditation device. The creators of the other mazes are unknown.

In the spirit of this continually shifting park, its name was changed from Round Top to the Robert Sibley Volcanic Preserve in 1972 to honor Robert Sibley, a "visionary who made his visions come true," according to friends. Sibley was one of the park district's founders and board president from 1949 until his death in 1958. He used to love to hike this park, which in 1936 became one of the first East Bay regional parks. It comprised only a couple hundred acres then. In 1977, the quarry site north of Round Top was added (381 acres). In 1991 came the northwest quarry and surrounding land (660 acres).

Start your walk facing the visitor center, where you can read interpretive plaques describing the geologic history of the park. There are samples of the different types of volcanic rock as well as lists of the plants and animals in the park. There are also benches, flush toilets, and drinking water.

Start to the left of the structure. You'll see a paved trail and to the right of it a beckoning single-track, dirt path heading into the hills. The marker identifies it as the Bay Area Ridge Trail. Take this trail to start your hike. (Warning: There is a lot of poison oak in the wooded sections of this hike. If you're sensitive, you may want to wear long pants.)

Soon, you can look down to your right and see the paved road that leads to the water tank and communications towers on the peak of Round Top. The peak is an easement, owned and controlled by the East Bay Municipal Utilities District. If there are hikers on the road, you may feel you have found a secret treasure on your more scenic path above them. In the distance to your right are homes on Skyline Boulevard.

You'll come to a trail marker. Follow signs toward Round Top Loop, not Volcanic Loop.

The Mazzariello Maze is modeled after the mazes of ancient Crete and was created by the artist as a gift to fellow hikers.

This takes you across the road, staying on the Bay Area Ridge Trail. Lift your feet to avoid roots along the trail. You may run into a squawking stellar jay or hear robins and wrens rustling in the bushes. Great-horned owls hoot at dawn and dusk.

When you see another sign for Round Top Loop Trail that points to the left, turn onto that trail. You may feel much farther away from the city during this section among the oaks. Breathe deeply. You will come upon an obvious and well-used trail on your right, though unmarked. Turn onto it. The two-person-wide trail through a eucalyptus grove is still Round Top Loop (a trailhead will soon confirm this). You can see here how the eucalyptus grew back after fires and freezes.

Hawks love to circle above these canyons. Keep an eye out for red-tailed hawks and even the rare golden eagles. After you climb a short hill, the terrain ahead of you opens up to grassland, golden in summer and fall, green in winter and early spring. Go through the cattle gate. To the right in the distance, you can see Mount Diablo. Farther up on the ridge, you will find more great views. To the east is Contra Costa County. As a matter of fact, you will cross back and forth between the two counties in this park. The line was originally drawn here to make equal division of the giant redwood forest that grew in these canyons until clearcut in 1860 (see Redwood Regional Park, page 250). Below you to the northeast are the cities of Orinda, Moraga, and Lafayette. The small body of water you see is the Lafayette Reservoir. The highway is Highway 24, just north of the Caldecott Tunnel. The westernmost end of the park takes hikers on the land above the tunnel.

In the foreground, you can see parts of hills cut away, a reminder that this area was heavily quarried prior to becoming parkland. Trek ahead, staying on Round Top Loop Trail. During the rainy season, come prepared for mud. Runoff from Round Top can make shady sections of the path a bit goopy.

There's a railing ahead. A wooden sign there is marker #4. The number refers to the self-guided geologic tour in the park (guide available at visitor center). Huge amounts of massive basalt lava were removed from this quarry pit. The result is a tremendous boon to geology, for the pit exposes the interior of the Round Top volcano.

At the base of the pit is Mazzariello's maze. For a quick, fun detour, head back to the main trail and turn left (east). Follow the trail down into the pit, where you can walk the maze, meditate if you wish, and make an offering in the middle. Past offerings may include anything from hairclips to Cliff Bars. This side journey offers a different perspective. Between the depth of the quarry, the exposed volcanic history in the walls, and the maze, many hikers report a sense of wonder here.

Go back the way you came, noticing the red-barked madrone trees to the east. Enjoy the view at the railing one more time, then go past marker #4, heading northwest on Round Top Loop Trail. At the next trail marker, go straight onto the Volcanic Trail, which comes up from the left. Have your self-guided tour brochure handy to read about more geological sights.

Site #5 on your right exposes Orinda Formation: river gravels, sands, and mudstones. The red streaks and layers in these riverbeds were caused by oxidation of iron in the sediments. Called redbeds, they are explored worldwide for plant and animal fossils. "Bake zones," areas of intense red, are rocks that were baked by brushfires and sunlight.

Site #6 is hidden from the trail. Follow the directions in the guide. Quarrymen took the lava but left "exotic" large sandstone blocks lying around. These rocks were torn from very ancient rocks by the ascending lavas.

Site #7 requires a short detour. The path leads to another quarry bed and spade-shaped maze. Go back the way you came, then turn right back onto the Volcanic Trail.

You'll come to markers #8 and #9. There's a gate that reads NOT FOR PUBLIC. It is part of the park, but is currently a Land Bank Area. Enter it and go 0.3 mile to see some intense examples of "bake zones" to the right. Go back on the Volcanic Trail. Stay on the trail past where it becomes the familiar Round Top Loop again. Just past marker #5, turn right onto the other curve of Round Top Loop Trail. You'll be coming back on the opposite side of the hill. This puts you near trees again on the slope of the little mountain.

At the cattle gate, you'll see a pedestrian gate on the left. Go through that to be back among the eucalyptus again. Just before it turns to paved road, you'll see the Bay Ridge Trail that started your hike to your right. Be sure to take the upper trail to the right of that. Steps take you down to a pretty viewing area with benches and interpretive plaques that tell you about the planting of the Australian eucalyptus in the early 1900s. Precipitation is precious here. North-face forests receive little sunlight. And in fog, the grove shields itself from parching Diablo winds. Winter rains penetrate the humus. Thus, moisture lingers, allowing decomposition to take place year-round. This safeguards a "new forest": bay laurel, madrone, and coast live oak, with an understory including coyote brush, blackberry, hazelnut, snowberries, toyon, and wild currant. Other plants include hounds tongue, sword fern, wood fern, ferrydells, woodland star, alum root, and angelica.

You can see Fish Ranch Road from here, where you may have driven in from; the KPFA (a popular local public radio station) transmitter station; and Grizzly, Chaparral and Volmer peaks. The way back to the parking lot is on a pleasant paved trail.

Miles/Directions

0.0 START at Robert Sibley Volcanic Regional Preserve entrance on Skyline Boulevard. Pick up a trail guide. Facing the visitor's center, walk to the right of it. To the right of a paved path is trailhead for Bay Area Ridge Trail. Take this single-track, dirt path.

0.2 Stay on Bay Area Ridge Trail as you cross over paved road that leads to Round Top.

0.4 Again, cross over paved road. Within about 30 feet, path will split again. Take fork to the left, Round Top Loop Trail. This leads around eastern side of Round Top.

0.6 Burned and cut logs are a result of the August 1998 fire.

0.9 Go through cattle gate.

1.0 Stop to admire views. Then go to railing and marker #4. (This corresponds to #4 on Self-Guided Tour of Round Top Volcanoes.) View the largest of quarry pits. Turn around and return to double-track trail; take the trail to the left for a diversion into the quarry.

1.1 Walk through the Mazzariello maze. Return to marker #4. Continue on Round Top Loop Trail heading northwest.

1.2 Go straight on Volcanic Trail.

1.3 Site #5 on Self-Guided Tour of Round Top Volcanoes; "redbeds" are on the right.

1.4 Take detour to the right to see site #6, sandstone from the age of the dinosaurs.

1.5 Trail splits. Stay on Volcanic Trail, the trail on the right, going straight ahead.

Hike Information

Trail Contacts:
Regional Parks Botanic Garden, Tilden Park (510) 841–8732
East Bay Regional Park District Headquarters, 2950 Peralta Oaks Court, P.O. Box 5381, Oakland, CA 94605 (510) 662–PARK or 662–7275; www.ebparks.org/parks/sibley.htm

Schedule:
Open daily year-round from 5:00 A.M. to 10:00 P.M. unless otherwise posted

Fees/Permits:
None

Local Information:
Oakland Convention and Visitors Bureau, 475 Fourteenth Street, Suite 120, Oakland, CA 94612 (510) 839–9000; www.oaklandcvb.com
Oakland.com www.oakland.com

Local Events/Attractions:
Oakland Museum of California, 1000 Oak Street, Oakland, CA (888) Oak–Muse or (510) 238–2200; www.museumca.org
Jack London Square, 30 Jack London Square, Oakland, CA (510) 814–6000
Yoshi's Japanese Restaurant and World Class Jazz House, Jack London Square, Oakland, CA (510) 238–9200
General information for Oakland www.oakland.com/arts/index.html; oakland.areaguides.net; www.sirius.com/~asta/oakland.html

Accommodations:
Berkeley and Oakland B&B Network, Berkeley and Oakland, CA (510) 547–6380; www.bbonline.com/ca/berkeley-oakland/index.html
Alameda County, San Francisco Bay Area hotels, B&Bs, inns, and resorts

pts.placestostay.com/script/node.asp?n=2177&pn=1098

Restaurants:
Piedmont Avenue Area:
Barney's Gourmet Hamburgers, 4162 Piedmont Avenue, Oakland, CA (510) 655–7180
Bay Wolf Restaurant, 3853 Piedmont Avenue, Oakland, CA (510) 655–6004
Cato's Ale House, 3891 Piedmont Avenue, Oakland, CA (510) 655–3349
Jack London Square Area:
Everett & Jones Barbeque, 126 Broadway Oakland, CA (510) 663–2350
Scott's Seafood Restaurant, 2 Broadway Oakland, CA (510) 444–3456

Local Outdoor Retailers:
Any Mountain, 2777 Shattuck Avenue, Berkeley, CA (510) 665–3939
Eddie Bauer, Inc., 2201 Shattuck Avenue, Berkeley, CA (510) 665–4801
Marmot Mountain Works, 3049 Adeline, Berkeley, CA (510) 849–0735
REI, 1338 San Pablo Avenue, Berkeley, CA (510) 527–4140
Wilderness Exchange, 1407 San Pablo Avenue, Berkeley, CA (510) 525–1255

Hike Tours:
Crabcove Visitor Center, 1252 McKay Avenue, Alameda, CA 94501 (510) 521–6887; www.ebparks.org

Maps:
East Bay Regional Park District Headquarters, 2950 Peralta Oaks Court, P.O. Box 5381, Oakland, CA 94605 (510) 662–PARK; www.ebparks.org/parks/sibley.htm
USGS maps: Oakland East, CA

1.6 Veer to the right to see smaller quarry and site #7.

1.7 The small quarry, marker #7. Turn around and head back to where trail veered.

1.8 To see sites #8 and #9, keep going northwest on Volcanic Trail.

2.1 Cattle gate to land bank area. Go through to view "bake zones."

2.3 "Bake zones" on the right. Turn around and head back through cattle gate and back to Volcanic Trail. Pass sites #6 and #5 again.

3.0 Turn right on Round Top Loop Trail. This heads around western side of Round Top.

3.1 Site #3 on the left. Site #2 comes up shortly after.

3.4 Walk about 10 feet or so on paved road. To the left are two dirt paths. Take upper, single-track path.

3.5 Viewing platform with interpretive plaques and benches. View of Grizzly, Chaparral, and Volmer peaks. Continue on paved path on opposite side of viewing area from which you entered.

3.6 Back at visitor center.

38 Sunol Regional Wilderness

Overview: *This loop in the 6,858-acre wilderness starts by bridging and paralleling Alameda Creek. You can borrow or buy a self-guided nature trail booklet at the visitor center to identify markers on the Indian Joe Nature Trail (wildflower identification kits and bird lists are also available). The hike will take you up through tranquil wooded canyons, past Indian Joe Cave Rocks, to grassy slopes covered with California poppies, lupine, and wild mustard in spring. The next landmark is Little Yosemite, with misting water cascading over boulders in the gorge, especially heavy in early spring and wet years. If you compare it to the real Yosemite, you'll be disappointed. But the falls are still picturesque and a wonderful discovery along your hike. You then traverse a ridge and head down a canyon with weathered green serpentine and sandstone outcrops, back through oak woodland, and finish by crossing the creek again. This is also your gateway to the Ohlone Wilderness for Bay Area backpacking.*

County: Alameda

Start: Indian Joe Nature Trail marker, by the bridge near the Sunol Regional Wilderness Visitor Center

Length: 6.0-mile loop

Approximate Hiking Time: 3.5 hours

Difficulty Rating: Moderate

Trail Surface: Single-track, dirt path rises steadily past creeks and through woodland to a double-track trail in grassland with vistas, back

down to woodland and Little Yosemite, then along a ridge on a footpath back into the canyon to the start

Land Status: Regional wilderness

Nearest Town: Sunol

Other Trail Users: Hikers only on the Indian Joe Creek Trail and Canyon View Trail; equestrians and bicyclists on Cave Rocks and Camp Ohlone Roads

Canine Compatibility: Dogs on leash

Getting There

By Car: From the Bay Bridge, head east on Highway 580 to Highway 680 in Pleasanton. Take Highway 680 south, and exit at Calaveras Road. Stay on Calaveras, past the nursery and San Francisco Water Department area, to Geary Road. Turn left on Geary Road, which leads directly to the park (sign will read SUNOL–OHLONE REGIONAL PARK). There is plenty of parking. Park near the visitor center to be close to the Indian Joe Trailhead, where this hike begins.

By Public Transportation: There is no public transportation to Sunol Regional Park. For the nearest location, contact AC Transit TravInfo (510–817 –1717; www.actransit.org).

Hike Description

The combination of landscapes here—riparian, woodland, and grassland—and abundant plant and wildlife provide for an invigorating and charming experience in Sunol, especially during the springtime, when you are sure to see dozens of species of wildflowers, birds, butterflies, and other critters, and maybe a cow feeding its calf up on the hill.

The Costanoan Indians first enjoyed this place. Sunol naturalists have found bedrock mortars used by the Native Americans for pounding acorns, reminders of their inhabitance. These early settlers found uses for most of the vegetation, rocks, and animals that thrived here, and we are lucky to find in this remote park a lot of native species not overrun by the exotics that also found their way here.

Alien species were most likely brought by the Spanish and later the American ranchers and farmers that settled here. In 1839, this park, along with 48,000 acres, most of the south-central portion of Alameda County, was granted as Rancho el Valle de San José to Antonio Mariá Suñol, the Bernal brothers, and Antonio Pico. They released cattle and sheep onto the land. The gold rush brought squatters onto the land in 1848. When California became a state in 1850, much of the land became government property, and large parcels of the ranch were sold off to settlers.

In 1865, Pat and Mary Ann Geary purchased 160 acres from the U.S. government for $2.50 an acre. They moved up here to the Sunol Valley from Mission San José, hoping to get away from it all.

The Gearys settled in a homesite next to Indian Joe Creek, about a half mile upstream from where it joins Alameda Creek (you pass the area on the Indian Joe Creek Trail). All that remains of their cabin is a pile of flat stones. Needing help to build the ranch, the Gearys hired some Indians recently released from San Quentin Prison. Indian Joe was among this group, most of whom had been jailed for stealing horses. Indian Joe, however, had been sent there for stabbing a fellow Indian. He lived in a shed located upstream from the Geary home. The shed was also used to store milk. Joe lived along the creek that would take his name until he died in the early 1950s.

The Gearys eventually acquired 1,500 acres and became prominent dairy farmers, providing milk and butter for the San Francisco market. They had eleven chil-

Sunol Regional Wilderness

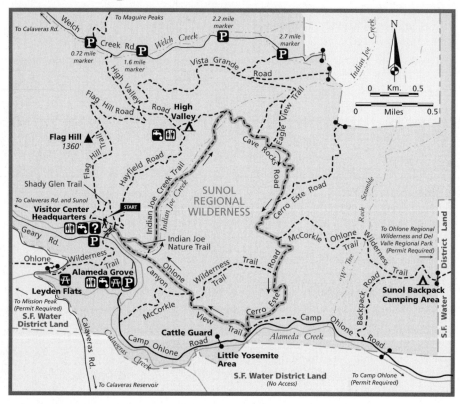

dren. In 1895, the oldest son, Maurice, built the house and Old Green Barn now used by the park as the visitor center and nature center. Later on, Maurice and his family moved into a larger house along Alameda Creek, and Pat and Mary Ann Geary moved into what is now the visitor center (the house was rebuilt after a 1954 fire). They lived in that house until they moved back to Mission San Jose, leaving the ranch to their son John.

The road you travel in on, Geary Road, was laid by Pat Geary with some help from neighbors. They constructed the whole thing with pick and shovel.

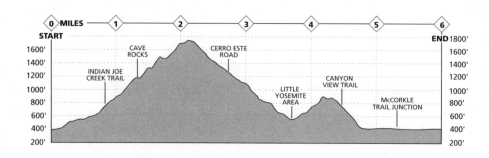

Cerro Este Road—heading downhill again with Del Valle Reservoir in the distance

A number of other families lived in the area now occupied by the regional wilderness. Two of Pat Geary's friends, Duffy and Leyden, also bought property about the same time Pat did. Leyden Creek is named after the one who built a house nearby. No signs of that house remain. Another family camped in gypsylike wagons on the spot where the lone Coulter pine tree now stands on Camp Ohlone Road.

Somewhere between Geary Road and Alameda Creek, the Rosedale School was built. The superintendent, Mr. A. A. Moore, named the school in honor of his wife, Rose. At its peak, Rosedale School had thirty students in eight grades, but enrollment declined until, in 1908, it was closed down.

To give you an idea of how much water used to flow in Alameda Creek, Rosedale's school year was arranged around the flow of water. Students had only the month of June for summer break because the school was closed from Christmas until April, when the creek was too high to cross.

Before the Calaveras dam was built (to provide water for San Francisco), Alameda Creek carried enough water to support large runs of steelhead trout, salmon, and Sacramento pike. Tule elk roamed this area (last one here killed in 1872), along with grizzly bears (last one killed in 1888), many deer, coyotes, mountain lions, and foxes. The deer and coyotes, made sparse by hunting, have been reestablished.

The last big private owner of these lands was Willis Brinker, a construction engineer from San Francisco. His company built the original San Francisco airport, the San Francisco Mint and part of the Bay Bridge, among other structures. In 1959, amid controversy, the East Bay Regional Parks District purchased 3,863 acres from Brinker to establish the Sunol Valley Regional Park. Fights to protect the land from developers in the 1960s were successful, and in 1962, the Sunol Regional Wilderness took its current name.

Miles/Directions

0.0 START at Indian Joe Nature Trail marker. To reach trailhead, facing park buildings, walk behind them and left until you see bridge crossing creek. Bridge starts hike on Indian Joe Nature Trail. After bridge, turn right and follow along bank of Alameda Creek. Stay on Indian Joe Nature Trail past Hayfield Road.

0.2 Junction with Indian Joe Creek Trail. After crossing over creek, come to trailhead for Indian Joe Creek Trail. Take a left onto single-track trail. Trail leads uphill. (*Note:* Watch for poison oak.)

0.4 Stay on Indian Joe Creek Trail past the junction with Canyon View Trail. This trail takes you through all three of the main botanical communities in Sunol Valley: riparian (river side), oak woodland, and grassland. During the next 0.92 mile, you go through cattle gate and cross creek. (*Note:* If it's running, you will cross the creek a few times.) Trail gets steeper toward the top.

1.3 Pass junction for Hayfield Road, staying on Indian Joe Creek Trail. Come to open area of sagebrush and grass and large rock outcropping. At the top of Indian Joe Creek Trail, terrain begins to change from oak woodland to grassland.

1.6 Indian Joe Creek Trail dead-ends onto Cave Rocks Road. Turn right on double-track, dirt trail. Path continues uphill. Trail allows equestrians and mountain bikers.

1.9 Junction with Eagle View Road. Turn right, staying on Cave Rocks Road. Trail continues uphill gradually.

2.6 Cerro Este overlook, Del Valle Reservoir in distance. Soon after, is trail marker for Cerro Este Road toward McCorkle Trail and Little Yosemite (1.6 miles to Little Yosemite from here). Head downhill on double-track, dirt Cerro Este Road. (*Note:* Area is prone to fire and is subject to closure or restrictions during the late summer and fall, California fire season.) Pass cattle ponds (ranchers still lease grazing rights here).

Hike Information

Trail Contacts:
Sunol Regional Wilderness Visitor Center, (510) 636–1684

East Bay Regional Park District Headquarters, 2950 Peralta Oaks Court, P.O. Box 5381, Oakland, CA 94605 (510) 662–PARK or 662–7275; www.ebparks.org/parks/sunol.htm

Schedule:
Open daily year-round from 7:00 A.M. to dusk. Gates are locked at night; campers must arrive and sign in before dusk

Fees/Permits:
$4.00 per vehicle weekends and holidays. Dog fee: $1.00 per day; free with membership. Ohlone Wilderness day permit $2.00; overnight backpacking $5.00 per person; call (510) 636–1684 for more information

Local Information:
Town of Sunol www.sunol.net
Pleasanton Chamber of Commerce, 777 Peters Avenue, Pleasanton, CA 94588 (925) 846–5858; www.pleasanton.org

Local Events/Attractions:
The Great Sunol Bed Race and Chili Cook-Off, early October (925) 862–0472
Mission San Jose, 43300 Mission Boulevard, Fremont, CA (510) 657–1797; www.pressanykey.com/missions
Niles Canyon Railway and Railroad Museum, Main Street and Kilkare Road, Sunol, CA (925) 862–9063; www.ncry.org

The Sunol Repertory Theatre at the Sunol Coffee House and Cafe, 11992 Main Street, Sunol, CA (925) 862–2020

Accommodations:
Camping in Sunol Regional Wilderness: (510) 636–1684
Lord Bradley's Inn, 43344 Mission Boulevard, Fremont, CA (510) 490–0520; www.lordbradleysinn.com; email: info@ lordbradleysinn.com

Restaurants:
Bosco's Bones & Brews Steak House and Saloon, 11922 Main Street, Sunol, CA (925) 862–2404; www.boscosbonesbrew.com
Elliston Vineyards, 463 Kilkare Road, Sunol, CA (925) 862–2377

Local Outdoor Retailers:
Fleet Feet Sports, 310 C Main Street, Pleasanton, CA (925) 426–5576
Nor-Ski and Sports, 4855 Hopyard Road, Pleasanton, CA (925) 460–0222

Hike Tours:
(510) 636–1684; www.ebparks.org/parks/sunol.htm

Maps:
East Bay Regional Park District Headquarters, 2950 Peralta Oaks Court, P.O. Box 5381, Oakland, CA 94605 (510) 662–PARK or 662–7275; www.ebparks.org/parks/sunol.htm
USGS maps: Niles, CA; LaCosta Valley, CA

3.0 Junction with McCorkle Trail. Stay on Cerro Este Road toward Little Yosemite. (*FYI:* Going west, McCorkle connects to Bay Area Ridge Trail and Ohlone Wilderness Trail that can take you all the way to Mission Peak. Going east, backpackers can take Backpack Road or make their way to Ohlone Wilderness through San Francisco Water District land to Del Valle Regional Park and beyond.)

3.8 Junction with Canyon View Trail. Stay on Cerro Este Road, continuing to Little Yosemite.

3.9 Cerro Este dead-ends at Camp Ohlone Road, a dirt and gravel service road. Turn right. Little Yosemite area starts here and continues to cattle gate. Continue on just past Little Yosemite to cattle gate.

4.2 Turn around at cattle gate and head back to Cerro Este Road Trail, the way you came.

4.5 Turn left on Cerro Este Road and walk about 0.2 mile to Canyon View Trail, just past water trough.

4.7 Trailhead for Canyon View Trail. Turn left on Canyon View Trail, which follows cattle fence through grassland corridor on single-track trail. Trail flattens out and goes along ridge, where it drops off steeply to the left (with Ohlone Road below). After the ridge, trail heads over a hill (where you may run into cows and calves), then downhill through wooded canyon.

5.3 Junction with McCorkle Trail. Stay on Canyon View Trail. Trail may be slightly eroded by hooves and rainwater, but is usually well maintained and dry.

5.7 Canyon View Trail becomes Indian Joe Nature Trail. Continue straight on Nature Trail.

5.9 Junction with Indian Joe Creek Trail. Continue straight, following Alameda Creek (on the left) to bridge.

6.0 Bridge and trailhead to park headquarters. Cross bridge back to Nature Center and parking lots.

39

Tilden Regional Park: From Jewel Lake to Wildcat Peak

Overview: *For seventy years, East Bay families have come to learn about nature, play, and create precious memories in Tilden Regional Park. That affection and wonder are tangible as you start your hike on a wooded canyon trail sloping upward to Wildcat Peak. You will likely see wildlife here, a speckled egg on the trail dropped from a nest, squirrels hopping through the trees, a banana slug. The view from Wildcat Peak (1,250 feet) is a breathtaking 360 degrees, including the San Francisco Bay and the Lamorinda areas. You will pass through Rotary Peace Grove, then enjoy a self-guided nature hike on Jewel Lake Trail on your way back to the Environmental Education Center, a well-equipped visitor center. Over the year, Tilden planners have aimed to "strike a healthy balance between the natural world and the man-made world." You see this on the drive in, passing the numerous picnic areas and trailheads, the Brazilian Room, steam train, carousel, Lake Anza swimming and fishing area, pony ride, Little Farm, education center, and protected nature area. Tilden is a great place to bring the kids (plan a shorter loop with them, Jewel Lake or the Pack Rat loop, about 0.9 mile).*

County: Alameda
Start: Tilden Nature Area on Central Park Road, behind the Environmental Education Center at the Laurel Canyon Trailhead
Length: 3.8-mile loop
Approximate Hiking Time: 2 hours
Difficulty Rating: Moderate, with a couple short but strenuous uphill sections
Trail Surface: Single-track, dirt path crossing

several sturdy bridges leads up the canyon to the double-track Wildcat Peak Trail, then loops back down into the woods again.
Land Status: Regional park
Nearest Town: Berkeley
Other Trail Users: Hikers only; equestrians permitted on Wildcat Creek Trail
Canine Compatibility: No dogs allowed in nature study area

Getting There

By Car: From the San Francisco–Oakland Bay Bridge, take Highway 580 east to Highway 24 east toward Walnut Creek. Before hitting the Caldecott Tunnel, get into the right lane. Immediately after the tunnel, exit on Fish Ranch Road. Turn right back over the freeway. Follow Fish Ranch to a four-way stop sign. Turn right on Grizzly Peak Road; signs read TO TILDEN. This is a scenic drive with great westward views, trailheads, and turnoffs to Tilden attractions like the Brazilian Room, steam train, Lake Anza, and carousel on the way. Turn right on Golf Course Drive. Golf course is on the right. Take a right on Shasta Road; again, a sign reads TO TILDEN PARK. Turn right on Wild Canyon Road. Turn right on Central Park Drive, the main entrance to Tilden Regional Park. Follow signs to the Nature Area and Little Farm. There is ample free parking.

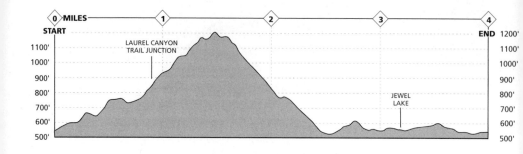

From the San Francisco–Oakland Bay Bridge, drive east on I–80. Take the Buchanan Street/Albany exit, turning right at the light onto Buchanan. After Buchanan crosses San Pablo, the name changes to Marin. Stay on Marin until you reach Spruce at a four-way stop sign. Turn left on Spruce, and go approximately 2 miles. After you cross Grizzly Peak, take a quick left down Canon Drive. At the bottom, turn left on Central Park Drive and take it to the parking lot at the end.

By Public Transportation: On weekends and holidays, take bus #67 from the Berkeley BART station to the park at Canon Drive, along Central Park Drive and Wildcat Canyon Road, and exit the park at Shasta Road. The route provides access to the Environmental Education Center and the Little Farm in Tilden Nature Area, the carousel, Lake Anza (a short walk), the Brazilian Room, the Botanic Garden, and several trailheads. On weekdays bus #67 operates only to the Canon Drive and Shasta Road entrances. For more information, contact AC Transit and BART TravInfo (510–817–1717; www.actransit.org).

Hike Description

Tilden is the East Bay's wilderness playground, combining barnyard animals, beloved pony rides, and a registered antique carousel with a protected nature area accessible to hikers only and home to readily seen wildlife and native and exotic plants (see sidebar, page 281). No park in the area better mirrors the intense public debate about balancing the preservation of parklands against the public use of these resources. It also illustrates changing ecophilosophies over the past seventy years. For example, a plan in the more development-oriented 1960s involving construction of an interpretive amphitheater, milk house, smoke house, milk bar, and nine-hole golf course never came to fruition. With twenty-first-century sensibilities, people are now more grateful for open space than fresh milk.

Despite the controversy, Tilden is truly the heart of the East Bay Regional Park District (EBRPD), part of the first land acquisition for wilderness preservation in the San Francisco Bay Area in 1934. The expansive park was named in honor of native Californian and champion of its cause Charles Lee Tilden in 1936. Part of the first graduating class of UC–Berkeley and the first EBRPD president, Tilden helped found the park system. With money from Bay Area real estate, lumber, mining, and shipbuilding, he made personal donations when necessary to uphold the

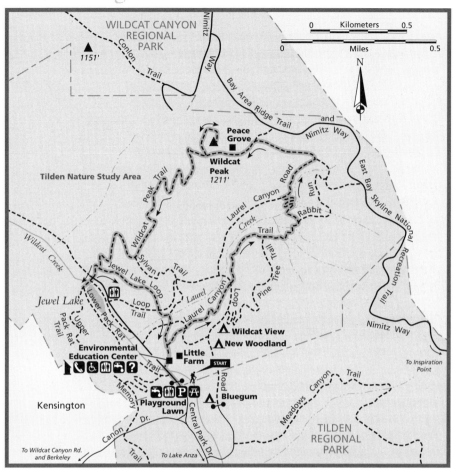

first goal of the park's board of directors: Acquire all available wilderness for parkland before it is lost forever.

On summer weekends, you will see a lot of people here. This is the most frequented park in the East Bay. But most visitors do not venture far past the manmade attractions and picnic areas. You can still find breathing space and a pleasing bit of wilderness in the canyons and hills.

Near the trailhead is the Little Farm, a community-created project designed to expose urban children to farm animals. The pint-size barn was built by Berkeley High School carpentry students in 1953 and has hosted countless schoolchildren since then. In the 1960s, horse-drawn farm implements were placed around the area to show youngsters how to raise and harvest a crop. In the 1970s, young people could ride noisy miniature tractors around an oval track.

The current Environmental Education (EEC) opened in 1974 and replaced the cluster of buildings used by the Civilian Conservation Corps (CCC) in the 1930s.

The Rotary Peace Grove of giant sequoias on Wildcat Peak Trail

The CCC cleared many of the trails here and built the stone signs, drinking fountains, and rest rooms you see today. CCC members planted trees for erosion control, lay roadways, and created the Tilden Golf Course.

The Tilden Nature Area's 740 acres are on the northern end of the park, adjacent to Wildcat Canyon Regional Park. Ten miles of hiking trails ramble through creekside woodlands, eucalyptus groves, grasslands, and coastal scrubland. The EEC (open from 10:00 A.M. to 5:00 P.M.) serves as the interpretive center for the nature area as well as the park headquarters. It's a great resource. Buy or borrow the self-guiding trail booklet for the Jewel Lake Trail. You will hit this easy trail on the way back down from the peak. All the trailheads in the nature area are marked by symbols. A leaf and berry represents the Laurel Canyon Trail, the first trail of the loop; a landing duck symbol tells you that you are on the Jewel Lake Trail.

The Laurel Canyon Trail offers the shade of two large eucalyptus groves, several small groves of conifers, dense oak/bay woodland, mature coastal brush, rich creek vegetation, grassland, and areas of coyote brush. The rare Oakland mariposa tree (*Calochortus umbellatus*) grows in the nature area about 150 yards north of the EEC. The ground is carpeted with leaves, branches, and long shreds of eucalyptus bark. Look for scurrying East Coast fox squirrels, introduced to the park in the 1960s.

Trickling Laurel Creek is a major tributary of Wildcat Creek, home to native steelhead trout. Several bridges cross the creek on your meander through Laurel Canyon. Among the riparian woodland are arroyo willow trees and white alder. Sword and wood ferns add to the lushness of the scene. It's a steady, moderately strenuous trek uphill that brings you to the Wildcat Peak Trail, a ridge trail where you can admire westward views. A surprising and pleasant sight along this sunny trail is the garden of redwoods in the Rotary Peace Grove.

The Peace Grove was established in 1955 by the Berkeley chapter to celebrate the golden anniversary of Rotary International. The one hundred giant sequoias are each monuments to individuals who have made a notable contribution to the advancement of international understanding, peace, and goodwill. Every year, Rotarians gather in a ceremony here to dedicate another tree. Take a moment to wander around these future giants.

The detour to Wildcat Peak (1,250 feet) is worth the short, steep trek, with 360-degree views that show off both the natural beauty and man-made splendor of the area. Hike in the morning if you want good photos of the bay.

Heading back down on the Peak Trail, you are likely to see native wildflowers: bright orange California poppies, lupine, wild hyacinth, buttercup, and mallow.

Attractions in Tilden

Tilden Park's **carousel** was built in 1911 by European artisans employed at the Hershell Spillman Company of Tonawanda, New York. It features fifty-nine hand-carved horses and other animals as well as a pipe organ. Purchased in 1953, it is another tribute to Charles Lee Tilden, in honor of his ninety-first birthday. It was added to the National Register of Historic Places in 1976.

The **pony ride** has been an attraction in Tilden since the late 1940s. A great many East Bay natives have ridden the ponies as children.

The **Brazilian Room** has a bronze statue of Tilden in front. The stone building was completed in 1941 to house the Brazilian Room, a popular exhibit that appeared at the San Francisco's World Fair of 1939 on Treasure Island, which is now halfway across the Bay Bridge. Used to entertain World War II soldiers for parties and high teas, it is currently one of the most popular wedding sites in the Bay Area.

The **Botanical Gardens** here cost $1 million to create back in 1953, but the twenty-acre site botanically represents the whole state of California.

Lake Anza opened to the public in 1939 with an aquatic sports carnival featuring synchronized swimmers. You can take a splash or fish for largemouth bass, rainbow trout, and catfish, among others.

The **Tilden Golf Course,** constructed by the CCC in 1937, is an eighteen-hole course operated by a private consessionaire.

The **steam train** is the Redwood Valley Railway (RVR), popularly known as the "Little Train." Constructed in 1952, it is one of the most authentic miniature steam trains in the United States. It was built at a scale of 5 inches to 1 foot, and it burns oil. The 1¼-mile ride is on narrow slopes and gives brief views of San Pablo Bay.

Most of the grass is Spanish annual, accidentally introduced along with cattle, but you can see patches of native perennial bunchgrasses too, mostly in wetter, shadier areas.

You may get a whiff of a maple tree or see the nuts of a buckeye tree that grow on the northwest-facing slopes of Wildcat Canyon. Shrubs include blackberry and hazelnut. Several common herbs grow here too: Solomon's seal, fairy bells, and alum root, among others. You are likely to see jackrabbits scurrying into this brush. A black-tailed deer may freeze and run while red-tailed and sparrow hawks soar through the sky above. You may not see the animals themselves, but look for prints of bobcats, coyotes, fox, and long-tailed weasel. Examples of their tracks are in the EEC.

Serenading your way are songbirds like the bushtit, northern mockingbird, song sparrow, western meadowlark, and American goldfinch. Despite a problem with feral cats, the songbirds still flourish here.

On the Jewel Lake Trail, numbered wooden markers correspond to the self-guided trail booklet. Learn about the spicy bay trees and all their uses. The bays were planted here in honor of Joshua Barkin, an eastern factory worker turned California naturalist who worked in Tilden for twenty years. Douglas fir, incense cedar, and Monterey pines also came to Tilden as memorial plantings. Standing on the bridge above Jewel Lake, see if you can spot western pond turtles among the cat-tails.

End your hike back at the EEC, where you can learn more about Tilden Park and freshen up. If you have the time and inclination, drive over for a ride on the carousel before you go.

Miles/Directions

0.0 START from parking lot for Tilden Nature Area. Walk across bridge to Environmental Education Center (EEC).

0.1 If starting hike between 10:00 A.M. and 5:00 P.M., visit EEC. If EEC is closed, go around building to right next to Little Farm to reach trailhead.

0.1 Look for Laurel Canyon Trail (trailhead to the left).

0.2 Pass over service road. Continue straight on Laurel Canyon Trail.

0.5 Cross over double-track road. Head down it about 50 feet to the left for continuation of Laurel Canyon Trail. (Note: Watch out for poison oak beside trail.)

0.8 Stay on Laurel Canyon Trail as you pass trailhead for Pine Tree Trail. Several more bridges pass over Laurel Creek.

0.9 Trail splits. Turn left on Laurel Canyon Trail. Path heads downhill then up switchbacks.

1.0 Turn right on Laurel Canyon Road, a double-track trail heading up to Wildcat Peak Trail.

1.2 At the Y, go left onto Peak Trail. It becomes single-track before becoming wider dirt road. You hit a strenuous but short uphill section.

Hike Information

Trail Contact:
East Bay Regional Park District
Headquarters, 2950 Peralta Oaks Court,
P.O. Box 5381, Oakland, CA 94605 (510)
662-PARK; www.ebparks.org/parks/tna.htm
or www.ebparks.org/parks/tilden.htm

Schedule:
Open daily year-round from 8:00 A.M. to
10:00 P.M. unless otherwise posted

Fees/Permits:
None

Local Information:
Berkeley Convention and Visitors
Bureau and Film Office, 2015 Center
Street, Berkeley, CA 94704-1204;
(510) 549-7040 or (800) 847-4823;
www.berkeleycvb.com
Berkeley Chamber of Commerce,
1834 University Avenue, Berkeley, CA 94703
(510) 549-7000; www.berkeleychamber.com
City of Berkeley
www.ci.berkeley.ca.us/default.asp
UC-Berkeley Visitor Services, 101 University Hall, 2200 University Avenue, Berkeley, CA 94703 (510) 642-5215 or
642-INFO; www.berkeley.edu; e-mail:
visitor_info@pa.urel.berkeley.edu

Local Events/Attractions:
Tilden Park (510) 662-PARK;
www.ebparks.org/parks/tilden.htm
Berkeley Art Museum, 2626 Bancroft
Way, Berkeley, CA (510) 642-0808
Berkeley Repertory Theatre, 2025
Addison Street, Berkeley, CA
(510) 845-4700; www.berkeleyrep.org
Freight and Salvage (live music), 1111
Addison Street, Berkeley, CA
(510) 548-1761; www.thefreight.org
Lawrence Hall of Science, University of
California at Berkeley, Centennial Drive,
Berkeley, CA (510) 642-5132;
www.lhs.berkeley.edu

Regional Parks Botanic Garden in
Tilden Regional Park, Anza View Road,
Berkeley, CA 94708 (510) 841-8732
Starry Plough (club and bar), 3101 Shat-
tuck Avenue, Berkeley, CA (510) 841-2082

Accommodations:
Berkeley and Oakland B&B Network,
Berkeley and Oakland, CA (510) 547-6380
www.bbonline.com/ca/berkeley-
oakland/index.html
Alameda County, San Francisco Bay
Area hotels, B&Bs, inns, and resorts
pts.placestostay.com/script/node.asp?n=
2177&pn=1098

Restaurants:
Ajanta (Indian), 1888 Solano Avenue,
Berkeley, CA (510) 526-4373
Cafe Venezia, 1799 University Avenue,
Berkeley, CA (510) 849-4681
Buttercup Restaurant, 3201 College
Avenue, Berkeley (510) 652-6157
Plearn (Thai), 2050 University Avenue,
Berkeley, CA (510) 841-2148

Local Outdoor Retailers:
Marmot Mountain Works, 3049 Ade-
line, Berkeley, CA (510) 849-0735
REI, 1338 San Pablo Avenue, Berkeley, CA
(510) 527-4140
Wilderness Exchange, 1407 San Pablo
Avenue, Berkeley, CA (510) 525-1255

Hike Tours:
Crabcove Visitor Center, 1252 McKay
Avenue, Alameda, CA 94501 (510)
521-6887; www.ebparks.org

Maps:
East Bay Regional Park District
Headquarters, 2950 Peralta Oaks Court,
P.O. Box 5381, Oakland, CA 94605 (510)
662-PARK; www.ebparks.org/parks/tna.htm
USGS maps: Oakland East, CA; Briones
Valley, CA

1.4 Keep to the left, continuing on Peak Trail.

1.6 Sequoias of Rotary Peace Grove.

1.7 Turn left up to Wildcat Peak, another strenuous, but short uphill section.

1.8 Wildcat Peak (1,250 feet). Great views from observation area—west: Bay Bridge, San Francisco, Marin Headlands, Berkeley Marina; north: Point Richmond, refineries of Martinez; east: San Pablo Dam Reservoir, Mount Diablo; south: Oakland, Alameda. Go back the way you came, returning to Peak Trail.

1.9 Turn right on Peak Trail. Sign reads TO NATURE AREA. It's downhill from here.

2.8 Trail splits. Go right to Jewel Lake Trail. Mark on trailhead is duck in flight.

3.1 Cross Wildcat Creek Trail to admire Jewel Lake. (There are a few markers for the self-guided nature trail along the way.)

3.2 Jewel Lake. From here, head back the way you came, across Wildcat Canyon Trail.

3.3 Turn right on Jewel Lake Trail. This part of loop heads back to EEC. Use self-guided nature guide along trail.

3.6 Pass over Loop Trail, continuing on Jewel Lake Trail back to EEC. Pass service areas. *(Note:* Look for mushrooms along the trail. NOT edible, but fun to identify.)

3.8 Return to EEC.

40 Anthony Chabot Regional Park

Overview: *In 1965, the East Bay Regional Park District (EBRPD) renamed Grass Valley Park the Anthony Chabot Regional Park. The area still reflects the small but mighty Chabot, who helped create and preserve this area as you see it today. Bold yet wily, stubborn, quiet, solid, generous of nature, restless, and ever changing describes both the man and the land. The 4,972-acre parkland offers walks by burbling creeks, through groves of eucalyptus, redwood, and oaks, over hills alive with swaying grasses, and along the rim of the well-loved Lake Chabot, rippling with bass looking for flies. The recommended hike takes you through a lush canyon along Grass Valley creek and dramatically arrives at the northern ridges of Lake Chabot. But there are many alternatives. The terrain ranges from gentle to rugged with flat uplands, steep-sided ravines, and the deep, narrow Grass Canyon. Elevation ranges from 235 feet at Lake Chabot to about 1,200 feet at Vulture's View. Besides the popular fishing and boating at Lake Chabot, recreational facilities in the park include Willow Park Public Golf Course, the Anthony Chabot Family Campground, the equestrian center, archery range, marksmanship range, motorcycle area, and several overnight group camps.*

County: Alameda
Start: Grass Valley Staging Area, Skyline Boulevard and Grass Valley Road
Length: 8.7 miles
Approximate Hiking Time: 4 hours
Difficulty Rating: Moderate
Trail Surface: Dirt trail, first double- then single-track, meandering through grassland, by a creek, and on a ridge overlooking Lake Chabot
Land Status: Regional park
Nearest Town: San Leandro and Castro Valley
Other Trail Users: Equestrians and mountain bikers on Goldenrod Trail and Jackson Grade
Canine Compatibility: Dogs on leash

Getting There

By Car: From the San Francisco Bay Bridge, take Highway 580 east. Off Highway 580, take Keller Street exit. Turn left onto frontage road, right onto Keller up the hill. (There is a small convenience market on the way up.) Keller dead-ends at Skyline. Turn right onto Skyline. At the end is the Grass Valley Staging Area for the Anthony Chabot Regional Park.

By Public Transportation: From San Leandro BART, head east on AC Transit bus #80 (frequency: every thirty minutes) to stop on MacArthur at Estudillo. Return in reverse; bus stop is on opposite side of Estudillo. Walk 0.4 mile to city of San Leandro's Chabot Park. The West Shore Trail leading to Anthony Chabot Regional Park is up to the left as you enter the park. The trail winds up and past the dam along the shoreline to the marina and picnic area.

Hike Description

Before the first Europeans arrived here in 1769, Chabot Park was home to the Jalquin. The women collected acorns, roots, bulbs, seeds, and greens, while the men hunted deer, abundant tule elk, small mammals, migratory waterfowl, and fish. There was no lake then, no eucalyptus trees. Giant redwoods populated the northern end of the park. The growl of a grizzly bear sometimes rumbled through the canyon. Then, between 1801 and 1807, Spanish missionaries sent at least sixty-two of the Jalquins to Mission San Jose (built in the Fremont area in 1797), and settlers took over this land.

The vegetation of Chabot changed with European habits. The Spanish introduced grazing animals and hunted to extinction the tule elk and California grizzly. Don't be alarmed if you hear shooting today. It echoes from the nearby shooting range. The Goldenrod Trail, where the hike begins, offers the grass-covered valleys characteristic of much of the park, reminding hikers of Grass Valley's equestrian and ranch past.

Victorian and twentieth-century Californians also influenced the land with the removal of grazing animals from most of the park, the suppression of wildfires, the logging of redwood trees, the planting and logging of eucalyptus trees, and the creation of Lake Chabot.

As you head down the Jackson Grade, brush and woodland cover become delightfully denser, especially on moist east-facing slopes. Above the monkey flowers and eucalyptus, vultures circle the canyon. Wild blackberries, live oaks, buckeyes, a few Monterey pine, and young redwoods share the grove. The People's Water Company began planting the eucalyptus in abundance about 1910 to stop land erosion. In the 1975 attack against the fire-dangerous eucalyptus, city and park officials cut down the Australian natives, and the local Rotary Club provided funds to plant 1,000 young redwoods and other trees over the twenty-five acres from Skyline Boulevard to the Stone Bridge. The hearty eucalyptus has come back to compete with the pack.

A railroad was supposed to come through here, connecting Oakland and Sacramento. The railroad companies bought and held a right-of-way across a part of the Grass Valley Ranch for years. Another location was finally selected in 1937.

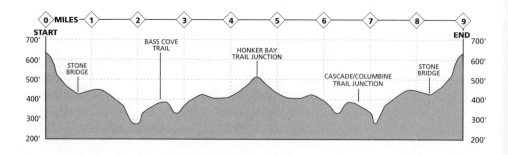

Anthony Chabot Regional Park

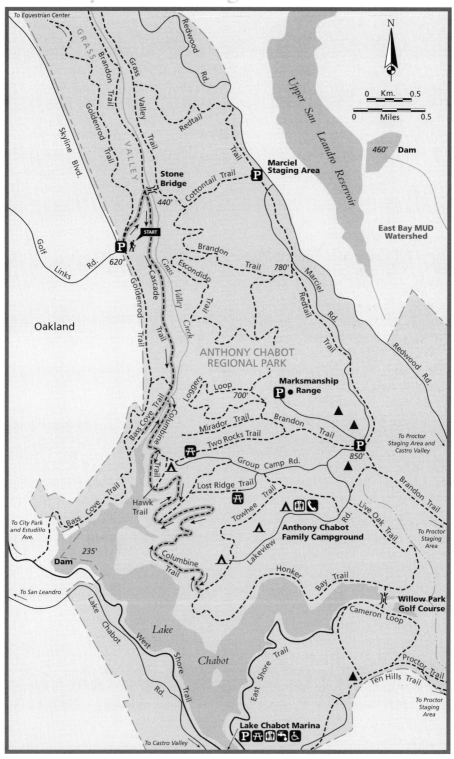

View of Lake Chabot (dam in background) from Columbine Trail

Just before the old Stone Bridge, made of quarried stone probably by the Civilian Conservation Corps (CCC) in the 1930s, you will see the single-track Cascade Trail, disappearing into thick brush and healthy creekside trees. This trail does not disappoint.

Lupine, Indian paintbrush, fairy bells, and geraniums grow along the dappled path. Clover and wild strawberries provide ground cover. Fifteen types of ferns and horsetails sprawl on the banks, including maidenhair, lady fern, bird's foot fern, and the common sword and wood ferns. Big-leaf maple trees, sweet cherry, madrones, black walnut, and black cottonwoods shade much of the path, their branches dripping with grandfather's beard and mistletoe. Grass Valley Creek trickles beside you, bursting into cascades in early spring.

The southern part of the Columbine Trail hosts more sun-loving flowers. Diverse native wildflowers take bloom among the Spanish grasses, especially in spring. As you make your way south on the trail, you enter seamlessly what was once called Rancho San Lorenzo, owned by Don Guillermo Castro.

Castro received the grant to the southern half of the park in 1843, part of his 27,722-acre ranch. He put grazing cattle on the land, and the hides of the cattle put money in his pocket. But it didn't stay there long. Don Castro was a gambler, and a pretty bad one. To pay losses from one unlucky game after the next, he started selling off portions of his land. Piece by piece, his ranch shrank.

Between 1855 and 1863, Faxen Dean Atherton accumulated many of Castro's promissory notes and several portions of his lands, then sued Castro for nonpayment of notes, asking that property be sold off to satisfy his claim. So, by 1864, Atherton owned all of Castro's remaining lands, and Don Castro left the country, still a fairly wealthy man looking for his next game of chance.

A businessman, not a farmer, Atherton sold off parcels of his new land to those who were interested in the agrarian life. Within what is now Chabot Regional Park, there were nine such farms. But just a few years later, the land was consolidated again, this time into watershed to provide a reliable source of water for the rapidly growing Oakland area. The largest of the ranches was the Grass Valley Ranch, where you begin the hike.

The search for water to quench the parched city of Oakland is eventually what saved this area from development. And leading the watery way was amateur engineer, businessman, and philanthropist Anthony Chabot.

Chabot and his associates, also known as the Contra Costa Water Company (CCWC), Oakland's first water supply, had built Lake Temescal in 1868. The supply was not nearly enough to satisfy the thirst of the skyrocketing suburban population with its lawns and gardens. Making matters even drier, these were drought years (a fairly frequent occurrence in the Golden State). To combat this, Chabot secured water rights to San Leandro Creek and began to acquire land in the narrow gorge around the creek.

In 1875, after a year of construction, he completed the San Leandro dam, creating Lake Chabot, the mainstay of the East Bay's water supply for forty years. You can see the dam from the beginning of the Columbine Trail. It is at the southern end of Bass Cove. The dam, 115 feet high, made of earthfill, is now a designated historic landmark.

There is one significant historic site located near Chabot Dam, but just outside Chabot Park: an encampment used by the Chinese immigrant laborers who constructed the dam and its associated tunnels. They called it Yema-po, or "Wild Horse Ridge," and lived there from the time of the initial dam construction (1874) until the turn of the century.

In 1952, the park district managed to turn 3,100 acres of Chabot, then still called Grass Valley Regional Recreation Area, into parkland. And in 1965, after Lake Chabot went on "standby" status by EBMUD, the park created today's Chabot Park by adding the lake for recreation.

Geologic features of the area include sandstone, shale, and bedrocks deposited during the Cretaceous period. Younger alluvial fan deposits are mapped in Grass Valley and along San Leandro Creek above the lake. The nearest active bedrock fault is the Hayward Fault located 1 mile west of the park. It is capable of producing a major, damaging earthquake. Not having much knowledge of fault lines in the nineteenth century, Chabot built the dam nearly on top of it, but it survived the 1906 earthquake without spilling a drop.

Miles/Directions

0.0 START at Grass Valley Staging Area. Trail from parking lot parallel to Skyline Boulevard is double-track Goldenrod Trail. Go left on Goldenrod Trail. *(FYI:* If you need drinking water, there is a fountain just up the hill heading right on Goldenrod. There are no toilets at staging area. Nearest bathrooms are at equestrian center and once you get near the lake at a group camp. Mutt mitts are available.) Trailhead for Jackson Grade ahead, less than 0.1 mile.

0.1 Trail splits. Take Jackson Grade to the right toward Cascade Trail. (It is downhill into the canyon on a double-track path shared by horses and mountain bikes.) Trail with lots of trees.

0.5 Around a bend is Stone Bridge. Trailhead for Cascade Trail is before bridge on the right, clearly marked. *(Note:* Watch for poison oak.) Trail is mostly level. Creek below on the left.

2.0 Cascade Trail becomes Columbine/Cascade Trail. Keep straight. Trail heads downhill after Columbine and Cascade merge, going deeper into canyon and woods. Creek is on the left of trail.

2.2 Cross creek. *(Note:* In wetter seasons [late winter, early spring], creek may flood the trail here, but it is very shallow, and branches and rocks make for easy crossing.)

2.4 Trailhead for Bass Cove Trail. Go left, staying on Columbine Trail. **Option:** Crossing creek to right would take you to Bass Cove Trail and eventually to Lake Chabot Marina (3.3 miles). Hiking either direction, this is a great hike for a shuttle car left on Lake Chabot Road by the main entrance to Lake Chabot.

3.4 Keep straight on Columbine Trail for view of Lake Chabot Marina. (*Bail-out.* If you have had enough, this is a turnaround and picnic stop. A short walk on Group Camp Road Trail to the left takes you to group camps, rest rooms, and drinking water.)

4.6 Columbine Trail meets Honker Bay Trail. Turn around and head back the way you came. **Option:** For a great one-way hike, leave a pick-up car at the marina and continue on Honker Bay around the lake.

5.8 Continue straight past trailhead to group camp.

6.7 Turn right on Cascade/Columbine Trail (Bass Cove to the left).

7.2 Continue straight on Cascade Trail. **Option:** Head left up Columbine to Goldenrod, which is double-track trail along golf course and neighborhood houses.

8.2 Cascade runs into Jackson Grade and Stone Bridge. Turn left, heading west up Jackson Grade.

8.6 Jackson Grade meets Goldenrod. Bear left back toward parking lot.

8.7 Parking lot of Grass Valley Staging Area.

Hike Information

📞 Trail Contacts:
East Bay Regional Park District Headquarters, 2950 Peralta Oaks Court, P.O. Box 5381, Oakland, CA 94605 (510) 662–PARK; www.ebparks.org/parks/anchabot.htm
Anthony Chabot Headquarters at Family Camp (510) 639–4751
Lake Chabot Marina (510) 247–2526

🕐 Schedule:
Open year-round daily from 5:00 A.M. to 10:00 P.M. unless otherwise posted

💲 Fees/Permits:
None at Grass Valley Staging Area; Lake Chabot Marina: $4.00 per car; $1.00 dog fee

❓ Local Information:
San Leandro Chamber of Commerce www.sanleandro.com/
Bay Area Insider (San Leandro): www.bayinsider.com/auto/yourtown/?94579

💡 Local Events/Attractions:
Anthony Chabot Equestrian Center (Sara Crary, operator), Anthony Chabot Regional Park, Oakland, CA (510) 569–4428
The Marksmanship Range (operated by the Chabot Gun Club), P.O. Box 2246, 9999 Redwood Road, Castro Valley, CA (510) 569–0213; www.chabotgunclub.com/
Lake Chabot Marina (boat rentals/fishing), Lake Chabot Road, Castro Valley, CA (510) 582–2198; www.ebparks.org/dropdown/boating.htm#CHABOT
Golden Tee Golfland, 2533 Castro Valley Boulevard, Castro Valley, CA (510) 537–4073

🛏 Accommodations:
Camping: Anthony Chabot Headquarters at Family Camp (510) 639–4751 or

(510) 562–CAMP; group camping: (510) 636–1684
San Leandro Marina Inn, 68 San Leandro Marina, San Leandro, CA (510) 895–1311 or (800) 786–7783
Bed and Breakfasts Online: www.bbonline.com/ca/region2.html

🍴 Restaurants:
Everybody's Bagel, 1099 MacArthur Boulevard, San Leandro, CA (510) 430–8700
Strizzi's (California cuisine), 1376 East Fourteenth Street, San Leandro, CA (510) 483–4883; www.strizzis.com/sanl.html

🎒 Local Outdoor Retailers:
Wilderness Supply, 18919 Lake Chabot Road, Castro Valley, CA (510) 886–4550
Sportmart, Inc., 1933 Davis, San Leandro, CA (510) 632–6100
Big 5 Sporting Goods, 15556 Hesperian Boulevard, San Lorenzo, CA (510) 278–0298

👥 Hike Tours:
East Bay Regional Park District Headquarters, 2950 Peralta Oaks Court, P.O. Box 5381, Oakland, CA 94605 (510) 662–PARK; www.ebparks.org/parks/anchabot.htm
Hayward Hiking Club, P.O. Box 367, Hayward CA 94543–0367; www.thellamaranch.com/hhc.html; dave@snakebite.com

📍 Maps:
East Bay Regional Park District Headquarters, 2950 Peralta Oaks Court, P.O. Box 5381, Oakland, CA 94605 (510) 662–PARK; www.ebparks.org/parks/anchabot.htm
USGS maps: San Leandro, CA; Hayward, CA

Honorable Mentions:
Three Ridges: San Pablo, the Oakland/ Berkeley Hills, and Sunol Ridge

P. Tilden Regional Park—Greater Tilden

Charles Lee Tilden Regional Park straddles the boundary between Alameda and Contra Costa counties in the hills above Berkeley. If you're hiking with your dog, the Nature Area is off-limits, but in the rest of Tilden you have miles of trails in canyon and ridge terrain to keep your feet and your pet happy. Also, if you want a longer hike or would like to visit some of the unique Tilden attractions by foot, this is a great way to do it. A full loop around the park starting at the steam train swings by Lake Anza, the Brazilian Room, the golf course, the botanical garden, and two peaks offering expansive vistas: Vollmer Peak (1,905 feet) and Grizzly Peak (1,795 feet). Vollmer can be reached on the Bay Area Ridge Trail, also part of the Skyline National Trail. You can enjoy 2 miles of views on the ridge, although the dirt path is roadwide and allows bike and horse traffic.

A 7-mile loop, it includes treks on Curran, Selby, and Grizzly Peak trails and takes 3.5 hours, not including stops at the sites, so bring lunch and plan for a whole day. For a shorter hike, you can start and end at a number of trailheads in the park. There are many delightful loops, some through eucalyptus, pine, or redwood groves, some with views from open grassland. Many, like Big Springs Trail, combine the two. For contact info and directions, see Hike 39 (Tilden Regional Park).

Q. Briones Reservoir

Briones Reservoir requires a permit ($10 a year, $2.50 for day pass) from East Bay Municipal Utilities District (EBMUD) (500 San Pablo Dam Road; 510-835-3000).

Start either at the Bear Creek Staging Area (left side of Bear Creek Road between Happy Valley Road and the Briones Regional Park entrance) or at the Briones Overlook Staging Area (on Bear Creek about a mile before the regional park, coming from Camino Pablo). Trails in this watershed interconnect with paths into the regional park area, around San Pablo Reservoir, and all the way to Inspiration Point in Tilden. Maps are available at the EBMUD office.

The Bear Creek Trail (4.5 miles) traverses the south slopes of Briones Reservoir, moderately steep in places, mostly forested. At the Bear Creek Staging Area enter the gate on the left, and cross the creek to the Bear Creek Trail. (Turning left would take you to the Briones Regional Park gate.) Instead, turn right and head along the reservoir through the tree farm to the shore. A dirt fire road follows the shoreline, then winds gradually higher up the slope, where it becomes a narrow path. With a brief stint on a service road, you are back on the serene single-track trail, home to rabbits, foxes, and deer that you are likely to see along this undisturbed path. The only drawback is the faint sound of occasional traffic from Bear Creek Road and some horse droppings on the narrow trail. At the Overlook Staging Area (a good place to drop a shuttle car for a group hike), you find a rest room. The trail continues on, following the lake's edge to the dam and down the grassy slope alongside the spillway to the junction with Oursan Trail.

Oursan Trail (10.2 miles) is a long, fairly easy trail through high, often windy meadows that descends lakeside again, skirting the northern shores of Briones Reservoir. It returns to the Bear Creek Staging Area.

R. Mission Peak Regional Preserve

When people think of mountains to climb in the Bay Area, they don't always think of Mission Peak, but perhaps they should. Shaped by the shifting of the earth, with quakes along the Hayward fault and landslides down its steep faces, nature is still sculpting this 2,517-foot mountain.

There are four ways to climb to the summit. The shortest, but steepest, starts at the end of Stanford Avenue. AC Transit bus #28 stops at the Mission Boulevard/Stanford Avenue corner from Fremont BART. The Hidden Valley Trail is a calf-burning climb, better in winter because it has few trees. Slightly longer, but a more gradual ascent through wildflowers and some woodland, the trail begins at Ohlone College on Mission Boulevard. The trailhead is behind the swimming pool at the college's southeast corner. A seldom-used path starts at Sunol Regional Wilderness and requires a wilderness permit (available at the park headquarters). This 11-mile round trip follows a gentle route west to the peak. The fourth route is from the Ed Levin County Park in Milpitas and follows the Bay Area Ridge Trail around 12 miles from Santa Clara County into Contra Costa.

For all the hikes, carry lots of water and wear layers. The mountain is either bathed in sun or white-capped for short days in winter. Your reward, besides a great workout, are views of Mount Hamilton, Mount Diablo, Mount Tamalpais, the Santa Cruz Mountains, Silicon Valley, San Francisco, and, if it's really clear, the Sierra Nevadas to the northeast (clearest views are after rains).

To get to the Stanford Avenue Trailhead, take the first Mission Boulevard exit northbound on I–680 and go east. Turn right on Stanford Avenue (look for MISSION PEAK REGIONAL PRESERVE sign), and drive to the end. Parking is free. For the Ohlone College trailhead, take the second Mission Boulevard exit (Highway 238) from I–680. Drive past Mission San Jose, and turn left into the Ohlone College parking lot. Parking costs $1.50 when classes are in session.

For the Sunol Regional Wilderness trailhead, take the Calaveras Road exit from I–680. Turn east on Calaveras, then go left on Geary Road, which goes into the park. Parking costs $3.00; trail permits are $2.00 per person. Sign in and out at trailheads. Take note of when the park gate closes (it varies by season) so you don't get locked in. For more information, call East Bay Regional Park District (510–562–PARK); interpretive hikes, Coyote Hills Visitor Center (510–795–9385).

S. Coyote Hills Regional Park

On the bay by the Dumbarton Bridge, the Coyote Hills Regional Park is a sanctuary for all kinds of wetland birds, wild pheasant, raptors, and for hikers and bicyclists as well. You can experience wind-swept grassland with wildflowers in spring and sounds and views of the San Francisco Bay. The paved Bayview Trail skirts around Red Hill by the marshes and bay levees, which are fun to explore. The Red Hill Trail takes you on packed dirt to the breezy top for a great workout and views of the Santa Cruz Mountains to the west and the east bay hills inland. The Tuibin Trail, Chochenyo Trail, and the trails over the boardwalks show off the marshes where white egrets and great blue herons feed at the water's edge. Check out the Ohlone Shellmound, accompanied by a reconstructed tule house, shade shelter, dance circle, and a sweat lodge. The waters to the west and south of Coyote Hills are part of the Don Edwards San Francisco Bay National Wildlife Refuge, operated by the U.S. Fish and Wildlife Service. The Shoreline, No Name, Apay Way and Alameda Creek trails provide access to the Refuge. Apay Way leads to the Refuge Visitor Center via a bridge over Highway 84. The Alameda Creek Trail stretches twelve miles south to Niles Canyon. The San Francisco Bay National Wildlife Refuge Visitor Center is worth a visit. Sitting pleasantly up on a rocky ridge, it provides information about the animals in the area as well as the surrounding salt flats that went into operation in the 1850s. The white hills south of the refuge are actually salt piles where the company is still in production. The family might enjoy a visit to nearby Ardenwood Historic Farm after the stroll as well, especially in the fall to pick out a pumpkin. Coyote Hills is at the west end of Patterson Ranch Road/ Commerce Drive in Fremont. From I-880, take Highway 84 west, exit at Paseo Padre Parkway and drive north. Turn left on Patterson Ranch Road (parking fee).

The Art of Hiking

When standing nose to nose with a mountain lion, you're probably not too concerned with the issue of ethical behavior in the wild. No doubt you're just wetting yourself. But let's be honest. How often are you nose to nose with a mountain lion? For most of us, a hike into the "wild" means loading up the 4-Runner with everything North Face and driving to a toileted trailhead. Sure, you can mourn how civilized we've become—how GPS units have replaced natural instinct and Gore-Tex, true-grit—but the silly gadgets of civilization aside, we have plenty of reason to take pride in how we've matured. With survival now on the back burner, we've begun to reason—and it's about time—that we have a responsibility to protect, no longer just conquer, our wild places; that they, not we, are at risk. So please, do what you can. Here are some rules to remember.

Zero impact. Always leave an area just like you found it—if not better than you found it. Avoid camping in fragile, alpine meadows and along the banks of streams and lakes. Use a camp stove versus building a wood fire. Pack up all of your trash and extra food. Bury human waste at least 100 feet from water sources under 6 to 8 inches of topsoil. Don't bathe with soap in a lake or stream—use prepackaged moistened towels to wipe off sweat and dirt, or bathe in the water without soap.

Stay on the trail. It's true, a path anywhere leads nowhere new, but purists will just have to get over it. Paths serve an important purpose; they limit impact on natural areas. Straying from a designated trail may seem innocent but it can cause damage to sensitive areas—damage that may take years to recover, if it can recover at all. Even simple shortcuts can be destructive. So, please, stay on the trail.

Keep your dog under control. You can buy a flexi-lead that allows your dog to go exploring along the trail, while allowing you the ability to reel him in should another hiker approach or should he decide to chase a rabbit. Always obey leash laws and be sure to bury your dog's waste or pack it in resealable plastic bags.

Yield to horses. When you approach these animals on the trail, always step quietly off the trail and let them pass. If you are wearing a large backpack, it's a good idea to sit down. From a horse's perspective, a hiker wearing a large backpack is a scary trail monster and these sensitive animals can be spooked easily.

Getting into Shape

Unless you want to be sore—and possibly have to shorten your trip or vacation—be sure to get in shape before a big hike. If you're terribly out of shape, start a walking program early, preferably eight weeks in advance. Start with a fifteen-minute walk during your lunch hour or after work and gradually increase your walking time to an hour. You should also increase your elevation gain. Walking briskly up hills really strengthens your leg muscles and gets your heart rate up. If you work in a storied office building, take the stairs instead of the elevator. If you prefer going to a gym, walk the treadmill or use a Stair-master. You can further increase your strength and endurance by walking with a loaded backpack. Stationary exercises you might consider are squats, leg lifts, sit-ups, and push-ups. Other good ways to get in shape include biking, running, aerobics, and, of course, short hikes. Stretching before and after a hike keeps muscles flexible and helps avoid injuries.

Preparedness

It's been said that failing to plan means planning to fail. So do take the necessary time to plan your trip. Whether going on a short day hike or an extended backpack trip, always prepare for the worst. Simply remembering to pack a copy of the *U.S. Army Survival Manual* is not preparedness. Although it's not a bad idea if you plan on entering truly wild places, it's merely the tourniquet answer to a problem. You need to do your best to prevent the problem from arising in the first place. These days the word "survival" is often replaced with the pathetically feeble term "comfort." In order to remain comfortable (and to survive if you really want to push it), you need to concern yourself with the basics: water, food, and shelter. Don't go on a hike without having these bases covered. And don't go on a hike expecting to find these items in the woods.

Water. Even in frigid conditions, you need at least two quarts of water a day to function efficiently. Add heat and taxing terrain and you can bump that figure up to one gallon. That's simply a base to work from—your metabolism and your level of conditioning can raise or lower that amount. Unless you know your level, assume that you need one gallon of water a day. Now, where do you plan on getting the water?

Preferably not from natural water sources. These sources can be loaded with intestinal disturbers, such as bacteria, viruses, and fertilizers. *Giardia lamblia*, the most common of these disturbers, is a protozoan parasite that lives part of its life-cycle as a cyst in water sources. The parasite spreads when mammals defecate in water sources. Once ingested, Giardia can induce cramping, diarrhea, vomiting, and fatigue within two days to two weeks after ingestion. Giardiasis is treatable with the prescription drug Flagyl. If you believe you've contracted giardiasis, see a doctor immediately.

Treating water. The best and easiest solution to avoid polluted water is to carry your water with you. Yet, depending on the nature of your hike and the duration, this may not be an option—seeing as 1 gallon of water weighs 8.5 pounds. In that case, you'll need to look into treating water. Regardless of which method you choose, you should always carry some water with you, in case of an emergency. Save this reserve until you absolutely need it.

There are three methods of treating water: boiling, chemical treatment, and filtering. If you boil water, it's recommended that you do so for ten to fifteen minutes. This is often impractical because you're forced to exhaust a great deal of your fuel supply. You can opt for chemical treatment (e.g., Potable Aqua), which will kill Giardia but will not take care of other chemical pollutants. Another drawback to chemical treatments is the unpleasant taste of the water after it's treated. You can remedy this by adding powdered drink mix to the water. Filters are the preferred method for treating water. Filters remove Giardia, organic and inorganic contaminants, and don't leave an aftertaste. Water filters are far from perfect as they can easily become clogged or leak if a gasket wears out. It's always a good idea to carry a backup supply of chemical treatment tablets in case your filter decides to quit on you.

Food. If we're talking about "survival," you can go days without food, as long as you have water. But we're talking about "comfort" here. Try to avoid foods that are high in sugar and fat like candy bars and potato chips. These food types are harder to digest and are low in nutritional value. Instead, bring along foods that are easy to pack, nutritious, and high in energy (e.g., bagels, nutrition bars, dehydrated fruit, gorp, and jerky). If you are on an overnight trip, easy-to-fix dinners include rice mixes with dehydrated potatoes, corn, pasta with cheese sauce, and soup mixes. For a tasty breakfast, you can fix hot oatmeal with brown sugar and reconstituted milk powder topped off with banana chips. If you like a hot drink in the morning, bring along herbal tea bags or hot chocolate. If you are a coffee junkie, you can purchase coffee that is packaged like tea bags. You can prepackage all of your meals in heavy-duty resealable plastic bags to keep food from spilling in your pack. These bags can be reused to pack out trash.

Shelter. The type of shelter you choose depends less on the conditions than on your tolerance for discomfort. Shelter comes in many forms—tent, tarp, lean to, bivy sack, cabin, cave, etc. If you're camping in the desert, a bivy sack may suffice, but if you're above the treeline and a storm is approaching, a better choice is a three or four season tent. Tents are the logical and most popular choice for most backpackers as they're lightweight and packable—and you can rest assured that you always have shelter from the elements (see Equipment: Tents on page 309). Before you leave on your trip, anticipate what the weather and terrain will be like and plan for the type of shelter that will work best for your comfort level.

Finding a campsite. If there are established campsites, stick to those. If not, start looking for a campsite early—like around 3:30 or 4:00 P.M. Stop at the first decent site you see. Depending on the area, it could be a long time before you find another suitable location. Pitch your camp in an area that's level. Make sure the area is at least 200 feet from fragile areas like lakeshores, meadows, and stream banks. And try to avoid areas thick in underbrush, as they can harbor insects and provide cover for approaching animals.

If you are camping in stormy, rainy weather, look for a rock outcrop or a shelter in the trees to keep the wind from blowing your tent all night. Be sure that you don't camp under trees with dead limbs that might break off on top of you. Also, try to find an area that has an absorbent surface, such as sandy soil or forest duff. This, in addition to camping on a surface with a slight angle, will provide better drainage. By all means, don't dig trenches to provide drainage around your tent—remember you're practicing zero-impact camping.

If you're in bear country, steer clear of creekbeds or animal paths. If you see any signs of a bear's presence (i.e., scat, footprints), relocate. You'll need to find a campsite near a tall tree where you can hang your food and other items that may attract bears such as deodorant, toothpaste, or soap. Carry a lightweight nylon rope with which to hang your food. As a rule, you should hang your food at least 20 feet from the ground and 5 feet away from the tree trunk. You can put food and other items in a waterproof stuff sack and tie one end of the rope to the stuff sack. To get the other end of the rope over the tree branch, tie a good size rock to it, and gently toss the rock over the tree branch. Pull the stuff sack up until it reaches the top of the branch and tie it off securely. Don't hang your food near your tent! If possible, hang your food at least 100 feet away from your campsite. Alternatives to hanging your food are bear-proof plastic tubes and metal bear boxes.

Lastly, think of comfort. Lie down on the ground where you intend to sleep and see if it's a good fit. For morning warmth (and a nice view to wake up to), have your tent face east.

First Aid

I know you're tough, but get 10 miles into the woods and develop a blister and you'll wish you had carried that first-aid kit. Face it, it's just plain good sense. Many companies produce lightweight, compact first-aid kits, just make sure yours contains at least the following:

- Band-Aids
- mole skin
- various sterile gauze and dressings
- white surgical tape
- an Ace bandage
- an antihistamine
- aspirin
- Betadine solution
- a first-aid book
- Tums
- tweezers
- scissors
- antibacterial wipes
- triple-antibiotic ointment
- plastic gloves
- sterile cotton tip applicators
- syrup of ipecac (to induce vomiting)
- thermometer
- wire splint

Here are a few tips to dealing with and hopefully preventing certain ailments.

Sunburn. In most parts of Northern California, summer sun can be an intense and constant companion on hikes. If you burn, it is a good idea to take along sunscreen or sun block, protective clothing, and a wide-brimmed hat. If you do get a sunburn, treat the area with aloe vera gel, and protect the area from further sun exposure. At higher elevations, the sun's radiation can be particularly damaging to skin. Remember that your eyes are vulnerable to this radiation as well. Sunglasses can be a good way to prevent headaches and permanent eye damage from the sun, especially in places where light-colored rock or patches of snow reflect light up in your face.

Blisters. Be prepared to take care of these hike-spoilers by carrying moleskin (a lightly padded adhesive), gauze and tape, or Band-Aids. An effective way to apply moleskin is to cut out a circle of moleskin and remove the center—like a donut— and place it over the blistered area. Cutting the center out will reduce the pressure applied to the sensitive skin. Other products that can help you combat blisters are Bodyglide and Second Skin. Bodyglide (888–263–9454) is applied to suspicious hot spots before a blister forms to help decrease friction to that area. Second Skin (made by Spenco) is applied to the blister after it has popped and acts as a "second skin" to help prevent further irritation.

Insect bites and stings. You can treat most insect bites and stings by applying hydrocortisone 1% cream topically and taking a pain medication such as ibuprofen or acetaminophen to reduce swelling. If you forgot to pack these items, a cold compress or a paste of mud and ashes can sometimes assuage the itching and discomfort. Remove any stingers by using tweezers or scraping the area with your fingernail or a knife blade. Don't pinch the area as you'll only spread the venom.

Some hikers are highly sensitive to bites and stings and may have a serious allergic reaction that can be life threatening. Symptoms of a serious allergic reaction can include wheezing, an asthmatic attack, and shock. The treatment for this severe type of reaction is epinephrine (Adrenaline). If you know that you are sensitive to bites and stings, carry a pre-packaged kit of epinephrine (e.g., Anakit), which can be obtained only by prescription from your doctor.

Ticks. As you well know, ticks can carry disease, such as Rocky Mountain spotted fever and Lyme disease. The best defense is, of course, prevention. If you know you're going to be hiking through an area littered with ticks, wear long pants and a long sleeved shirt. You can apply a permethrin repellent to your clothing and a DEET repellent to exposed skin. At the end of your hike, do a spot check for ticks (and insects in general). If you do find a tick, coat the insect with Vaseline or tree sap to cut off its air supply. The tick should release its hold, but if it doesn't, grab the head of the tick firmly—with a pair of tweezers if you have them—and gently pull it away from the skin with a twisting motion. Sometimes the mouthparts linger, embedded in your skin. If this happens, try to remove them with a disinfected needle. Clean the affected area with an anti-bacterial cleanser and then apply triple antibiotic ointment. Monitor the area for a few days. If irritation persists or a white spot develops, see a doctor for possible infection.

Poison oak

Poison ivy, oak, and sumac. These skin irritants can be found most anywhere in North America and come in the form of a bush or a vine, having leaflets in groups of three, five, seven, or nine. Learn how to spot the plants. The oil they secrete can cause an allergic reaction in the form of blisters, usually about twelve hours after exposure. The itchy rash can last from ten days to several weeks. The best defense against these irritants is to wear clothing that covers the arms, legs and torso. For summer, zip-off cargo pants come in handy. You can also apply a non-prescription product called IvyBlock to exposed skin. This lotion is meant to guard against the affects of poison ivy/oak/sumac and can be washed off with soap and water. If you think you were in contact with the plants, after hiking or even on the trail during longer hikes scub Technu on exposed areas and rinse with cold water or a wet towel. It is one of the few products on the market that washes off the hard-to-remove oils. Taking a hot shower with soap after you return home from your hike will also help to remove any lingering oil from your skin. Should you contract a rash from any of these plants, use Benadryl or a similar product to reduce the itching. If the rash is localized, create a light Clorox /water wash to dry up the area. If the rash has spread, either tough it out or see your doctor about getting a dose of Cortisone (available both orally and by injection).

Snakebites. First off, snakebites are rare in North America. Unless startled or provoked, the majority of snakes will not bite. If you are wise to their habitats and keep a careful eye on the trail, you should be just fine. Though your chances of being struck are slim, it's wise to know what to do in the event you are.

If a *nonpoisonous* snake bites you, allow the wound to bleed a small amount and then cleanse the wounded area with a Betadine solution (10% povidone iodine). Rinse the wound with clean water (preferably) or fresh urine (it might sound ugly, but it's sterile). Once the area is clean, cover it with triple antibiotic ointment and a clean bandage. Remember, most residual damage from snakebites, poisonous or otherwise, comes from infection, not the snake's venom. Keep the area as clean as possible and get medical attention immediately.

If you are bitten by a poisonous snake, remove the toxin with a suctioning device, found in a snakebite kit. If you do not have such a device, squeeze the wound—DO NOT use your mouth for suction, as the venom will enter your bloodstream through the vessels under the tongue and head straight for your heart.

Then, clean the wound just as you would a nonpoisonous bite. Tie a clean band of cloth snuggly around the afflicted appendage, about an inch or so above the bite (or the rim of the swelling). This is NOT a tourniquet—you want to simply slow the blood flow, not cut it off. Loosen the band if numbness ensues. Remove the band for a minute and reapply a little higher every ten minutes.

If it is your friend who's been bitten, treat him or her for shock—make the person comfortable, have him or her lie down, elevate the legs, and keep him or her warm. Avoid applying anything cold to the bite wound. Immobilize the affected area and remove any constricting items such as rings, watches, or restrictive clothing—swelling may occur. Once your friend is stable and relatively calm, hike out to get help. The victim should get treatment within twelve hours, ideally, which usually consists of a tetanus shot, antivenin, and antibiotics.

If you are alone and struck by a poisonous snake, stay calm. Hysteria will only quicken the venom's spread. Follow the procedure above, and do your best to reach help. When hiking out, don't run—you'll only increase the flow of blood throughout your system. Instead, walk calmly.

California has six poisonous snakes, all of them rattlesnakes. Of these, only the western rattlesnake is common to Northern California. Although occasionally found as high as 11,000 feet above sea level, rattlesnakes are rare above 5,000 feet. Snakes generally leave the area when they feel the ground vibrations of approaching hikers, but care should be taken when in rattlesnake country. Rattlesnakes will not usually bite unless provoked or surprised. Pay particular attention in areas of dense brush and jumbled rocks, and watch where you put your hands and feet. When stepping over logs, first step on the log, making sure you can see what's on the other side before stepping down.

Scorpions and spiders. Other insects exist in Northern California. Black widow spiders are found in woodpiles and debris, as well as sheltered locations in buildings. Only the female of the species bites, and the bite can be very painful, and in rare cases fatal. Black widows are about ¾ inch long, and shiny black with a red hourglass mark on the underside of the abdomen. Small scorpions, up to 1¼ inches long, are occasionally found here also. The sting of these animals is very painful but not especially dangerous. Take care when picking up rocks, and when sitting or sleeping on loose stone debris.

Dehydration. Have you ever hiked in hot weather and had a roaring headache and felt fatigued after only a few miles? More than likely you were dehydrated. Symptoms of dehydration include fatigue, headache, and decreased coordination and judgment. When you are hiking, your body's rate of fluid loss depends on the outside temperature, humidity, altitude, and your activity level. On average, a hiker walking in warm weather will lose 4 liters of fluid a day. That fluid loss is easily replaced by normal consumption of liquids and food. However, if a hiker is walking briskly in hot, dry weather and hauling a heavy pack, he or she can lose 1 to 3 liters of water an hour. It's important to always carry plenty of water and to stop often and drink fluids regularly, even if you aren't thirsty.

Heat exhaustion is the result of a loss of large amounts of electrolytes and often occurs if a hiker is dehydrated and has been under heavy exertion. Common symptoms of heat exhaustion include cramping, exhaustion, fatigue, lightheadedness, and nausea. You can treat heat exhaustion by getting out of the sun and drinking an electrolyte solution made up of 1 teaspoon of salt and 1 tablespoon of sugar dissolved in a liter of water. Drink this solution slowly over a period of one hour. Drinking plenty of fluids (preferably an electrolyte solution like Gatorade) can prevent heat exhaustion. Avoid hiking during the hottest parts of the day, and wear breathable clothing, a wide brimmed hat, and sunglasses.

Hypothermia is one of the biggest dangers in the backcountry, especially for day hikers in the summertime. That may sound strange, but imagine starting out on a hike in mid-summer when it's sunny and 80 degrees out. You're clad in nylon shorts and a cotton T-shirt. About halfway through your hike, the sky begins to cloud up, and in the next hour a light drizzle begins to fall and the wind starts to pick up. Before you know it, you are soaking wet and shivering—the perfect recipe for hypothermia. More advanced signs include decreased coordination, slurred speech, and blurred vision. When a victim's temperature falls below 92 degrees, the blood pressure and pulse plummet, possibly leading to coma and death.

To avoid hypothermia, always bring a windproof/rainproof shell, a fleece jacket, Capilene tights, gloves, and hat when you are hiking in the mountains. Learn to adjust your clothing layers based on the temperature. If you are climbing uphill at a moderate pace you will stay warm, but when you stop for a break you'll become cold quickly, unless you add more layers of clothing.

If a hiker is showing advanced signs of hypothermia, dress him or her in dry clothes and make sure he or she is wearing a hat and gloves. Place the person in a sleeping bag in a tent or shelter that will protect him or her from the wind and other elements. Give the person warm fluids to drink and keep him awake.

Frostbite. When the mercury dips below 32 degrees, your extremities begin to chill. If a persistent chill attacks a localized area, say, your hands or your toes, the circulatory system reacts by cutting off blood flow to the affected area—the idea being to protect and preserve the body's overall temperature. And so it's death by attrition for the affected area. Ice crystals start to form from the water in the cells of the neglected tissue. Deprived of heat, nourishment, and now water, the tissue literally starves. This is frostbite.

Prevention is your best defense against this situation. Most prone to frostbite are your face, hands, and feet, so protect these areas well. Wool is the material of choice because it provides ample air space for insulation and draws moisture away from the skin. However, synthetic fabrics have recently made great strides in the cold weather clothing market. Do your research. A pair of light silk liners under your regular gloves is a good trick to keeping warm. They afford some additional warmth, but more importantly they'll allow you to remove your mitts for tedious work without exposing the skin.

If your feet or hands start to feel cold or numb due to the elements, warm them as quickly as possible. Place cold hands under your armpits or bury them in your crotch. If your feet are cold, change your socks. If there's plenty of room in your boots, add another pair of socks. Do remember, though, that constricting your feet in tight boots can restrict blood flow and actually make your feet colder more quickly. Your socks need to have breathing room if they're going to be effective. Dead air provides insulation. If your face is cold, place your warm hands over your face, or simply wear a head stocking.

Should your skin go numb and start to appear white and waxy, chances are you've got or are developing frostbite. Don't try to thaw the area unless you can maintain the warmth. In other words, don't stop to warm up your frostbitten feet only to head back on the trail. You'll do more damage than good. Tests have shown that hikers who walked on thawed feet did more harm, and endured more pain, than hikers who left the affected areas alone. Do your best to get out of the cold entirely and seek medical attention—which usually consists of performing a rapid rewarming in water for twenty to thirty minutes.

The overall objective in preventing both hypothermia and frostbite is to keep the body's core warm. Protect key areas where heat escapes, like the top of the head, and maintain the proper nutrition level. Foods that are high in calories aid the body in producing heat. Never smoke or drink when you're in situations where the cold is threatening. By affecting blood flow, these activities ultimately cool the body's core temperature.

Navigation

Whether you are going on a short hike in a familiar area or planning a weeklong backpack trip, you should always be equipped with the proper navigational equipment—at the very least a detailed map and a sturdy compass.

Maps. There are many different types of maps available to help you find your way on the trail. Easiest to find are Forest Service maps and BLM (Bureau of Land Management) maps. These maps tend to cover large areas, so be sure they are detailed enough for your particular trip. You can also obtain National Park maps as well as high quality maps from private companies and trail groups. These maps can be obtained either from outdoor stores or ranger stations.

U.S. Geological Survey topographic maps are particularly popular with hikers—especially serious backcountry hikers. These maps contain the standard map symbols such as roads, lakes, and rivers, as well as contour lines that show the details of the trail terrain like ridges, valleys, passes, and mountain peaks. The 7.5-minute series (1 inch on the map equals approximately $^2/_5$ mile on the ground) provides the closest inspection available. USGS maps are available by mail (U.S. Geological Survey, Map Distribution Branch, P.O. Box 25286, Denver, CO 80225), or online at mapping.usgs.gov/esic/to_order.html.

If you want to check out the high-tech world of maps, you can purchase topographic maps on CD-ROM. These software-mapping programs let you select a route on your computer, print it out, then take it with you on the trail. Some software mapping programs let you insert symbols and labels, download waypoints from a GPS unit, and export the maps to other software programs. Mapping software programs such as DeLorme's TopoUSA (www.delorme.com) and MAPTECH's Terrain Navigator (www.maptech.com) let you do all of these things and more.

The art of map reading is a skill that you can develop by first practicing in an area you are familiar with. To begin, orient the map so the map is lined up in the correct direction (i.e. north on the map is lined up with true north). Next, familiarize yourself with the map symbols and try and match them up with terrain features around you such as a high ridge, mountain peak, river, or lake. If you are practicing with a USGS map notice the contour lines. On gentler terrain these contour lines are spaced further apart, and on steeper terrain they are closer together. Pick a short loop trail, and stop frequently to check your position on the map. As you practice map reading, you'll learn how to anticipate a steep section on the trail or a good place to take a rest break, and so on.

The compass. First off, the sun is not a substitute for a compass. So, what kind of compass should you have? Here are some characteristics you should look for: a rectangular base with detailed scales, a liquid-filled housing, protective housing, a sighting line on the mirror, luminous alignment and back-bearing arrows, a luminous north-seeking arrow, and a well-defined bezel ring.

You can learn compass basics by reading the detailed instructions included with your compass. If you want to fine-tune your compass skills, sign up for an orienteering class or purchase a book on compass reading. Once you've learned the basic skills on using a compass, remember to practice these skills before you head into the backcountry.

If you are a klutz at using a compass, you may be interested in checking out the technical wizardry of the **GPS (Global Positioning System)** device. The GPS was developed by the Pentagon and works off twenty-four NAVSTAR satellites, which were designed to guide missiles to their targets. A GPS device is a handheld unit that calculates your latitude and longitude with the easy press of a button. However, the crafty defense department doesn't want civilians (or spies) to have the same pinpoint accuracy, so they have purposefully mixed the signals a bit so a GPS unit's accuracy is generally within 100 meters or 328 feet.

There are many different types of GPS units available and they range in price from $100 to $400. In general, all GPS units have a display screen and keypad where you input information. In addition to acting as a compass, the unit allows you to plot your route, easily retrace your path, track your travelling speed, find the mileage between waypoints, and calculate the total mileage of your route.

Before you purchase a GPS unit, keep in mind that these devices don't pick up signals indoors, in heavily wooded areas, on mountain peaks, or in deep valleys.

A pedometer is a handy device that can track your mileage as you hike. This device is a small, clip-on unit with a digital display that calculates your hiking distance in miles or kilometers based on your walking stride. Some units also calculate the calories you burn and your total hiking time. Pedometers are available at most large outdoor stores and range in price from $20 to $40.

Trip Planning

Planning your hiking adventure begins with letting a friend or relative know your trip itinerary so they can call for help if you don't return at your scheduled time. Your next task is to make sure you are outfitted to experience the risks and rewards of the trail. This section highlights gear and clothing you may want to take with you to get the most out of your hike.

Day Hikes
- camera/film
- compass/GPS unit
- pedometer
- daypack
- first-aid kit
- food
- guidebook
- headlamp/flashlight with extra batteries and bulbs
- hat
- insect repellant
- knife/multipurpose tool
- map
- matches in waterproof container and fire starter
- Polar Fleece jacket
- raingear
- space blanket
- sunglasses
- sunscreen
- swimsuit
- watch
- water
- water bottles/water hydration system

Overnight Trip
- backpack and waterproof rain cover
- backpacker's trowel
- bandanna
- bear repellant spray
- bear bell
- biodegradable soap
- pot scrubber

- collapsible water container (2–3 gallon capacity)
- clothing—extra wool socks, shirt and shorts
- cook set/utensils
- ditty bags to store gear
- extra plastic resealable bags
- gaiters
- garbage bag
- ground cloth
- journal/pen
- nylon rope to hang food
- long underwear
- permit (if required)
- rain jacket and pants
- sandals to wear around camp and to ford streams
- sleeping bag
- waterproof stuff sack
- sleeping pad
- small bath towel
- stove and fuel
- tent
- toiletry items
- water filter
- whistle

Equipment

With the outdoor market currently flooded with products, many of which are pure gimmickry, it seems impossible to both differentiate and choose. Do I really need a tropical-fish-lined collapsible shower? (No, you don't.) The only defense against the maddening quantity of items thrust in your face is to think practically—and to do so before you go shopping. The worst buys are impulsive buys. Since most name brands will differ only slightly in quality, it's best to know what you're looking for in terms of function. Buy only what you need. You will, don't forget, be carrying what you've bought on your back. Here are some things to keep in mind before you go shopping.

Clothes. Clothing is your armor against Mother Nature's little surprises. Weather in Northern California can range from blistering heat to brutal cold, and hikers should be prepared for any possibility, especially when hiking in mountainous areas. Adequate rain protection and extra layers of clothing are a good idea. In summer, a wide-brimmed hat can help keep the sun at bay. In the winter months the first layer you'll want to wear is a "wicking" layer of long underwear that keeps perspiration away from your skin. Wearing long underwear made from synthetic fibers such as Capilene, Coolmax, or Thermax is an excellent choice. These fabrics wick moisture away from the skin and draw it toward the next layer of clothing where it then evaporates. Avoid wearing long underwear made of cotton as it is slow to dry and keeps moisture next to your skin.

The second layer you'll wear is the "insulating" layer. Aside from keeping you warm, this layer needs to "breathe" so you stay dry while hiking. A fabric that provides insulation and dries quickly is fleece. It's interesting to note that this one-of-a-kind fabric is made out of recycled plastic. Purchasing a zip-up jacket made of this material is highly recommended.

The last line of layering defense is the "shell" layer. You'll need some type of waterproof, windproof, breathable jacket that'll fit over all of your other layers. It should have a large hood that fits over a hat. You'll also need a good pair of rain pants made from a similar waterproof, breathable fabric. A fabric that easily fits the bill is Gore-Tex. However, while a quality Gore-Tex jacket can range in price from $100 to $450, you should know that there are more affordable fabrics out there that work just as well.

Now that you've learned the basics of layering, you can't forget to protect your hands and face. In cold, windy, or rainy weather you'll need a hat made of wool or fleece and insulated, waterproof gloves that will keep your hands warm and toasty. As mentioned earlier, buying an additional pair of light silk liners to wear under your regular gloves is a good idea. They'll allow you to remove your outer gloves for tedious work without exposing the skin.

During the summer, your main consideration is protecting your skin from sunburn and poison oak that can be found in many parts of Northern California. Wearing long pants and a long-sleeved shirt made out of materials such as Supplex nylon will protect your skin from the damaging rays of the sun and from any poison oak that may be lurking along the trail.

Footwear. If you have any extra money to spend on your trip, put that money into boots or trail shoes. Poor shoes will bring a hike to a halt faster than anything else. To avoid this annoyance, buy shoes that provide support and are lightweight and flexible. A lightweight hiking boot is better than a heavy, leather mountaineering boot for most day hikes and backpacking. Trail running shoes provide a little extra cushion and are made in a high-top style that many people wear for hiking. These running shoes are lighter, more flexible, and more breathable than hiking boots. If you know you'll be hiking in wet weather often, purchase boots or shoes with a Gore-Tex liner, which will help keep your feet dry.

When buying your boots, be sure to wear the same type of socks you'll be wearing on the trail. If the boots you're buying are for cold weather hiking, try the boots on while wearing two pairs of socks. Speaking of socks, a good cold weather sock combination is to wear a thinner sock made of wool or polypropylene covered by a heavier outer sock made of wool. The inner sock protects the foot from the rubbing effects of the outer sock and prevents blisters.

Once you've purchased your footwear, be sure to break them in before you hit the trail. New footwear is often stiff and needs to be stretched and molded to your foot.

Backpacks. No matter what type of hiking you do you'll need a pack of some sort to carry the basic trail essentials. There are a variety of backpacks on the market, but let's first discuss what you intend to use it for. Day hikes or overnight trips?

If you plan on doing a day hike, a daypack should have some of the following characteristics: a padded hip belt that's at least two inches in diameter (avoid packs with only a small nylon piece of webbing for a hip belt); a chest strap (the chest strap helps stabilize the pack against your body); external pockets to carry water and other items that you want easy access to; an internal pocket to hold keys, a knife, a wallet, and other miscellaneous items; an external lashing system to hold a jacket; and a hydration pocket for carrying a hydration system (which consists of a water bladder with an attachable drinking hose).

For short hikes, some hikers like to use a fanny pack to store just a camera, food, a compass, a map, and other trail essentials. Most fanny packs have pockets for two water bottles and a padded hip belt.

If you intend to do an extended, overnight trip, there are multiple considerations. First off, you need to decide what kind of framed pack you want. There are two backpack types for backpacking: the internal frame and the external frame. An internal frame pack rests closer to your body, making it more stable and easier to balance when hiking over rough terrain. An external frame pack is just that, an aluminum frame attached to the exterior of the pack. An external frame pack is better for long backpack trips because it distributes the pack weight better and you can carry heavier loads. It's easier to pack, and your gear is more accessible. It also offers better back ventilation in hot weather.

The most critical measurement for fitting a pack is torso length. The pack needs to rest evenly on your hips without sagging. A good pack will come in two or three sizes and have straps and hip belts that are adjustable according to your body size and characteristics.

When you purchase a backpack, go to an outdoor store with salespeople who are knowledgeable in how to properly fit a pack. Once the pack is fitted for you, load the pack with the amount of weight you plan on taking on the trail. The weight of the pack should be distributed evenly and you should be able to swing your arms and walk briskly without feeling out of balance. Another good technique for evaluating a pack is to walk up and down stairs and make quick turns to the right and to the left to be sure the pack doesn't feel out of balance.

Other features that are nice to have on a backpack include a removable day pack or fanny pack, external pockets for extra water, and extra lash points to attach a jacket or other items.

Sleeping bags and pads. Sleeping bags are rated by temperature. You can purchase a bag made of synthetic fiber such as Polarguard HV or DuPont Hollofil II, or you can buy a goose down bag. Goose down bags are more expensive, but they have a higher insulating capacity by weight and will keep their loft longer. You'll want to purchase a bag with a temperature rating that fits the time of year and conditions you are most likely to camp in. One caveat: the techno-standard for temperature ratings is far from perfect. Ratings vary from manufacturer to manufacturer, so to protect yourself you should purchase a bag rated 10 to 15 degrees below the temperature you expect to be camping in. Synthetic bags are more resistant to water than down bags, but many down bags are now made with a Gore-Tex shell that helps to repel water. Down bags are also more compressible than synthetic bags and take up less room in your pack, which is an important consideration if you are planning a multiday backpack trip. Features to look for in a sleeping bag include a mummy style bag, a hood you can cinch down around your head in cold weather, and draft tubes along the zippers that help keep heat in and drafts out.

You'll also want a sleeping pad to provide insulation and padding from the cold ground. There are different types of sleeping pads available, from the more expensive self-inflating air mattresses to the less expensive closed-cell foam pads (e.g., Ridge Rest). Self-inflating air mattresses are usually heavier than closed-cell foam mattresses and are prone to punctures.

Tents. The tent is your home away from home while on the trail. It provides protection from wind, snow, rain, and insects. A three-season tent is a good choice for backpacking and can range in price from $100 to $500. These lightweight and versatile tents provide protection in all types of weather, except heavy snowstorms or high winds, and range in weight from four to eight pounds. Look for a tent that's easy to set up and will easily fit two people with gear. Dome type tents usually offer more headroom and places to store gear. Other tent designs include a vestibule where you can store wet boots and backpacks. Some nice-to-have items in a tent include interior pockets to store small items and lashing points to hang a clothesline. Most three-season tents also come with stakes so you can secure the tent in high winds. Before you purchase a tent, set it up and take it down a few times to be sure it is easy to handle. Also, sit inside the tent and make sure it has enough room for you and your gear.

Hiking with Children

Hiking with children isn't a matter of how many miles you can cover or how much elevation gain you make in a day; it's about seeing and experiencing nature through their eyes.

Kids like to explore and have fun. They like to stop and point out bugs and plants, look under rocks, jump in puddles, and throw sticks. If you're taking a toddler or young child on a hike, start with a trail that you're familiar with. Trails that have interesting things for kids, like piles of leaves to play in or a small stream to wade through during the summer, will make the hike much more enjoyable for them and will keep them from getting bored.

You can keep your child's attention if you have a strategy before starting on the trail. Using games is not only an effective way to keep a child's attention, it's also a great way to teach him or her about nature. Play hide and seek, where your child is the mouse and you are the hawk. Quiz children on the names of plants and animals. If your children are old enough, let them carry their own daypack filled with snacks and water. So that you are sure to go at their pace and not yours, let them lead the way. Playing follow the leader works particularly well when you have a group of children. Have each child take a turn at being the leader.

With children, a lot of clothing is key. The only thing predictable about weather is that it will change. Especially in mountainous areas, weather can change dramatically in a very short time. Always bring extra clothing for children, regardless of the season. In the winter, have your children wear wool socks, and warm layers such as long underwear, a polar fleece jacket and hat, wool mittens, and good rain gear. It's not a bad idea to have these along in late fall and early spring as well. Good footwear is also important. A sturdy pair of high top tennis shoes or lightweight hiking boots are the best bet for little ones. If you're hiking in the summer near a lake or stream, bring along a pair of old sneakers that your child can put on when he wants to go exploring in the water. Remember when you're near any type of water, always watch your child at all times. Also, keep a close eye on teething toddlers who may decide a rock or leaf of poison oak is an interesting item to put in their mouth.

From spring through fall, you'll want your kids to wear a wide brimmed hat to keep their face, head, and ears protected from the hot sun. Also, make sure your children wear sunscreen at all times. Choose a brand without Paba—children have sensitive skin and may have an allergic reaction to sunscreen that contains Paba. If you are hiking with a child younger than six months, don't use sunscreen or insect repellant. Instead, be sure that their head, face, neck, and ears are protected from the sun with a wide brimmed hat, and that all other skin exposed to the sun is protected with the appropriate clothing.

Remember that food is fun. Kids like snacks so it's important to bring a lot of munchies for the trail. Stopping often for snack breaks is a fun way to keep the trail interesting. Raisins, apples, granola bars, crackers and cheese, Cheerios, and trail mix all make great snacks. If your child is old enough to carry his/her own backpack, fill it with treats before you leave. If your kids don't like drinking water, you can bring boxes of fruit juice.

Avoid poorly designed child-carrying packs—you don't want to break your back carrying your child. Most child-carrying backpacks designed to hold a 40-pound child will contain a large carrying pocket to hold diapers and other items. Some have an optional rain/sun hood. Tough Traveler (800–GO–TOUGH; www. toughtraveler.com) is a company that specializes in making backpacks for carrying children and other outdoor gear for children.

Hiking with Your Dog

Bringing your furry friend with you is always more fun than leaving him behind. Our canine pals make great trail buddies because they never complain and always make good company. Hiking with your dog can be a rewarding experience, especially if you plan ahead.

Getting your dog in shape. Before you plan outdoor adventures with your dog, make sure he's in shape for the trail. Getting your dog into shape takes the same discipline as getting yourself into shape, but luckily, your dog can get in shape with you. Take your dog with you on your daily runs or walks. If there is a park near your house, hit a tennis ball or play Frisbee with your dog.

Swimming is also an excellent way to get your dog into shape. If there is a lake or river near where you live and your dog likes the water, have him retrieve a tennis ball or stick. Gradually build your dog's stamina up over a two- to three-month period. A good rule of thumb is to assume that your dog will travel twice as far as you will on the trail. If you plan on doing a 5-mile hike, be sure your dog is in shape for a 10-mile hike.

Training your dog for the trail. Before you go on your first hiking adventure with your dog, be sure he has a firm grasp on the basics of canine etiquette and behavior. Make sure he can sit, lie down, stay, and come. One of the most important commands you can teach your canine pal is to "come" under any situation. It's easy for your friend's nose to lead him astray or possibly get lost. Another helpful command is the "get behind" command. When you're on a hiking trail that's narrow, you can have your dog follow behind you when other trail users approach. Nothing is more bothersome than an enthusiastic dog that runs back and forth on the trail and disrupts the peace of the trail for others. When you see other trail users approaching you on the trail, give them the right of way by quietly stepping off the trail and making your dog lie down and stay until they pass.

Equipment. The most critical pieces of equipment you can invest in for your dog are proper identification and a sturdy leash. Flexi-leads work well for hiking because they give your dog more freedom to explore but still leave you in control. Make sure your dog has identification that includes your name and address and a number for your veterinarian. Other forms of identification for your dog include a tattoo or a microchip. You should consult your veterinarian for more information on these last two options.

The next piece of equipment you'll want to consider is a pack for your dog. By no means should you hold all of your dog's essentials in your pack—let him carry his own gear! Dogs that are in good shape can carry up to 30 percent to 40 percent of their own weight.

Companies that make good quality packs include RuffWear (888–RUFF–WEAR; www.ruffwear.com) and Wolf Packs (541–482–7669; www.wolfpacks.com). Most packs are fitted by a dog's weight and girth measurement. Companies that make dog packs generally include guidelines to help you pick out the size that's right for your dog. Some characteristics to look for when purchasing a pack for your dog include a harness that contains two padded girth straps, a padded chest strap, leash attachments, removable saddle bags, internal water bladders, and external gear cords.

You can introduce your dog to the pack by first placing the empty pack on his back and letting him wear it around the yard. Keep an eye on him during this first introduction. He may decide to chew through the straps if you aren't watching him closely. Once he learns to treat the pack as an object of fun and not a foreign enemy, fill the pack evenly on both sides with a few ounces of dog food in resealable plastic bags. Have your dog wear his pack on your daily walks for a period of two to three weeks. Each week add a little more weight to the pack until your dog will accept carrying the maximum amount of weight he can carry.

You can also purchase collapsible water and dog food bowls for your dog. These bowls are lightweight and can easily be stashed into your pack or your dog's. If you are hiking on rocky terrain or in the snow, you can purchase footwear for your dog that will protect his feet from cuts and bruises. All of these products can be purchased from RuffWear (888–RUFF–WEAR; www.ruffwear.com).

Always carry plastic bags to remove feces from the trail. It is a courtesy to other trail users and helps protect local wildlife.

The following is a list of items to bring when you take your dog hiking: collapsible water bowls, a comb, a collar and a leash, dog food, plastic bags for feces, a dog pack, flea/tick powder, paw protection, water, and a first-aid kit that contains eye ointment, tweezers, scissors, stretchy foot wrap, gauze, antibacterial wash, sterile cotton tip applicators, antibiotic ointment, and cotton wrap.

First aid for your dog. Your dog is just as prone—if not more prone—to getting in trouble on the trail as you are, so be prepared. Here's a rundown of the more likely misfortunes that might befall your little friend.

Bees and wasps. If a bee or wasp stings your dog, remove the stinger with a pair of tweezers and place a mudpack or a cloth dipped in cold water over the affected area.

Heat stroke. Avoid hiking with your dog in really hot weather. Dogs with heat stroke will pant excessively, lie down and refuse to get up, and become lethargic and disoriented. If your dog shows any of these signs on the trail, have him lie down in the shade. If you are near a stream, pour cool water over your dog's entire body to help bring his body temperature back to normal.

Heartworm. Dogs get heartworms from mosquitoes which carry the disease in the prime mosquito months of July and August. Giving your dog a monthly pill prescribed by your veterinarian easily prevents this condition.

Plant pitfalls. One of the biggest plant hazards for dogs on the trail are foxtails. Foxtails are pointed grass seed heads that bury themselves in your friend's fur, between his toes, and even get in his ear canal. If left unattended, these nasty seeds can work their way under the skin and cause abscesses and other problems. If you have a long-haired dog, consider trimming the hair between his toes and giving him a summer haircut to help prevent foxtails from attaching to his fur. After every hike, always look over your dog for these seeds—especially between his toes and his ears.

Other plant hazards include burrs, thorns, thistles, and poison oak. If you find any burrs or thistles on your dog, remove them as soon as possible before they become an unmanageable mat. Thorns can pierce a dog's foot and cause a great deal of pain. If you see that your dog is lame, stop and check his feet for thorns. Dogs are immune to poison oak but they can pick up the sticky, oily substance from the plant and transfer it to you.

Protect those paws. Be sure to keep your dog's nails trimmed so he avoids getting soft tissue or joint injuries. If your dog slows and refuses to go on, check to see that his paws aren't torn or worn. You can protect your dog's paws from trail hazards such as sharp gravel, foxtails, lava scree, and thorns by purchasing dog boots.

Sunburn. If your dog has light skin he is an easy target for sunburn on his nose and other exposed skin areas. You can apply a non-toxic sunscreen to exposed skin areas that will help protect him from over-exposure to the sun.

Ticks and fleas. Ticks can easily give your dog Lyme disease, as well as other diseases. Before you hit the trail, treat your dog with a flea and tick spray or powder. You can also ask your veterinarian about a once-a-month pour-on treatment that repels fleas and ticks.

When you are finally ready to hit the trail with your dog, keep in mind that national parks and many wilderness areas do not allow dogs on trails. Your best bet is to hike in national forests, BLM lands, and state parks. Always call ahead to see what the restrictions are.

Appendix A: Hiking Clubs

Antioch Trail Masters
Sponsors local day hikes, backpacks, bike rides, trail building and maintenance and activism in all trail-related issues.
(925) 778–0490; www.geocities.com/yosemite/trails/4849/atm/atmnewshead.html

Bay Area Bad Weather Hiking Group (e-mail list group)
"No matter what the weather man says. No matter what's falling from the sky. You want to hike. But for some reason, no one will go with you. Maybe they think you're reckless. But we don't. Hikes most likely occur on weekends, and destinations are in the San Francisco Bay Area."
groups.yahoo.com/group/bad_weather_hiking/

Bay Area Orienteering Club
"In orienteering, the thinking sport, you use a map and compass to navigate a course through unfamiliar terrain. It can be enjoyed as a walk in the woods or as a cross-country competition."
(408) 255–8018; www.baoc.org

Bay Area Hiking (e-mail list group)
A forum for discussing hiking and backpacking in and near the San Francisco Bay Area. Also a forum for finding hiking partners and setting up group hikes.
www.pair.com/hiking/bayareahiking

Berkeley Hiking Club
"Purpose: To draw together, in mutual consideration, persons interested in hiking to develop an appreciation of the out-of-doors; to foster the preservation and extension of them and to furnish such recreation as many seem desirable."
P.O. Box 147, Berkeley, CA 94701 (510) 663–0263; www.berkeleyhikingclub.pair.com

Berkeley Path Wanderers
"Dedicated to the preservation and restoration of public paths, steps, and walkways in Berkeley for the use and enjoyment of all."
1442A Walnut Street, #269, Berkeley, CA 94709 (510) 525–4064; www.internettime.com/bpwa

Cal Hiking and Outdoor Society (CHAOS)
"CHAOS is a group of University of California–Berkeley students, staff, Berkeley area residents, and assorted other friendly souls who meet regularly to experience

the outdoors, have fun and eat chocolate."
www.uc-hiking-club.berkeley.ca.us

California Adventure Club

"We are an overly ambitious group of athletes, trailrunners, hikers, backpackers, snowshoers and mountaineering fools who are looking for others to join us in our madness. The parent organization to the popular Mount Diablo Family Trekkers of Eastern Contra Costa County, we organize extended overnight, exotic trips, to unique venues in and out of state."
e-mail: hiking@signatureEsolutions.com (contact: Allen Tatomer); www.geocities.com/mtdiablohiking/caladventureclub.html

California Alpine Club

"The purpose of this club is to explore, enjoy and protect the natural resources of our land, including wildlife, forests and plants, water and scenic values; to support and promote educational programs on these and related topics; and at all times to protect and, as far as we are able, to improve the environment in which we live."
P.O. Box 2180, Mill Valley, CA 94942–2180; www.calalpine.org

Commonwealth of Nature Fanatics Unofficial SF/South Bay Excursion Division (CONFUSED)

"We're an informal group of outdoor enthusiasts based in the greater San Francisco Bay Area who get together to organize and enjoy outdoor activities of all kinds."
www.confused.org

Contra Costa Hills Club

"Plant a seed. Grow a tree. Conservation–Companionship–Hiking."
1515 Webster Street, Oakland, CA 94612–3355; www.geocities.com/evbuck/cchc

Diablo Hiking Club

"Sponsored by the Pleasant Hill Recreation and Park District. Founded in 1965. Come and enjoy rewarding outdoor adventures with us. All trips begin at the Pleasant Hill Recreation and Park District, 320 Civic Drive, Pleasant Hill, CA."
e-mail: diablohike@yahoo.com; www.geocities.com/yosemite/trails/7733

East Bay Barefoot Hikers

"Enjoy walking barefoot? So do we!! The East Bay Barefoot Hikers take to the trails every 2 to 3 weeks, year-round. It's fun, it's healthy and it's FREE."
(925) 680–1048; www.unshod.org/ebbfhike

EnviroSports

"Enviro-Sports is a club specializing in unique environmental outings and environmental education, and supports trail maintenance and habitat restoration in the

various parks in which we run to preserve wilderness and parklands."
P.O. Box 1040, Stinson Beach, CA 94970 (415) 868–1829; e-mail: info@
envirosports.com; www.envirosports.com

Gourmet Hikers Club

"In the mid-1960s three families rode their bikes on Point Reyes, returning to the trailhead for a potluck supper. The children grew and other families joined in. As trail usage increased, bikers became hikers and began to seek other places to explore. The children went off to college, but the expanded adult group continued to explore hiking areas. The children, now young adults, have returned and brought their friends. By year 2000, there were about 40 people on the hikers' e-mail list. The formula remains the same. After walking for a couple of hours, the most amazing gourmet feast appears from backpacks and we enjoy once again . . . food, nature and friends."
e-mail: Wwmabenson@aol.com

Hayward Hiking Club

"The Hayward Hiking Club invites you to try a hike with us. Have fun, get plenty of exercise, make friends, and experience nature all in one activity. Our hikes are scheduled every Saturday and range from easy to strenuous."
P.O. Box 367, Hayward, CA 94543–0367; www.thellamaranch.com/hhc

HikanByke

"We are a nonprofit group of single friends, dedicated to sharing the enjoyment of activities, such as biking, hiking, skiing, jogging, dining and camping, in a support-ive, nonthreatening atmosphere."
125 Lees Place Martinez, CA 94553; e-mail: hiknbyke@netscape.net; www.hikanbyke.org

Intrepid Northern California Hikers (INCH)

"Some people hike to enjoy the beauty of nature . . . some people hike to achieve inner serenity . . . some people hike for the physical and mental challenge . . . we hike because we love to eat!"
e-mail: peter.saviz@intel.com; www.members.tripod.com/%7Einch_hike/index.html

Lafayette Hiking Club

The Lafayette Parks and Recreation Commission schedules hikes on the average of two hikes a month as a service to the community. Generally, no fee or advance reg-istration is required.
(925) 284–2232; www.lafayettechamber.org

Livermore Hiking Club

The Livermore Hiking Club is an informal group with no published schedule. Hikers meet every Friday at 8:30 A.M. sharp in front of the Old Carnegie Library in Livermore, on South K Street between Third and Fourth Streets. (925) 447–4280; geocities.com/evbuck/lhc/lhcblurb.html

Mike and Kathy Wimbles' Hikes

"We are a loose group of a dozen or two people whose only connection is that they usually find out about the group by being a friend of Michael or Kathy Wimble." e-mail: hike@wimble.org; www.webself.com/~hiking

Montclair Hiking Club

"City of Oakland, Life Enrichment Agency Office of Parks and Recreation. Hikes are open to everyone. There are no fees. To attend, be at the Montclair Rec. Center on Tuesday at 9:00 A.M. sharp (unless noted) to make up car pools." Montclair Recreation Center, 6300 Moraga Avenue, Oakland, CA 94611 (510) 482–7812; e-mail: Montclairhikers@topica.com; geocities.com/evbuck/mhc/schedule.html

Mount Diablo Family Hiking Club

"We are a loose group of outdoor-loving, fresh air–breathing, underexercised and overstressed hiking enthusiasts who are put off by the exclusionary 'adults-only' hiking clubs of the East County of Northern California." www.geocities.com/mtdiablohiking/familyhikingclub.html

North of SF Bay Hiking

"Our list of hiking groups includes those in Sonoma, Marin, and Napa counties, as well as San Francisco area groups that often hike in Sonoma and Marin counties." e-mail: laura@hikenorthbay.com; www.hikenorthbay.com

Orinda Hiking Club

The Orinda Hiking Club sponsors weekend hikes, Wednesday hikes, and evening strolls. P.O. Box 934, Orinda, CA 94563 (925) 254–3689 or (925) 254–1465

Pacific Trail Society

The Pacific Trail Society is an informal group that hikes in Marin, Point Reyes, and the East Bay two to four times a month. Most of the hikes are 5 to 10 miles long and moderate in difficulty. www.geocities.com/Pacific_Trail_Club

San Francisco Hiking Club

The San Francisco Hiking Club organizes hikes and similar outings for gays, les-

bians, and friends. An event is generally planned on either Saturday or Sunday each weekend.
P.O. Box 14065, San Francisco, CA 94114 www.sfhiking.com

Stanford Outing Club
"Our most common activity is hiking (day trips) at one of the Bay Area's many parks, such as Point Reyes, Big Basin, Mount Tamalpais, or Pinnacles, to name a few. Our activities are open for everyone (i.e., also for people not affiliated with Stanford University)."
e-mail: cfoster01@yahoo.com; www.stanford.edu/group/outing/about.html

Yahoo Clubs—Bay Area Hiking (e-mail list group)
"This is a place to find people who want to go hiking in Northern California's Bay Area. All levels are welcome."
www.clubs.yahoo.com/clubs/bayareahiking

Organizations That Offer Hikes in the Bay Area
Bay Area Ridge Trail
The Bay Area Ridge Trail Council offers a variety of activities, open to the public, along the Bay Area Ridge Trail. Activities include hikes, trail bike rides, and horse rides.
1007 General Kennedy Avenue, Suite 3, San Francisco, CA 94129 (415) 561–2595; e-mail: info@ridgetrail.org; www.ridgetrail.org/trlevnt.htm

California Coastwalk
"Our purpose is to explore and promote the opening of remote and heretofore inaccessible sections of our coastline, and to shift perception of the coastline from one of a few isolated beaches and accesses to one of a continuous 55 (now 1,156) miles of unbroken beauty."
7207 Bodega Avenue, Sebastopol, CA 95472 (707) 829–6689; e-mail: hshane@coastwalk.org; www.coastwalk.org

East Bay Regional Park District
The East Bay Regional Park District has hundreds of events scheduled all year long.
2950 Peralta Oaks Court, P.O. Box 5381, Oakland, CA 94605 (510) 562–PARK; www.ebparks.org

Fifty-Plus Fitness Association (FPFA)
The Fifty-Plus Fitness Association is a twenty-year old nonprofit organization whose mission is to promote an active lifestyle for older people.
P.O. Box 20230, Stanford, CA 94309 (650) 323–6160; www.50plus.org

Greenbelt Alliance

"Our mission is to make the nine-county San Francisco Bay Area a better place to live by protecting the region's Greenbelt and improving the livability of its cities and towns. FREE hikes, bikes rides and more."

530 Bush Street, Suite 303, San Francisco, CA 94108 (415) 398–3730; fax: (415) 398–6530; e-mail: info@greenbelt.org; www.greenbelt.org

Midpeninsula Regional Open Space District

The twenty-four Midpeninsula Regional Open Space District preserves include over 45,000 acres of permanently protected open space, from redwood forests to bay shoreline.

330 Distel Circle, Los Altos, CA 94022 (650) 691–2150; www.openspace.org

Mount Diablo Interpretive Association (MDIA)

The MDIA sponsors walks and hikes, which are led by Mount Diablo State Park volunteers.

P.O. Box 346, Walnut Creek, CA 94597–0346 (925) 837–5245; www.mdia.org/events.htm

Mount Tamalpais Interpretive Association

The Mount Tamalpais Interpretive Association is a volunteer organization whose purpose is to promote the conservation, education, and interpretation of California state parks, primarily at Mount Tamalpais State Park. Sponsors interpretive hikes open to the public.

P.O. Box 3318, San Rafael, CA 94912 (415) 258–2410; www.mttam.net/index.html

Santa Cruz Mountains Trail Association (SCMTA)

"Founded in 1969, the Trail Association was formed under the guidance of the California State Parks and Sempervirens Fund (a nonprofit land conservancy) to build and maintain trails in the Santa Cruz Mountains. The building of the Skyline-to-the-Sea Trail that year inaugurated Trail Days in the Santa Cruz Mountains. Since then our activities have broadened to include weekly hikes."

P.O. Box 1141, Los Altos, CA 94023 e-mail: MHD@slac.stanford.edu; www.stanford.edu/~mhd/trails/

Sierra Club

Most regional chapters offer regular outings.

85 Second Street, 2nd floor, San Francisco, CA, 94105 (415) 977–5500; www.sierraclub.org

San Francisco Bay Chapter

The Hiking Section of the San Francisco Bay chapter of the Sierra Club sponsors a variety of day hikes in Marin, Alameda and Contra Costa Counties, and city hikes in San Francisco. Fifty to sixty hikes are scheduled each month on Saturdays, Sundays, Wednesdays, and most holidays.

For schedule: Tom Foote, 53 Jersey Street, San Francisco, CA 94114–3915 (925) 631–0751; sanfranciscobay.sierraclub.org/hiking

Mount Diablo Regional Group
San Francisco Bay Chapter Office, 2530 San Pablo Avenue, Suite I, Berkeley, CA 94702 (510) 848–0800; www.sanfranciscobay.sierraclub.org/mdhikes.html

Sierra Singles
Sierra Singles is an activity section of the San Francisco Bay chapter of the national Sierra Club. Includes volunteer leaders who organize activities including day hiking, backpacking, cross-country and downhill skiing, river rafting, bicycling, car camping, sea kayaking, environmental education programs, social events such as dances, and cultural events such as visits to special museum exhibits. Sponsors approximately fifty activities each month.

5337 College Avenue, Suite 541, Oakland, CA 94618; www.sanfranciscobay. sierraclub.org/singles

Loma Prieta Chapter
Chapter sponsors a variety of outdoor activities. All are led by trained, certified, volunteer Sierra Club leaders.

3921 East Bayshore Road, Suite 204, Palo Alto, CA 94303 (650) 390–8411; www. lomaprieta.sierraclub.org/outingsmain.html

Loma Prieta Day Hiking Section
"The DHS provides well-organized access to the many parks, open spaces, and other legally accessible lands primarily (but not exclusively) in the San Francisco Bay Area. Hikers may thus learn the ways and means of visiting these areas on their own. The DHS promotes and schedules one-day hikes for enjoyment and to increase awareness for the need to preserve our open space. Most hikes are over 10 miles in length and quite a few are over 20 miles, distances necessary to get a full view of the areas being hiked."

www.lomaprieta.sierraclub.org/dayhiking

Loma Prieta Sierra Singles
"Sierra Singles is a group of more than 800 singles of all ages, who enjoy a wide range of activities, from outdoor to social. Most of our events are centered in Santa Clara, San Benito, and San Mateo Counties, near the beautiful San Francisco Bay."

P.O. Box 391775, Mountain View, CA 94039–1775 (408) 795–3237; e-mail: datsrex@netzero.net; www.lomaprieta.sierraclub.org/lpss

Black Mountain Group
"Many of our activities are hikes. Unless you are familiar with the hike or hike regularly, please consider contacting the leader. While we maintain a moderate pace, we do occasionally encounter a steep hill. We use the common number and letter code to denote a hike's difficulty."
www.lomaprieta.sierraclub.org/bmg/schedule.html

Appendix B: Hike Finder

This guidebook contains trails for all levels of hikers in all kinds of terrain. Here, at a glance, the hikes are categorized by favorite features to help you choose your next Bay Area adventure.

Hikes for Anglers
8. Phoenix Reservoir: Tucker and Bill Williams Trail
12. Marin Municipal Water District: Kent Trail along Alpine Lake
34. Briones Regional Park (San Pablo Reservoir)
40. Anthony Chabot Regional Park (Lake Chabot)

Hikes for Animal Lovers
2. Point Reyes National Seashore: Tomales Point (tule elk)
3. Point Reyes: Lighthouse and Chimney Rock Trails (whale-watching)
22. Año Nuevo State Park
24. James V. Fitzgerald Marine Reserve: The Tide Pool Loop
39. Tilden Regional Park: From Jewel Lake to Wildcat Peak

Hikes for Backpackers
4. Point Reyes National Seashore: Palomarin Trailhead to Alamere Falls (Coastal Trail)
27. Castle Rock State Park
38. Sunol Regional Wilderness
I. Skyline Ridge Open Space Preserve

Hikes for Beach/Coast Lovers
1. Mount Wittenberg and Bear Valley Loops
4. Point Reyes National Seashore: Palomarin Trailhead to Alamere Falls
5. Tomales Bay State Park: Heart's Desire Beach to Shell Beach
9. Steep Ravine Loop to Stinson Beach
11. Marin Headlands: Miwok Trail to Point Bonita
20. Pescadero Marsh Trail
22. Año Nuevo State Park
24. James V. Fitzgerald Marine Reserve: The Tide Pool Loop

Hikes for Bird Lovers
4. Point Reyes National Seashore: Palomarin Trailhead to Alamere Falls
11. Marin Headlands: Miwok Trail to Point Bonita (raptors)
20. Pescadero Marsh Trail
H. Russian Ridge Open Space Preserve (raptors)
I. Skyline Ridge Open Space Preserve
S. Coyote Hills Regional Park

Hikes Best for Camping
6. Samuel P. Taylor State Park: To the Top of Barnabe Peak
9. Steep Ravine Loop to Stinson Beach
15. Angel Island State Park
21. Butano State Park
26. Big Basin State Park: Berry Creek Falls Trail Loop
28. Portola Redwoods State Park
N. Pescadero Creek County Park

Hikes for Children and Beginning Hikers
3. Point Reyes: Lighthouse and Chimney Rock Trails
8. Phoenix Reservoir: Tucker and Bill Williams Trails
24. James V. Fitzgerald Marine Reserve: The Tide Pool Loop
25. San Pedro Valley County Park
26. Big Basin State Park: Berry Creek Falls Trail Loop
36. Huckleberry Botanic Regional Preserve
39. Tilden Regional Park: From Jewel Lake to Wildcat Peak
B. Point Reyes on Rainy Days
L. Rancho San Antonio Open Space Preserve and County Park
N. Pescadero Creek County Park
S. Coyote Hills Regional Park

Hikes for Geology Lovers
27. Castle Rock State Park
30. Las Trampas Regional Wilderness
33. Rock City to the Summit
37. Robert Sibley Volcanic Regional Preserve
B. Point Reyes on Rainy Days

Hikes for Hill Climbers
6. Samuel P. Taylor State Park: To the Top of Barnabe Peak
10. East Peak Loop
13. Burdell Mountain Open Space Preserve
19. San Bruno State Park: Summit Loop Trail
23. McNee Ranch State Park and Montara State Beach
33. Rock City to the Summit

L. Rancho San Antonio Open Space Preserve and County Park
R. Mission Peak Regional Preserve

Hikes for History Lovers
3. Point Reyes: Lighthouse and Chimney Rock Trails
11. Marin Headlands: Miwok Trail to Point Bonita
15. Angel Island State Park
16. Cliff House Walk at Land's End
18. The Presidio: Lovers' Lane and the Ecology Trail
32. Black Diamond Mines Regional Preserve
B. Point Reyes on Rainy Days
D. Golden Gate Park
O. Las Trampas Regional Wilderness: Eugene O'Neill Loop

Hikes for Lake Lovers
4. Point Reyes National Seashore: Palomarin Trailhead to Alamere Falls
8. Phoenix Reservoir: Tucker and Bill Williams Trails
12. Marin Municipal Water District: Kent Trail along Alpine Lake
40. Anthony Chabot Regional Park
I. Skyline Ridge Open Space Preserve
Q. Briones Reservoir

Hikes for Lighthouse Lovers
3. Point Reyes: Lighthouse and Chimney Rock Trails
11. Marin Headlands: Miwok Trail to Point Bonita

Hikes for Redwood Lovers
6. Samuel P. Taylor State Park: To the Top of Barnabe Peak
7. Muir Woods: Bootjack Trail to Dipsea Trail Loop
9. Steep Ravine Loop to Stinson Beach
21. Butano State Park
26. Big Basin State Park: Berry Creek Falls Trail Loop
28. Portola Redwoods State Park
29. Purisima Creek Redwoods Open Space Preserve
35. Redwood Regional Park: East to West Ridge Trails
E. Huddart County Park and Phleger Estate
F. Wunderlich County Park
N. Pescadero Creek County Park (Heritage Grove)

Hikes Best for Variety
1. Mount Wittenberg and Bear Valley Loops
4. Point Reyes National Seashore: Palomarin Trailhead to Alamere Falls
5. Tomales Bay State Park: Heart's Desire Beach to Shell Beach
6. Samuel P. Taylor State Park: To the Top of Barnabe Peak

9. Steep Ravine Loop to Stinson Beach
10. East Peak Loop
12. Marin Municipal Water District: Kent Trail Along Alpine Lake
21. Butano State Park
40. Anthony Chabot Regional Park
J. Monte Bello Open Space Preserve

Hikes Best for Views
2. Point Reyes National Seashore: Tomales Point
10. East Peak Loop
11. Marin Headlands: Miwok Trail to Point Bonita
14. Ring Mountain
15. Angel Island State Park
17. Sweeney Ridge: The Portolá Discovery Site
19. San Bruno State Park: Summit Loop Trail
23. McNee Ranch State Park and Montara State Beach
26. Big Basin State Park: Berry Creek Falls Trail Loop
29. Purisima Creek Redwoods Open Space Preserve
33. Rock City to the Summit
35. Redwood Regional Park: East to West Ridge Trails
38. Sunol Regional Wilderness
G. Windy Hill Open Space Preserve
M. Long Ridge Open Space Preserve
N. Pescadero Creek County Park
P. Tilden Regional Park—Greater Tilden
R. Mission Peak Regional Preserve
S. Coyote Hills Regional Park

Hikes for Waterfall Lovers
4. Point Reyes National Seashore: Palomarin Trailhead to Alamere Falls
9. Steep Ravine Loop to Stinson Beach
25. San Pedro Valley County Park
26. Big Basin State Park: Berry Creek Falls Trail Loop
31. Donner Canyon to the Falls Trail
38. Sunol Regional Wilderness
C. Cataract Trail

Hikes for Wildflower Lovers
2. Point Reyes National Seashore: Tomales Point
3. Point Reyes: Lighthouse and Chimney Rock Trails
14. Ring Mountain
31. Donner Canyon to the Falls Trail
38. Sunol Regional Wilderness

About the Author

A native to the Bay Area, Linda Hamilton has been elated to rediscover the incredible beauty of her home region, beyond the crowded highways. Her first (of so many) solo hiking adventures occurred at age four, when she happily wandered off to explore nature, scaring the daylights out of her family. After nine years of exploring high school and college teaching and with an M.A. in English under her belt, she set out to achieve her true dream of writing for a living. Her work has appeared in the *San Francisco Chronicle, American Heritage of Invention and Technology Magazine, MyFamily Travel* newsletters, Americaslibrary.gov, and many online sites. When not on foot or hugging her laptop, Linda is singing with a band or laughing with her husband Doug in their Oakland home.

Contact

Help Us Keep This Guide Up to Date

Every effort has been made by the author and editors to make this guide as accurate and useful as possible. However, many things can change after a guide is published—trails are rerouted, regulations change, techniques evolve, facilities come under new management, etc.

We would love to hear from you concerning your experiences with this guide and how you feel it could be improved and kept up to date. While we may not be able to respond to all comments and suggestions, we'll take them to heart and we'll also make certain to share them with the author. Please send your comments and suggestions to the following address:

> The Globe Pequot Press
> Reader Response/Editorial Department
> P.O. Box 480
> Guilford, CT 06437

Or you may e-mail us at:

> editorial@globe-pequot.com

Thanks for your input, and happy travels!